In Search of Brightest Africa

RACE IN THE ATLANTIC WORLD, 1700–1900

SERIES EDITORS

Richard S. Newman, *Rochester Institute of Technology*
Patrick Rael, *Bowdoin College*
Manisha Sinha, *University of Massachusetts, Amherst*

ADVISORY BOARD

Edward Baptist, *Cornell University*
Christopher Brown, *Columbia University*
Vincent Carretta, *University of Maryland*
Laurent Dubois, *Duke University*
Douglas Egerton, *LeMoyne College*
Leslie Harris, *Emory University*
Joanne Pope Melish, *University of Kentucky*
Sue Peabody, *Washington State University, Vancouver*
Erik Seeman, *State University of New York, Buffalo*
John Stauffer, *Harvard University*

In Search of Brightest Africa

REIMAGINING THE DARK CONTINENT

IN AMERICAN CULTURE, 1884–1936

Jeannette Eileen Jones

The University of Georgia Press | Athens and London

Paperback edition, 2011
© 2010 by the University of Georgia Press
Athens, Georgia 30602
www.ugapress.org
All rights reserved
Set in 10.5/13.5 Adobe Caslon Pro by BookComp, Inc

Printed digitally in the United States of America

The Library of Congress has cataloged the hardcover
edition of this book as follows:

Jones, Jeannette Eileen, 1970–
  In search of brightest Africa : reimagining the dark continent
in American culture, 1884–1936 / Jeannette Eileen Jones.
    xviii, 296 p. : ill. ; 24 cm.
    Includes bibliographical references and index.
    ISBN-13: 978-0-8203-3320-5 (hardcover : alk. paper)
    ISBN-10: 0-8203-3320-4 (hardcover : alk. paper)
  1. Africa—Foreign public opinion, American.
  2. Public opinion—United States.
  3. Africa—Relations—United States.
  4. United States—Relations—Africa.
  5. Africa—Civilization.
  6. United States—Civilization—1865–1918.
  7. United States—Civilization—1918–1945.
  8. United States—Intellectual life. I. Title.
  DT38.1.J66 2010
  327.607309'034—dc22   2009047895

Paperback ISBN-13: 978-0-8203-4029-6
        ISBN-10: 0-8203-4029-4

British Library Cataloging-in-Publication Data available

For my parents,

Joseph Edward and Frances Jeannette Jones

Wake up Ethiopia! Wake up Africa! Let us work towards
the one glorious end of a free, redeemed and mighty nation.
Let Africa be a bright star among the constellation of nations.

 Marcus Garvey, *Philosophy and Opinions of Marcus Garvey*, 1923

Africa Hall will tell the story of jungle peace, a story that is
sincere and faithful to the Africa beasts as I have known them,
and it will, I hope tell the story so convincingly that the traditions
of jungle horrors and impenetrable forests would be obliterated.

 Carl E. Akeley, *In Brightest Africa*, 1923

Today the Congo has undergone transformation, like the
remainder of the great continent. No longer can it claim the
title of "Darkest Africa," the land of pestilence, terrors and black
magic. "Brightest Africa" has come to stay—a land in which a
sovereign of Europe can travel safely, comfortably and swiftly by
mail plane, by steamer and by motor safari, while he is afforded
wireless communication with his capital from every important Post.

 Mary Jobe Akeley, "Darkest Africa Becomes a Wonderland," 1932

CONTENTS

Preface: What Is Africa to Me?   xi

Acknowledgments   xv

INTRODUCTION
In Search of Brightest Africa   1

ONE
A Cry from Africa: Victorians, New Women, New Negroes, and Moderns Confront the Dark Continent   13

TWO
To Bunco a Yankee: America and the Congo Question   47

THREE
Written on the Wall: Pan-African Dreams of African Empires and Republics   83

FOUR
To Capture a Vanishing World: Naturalist-Environmentalist Discourses and Displays of Africa   132

FIVE
Reel Africa: American Filmmaking and Criticism in Defense of Africa   177

CONCLUSION
The Wonders of Africa Brought to America   211

Chronology of Events   227

Notes   231

Bibliography   253

Index   277

PREFACE
What Is Africa to Me?

Technically, the genesis of this project can be located in that long ago fateful semester (1996 to be precise) in Gail Radford's Twentieth-Century United States seminar at the University of Buffalo, when I had to come up with a research topic. Knowing that I would be returning to "Strong Island" for the upcoming break, I decided to select a topic that I could research while at home. A year earlier, I had written a research paper on the Shinnecock Indian Nation, whose reservation is in Southampton, Long Island. In that paper, I explored the ways in which colonial and U.S. constructions of race—particularly with regard to "Indian" intermixing with "Negroes"—circumscribed the Shinnecock's campaign for federal recognition. Out of respect for their quest for federal status as Native American, I abandoned researching their African ancestry as a possible dissertation topic. Yet, it was this paper that stirred my intellectual curiosity about race and representation in American history; more specifically, I was interested in how America arrived at its metanarratives about race.

The scholarly journey from the Shinnecock reservation to the American Museum of Natural History was a long one, despite its ninety-mile distance. On my intellectual passage from Southampton to New York City, I took a detour across the Atlantic to explore the ways in which Western racial ideologies influenced museum classifications of the Benin Bronzes seized in the British Punitive Expedition of 1897. I also decided to investigate generally how Western museums displayed Africa during the early decades of European imperialism on the continent. My findings confirmed what I learned throughout my graduate career. Race was not simply a pseudobiological category, but an ideological trope, a metanarrative that organized and produced Western knowledge about everything from aboriginal rights to museum displays.

Although the two research papers that resulted from my foray into museum culture inspired my decision to examine representations of Africa in museums closer to home, my fascination with Africa dated back to my childhood and youth. As I visited the American Museum of Natural History, the Metropolitan Museum of Art, and the United Nations, I also sorted through elusive memories: my grandmother's African "male friend" who worked at the United Nations, the painful departure (for me) of four of my cousins and their mom to live in Africa while their dad completed his dissertation, and my cousin's expatriation to and later death in Africa. I loved Africa. I had no clue why. I had never traveled there, and although I resented Africa for stealing away parts of my family, secretly I wanted to understand its allure to them. Was it simply that Africa was the land of our ancestors cruelly brought to these American shores as slaves?

I reread Countee Cullen's poem "Heritage" (1925) in preparation for my return to the Akeley African Hall at the American Museum of Natural History. This was a tour that I had taken several times as a child and teenager. I recall the tour guide's descriptions of the African mammals and statements about the importance of Carl Akeley to animal preservation in Africa. All the while, Cullen's images of "jungle herds" and "defiant grass" ran through my head.

> So I lie, who all day long
> Want no sound except the song
> Sung by wild barbaric birds
> Goading massive jungle herds,
> Juggernauts of flesh that pass
> Trampling tall defiant grass

Indeed, the dioramas were a spectacle to behold. The expressions on the faces of the children as they marveled at the sight of stuffed elephants, lions, and Grevy's zebras must have matched my own at their age. My mother tells a different story of an inquisitive child who was more interested in the dinosaurs than any posthistoric mammal. Nevertheless, I remembered seeing and admiring "The Herd"—the seven elephants that stood in the center of the hall.

After leaving the group, I walked into the Hall of African Peoples. My memory of my first time in this hall is lost to me, but my father recalls my becoming upset with a guide who could not adequately explain to me, a child, why the Egyptians were not in the Hall of African Peoples. Apparently, in the heated exchange, the guide told me that the cultures of "white people" were not exhibited in natural history museums. If I was interested in them and the Egyptians, he said, I should go across the park to the Met.

I suspect the scene was a set-up. My father, of course, knew the answer that I would receive, and I imagine he encouraged me to ask questions to provoke the guide. He was trying to teach me a lesson that I would only begin to comprehend fully after years of exposure to a variety of images of

Africa, running the gamut from that of mainstream Pan-Africanists, Nubian Islamic Hebrews, the Five Percent Nation, National Geographic, Jane Goodall, Sigourney Weaver (portraying Dian Fossey), and most important, my family.

I headed to the museum library (now Archives and Special Collections) and filled out a request slip. I wanted to read Carl Akeley's much-praised *In Brightest Africa* (1924). As I waited, Cullen summoned me again—a stanza I had memorized for my undergraduate African American Literature class with Joseph McLaren.

> What is Africa to me:
> Copper sun or scarlet sea,
> Jungle star or jungle track,
> Strong bronzed men, or regal black
> Women from whose loins I sprang
> When the birds of Eden sang?
> One three centuries removed
> From the scenes his fathers loved,
> Spicy grove, cinnamon tree,
> What is Africa to me?

Ten-odd years after visiting Ghana, Benin, Togo, and South Africa and receiving a brilliant tattoo of Africa superimposed on Mosi-oa-Tunya (Victoria Falls), I still ask myself: "What is Africa to me?"

ACKNOWLEDGMENTS

This project was conceived in the true spirit of communalism despite its status as "my book." Without the intellectual, emotional, and financial support of a myriad of individuals and institutions, this book would have remained a dissertation filed with UMI. First I would like to thank all of the institutions and individuals that provided financial support for researching and writing this book: the University of Nebraska–Lincoln's Grant-in-Aid and Layman Awards from the Office of Research, the Deutsche Bank Junior Scholar in Residence Fellowship at the Heidelberg Center for American Studies (Universität Heidelberg, Germany), the Arthur A. Schomburg Fellowship from the University at Buffalo (UB), the Plesur Research Study Grant and Lockwood Dissertation Grant from the UB Department of History, and the Frederick Douglass Teaching Fellowship at the West Chester University of Pennsylvania. I would also like to thank my parents for cofunding my trips to London and Brussels and Evelyn McKenzie, Alison Bramble, and Nah Dove's family for sheltering a foreigner in a strange land. Additional thanks to my sister Stephanie and my brother-in-law "Big Ian" for giving me a place to lay my head as I conducted research in New York, and to cousins Henry, (the late) Sherile, and Donielle for putting me up in Chicago. Lastly, thanks to my former partner of five years, Louie Tyler Veasey Jr.

I could not have completed this book without the help of librarians, archivists, and museum personnel. First and foremost, I must thank the wonderful staff of the Department of Library Services at the American Museum of Natural History—Mary DeJong, Reference Librarian; (the late) Roscoe Thompson, former Acting Director of the Library; Barbara Mathe, Museum Archivist; Annette Springer, Reference Clerk; Emily Lanzara, Special Collections Clerk; Matthew Pavlick, Project Archivist; Paula Wiley, Special Collections Clerk; and Tom Baione, Assistant Director for Client Services. Special thanks go to the following institutions, their staff, and selected persons: the Interlibrary Loan Offices at the University at Buffalo, University of Nebraska, and Universität Heidelberg; the New York Public Library; Michael L. Perry and the Schomburg Center for Research in Black Culture; the Brooklyn Public Library; the New York Historical Society; the George Eastman House; Rare Books and Special Collections at the University of Rochester Library; Susan Persia and the

Town of Clarendon Town Hall; the University of Brockport; the Library of Congress; the Buffalo Museum of Science; the Buffalo and Erie County Public Library; Judy Turner and the Milwaukee Public Museum; Armand Esai and the Field Museum of Natural History; the University of Chicago; Carl Hallberg and the University of Wyoming American Heritage Center; the Martin and Osa Johnson Safari Museum; Duke University; Mahmood Mamdani (formerly of) the University of Cape Town; Cape Town Public Library; J. C. Thackray and the Natural History Museum (UK); the Public Record Office at Kew (UK); the British Library; the Wellcome Center for the History of Medicine (UK); Madame DeKais and le Ministère des Affaires étrangères, Bibliothèque Africaine (Belgium); le Musée Royal de l'Afrique Centrale (Belgium); and Raphaël de Smedt (le Minstère de l'Education Nationale) and Bibliothèque Royale Albert Ier (Belgium).

I cannot say enough about my dissertation committee, Michael Frisch, Tamara Plakins Thornton, and James Bono, whom I affectionately refer to as my academic Triple Threat or one-two-three punch. Special thanks to them and my outside reader, James Oliver Horton, for his insightful comments. Collectively, their guidance could have been grim, leading me to dub them the Four Horseman of the Apocalypse. Instead, they mentored me as much as with words as with deeds. Mike helped me to see the big picture—that is, how my work engaged urban, public, cultural, and intellectual history. His own work in the fields of public and urban history served as examples to follow in approaching the American Museum of Natural History as both a public site/artifact and an intrinsic part of the urban landscape. Tamara grounded me in the fields of American cultural and intellectual history, reminding me that what I researched was indeed cultural phenomena. Moreover, she helped me come to grips with the fact that even as I explored the intellectual productions of elite dead white people, in no way did I compromise my interests in the history of race as a construct and its impact on the lives of people of African descent. Jim deserves praise for opening my mind to the history of science. His presence on my committee ensured that I would not lose sight of the fact that many of the historical actors in my narrative fashioned themselves as naturalists who believed that their work was scientific. Without these three towering intellects, I could not have realized this project. What an awesome committee! Special thanks to Michael Vorenberg (formerly of UB and now at Brown) for convincing me to revise the dissertation by placing African Americans alongside white naturalists in my exploration of American reinventions of Africa.

The revising and editing of the manuscript could not have been possible without the dedication of my research assistant, Robert "Bobby" Lee, at the Heidelberg Center for American Studies. Thanks to generous funding from Deutsche Bank, I enjoyed nine months of Bobby's research skills, as well as eyes and ears. From listening to me work through a chapter aloud, to reading revised chapter sections, to checking my formatting, Bobby served as an endless resource who kept a fellow New Yorker sane. Also, special thanks to my "sisters" Kalenda Eaton and Seanna Sumalee Oakley, my "big brother" Mark Anthony Neal, and my gracious colleague Davarian Baldwin for their advice on revising the manuscript. I would also like to thank my editor, Derek Krissoff.

I presented portions of this book at the American Studies Association and Social Science History Association national conferences and at other scholarly conventions. Parts of chapter four appeared in somewhat different form as "'Gorilla Trails in Paradise': Carl Akeley, Mary Bradley, and the American Search for the Missing Link" in the *Journal of American Culture* 29, no. 3 (September 2006): 321–36. The introduction and parts of chapter one (in earlier forms) appear in *Images of Africa: Stereotypes and Realities*, edited by Daniel Mengara (New York: African World Press, 2001). The opportunity to publish and to deliver lectures at these various venues exposed me to much appreciated peer review and commentary.

Thanks to the University of North Carolina at Chapel Hill for making available the electronic edition of John Wesley Edward Bowen's edited collection *Africa and the American Negro: Addresses and Proceedings of the Congress on Africa*.

Much emotional and intellectual support came from the following: Thomas Kierstead, Peter Ekeh, Liana Vardi, Bill Graebner, Ellen Litwicki, Richard Filipink Jr., Najia Aarim-Heriot, Peter Ekeh, Michael Boston, Bertha Boston, James Jones, Michelle Scott, Anthony Grajeda, Barry Jackisch, Joel Siepierski, Sara Abosch, Stephanie Petkovsek, Jeanne and Roger Cross, Tara Wood, Anika Johnson, Kawain Lane, Michelle Rivera, and the Alabis and Allon Chapel SDA. Special thanks to all of my colleagues in the Department of History and the Institute for Ethnic Studies at the University of Nebraska–Lincoln, especially Carole Levin, Alan Steinweis, Susanna Schrafstetter, Jim LeSueur, Benjamin Rader, Andrew Graybill, Kwakiutl Dreher, Douglas Seefeldt, Learthen Dorsey, and the late, great Oyekan Owomoyela for their indispensable advice in making the transition from graduate student to assistant professor. Additional thanks to my colleagues at the HCA, particularly Detlef Junker, Wilfried Mausbach, Jana Freihöfer, Martin Thunert, Mischa Honeck, and Elizabeth Borgwardt. To my former and present students at UB, Buffalo State College, SUNY Fredonia, Universität Heidelberg, and UNL, and my mentees in the Fredonia Black Student Union and UNL Black Graduate Student Association, thanks for reminding me why I got into academia in the first place.

Last, but not least, and most important, I would like to thank my family for their untiring support: Mommy and Daddy; my siblings, Antoinette, Stephanie, and Jelani; my niece, Shianna; my nephew, Ian; and my brother-in-law, Ian. Special thanks go to cousin Dr. Barry Colley for opening my eyes to the wonders of Africa. Last but not least, thanks to Mein Mann Alexander Vazansky. We'll always have Heidelberg, Schwetzingen, Munich, Paris, Vienna.... I close with words from Deah Love Harriot's "The Potter," which inspired me throughout the writing of this book: "YOU are the potter, I'm the clay."

INTRODUCTION
In Search of Brightest Africa

On May 18, 1936, Colonel J. C. Robinson, variously known as the Black Condor or Brown Condor, returned to the United States after several years serving as Ethiopian Emperor Haile Selassie's personal aviator and trusted lieutenant. Disembarking the German ocean liner *Europa* in downtown New York, Robinson greeted friends from his native Chicago, including Claude Barnett, the director of the Associated Negro Press, as well as members of the mainstream national press. Robinson commented on the ongoing struggle between Italy and Ethiopia and predicted Ethiopian victory as trained soldiers and guerilla fighters mobilized to expel the Italian invaders. He also revealed that he had returned to America to teach aviation at his alma mater, Tuskegee Institute. None of his greeters that day could foresee the irony of his return. The thirty-one-year-old citizen, whose government denied him the right to fly combat planes in its air force, had returned from fighting in a foreign land to train pilots who would become the decorated Tuskegee Airmen of World War II. Yet, that day, Robinson served as a symbol not only of resistance to imperialism in Africa but also of the intertwining fates of Africa and her sons and daughters in America. Marcus Garvey's Africa, "a bright star among the constellation of nations," made so by continuing cooperation between "Africans at home and abroad," awaited its rise.[1]

Although the forecast called for rain, on the day following Robinson's return thousands of New Yorkers came outdoors to pay homage to Africa in their own distinctive ways. Early that morning "sympathizers with Ethiopia in her struggle against the Italian invasion" congregated in front of Patsy's Fish Market on Lenox Avenue in Harlem to hold a "street meeting." By the late afternoon, at an unrelated event some fifty blocks downtown, nearly two thousand members and their guests gathered on the steps of the American Museum of Natural History (AMNH) around the Theodore Roosevelt Memorial statue awaiting the dedication of the Akeley Memorial Hall of African Mammals. The *New York Times*, which had also covered Robinson's arrival, reported that the sympathizers with Ethiopia at the Lenox Avenue meeting "dispersed without disorder," but twelve "hoodlums" disrupted their departure by throwing bricks through Patsy's window, and a "riot" ensued. The journalist explained how a "mob" of twelve seemed to grow exponentially to one hundred and then to four hundred in minutes. The reporter's description of the twelve men as a "mob" suggests that the number of protestors may have been exaggerated. Meanwhile, in two separate articles, one of which included a pictorial spread, the newspaper described how Africa had come to the Akeley Memorial Hall of African Mammals in the form of fifteen habitat dioramas and an elephant centerpiece titled "The Herd." The correspondents hailed the dioramas for "their artistic beauty, dramatic realism, and scientific accuracy" but most important for their enabling the AMNH to achieve the impossible: the dioramas brought Africa to America.[2]

Competing images of Africa as a space of egalitarian celebrity and military manhood, a site for black international and antifascist consciousness, and a foreign artifact all converged on New York City that May. However, it is insufficient to treat the events discussed above as simply representative of radically different views of Africa—those of black elites, middle- and working-class "New Negroes," New York socialites, middle-class whites, and white naturalists.[3] Instead, the events' interconnectedness becomes apparent when their narratives are placed within the cultural and political context of American knowledge production about Africa. Although these events took place in 1936, they encapsulated a decades-long discursive process of reimagining Africa in American intellectual and popular discourses that spread through film, literature, academia, museum exhibits, and political thought. Using these events as a springboard, this book examines the idea of Africa as both a geographic place and a political marker in American intellectual and cultural history. Located on one end of the spectrum was the "Darkest Africa" trope associated with impenetrable jungles, wild beasts, savages, and primitive governments. On the other end lay several iterations of "Brightest Africa": the continent as a pristine wilderness, a site for black repatriation, a space for white masculine regeneration, and a place for black empowerment. This work concerns the development of this counterimage as it reveals an epistemological break, a discursive rupture with centuries-old Western imagery of Africa. Although the Dark Continent construct never disappeared from the Western cultural and intellectual landscape, Brightest Africa posed a considerable challenge to that paradigm, becoming a pervasive part of American intellectual history, scientific debate, and institution building from 1884 to 1936. From the Berlin Conference of 1884–1885, which inaugurated the European "scramble for Africa," to the annexation of Ethiopia by Italy on May 7, 1936, American debates over the significance of Africa to both the United States and the broader Atlantic world reached unprecedented levels. As Penny Von Eschen has convincingly argued, "the Italian invasion of Ethiopia in 1935 marked an especially critical moment in the articulation of diaspora thought and politics." After the annexation, "the politics of the African Diaspora" assumed a different posture with the founding of the International African Service Bureau in 1937.[4] The European quest to control the entire African continent coinciding with America's mounting racial tensions fostered a unique atmosphere for reimagining Africa as a bright continent, visions in themselves multifaceted and stemming from a variety of motivations.

On the one hand, a new generation of African American intellectuals and ordinary black folk (as well as other diaspora blacks) challenged the Dark Continent thesis that whites perpetuated to justify the enslavement and political subjugation of peoples of African descent. For these African Americans, vindicating Africa—that is, removing the stigma of savagery attached to its people and challenging the European invasion of the continent—would aid in the realization of their own redemption. On the other hand, primarily white American environmental writers and naturalists began using Africa as a portent of the destruction of pristine wildlife by the forces of civilization and modernity. My term *naturalist-environmentalists* refers to those individuals trained in natural history, specifically zoology, who advocated for the protection of the natural environment, including wildlife. These men and women strove to save Africa as part of a larger project tied to preservation and conservation movements emerging in Western metropolises. Although naturalists conceived of their project as providing an alternative to the Darkest Africa trope, their critiques reflected an embedded essentialist image of Africa as a site of primitivism. In an interesting parallel, American critiques of imperialism in Africa selectively linked Africa's fate to that of the United States. Where white naturalists drew connections between Africa and America as sites of environmental degradation, blacks linked the two via their black populations and their quests for self-determination. Both groups' missions represented a struggle over shared terms—*redemption* or *preservation*—that were given meaning within localized systems of logic that assumed not only a virtually homogeneous Africa but also a continent locked in stasis.

In discussing black and white imaginings of Africa it is important to note that they at times defy placement into neat categories of Pan-Africanism and naturalist-environmentalism. Some white Americans, predominantly anti-imperialists and missionaries, envisioned an Africa free from colonial dominance or "redeemed" by the "light" of Christianity. Similarly, African Americans also articulated their own naturalist and environmentalist agenda. Some blacks' participation in safaris, American world fairs, the Cotton States Exposition in 1895, the Paris International Exposition of 1900, and the 1907 Jamestown Tercentennial Exposition reveals a refusal to cede naturalist discourses to whites. In addition, African American engagement with museum culture as patron, critic, or curator discloses the interconnectedness of black political and scientific thought. However, the focus of this study remains on the predominantly white naturalist-environmentalist and Pan-African discourses.[5]

That American naturalists, environmentalists, Pan-Africanists, missionaries, black intellectuals, and ordinary black folk alike viewed themselves as redeemers of a continent besieged by the forces of European imperialism obliges us to consider the memetic nature of the Darkest Africa myth in American culture. Yet, one need not be a meme theorist to recognize the dynamism and functionality of the idea of Darkest Africa—often treated by scholars as an a priori Western image of the continent—and how it was sustained not only from its replication via old and new information technologies but also from challenges posed by proponents of Brightest Africa. Ultimately, many images of Brightest Africa found congruence with the underlining premise of the trope of the Dark Continent wielded by imperialists.[6] The very notion that Africa needed saving, articulated either as environmentalist discourse or as Pan-Africanist politics, presupposed a continent whose people were incapable of enforcing environmental protection or enacting self-determination on their own terms. Thus, in one context, locating Brightest Africa in natural history (flora and fauna) or in a future uniform nation-state constituted a radical epistemological move—seeing brightness in a geography described as inhospitable or in people dismissed as apolitical savages. But in another context, it sustained the dominant image of Africa and Africans as helpless victims of Western expansion. The tendency of American environmental and political defenders of Africa to downplay the role of Africans in the continent's redemption discloses the potency of this image.

The subject of the Western image of Africa is not a new topic in cultural and intellectual history or cultural studies. Scholarly literature abounds that documents the myriad ways in which Europeans (and later Americans) propagated the trope of Darkest Africa over centuries of contact with the continent, specifically in the context of the transatlantic slave trade and imperialism. Scholars have argued that during the medieval period Africans enjoyed a favorable image in Europe as some Africans were part of the courtly system, referred to as Moors, moriscos, or mohren rather than as Negroes or its racialized derivatives. Court records described African courtiers as noble, comely, and intelligent; literature and paintings depicted Africans positively; and the Prester John legend circulated Europe. Other scholars have examined stereotypical images of black Africans that emerged during the Renaissance as vital to unearthing the origins of the Dark Continent myth. Complementing these scholars, Winthrop Jordan's seminal work *White over Black* (1968) locates the American demonization of Africa and blacks in the early years of the slave trade. Jordan argued that Europeans, particularly the English, tapped into their pre-existing linguistic devaluation of all things dark or black to reimagine Africa and Africans as inferior and evil in order to justify their enslavement. He also posited that colonial Americans and New Republicans helped reinforce the image of the Dark Continent to rationalize their legal sanctioning of a racialized system of slavery. The Jordan thesis, specifically its depiction of the adoption of racial slavery as an "unthinking decision," has been criticized and reconsidered over the last four decades. However, Jordan's basic premise—that Europeans did not always view Africans as savages and Africa as dark—points to an evolving Western image of Africa inflected by American ideas about its own African population.[7]

Scholars have also explored the role of museums and environmentalists in shaping popular images of Africa, often as discreet episodes in Western imaginings of Africa. Jonathan S. Adams and Thomas O. McShane's *The Myth of Wild Africa* discusses the origins of conservation/preservation rhetoric in the European travel narrative trope of Africa as the "empty wilderness." However, the authors' interest lies primarily in the ways in which these narratives have served as models for contemporary conservation policies in Africa that often deny local Africans roles in shaping environmental policies. Similarly, William Beinart and Peter A. Coates's comparative analysis of the reinforcing histories of environmentalism in South Africa and the United States unveils them to be critical markers of their respective racial pasts with relation to land policies and native rights. However, the authors' goal is to understand this complex history in order to reform current environmental policies. The works of Donna Haraway, Fatimah Tobing Rony, and Tracy Lang Teslow offer compelling discussions of the ways in which museums have historically represented race to the public. However, exploring the discursive relationship between museum culture, science (for example, natural history), conservation movements, popular culture, and politics in shaping American images of Africa brings those ideas of Africa viewed principally through the eyes of white Western scientists into conversation with those of African Americans who at the same moment reinvented Africa and offered an alternative representation of race to the public. In such an analysis, images of Africa are not treated as a subtheme in a broader analysis of patriarchy in primate studies, race in ethnographic film, indigenous hunting rights, or a need for reform in contemporary conservation policies.[8]

Arguably Dennis Hickey and Kenneth Wylie's *An Enchanting Darkness* (1993) represents the most comprehensive treatment to date of American images of Africa that includes the perspectives of both white Americans and African Americans. The book offers a survey of American writing (and sometimes those of selected Europeans and West Indians residing in America) about Africa, irrespective of genre, to support their argument that the Dark Continent stereotype continues to dominate the American popular imagination. Hickey and Wylie contend that the intervention of African American intellectuals and anthropologists, among other progressive writers, played and continues to play significant roles in undermining American images of Darkest Africa popularized in mass media. Their assessment does not argue for a watershed in American visions of Africa but rather offers overviews of the political circumstances that produced certain images of Africa in a given space and time.

Hickey and Wylie's study laid the groundwork for further research, including this study, which emphasizes two watershed dates in American visions of Africa—1884 and 1936—which reveal the complex processes of invention, propagation, imitation, competition, mutation, and modification with regard to the image of Darkest Africa. Although the resilience of the trope of the Dark Continent cannot be understated, serious challenges to that myth emerged within the political and cultural contexts outlined in this introduction. Multiple forms of media other than the printed text emerging during this period also disseminated images of Africa, arguably more effectively in this early unprecedented era of mass communication, media, and culture. Images of Africa found in the novel, scientific treatise, and travel narrative informed and enjoyed a symbiotic relationship with those that appeared in film, radio, and museum exhibits.

Reimagining Africa as either a wilderness utopia or a future political Canaan exteriorized the identity politics of the participants in these new discourses. Those invested in these crusades used their proverbial battlegrounds to perform their racial and gender identities and assert their intellectual authority as "race men" and "men of science" in America. Their use of the noun "men" is misleading, as women played significant roles in naturalist culture (for example, safari) and what historian Davarian Baldwin terms "New Africanisms." White naturalists Delia Akeley, Mary Jobe Akeley, and Osa Johnson and black political thinkers Anna Julia Cooper and Amy Jacques Garvey fought to be heard in what many considered masculine spheres and pursuits, yet they strove to maintain their "feminine" traits. However, the commanding figures in these movements were often white and black men on whom their communities and outsiders alike conferred authority. In their own discrete racialized performances of masculinity, naturalists Carl Akeley, Theodore Roosevelt, and Martin Johnson and Pan-Africanists Marcus Garvey, W. E. B. Du Bois, and Alexander Crummell affirmed that the initiative to "save" Africa would be a transatlantic effort spearheaded by intellectual men in the Western Hemisphere.

With respect to the various articulations of Pan-Africanism—from elite social clubs to mass political movements to black soldiers' linking up in European metropolises and Africa—male and female thinkers alike emphasized the "manhood of the race." Their desire to contest images of black men as feminized—rendered docile through slavery or as emasculated spectators to the ruination of their women and children—translated into frequent calls for whites and Europeans to "recognize the manhood of the Negro."[9] Moreover, as Martin Summers argues, African American men often articulated their "demands for remedies" against the dehumanizing realities of Jim Crow and lynching "within the discourse of 'manhood rights.'"[10]

Arguably, Pan-Africanist laudations of an African past characterized by cultural diversity, aesthetic achievement, and multivariate political formations, most notably a comparable aristocratic empire (mostly under the leadership of men), served simultaneously to redeem the image of Africa and reclaim an idealized black manhood and womanhood historically denied to African Americans through slavery. This reclamation often entailed remaking the Victorian politics of respectability to meet the needs of the black community.

Elite and middle-class Pan-Africanists, as well as racial uplift ideologues, often accentuated the need for blacks to conform to Victorian morality and gender roles. The man as protector of the home, and by extension the race, reverberated among some black women weary of defending their moral and civic virtue against charges of harlotry and political ignorance. The black elite and middle class were in the vanguard of these efforts to merge Victorianism with Pan-Africanism, primarily through print media, the public square, or the pulpit. However, many working-class and other blacks with limited or no opportunities to publish or deliver stump speeches used their bodies and voices to perform their own form of Pan-Africanism by participating in urban public protests and street meetings. Although the guardians of black respectability shunned the more raucous demonstrations, believing they reinforced images of blacks and Africans as savages, they approved of African Americans publicly championing Africa as long as they were properly coiffed and adorned. Defending Africa was as much a political act as a performance of a respectable, unashamed "blackness."[11] As Summers argues, when African American men deployed the discourse of manhood to laud black men's military service, leadership in the church, or missionary efforts in Africa, "they engaged the same discourse that white men did—discourses that grounded manhood in, among other things, independence, citizenship, engagement in the marketplace, mastery over self and environment, and patriarchy."[12]

Africa also played a key role in constructing modern manhood for white men. Concurrent with black men's assertions of a new manhood, a "new style of masculinity" tied to whiteness surfaced, as observed by E. Anthony Rotundo. This quest for renewed manhood intersected with American nostalgia for the lost frontier. Although this masculinity exalted the agrarian past, it did not repudiate civilization entirely. Members of the white middle and upper classes and transplanted rural men living in urban centers embraced this manliness, perhaps best epitomized in the figure of Theodore Roosevelt, partially as a result of his distinguished service in the Spanish-

American War. When Roosevelt announced on December 6, 1908, that he would safari in the Dark Continent, he challenged white men to embrace the "strenuous life" and renew their manhood. As Gail Bederman argues: "By projecting pure primitivism onto Africa, Roosevelt constructed it as a place where Stone Age men battled large, fierce animals—where he could fully savor both the advancement of his own superior civilized manliness, and the violent power of his primitive masculinity."[13] A chance to safari in Africa could lead to the regeneration of white manhood.

The identity politics that underlay the efforts of Pan-Africanists and naturalists to reframe Africa in the popular imagination informed their perceptions of their cultural projects. (Here, Edward Said's notion of projects as actions undertaken with the purpose of uncovering or producing knowledge of the Other is helpful.)[14] Adopting a paternalistic rhetoric akin to that employed by imperialist powers claiming a civilizing influence on a backwards continent, many white naturalists and Pan-Africanists saw themselves as saviors of Africa. Although most Pan-Africanist thinkers accentuated the need for cooperation between Africans "at home and abroad," a conspicuous number of high-profile activists believed that the American "Negro" had either a political duty or providential mission to reclaim the continent for all blacks. Men like the influential Liberian Edward Wilmot Blyden (considered to be the father of Pan-Africanism) theologized the enslavement of Africans in the Americas as part of a divine plan to place God's chosen people in the fire so that they would come out as pure gold. "Trained in the house of bondage," these tried and tested men and women would fulfill their ultimate purpose—to bring Christianity and democracy to their ancestral continent. Like Garvey, Blyden argued that the descendants of Africans in the Americas (predominantly Anglophone) possessed the educational, commercial, political, and industrial experience necessary for the "regeneration" of the continent.[15]

White naturalists who extended their campaign beyond the museum to save Africa became active participants in preservation movements in Africa. For them the "white man's burden" was not to bring Christianity, commerce, and civilization to Africa but rather to use science to save a fast-disappearing continent. Terence Ranger's case study of the establishment of Matobo National Park demonstrates how the image of Africa as a vanishing continent appealed to "a rather romantic sort of science." E. A. Nobbs's lobbying efforts in 1919 to establish a national park in Matopos (a region south of Bulawayo in Zimbabwe) prove particularly illustrative. Nobbs hoped to retain the area in its "pristine condition for scientific interests" and believed that the park would "preserve in perpetuity the pristine conditions of South Africa—rapidly vanishing throughout the rest of the subcontinent."[16] Similarly, American naturalists affiliated with the AMNH and the National Geographic Society worked tirelessly with the Belgian government to establish Parc National Albert in the Congo to protect the gorilla from extinction. The park was the brainchild of Carl Akeley, who proposed that it be guarded by a combination of a foreign conservation corps and a native police force. Insightfully, Akeley argued that the protection of the park required the cooperation of Africans, which could "be obtained through giving careful thought and considerations to their needs and rights." He observed: "The natives of this region have disturbed the gorillas very little, nor have the gorillas disturbed the natives. Certain it is that the gorillas got along very well till the white men came along with guns."[17] Although Akeley and groups such as the British Society for the Preservation of Fauna in the Empire recognized the need for Africans to play a role in the conservation movement, the paternalism of colonial politics denied them any voice in policy making. These naturalists turned environmentalists declared that the decision making be left to white men, thereby physically and ideologically converting the land and its resources into a white imperial space.

The dissemination of images of Brightest Africa by way of new and old technologies reflected a form of knowledge production about Africa constructed and empowered by those outside of the continent. Although white American naturalists collaborated with their European counterparts, some who resided in Africa, the ideas that they created about the continent did not reflect indigenous ways of knowing the environment. For sure, they consulted native informants—predominantly porters, gun bearers, and occasionally nobles—to gather information about the location of herds or the habits of animals. However, naturalists often dismissed indigenous knowledge as unscientific, sensational, or superstitious. Similarly, many Pan-Africanists and black intellectuals in America privileged their own knowledge of Africa derived from their personal travels to the continent or those of other reputable diasporic Africans. Although they often enjoyed close relationships with Africans whom they met, their public veneration of the continent rested primarily on images of historic kings, queens, empires, and kingdoms—with the exception of the Emperors Menelik II and Haile Selassie of Ethiopia. As Clare Corbould has argued regarding African American identity formation in Harlem, "Africa's past splendor was something of which to be proud, not ashamed, just as Americans were proud of the republican democracy they had built and defended."[18] Historic African kings epitomized black masculinity and leadership and, thus, served as beacons of a Brightest Africa to come. Garvey's self-designation as "Provisional President of Africa" reflected his own conviction that he would play a vital role—perhaps more so than Africans themselves—in uniting Africa and elevating its global status. Other Pan-Africanists extolled the success of black missionary activities in Africa as evidence of a continent inhabited by godly people willing to turn away from their false gods and return to their monotheistic roots—arguing that the slave trade disrupted Africa's historic embrace of Christianity. However, Pan-Africanist-minded blacks like Max Yergan, a missionary who worked for the YMCA in South Africa, embraced a "liberating interpretation of Christianity" or "Christian radicalism" that emphasized the cooperation of African Americans and Africans toward the "redemption of Africa." They envisioned an alliance that would transcend class and national hierarchies.[19]

To analyze the search for Brightest Africa as a challenge to the trope of Darkest Africa, this book takes the form of an intellectual and cultural history, informed by the methodologies of the history of science, critical race studies, museum studies, environmental studies, and the new imperial history.[20] These approaches facilitate an interrogation of the reimagining of Africa that not only is descriptive but also seeks to explain which Americans envisioned Africa in distinct ways and why. Thus, the book attends to the intersections of race, gender, and class in determining who had the power to contest and shape dominant discourses about Africa in particular communities. To tell this complex story, the book uses a range of sources that reflect the role of both traditional cultural forms—such as autobiographies, speeches, political pamphlets, travel narratives, journal and newspaper articles—and new technologies—predominantly film, museum exhibits, and radio—in shaping American images of Africa. Archival source materials, which include colonial office records, personal correspondences, and official museum records, help to contextualize these other primary sources as entrenched within particular sites of knowledge production.

The political conditions that coalesced to favor an American re-envisioning of Africa from 1884 to 1936 coincided with critical issues in American cultural life. The European partition of Africa impacted the emergence of modern Pan-Africanism, which linked the fate of Africans to the Negro Problem in America and thus, informed the African American search for a usable identity. Thus, reimagining Africa informed not only the fashioning of a new assertive racial identity—the New Negro—but also the politics of black masculinity and femininity as well. The advent of American anti-imperialism that condemned the European project in Africa also swayed environmentalist sentiment that linked American nostalgia for the frontier to the crisis of masculinity among white men, as well as women's pursuit of "New Woman identities" associated with first-wave feminism and the crisis of womanhood.[21] The new technologies made available during this period democratized old spaces and created new sites in which these men and women could challenge the dominant image of Africa as the Dark Continent. Ultimately, the invention of Brightest Africa was a dialogic process by which Pan-Africanists, anti-imperialists, naturalists, and environmentalists alike challenged and informed imperialist narratives about the continent.

ONE

A Cry from Africa

Victorians, New Women, New Negroes, and Moderns Confront the Dark Continent

In December 1882, the black newspaper the *Virginia Star* ran two articles addressing the need for Christian evangelization in Africa under African American impetus, citing clergymen who argued that such work would result in the "spiritual regeneration of Africa." The article "A Noble African" summarized a sermon delivered by Edward Wilmot Blyden at the First African Baptist Church in Richmond, in which he discussed the successes and failures of foreign evangelizing in Africa. At the time of the lecture, Blyden was president of Liberia College, where he had begun teaching in 1881.[1] Calling on congregants to support the college, Blyden noted the success of former slave Lott Cary (also Carey) and other members of the First African Baptist Church in establishing sister churches in Liberia. Founded as a colony for freed blacks from the United States in 1822, Liberia gained its independence in 1847. Blyden argued that "Africans must be agents under God" if the continent wished to discard practices that kept "the heathen in his blindness." According to him, the "noble crusades" of European Christians, white American Protestants, and Roman Catholics failed foremost

13

because they were ignorant of African realities. He also argued that white missionaries could not withstand the climatic conditions of the continent. Like many intellectuals of the era, Blyden believed that God created races to live in specific environments.[2]

Fourteen days after Blyden's speech, another article, "A Cry from Africa," appeared in the *Virginia Star* reproving African Methodist Episcopal (AME) bishop Rev. W. R. Carson for claiming that evangelism in the American South should take precedence over any overseas missionary activities, as according to Carson, the disadvantages facing southern blacks outweighed those experienced by their African brethren. Echoing Bishop R. H. Cain, who held that the duties of the church to the South and Africa were equal, the article chided Carson. "This reverend gentleman must not forget the command of his Lord and Master: 'Go ye into all the world and preach,' and not make an excuse for not going or sending the Gospel to poor Africa, who is crying loudly for it now in such ways as not to be misunderstood." Cain was a former president of Paul Quinn College founded by traveling ministers of the AME church in Austin, Texas. Although Cain was dedicated to educating black youth, he embraced African missionary work, which the AME Church viewed as vital to its outreach ministries.[3]

Addressing the question of the Christianization of Africa, these two articles reflected one emerging interpretation African Americans' relationship to Africa in the wake of Emancipation. Specifically, black clergymen and intellectuals began to argue for the providential mission and "racial destiny" of black missionaries to bring their brethren in Africa into the Christian fold. This new understanding of Africa as a site for black racial uplift, while rooted in discourses of heathenish Darkest Africa, made the continent directly relevant to the lives of African Americans. As Michele Mitchell has argued, this belief that African Americans had a duty to Christianize Africa was one manifestation of the so-called "black man's burden"—the embrace of imperialism tied to "racial manhood."[4] What united Blyden's and Cain's calls for Christian proselytizing in Africa was a conviction that in the wake of European imperialism African Americans had to stake their claim on the continent—not with the spirit of the conqueror but with that of a helper. Yet, Blyden moved beyond missionary efforts, connecting the fate of all Africans in the diaspora to the prosperity of the lone African republic. As he would in many speeches to follow, Blyden argued that freedom in Liberia was preferable to second-class citizenship and economic subservience in the Americas, particularly the United States.

A Cry from Africa

The "cry from Africa" heard by Bishop Cain and other black leaders came at a time when African Americans suffered under the strictures of Jim Crow and political disenfranchisement, faced economic malaise and racial violence, and sought new avenues to achieve self-determination and to challenge white supremacy. Some blacks chose to turn inward, to reject assimilation and integration into the dominant white society, opting instead to continue to build independent black communities and institutions. Some decided to migrate out of the South and the North, heading for the mythic West, where supposedly rugged individualism and frontier democracy would allow blacks to own their own land and businesses and enjoy a measure of autonomy. Still others began looking outward, toward Africa, as a source of not only identity but also potential residence.

Societies and organizations such as Benjamin "Pap" Singleton's United Trans-Atlantic Society, the Liberian Emigration Association, and the Liberian Exodus Joint-Stock Steamship Company, to name a few, emerged in response to the oppressions that southern African Americans faced at the close of Reconstruction. The black community fiercely debated the merits of wide-scale emigration of African Americans to Africa, and the church often operated as a forum for these discussions. Indeed, blacks looked to their clergymen for guidance on this crucial issue and its implication—namely that African Americans would never achieve equality in the United States. Not coincidently, these conversations took place as the United States embraced the new imperialism of the era, which included European expansion in Africa and Asia and interference in Latin American affairs.

The new imperialism that gripped Europe beginning in the 1870s, culminated in the establishment of colonies, protectorates, and economic spheres of influence in Asia and Africa. This imperialism differed starkly from older forms of expansionism as the goal of its proponents was foremost economic—to create new markets and control new sources of raw materials. New imperialists essentially abandoned the creation of settler colonies in favor of treaties that gave them effective dominion over entire countries, kingdoms, and their peoples. Fearing that European nations would surpass its international trade and economic growth, the United States at the behest of American public officials and politicians went in search of its own overseas possessions. Looking westward, the United States signed a treaty with Samoa in 1878 and a reciprocal trade agreement with Hawaii in 1875, giving America a base for naval operations at Pago Pago and a near monopoly in sugar production in Hawaii.[5] Despite continued American penetration into the Pacific, Europeans still eclipsed the United States as imperial powers, due in large part to the designs of Britain, France, Germany, Italy, Belgium, and Portugal on Africa.

European exploration in Africa had begun in earnest as early as 1768 with Scottish explorer James Bruce's trip to Ethiopia. His travels inaugurated a new era of European penetration into Africa, which included the famed expeditions of Mungo Park (1795–1797, 1805–1806), René Caillié (1827–1828), John and Richard Lander (1830), Richard Burton, John Speke, and James Grant (1857–1863), David Livingstone (1852–1856, 1858–1864, 1866–1873), Hienrich Barth (1850–1855), Gustav Nachtigal (1870–1874), and Henry Morton Stanley (1874–1877). It was the latter's journeys in the Congo and his crossing of the Lualaba River in 1876 that opened up the continent and led to the partition of Africa south of the Sahara. When European nations gathered in Berlin during the winter of 1884–1885 at the Kongokonferenz to discuss open access to trade and the waterways of the Congo basin, much of Africa had fallen under European control. Thus, the General Act of the Berlin Conference signed by the participants only formalized, regulated, and sanctioned a process that had unfolded over the past decade. By 1902, after the Ashanti War and the annexation of Ashanti territories into the Gold Coast colony, all of Africa—with the exception of Liberia and Ethiopia—was under European domination.[6]

Although Americans were present at the Berlin conference, the United States expressed no formal imperial designs on Africa. That Liberia maintained its independence as European signatories to the act carved up their neighbors into colonies and protectorates assuaged American public officials who feared that their only tie to Africa would fall prey to the scramblers. Additionally, American businessmen reveled at the opportunity to engage in lucrative trade with Africa. Their missionary counterparts also conceded (at least initially) that the European presence on the continent would aid their evangelistic efforts. For other Americans, their interest in Africa during this period (1884–1902) was refracted through the imperialist eye—specifically Stanley's, whose tales of Darkest Africa intrigued a cross-section of Americans.

Prior to the scramble for Africa, the average American knew little about Africa, other than it was the aboriginal homeland of the enslaved men and women from which the African American population descended. For over a century, Americans had pictured Africa as the Dark Continent, "in pigments of shadow-drenched jungles, viciously charging animals, superstitious savages, and black slavery."[7] Public defiance of that imagery in America—as early as the late eighteenth century—invariably came from free black men and women who had access to letters, the public square, and the printing press. Prince Hall, David Walker, and Robert Alexander Young, among others who eulogized the glories of ancient Egypt and Ethiopia as the slave's stolen birthright, constituted a minority of American voices challenging the trope of Darkest Africa.[8] However, as the majority of African Americans remained illiterate or resided in communities with little access to the black press, their knowledge of Africa came mostly from oral tradition. Nevertheless, even facing the crucible of antebellum slavery or a quasi-free status in the United States, free and enslaved blacks developed a sense of kinship with one another and other diaspora blacks rooted in their African ancestry.

Political theorists attribute the evolution of Pan-Negro Nationalism—the idea that all persons of African descent constituted a metaphorical nation with shared interests—to the growth of the antebellum free, literate African American population, specifically elites and missionaries who traveled to Africa. Emphasizing the consanguine alliance between all persons of African descent, Pan-Negro Nationalists defended Africa as a land of redemption, thereby joining the phalanx of the emigration movement that advocated repatriation or return to Africa. Although blood ties to Africa remained an integral part of many African Americans' racial identity and political consciousness, it was not until the late nineteenth century that modern Pan-Africanism emerged. In contrast to Pan-Negro Nationalists, Pan-Africanists claimed a racial kinship or brotherhood with all persons of African descent, without necessarily advocating emigration or Black Nationalism.[9] Instead of wedding themselves exclusively to a policy of emigration, Christianization, and "civilizing," they expanded their political agenda to include the unification of the entire continent (south of the Sahara) in a federal-like system, often downplaying or rejecting the religious agenda of the old guard.

During the nadir (1877–1901), marked by lynching, race riots, Jim Crow, and legislative suppression of African American freedom, blacks began to publish newspapers widely, establish race institutions, and create counterpublic spaces where they could fashion their own culture and political ideologies. This included assigning cultural and political meaning to Africa. While Trinidadian Henry Sylvester Williams would not organize the Pan-African Association until 1897 and the first Pan-African Conference would not convene until 1900, black elites, intellectuals, clergymen, and ordinary black folk publicly condemned imperialism in Africa, performing their own iterations of Pan-Africanism.[10] Whether expressed orally, in print, or via the body in street meetings, African American opposition to the partition of Africa linked inextricably to their own struggle for equality in America. Their imaginings of a bright Africa, expressed either as nostalgia for the glorious past of the idolized Ethiopia or as prophecy of a postcolonial united continent, inaugurated a sustained critique of the Dark Continent thesis that would survive well into the 1930s in African American political speeches, literature, and in the platforms and activities of racial uplift, anti-imperialist, and social justice organizations. However, blacks were not alone in their reappraisal of dominant images of Africa in response to the 1885 partition of the continent.

White Americans also grappled with relating Africa to the United States in the wake of the Berlin Conference. Most of the postbellum white-authored American literature on Africa published before the 1884 conference took the form of travel narratives, geography textbooks, and scientific treatises on race. The popular white imagination clung to the descriptions of Africa and its inhabitants found in texts such as *Mitchell's Geography* primer (1873) and Stanley's descriptions of the Congo in *Through the Dark Continent* (1878), while white intellectuals engaged emerging scientific literature on race. Race science gained increasing legitimacy in the late nineteenth century, and with respect to Africans and "Negroes," the majority of race scientists brandished their findings to uphold extant doctrines of white supremacy. However, as Lee D. Baker argues, on the eve of the fin de siècle progressive American scientists began to challenge images of Africans as savages. Chief among these revisionists were anthropologists who studied in Europe (mostly Germany) but worked in the United States or trained under men like Franz Boas who were committed to political and social equality. While American anthropologists worked to discredit the accepted scientific notion of "savagery," helping set the stage for naturalists who would contest images of Africa as the Dark Continent, they did not launch a coordinated campaign to save Africa for future generations. Their paradigmatic shift to cultural relativism held implications for studying all so-called savages, not just Africans. In contrast, naturalists devoted to rescuing Africa interpreted their environmentalist work as uniquely tied to the African landscape, despite drawing comparisons between North American and African topography.

For white naturalists, many who grew up in the Wild West or in rural America, Africa reminded them of the lost frontier, which officially closed in 1890 according to the United States Census Bureau.[11] Frederick Jackson Turner's historic essay "The Significance of the Frontier in American History" delivered at the 1893 Chicago's Columbian Exposition meeting of the American Historical Association had several imperial implications for American images of Africa at home and abroad. Turner's valorization of the frontier as a space where Americans "return to primitive conditions," strip "off the garments of civilization," and "win" a wilderness validated the imperial past of the United States. Noting the "expansive character of American life," Turner argued: "Movement has been its dominant fact, and unless this training has no effect upon a people, the American energy will continually demand a wider field for its exercise." Romanticizing the "Indian wars" and the farmers and ranchers who encroached on Native American lands, Turner's eulogy for the frontier served as a clarion call to Americans to seek out new frontiers.[12]

Indeed, witnessing the decimation of the buffalo or destruction of forests under the forces of industrialization encouraged Americans to look elsewhere for communion with nature. Other popular concerns about the closing of the American frontier bolstered nascent prognoses of "race suicide" and "degeneration" among whites who had not benefited from exposure to unfettered nature. Fears that cosmopolitan life feminized white men led Teddy Roosevelt to advocate the pursuit of "the strenuous life." He warned Americans of the dangers of living a life of "ignoble ease," lambasted "over-civilized" men for their laziness, and scorned men of "dull mind," urging them to seek rebirth through communion with nature. For Roosevelt and other naturalists, Africa hearkened as a beacon of earth's primeval past—an ideal site for regeneration. Roosevelt quoted Shakespeare's *Henry IV, Part II* to open his safari narrative, *African Game Trails* (1910). Explaining the lure of Africa, he wrote: "I speak of Africa and golden joys, the joy of wondering through lonely lands."[13] Roosevelt and many of his naturalist contemporaries extolled the African landscape and wildlife as emblematic of a pristine world endangered by modernity. However, as they chided colonial powers for their failure to protect the environment, American naturalists fashioned their own imperialist gaze that rendered Africa a fertile resource in preservationist rhetoric.

These naturalists who championed Africa often wrote of being enthralled by Stanley's descriptions of great rivers, Paul Belloni Du Chaillu's accounts of Pygmies and gorillas, and Speke's claim of discovering the source of the Nile in the East African interlacustrine region. They dreamed of traveling to Africa to recapture the lost innocence of the frontier and their manhood.

Until 1884 when Europeans opened up Africa to further exploration and settlement, these naturalists stood little chance of traveling to the continent that they began to see as bright. Revealingly, although white American naturalists, some of whom became "Great White Hunters," appreciated the colonial administrations that allowed them to travel across the continent relatively unmolested, they regretted the destruction that imperialism wrought on the African landscape. Affiliating themselves with urban museums of natural history, these men and women envisaged a vanishing continent and waged a campaign to save Africa for posterity. Concomitant with this objective was a desire to convince their fellow Americans (and indeed the broader Western world) that Africa was not the proverbial Dark Continent. They reasoned that if one viewed Africa as "that most interesting animal kingdom," one would see its true beauty.[14]

American reactions to European imperial conquest in Africa—particularly to the Congo question—coincided with articulations of new forms of identity and political thought in the United States during the formation of modern America, around 1890 to 1930.[15] Pinpointing exact dates for the rise of modernity in America has always been contested by historians. Yet, there exists an overwhelming consensus that rapid urbanization, increased immigration, mass internal migration, and industrialization as well as America's quest for empire during the 1890s composed the forces that irrevocably transformed the nation. In addition, shifts in cultural, political, and intellectual expressions corresponded to these processes that reshaped the American landscape and everyday life. Modernity as a signifier of progress came to represent different things to diverse groups in America, such that living modern lives could mean participating in the mass consumer marketplace, voting in a national election, riding on a train absent Jim Crow, or traveling to far-away places. Yet, as Americans approached the end of the nineteenth century marveling at the changes taking place across the nation, many continued expressing their discontent with the status quo with regard to racism, gender oppression, nativism, and other "isms" that seemed to belie the moral progress of the United States.[16]

The introduction of mass media and mass cultural forms in America during this period proved instrumental in shaping American cultures of dissent and struggles for equality. Commercial amusements, film, and radio threatened to destabilize the authority of the printed text, the traditional museum exhibit, and the gallery. The appeal of these new cultural forms to the masses increasingly challenged reigning distinctions between highbrow and lowbrow culture, elevating the popular in American life. As a result, the technological innovations that produced new media and improved old ones actualized new sites for the production of knowledge. While much of these new technologies served the hegemonic interests of their industrial producers, as access to these media democratized, spaces opened up for cultural producers and social groups to use these forms to contest existing bodies of knowledge and invent their own.[17] Thus, those Americans in search of Brightest Africa conscientiously used cinema, radio, print media, and the new technologies of display for modern fairs and expositions and museum exhibits to engage the masses or public in reimagining Africa. However, unequal access to these technologies, often as a result of racial discrimination and class stratification, in many ways determined the success of Pan-Africanists and naturalist-environmentalists in promoting their new images of Africa.

As noted, Pan-Africanist thought, although owing its origins to late eighteenth- and nineteenth-century African American emigrationist platforms, concretized in the late nineteenth century as a direct result of the partition of Africa. Africa entered African American political discourse and social thought as integral to black self-determination at home and abroad, informing the identity politics of many New Negroes, including New Women. In religious circles, some African Americans looked to Africa for spiritual inspiration, searching for a more indigenous Christianity or to reclaim Islam. Others, such as Christian missionaries, interpreted the European penetration of Africa as a call for them to evangelize the natives, not as foreigners, but as men and women returning to the home of their ancestors. During the Harlem Renaissance, as Kathy Ogren argues, artists, writers, political thinkers, and intellectuals mediated their engagement with European and American forms as sources of inspiration by employing "African strategies"—evoking Africa literally and figuratively in their work.[18] Outside this circle of elite and middle-class African Americans, Africa took on new meaning and significance for some white New Women and Moderns looking to throw off the strictures of Victorianism. As Lynn Dumenil points out, Victorians "valued hierarchy, order, and a single standard, of culture, morality, and values" whereas Moderns in the new consumer culture valued leisure, a flexible morality, and "personal pleasure."[19] Inspired by Stanley, white Americans began traveling to Africa for pleasure, sport, and science, among them New Women explorers as well as "great white hunters." Some whites joined the crusade to Christianize Africa as part of the white man's burden to bring civilization to the Dark Continent. Other white Moderns celebrated Africa for its primitivism, reevaluating its musical, art, literary, and dance traditions.

Situating the cultural work of Pan-Africanists and naturalist-environmentalists interested in Africa requires a consideration of the advent of the woman's era, the rise of the New Woman (and her "hybridities"), the emergence of the New Negro, and the fashioning of American modernism. Such an exploration prompts several questions: To what extent did Africa factor into concepts of black New Womanhood or ideas of a "new race of colored women?"[20] How did New Negroes, both men and women, mediate Africa toward political, artistic, social, religious, and cultural ends? In what ways did the cult of primitivism undergird black and white Moderns' involvement with Africa? To what degree, if any, did Pan-Africanists and naturalists align themselves with modernism's fascination with the exotic and the primitive? How did transformations in American femininities and masculinities divulge themselves in Pan-Africanist and naturalists campaigns to "save" Africa? Ultimately, American imaginings of Africa in the wake of Stanley's legendary travels to Darkest Africa and European partition of the continent manifested sincere concerns about the future of the continent, as well as externalized myriad cultural anxieties and ambiguities about modernity at home and abroad.

Stanley's "Darkest Africa"

In 1871, Henry Morton Stanley began his mission to find Livingstone, a British medical missionary and explorer who had set out in 1864 to find the source of the Nile River. Stanley, who was born in Wales as John Rowlands, moved to America at the age of eighteen and took the given and surname of the wealthy American who took him in. Fashioning an American accent, he began his career as a journalist during the Civil War after failing to distinguish himself in either the Confederate or Union armies. At the end of the war he began traveling abroad as a foreign correspondent. Stanley's reputation as an intrepid reporter led James Gordon Bennett Jr., owner of the *New York Herald*, to send Stanley to Africa to find the man whose dual mission to convert the heathen and stamp out the slave trade endeared him to both the British public and crown. Indeed, Stanley did find Livingstone in 1872, and after celebrating the moment, the two men parted. Stanley returned to England as a hero, gaining increased fame after the publication of *How I Found Livingstone: Travels, Adventures, and Discoveries in Central Africa* (1872). In 1874, the *New York Herald* and the British *Daily Telegraph* financed Stanley's expedition to follow the course of the Congo River to its termination and to chart its estuaries. This expedition and Stanley's account of it narrated in *Through the Dark Continent* (1878), and his subsequent works *The Congo and the Founding of Its Free State* (1885) and *In Darkest Africa* (1890), helped shape American and European cultural perceptions of the Congo, contributing to and strengthening the Victorian conception of Africa as the Dark Continent.[21]

As Dennis Hickey and Kenneth Wylie have argued, "Stanley played a crucial role in acquainting the American public with the enduring reality that was Africa." Drawing on extant images of Africa and Africans found predominantly in Anglophone European texts and forging them with American stereotypes about the domestic "Other," principally Native Americans and African Americans, Stanley invented a new Africa for popular consumption. In the process, he revived and revised the standard travel narrative genre, infusing his books with language that resonated with the masses without totally sacrificing his appeal to the learned elite. The fanfare that accompanied the publishing of his travelogues conferred celebrity on Stanley, as his works became popular reading for ordinary Americans and Britons alike. Soon Africa became known by the appellative "Stanley's Africa" in elite circles, popular discourses, and public spaces.[22]

The literary aspects of Stanley's imaginary geography of Africa are critical to charting the genealogy of nature writing on Africa in the imperialist era of the late nineteenth and early twentieth centuries. While Stanley's writings contributed to an existing canon of travel narratives about Africa (for example, those penned by Du Chaillu, Livingstone, and Speke), they represented a phase of writing about Africa from which many naturalists would later distance themselves.[23] Much of the scholarship on Stanley's role in perpetuating the myth of Darkest Africa stresses the "full panoply of dark and secret rites, gloomy forests, cannibalism, untrammeled primitivism, and unspeakable lusts" found in his works. Indeed, these themes abound in Stanley's depictions of Africa. Yet, what is additionally noteworthy is how Stanley's writings invented a paradoxically Romantic portrait of Africa that simultaneously upheld longstanding tropes about the continent's supposed darkness while positing it as a place for retreat into the sublime.[24]

Hickey and Wylie's reading of Stanley's narratives as part of a broader discourse on Africa's "enchanting darkness" provides a starting point for further disarticulating the complexity of Stanley's version of the Darkest Africa trope. The emotionality that undergirded his narratives of traveling through the bush hearkened back to Romanticists' emphasis on individual confrontation with nature, characterized by an aestheticization of the untamed wilderness not only as the manifestation of the sublime and picturesque but also as a site for personal liberation from the strictures of civilization. However, the synchronous feelings of reverence, awe, repulsion, and horror that Stanley evoked to describe his wanderings through the primeval forest complicates—if not belies—the Romanticists' idyllic Nature. He narrates: "Now let us look at this great forest, not for scientific analysis of its woods and productions, but to get a real idea of what it is like.... Lean but your hand on a tree, measure but your length on the ground, seat yourself on a fallen branch, and you will then understand what venom, fury, voracity, and activity breathes around you.... And yet it is all beautiful—but there must be not sitting or lying down on this seething earth. It is not like your pine groves and your dainty woods in England. It is a tropic world, and to enjoy it you must keep slowly moving."[25] Stanley approached the African forest as an object of scientific curiosity, marveling at its dangerous beauty—constituting the forest as an object of aesthetic appreciation. It is so Other in its wild beauty that Stanley juxtaposes it to the woods in England, which appear refined in comparison.

Stanley's anthropomorphic descriptions of the forest complement what Onno Oerlemans posits as Romanticism's concern with the "materiality of nature."[26] Attempting to convey to his readers the physical dimensions of nature, Stanley consistently analogized trees to humans and the forest ecosystem to a community. Closing his ruminations on the "ruthless forest," Stanley writes: "As I have already said, the forest is typical of the life of humanity. No single glance can be taken of it without becoming conscious that decay, death, and life, are at work there as with us. I never could cast a leisurely look at it but I found myself, unconsciously, wondering at some feature which reminded me of some scene in the civilized world."[27] Going on to describe his morning forays in London when he witnessed "the human tide flowing into the city over the London Bridge," Stanley not only transgresses the Romanticist separation of the wilderness and the urban center but also inverts the Gilded Age nature writers' diametric positioning of the human and nonhuman world.[28]

Many American naturalist-explorers who paid homage to Stanley's pioneering role in furthering Western geographical and literary knowledge about Africa conspicuously avoided comparing the floral and faunal environment to the human cultural landscape. Moreover, they went to great pains to announce that they broke with his descriptions of the African nonhuman environment as a dark and hostile place. American Museum of

Natural History naturalist and landscape artist William Robinson Leigh wrote in his memoirs that, like many Americans, he had "gathered the impression that Africa was mostly jungle, extremely hot, pestilential, with cannibals, tsetse flies, fever, snakes, and man-eating lions." As a child and young adult, he had read the works of Livingstone, Stanley, and Colonel J. H. Patterson (author of *The Man-Eaters of Tsavo*), and as he prepared to leave on his first trip to Africa in 1926, he admitted to not believing the continent had changed that much. However, when he reached the continent he found his "preconception of it very faulty." Through his own eyes he saw that Africa was "not hot, but gloriously delightful; a land not dark, but bright; not jungle, but open; not pestilential but extremely salubrious." Attempting to locate the source of negative portrayals of Africa, Leigh reasoned that the "men who had written so ably about Africa ... did not speak my language." Essentially, because they were not artists, they lacked aesthetic appreciation for the details of Africa, which made it "glamorous" and "romantic." Thus, he concluded that "the historian and scientist need the artist to supplement their African studies—to make these more understandable, more nearly complete, more human and truthful."[29] Leigh was part of the new generation of American naturalists coming of age during the scramble for Africa who contested the dominant image of the Dark Continent by romanticizing Africa's landscape.

Although Stanley's contemporaries and scholars alike have read his travel narratives as commentaries on Africa as a homogenous entity (and understandably so as he often used "Africa" and "Congo" interchangeably), it must not be underemphasized that many of his accounts related his experiences in the Congo. Thus, in the same way that Conrad's "heart of darkness" served as colonialist metonym for Africa, it can be argued that Stanley's "Darkest Africa" represented a metalepsis of his "Dark Continent" that itself functioned as a metaphor for Central Africa and the Congo.[30] Essentially, although it appears as if Stanley progressed sequentially from a specific description of Africa to a more generic one, the contents of his three travel narratives disclose an attention to geographic specificity and detail. Nevertheless, the performative power of Stanley's use of "dark" as a descriptor for Africa was so great that most Americans who had never read Stanley's works imagined the continent according to the negative attributes of "darkness"—evil, gloomy, unenlightened. Only a minority of Americans, predominantly naturalists and nature writers, claimed to find Stanley's descriptions of the African landscape intriguing and worthy of further exploration. Many Americans who ascribed to Stanley's ideas about Africa often perpetuated the Dark Continent mythology to support missionary, imperialist, and capitalist ventures in Africa.

In African American newspapers, Stanley's exploits in the Congo generally received favorable coverage, as he allegedly opened up the area to the spread of civilization, commerce, and Christianity. Ostensibly, this opening up would benefit intrepid black missionaries and businessmen. The *New York Freeman*, the precursor to the *New York Age*, ran several articles on Africa after the publication of *Through the Dark Continent*, many which reinforced images of Africa as a continent filled with pestilential jungles, native slave traders, marauding savages, and benighted heathens. In 1886, the newspaper printed an excerpt from African American Baptist missionary Rev. John J. Coles's book *Africa in Brief*, published the same year. "A Thrilling Experience: Forty-eight Hours in the African Jungles" recounts an incident in Coles's "efforts to carry the light of the Gospel to the heathen." Coles describes his many encounters with Africans, which he referred to as "heathens," and his dismay at being left in the forest by an African woman whom he asked for directions to Jundoo. He writes: "Now, I was left alone in the wild woods; though I went onward through this thick bush and pineapple forest, with my eyes flashing to the right and left, fearing the attack of some ferocious beast or heathen robber." Coles ends his narrative of his over one-hundred-mile walk with a description of a "civilized man" who bathed and oiled his legs and feet and invited him to share his camp. Following a similar narrative, in "A Noted Africa Trader," originally printed in the *New York Sun*, the reporter provides an update on the African slave trader Tippu Tib (Muhammad bin Hamid), who became a household name among readers of African travel books, particularly those who read Verney L. Cameron's *Across Africa* (1877). The reporter describes Tippu Tib as "45 years old, as black as coal, and of Negroid blood," showing no "Arab blood in his veins," but whose dandified manners and "ideas" aligned him more with Arabs than "Negroes." The article explains that Tib had amassed more power and wealth since he aided Stanley in navigating the Congo River from Nyangwe and ends by noting that Tib had established "amicable relations" with the white imperialist and promised missionaries his protection as they spread the Gospel.[31]

In 1889, the newspaper (now the *New York Age*) published a syndicated article from the *Boston Herald*, "He Saw Stanley in Africa: A Native Prince on the Great Explorer." The reporter recounted an interview with Prince Frederick Nicholas Smith (his English name) in which he told reporters of his experiences working as a clerk in Floridian Henry Sanford's offices in Kinshasa. At age twenty-five the prince from Freetown, Sierra Leone, attended Phillips Exeter Academy in New Hampshire. Smith described Stanley as a man with the "voice of a lion" who commanded the respect of the Congolese. When asked by the reporter, "What kind of country is the Congo?" he described commerce activities, elephants, and the "half-civilized" and "half-wild" peoples of the Lower and Upper Congo. However, he explained to the reporter that Belgium was determined to "make the Congo a great and profitable country for its own benefit," alluding to policies—"far from praiseworthy"—that undermined the efforts of Christian missionaries. The prince limited his critique of the Belgian government to its fostering of drunkenness and tobacco consumption among Africans. He did not overtly condemn the mobilization of African labor but rather remonstrated the imperialists for showing more concern for increasing their coffers than for the spiritual salvation of the African workers.[32]

The *National Reflector*, published in Kansas, proved equally interested in dark Africa and exceptional Africans. "His Bloody Life: The Man Who Has Ended Many Careers" (1897) told of the "Great Executioner" for the "King of the Ashanti" (the Asantehene), whose executions of Ashanti subjects for treason and criminal offenses the British considered human sacrifice. The executioner went into hiding after British forces launched a punitive expedition to Kumasi in 1896. According to the reporter, "One of the chief reasons for the British advance in hostile array was the failure of the king to put a stop to human sacrifices at his capital, as he had promised to do." After arresting the Asantehene, the British could not locate the golden stool (a symbol of both the king's leadership and the spirit of the people) and pursued the executioner, who, they believed, knew where it was hidden. However, after his capture, the executioner professed no knowledge of the stool's whereabouts. The article mentions Stanley's graphic description of the "horrible sacrificial grove," which "is no more," as the British used dynamite to destroy the cottonwood trees under which the executioner placed the skulls and skeletons of his victims. The reporter closes with a quip that the Ashanti and neighboring people can "breathe easier" now that the British abolished human sacrifice and imprisoned the Asantehene and his executioner.[33]

The above cited articles upheld the narrative of Darkest Africa, doing little to challenge images of Africans as savages and heathens who engaged in slave trading, human sacrifice, and superstitious practices. Interestingly, the editor of the newspapers neither offered commentary as to the veracity of these reports nor remarked on the imperialist aims of Europeans in Africa. Such articles confirmed Stanley's and other white explorers' narratives of savagery in Africa and the benevolence of imperialism. Although they appeared somewhat critical of the flourishing of slavery under colonial rule and the desecration of revered objects by European expeditionary forces, they praised the work of missionaries and the suppression of "immoral" indigenous practices under colonial rule. By the turn of the twentieth century, American popular images of Stanley and his Africa could still be found in textbooks, popular magazines, and mainstream newspapers, reflecting Americans' fascination with tales of impenetrable jungles, savage men, and wild beasts.

Celebratory American accounts of Stanley's travels and face-value acceptance of his descriptions of Africa as dark, even among some African Americans, amounted to a propaganda campaign for imperialist, missionary, and commercial efforts in Africa. American nostalgia for the lost frontier, as well as their emergent sense of being an imperialist nation (particularly after the Spanish-American War), fueled further interest in Africa. Wielding the imperial gaze, Secretary of State Elihu Root (under Teddy Roosevelt from 1905 to 1909) would claim Liberia as an American colony, despite its actual status as an independent republic.[34] While Root's claim can be dismissed as hyperbole, among some Americans there was an increasing sense of connectedness to Africa post-1900. For many white naturalist-environmentalists and Pan-Africanists, Stanley's Dark Continent served as a foil against which they defined their selves and imagined a Brightest Africa.

Constructing the Negro Self and Africa in the Fin-de-siècle

In 1890, former slave turned Methodist preacher John Wesley Edward Bowen read a chapter of his work on African ethnology before the Bethel Historical and Literary Association in Washington, D.C. Bowen had received his bachelor of arts degree at the University of New Orleans, his bachelor of divinity at Boston University, and his doctorate and doctorate of divinity at Gammon Theological Seminary. His paper, which he would later present as "Africa and the American Negro" at the Congress on Africa in 1895, argued that "distinctively Negro Tribes" were "unquestionably, though remotely" related to the ancient Egyptians. Presaging the work of twentieth-century Afrocentrists, Bowen cited as evidence of his thesis linguistic and artistic similarities between the two groups despite thousands of miles of separation. Bowen's implication was clear: the Egyptians, whom

Westerners recognized as the originators of civilization, connected culturally to West and Central Africans, the ancestors of African Americans.[35] While Smith hoped his findings would inspire race pride and a sense of mission in blacks, such theories about the American Negro's relationship to the continent did not go uncontested in the black community. Speaking at the seventy-third anniversary of the American Colonization Society, also in 1890, Blyden stated: "I freely admit the fact, to which attention has been recently called, that there are many Afro-Americans who have no more to do with Africa than with Iceland, but this does not destroy the truth that there are millions whose life is bound up with that continent. It is to them that the message comes from their brethren across the deep, 'Come over and help us.'"[36]

Despite the overwhelmingly partisan coverage of Stanley's adventures in Africa in the black press, African Americans became demonstrably more critical of Western images of Africa and of European imperialism in the continent at the close of the nineteenth century. New configurations of "Negro" identity as iterated by Smith and Blyden accounted, in part, for more censorious tales of the scramble for Africa. African American engagement with the continent became progressively if not inextricably linked to the politics of race and notions of consanguinity. Being "Negro" meant recognizing one's membership in a distinct race that hailed from Africa and, for many blacks, it demanded sharing a sense of race mission—embracing race manhood, womanhood, and consciousness that took pride in African heritage and defended Africa against European colonialism.

In August 1886, the future editor of the *Philadelphia Times*, Eugene M. Camp, published "Our African Contingent" in *Forum* magazine. In the article, Camp addressed the "debt" that white Americans owed African Americans for their over three hundred years of toil in the British North American colonies and subsequently the United States. Previewing the article in the July 31 issue of the *New York Freeman*, the editor T. Thomas Fortune commended Camp for his support of financial compensation for slavery, as he had himself in his book *Black and White: Land, Labor, and Politics in the South* (1884). Fortune quoted Camp's declaration: "It follows then, that until the debt for wages is paid by the white to the black race to the last farthing, accumulated interest and all, silly becomes a justice loving people to prate about the colored man's poverty, his ignorance, or his crimes. Nay, more, the white race must either admit its civilization to be a pretentious sham, a non-debt paying fraud, or it must proceed to liquidate, either in work or money, the debt due its creditors." Despite his praise for Camp's views, Fortune held no hope that white Americans would return what they had "stolen" through "roguery" from Africans and their descendants. Overall, he applauded Camp's assessment of the situation of African Americans and his assertion that the "Negro is no longer a grown up child" and that the nation had to resign itself to the fact that he is a citizen and "he is here to stay." Fortune's only objection was to Camp's statement that the Africans enslaved in the colonies "were the refuse of the African Continent." In umbrage, he argued that the slave traders stole the good and worthless alike, and he cited the achievements of Blyden, Henry Highland Garnet, and Alexander Crummell as proof that "such men came not from the refuse population of Africa."[37] In addressing Camp's comment on the origins of America's African population, Fortune not only dismissed a widely held belief among some whites that slavery removed undesirable Africans from a land in which they would not have prospered but also claimed Africa's upper echelon as the progenitors of distinguished African Americans. More important, he offered his readers an alternative narrative of their racial ancestry and future. Fortune's response to Camp's characterization of the relationship between Africa and African Americans in his exegesis of the "Negro question" points to the ambivalence felt by many blacks about linking their post-Emancipation identities and futures to Africa.

Fortune highlighted the black community's continuing crisis of masculinity—its debates over respectable manhood and manliness and their significance for what he called "sovereign citizenship" in America. The *New York Age* did not stand alone in journalistic discussions of black manhood. Since their founding, black newspapers such as the *N.C. Republican and Civil Rights Advocate* and the *Baltimore American* linked citizenship and civil rights issues not only to black manhood but also to womanhood. The *N.C. Republican* commended emigrationist Bishop Henry McNeal Turner for in "a spirit of manly dignity and forbearance" calling attention to the "wrongs and indignities to which colored citizens" had been subjected. Featuring a section entitled "Colored Men of Mark," the weekly reported on the actions of other bishops of the AME Church to secure civil rights for African Americans. The newspaper also discussed members of "the Black Phalanx" working to uplift the race. In 1887, the *New York Age* reprinted the a report from the editor of the *Boston Advocate*, W. H. Bonaparte, titled "An Open Letter to the American Negro," which endorsed the formation of the Afro-American League and called on African Americans "to act"—to "demand 'liberty or death.'" Bonaparte argued that the political parties fed blacks empty promises and that white Christians continued to stand in silence as "our women" are "outraged by pale scoundrels" and "our men ... hanged by brutish mobs." African Americans endured many injustices at polling booths and public spaces, while ex-Confederate soldiers paraded down streets hurling racial epithets at them. Bonaparte exhorted: "Colored men of America, you are to answer whether or not you are ready to pitch an endless battle for the rights of manhood and womanhood," for "human liberty and rights."[38] The rhetoric of Bonaparte's letter attests to the inextricability of matters of social equality, legal justice, civil rights, manhood, and womanhood in African American political discourses in the fin de siècle. To be a respectable man or woman meant not only exercising the rights of citizenship but embracing an identity that imparted no shame on the behalf of African Americans for their slave past or, in some instances, for their African ancestry.

In March 1893, the Milwaukee-based black newspaper the *Northwestern Recorder* published the article "Future for Africa." Originally written by G. Washington in 1892, it told of the "faithful labor of the black man," who "while in a state of bondage" remained "obedient to his master" and in doing so created wealth for the United States and white individuals via the cotton industry. Washington argued that since Emancipation, the black man had proven himself worthy of citizenship, pledging fealty to his country and to the flag. In the process, he made strides in education, industrial labor, entrepreneurship, and some professional occupations. However, although the black man had "passed through the probationary period and come forth a freeman, endowed with all the faculties and functions of manhood," Washington held that "his race must now enter a new stage of life, as a people, and establish his ultimate nationalization among the peoples of the earth." According to the article, Africa offered the perfect opportunity for the black man rejected by his own country to "establish an enlightened nation," as the continent was the home of his ancestors. Reemphasizing that the black race had proved its "manhood and womanhood," Washington urged African Americans interested in Africa to illicit financial support from whites in order to raise their own nation. Envisioning a transatlantic alliance between people in Monrovia, Liberia, and white philanthropists and peoples of African descent in Philadelphia, he looked forward to the day when Africa would "lift the dark cloud that has so long darkened her country" and "rank among the nations of the world."[39]

The Wichita, Kansas, newspaper the *National Baptist World*, which claimed to operate "in the interest of the Negro Baptist Church and the race," published a dissenting opinion from "the false prophets" of emigration. In a three-part series, "Fifty Days in Africa," Rev. W. E. Gladden, ironically one of the founders of the African Emigration Society in 1888, explained how his trip to Liberia in 1889 revealed how badly mistaken he was in his dreams of Liberia. In 1888, Gladden along with two other delegates from the society requested an audience with the president to obtain documents certifying their citizenship to be used during their reconnaissance mission to Liberia. They hoped to resettle African Americans from Kansas, Louisiana, and Mississippi, especially from Jackson, where blacks suffered from "recent election outrages." According to the city's mayor, John McGill: "Not a single colored man was permitted to vote.... They were as completely disenfranchised as though they had never had the privilege of citizenship conferred upon them." Gladden arrived in Monrovia in 1889 with fifty-four emigrants "who were shipped off to their destination like so many cattle." In his recollection of the trip, he called attention to the ill-treatment of emigrants compared to that received by visitors. He also described receiving a "cool reception" from Blyden, who lectured him on the many opportunities for African Americans in Liberia, which they would never receive in the United States. Gladden stated that he was unable to see these advantages and all indications were that the emigrants, missionaries, and natives in Liberia "were going backward instead of forward." In a reversal of opinion on emigration, Gladden warned: "'Beware of false prophets' who tell you that Africa is a place for the American negro and continually try to get others to go but stays here himself. I have learned that 'what is sauce for the goose is sauce for the gander.' We are Americans just as much as the white man and we can no more live in Liberia than he can." Although Gladden's trip took place in 1889, the newspaper published the article series in 1894—four years after the introduction of the Butler Bill in the U.S. Senate, which if passed would have allocated five million dollars per annum to relocate African Americans to Africa.[40]

Despite the bill's popularity among some black elites and working-class African Americans frustrated with their status in American society, emigration still remained a last resort for self-determination in the larger black community. However, Gladden and other antiemigrationists clearly feared the attraction of the emigration movement and urged black missionary activity as a more appropriate course of action for African Americans interested in the continent. In this vein, their rhetoric of "redeeming" Africa through Christianization strengthened the Victorian notion of the civilizing mission. For example, when the African Baptist Mission convened in Xenia, Ohio, in October 1894, they urged support for missions in southern Africa. Daniel Payne, a South African attending Wilberforce University, delivered a speech asking that African American teachers and preachers travel to his country to educate his countrymen. Payne accused white missionaries of establishing schools and Sunday schools under the guise of spreading Christianity and education, when in reality they sought "selfish gains." A reporter interpreted his message thusly: "He said that Africa would not be saved until the American Negro came over there." Indeed, during the 1890s, African American missionaries from the African Baptist, Black Baptist, and AME churches arrived in South Africa only to discover an incipient independent-church movement called Ethiopianism. In 1892, Rev. Mangena Makke Mokone left the Wesleyan Methodist church in the Transvaal and founded the Ethiopian Church of South Africa. This church became affiliated in 1898 with the AME Church as its fourteenth district, so that the Ethiopian Church could operate legally under the freedom of religious expression extended to American missionaries. In the first decade of the twentieth century this alliance came under increasing suspicion by the South Africa government, with whites arguing for the deportation and/or "disbarring" of African Americans from the country. The "redemption of Africa" entailed African American missionary and educational work, not permanent emigration.[41]

Black newspapers' extensive coverage of African American missionary conventions in America and missionary activities in Africa evince the importance that Christianity held in performances of respectable manhood and womanhood in the late nineteenth century. In the words of the *National Baptist World*, the Xenia convention "consisted of christian [sic], brainy and progressive men and women, than which, a more loyal number of disciples—free from bickering and harmonious, never convened on this continent." Articles featuring journal excerpts from male and female missionaries highlighted their civility, intelligence, daring, and morality. As John G. Turner has argued in his study of missionary William H. Sheppard, evangelizing in Africa figured prominently in Sheppard's public image of "robust manhood" in the late nineteenth and early twentieth centuries. More pointedly, Sheppard's performances of middle-class manhood shifted from "a late-Victorian 'civilized' manhood early in his career" to a "more 'primitive' and robust masculinity as an 'imperial male,' and then to a dignified domesticity after his resignation from the mission field."[42] Similarly, many of Sheppard's cohorts negotiated their manhood and womanhood according to their geographical locale, often emerging as more forceful and militant "race men" in Africa.

As indicated, African Americans outside of missionary circles evoked Africa to assert a variety of respectable masculinities and femininities. At the July 21, 1896, afternoon session of the convention of the National Association of Colored Women (NACW) in Washington, D.C., delegates from various women's clubs around the United States met to discuss the union of the National League of Colored Women and the National Federation of Afro-American Women. At the afternoon session of the convention, delegates met to discuss the merger. Called to order by Mrs. Booker T. Washington and attended by Ida B. Wells Barnett, Lucy Thurman, Mary Church Terrell, and other influential middle-class and elite black women, the delegates resolved to call the new organization the National Association of Colored Women. However, Victoria Mathews of New York City voiced her opposition to the term *colored*, despite its use by the U.S. Census Bureau to identify African Americans. According to the 1896 NACW articles of agreement, Mathews informed the attendees that

> she had African blood in her veins and was of African descent, which entitled her to the name Afro. While this was true, having been in America, she was an American citizen and entitled to all the privileges of such, although many of these rights are constantly denied, she was entitled to the name American, therefore she claimed that the Negro in America was entitled to the name Afro-American as much as the French, Franco-American, or the English, Anglo-American; as for the name "colored," it meant nothing to the Negro race. She was not a colored American, but an Afro-American.

Although Mathews's position constituted a minority of the voters for that session, her sentiments echoed a feeling among many African Americans that the terminology used to designate them and their organizations should reflect their ancestral origins and not what many perceived as superficial racial categories. To claim to be Afro or African was to link oneself to a place or heritage, not a skin color; more important, such a declaration defied American popular discourses that degraded Africans and their descendants. The problematic nature of identifying oneself with an entire continent was not lost on many advocates and opponents of African-based nomenclature; however, in an era where "blackness" appeared to be a scourge, imagining

Africa as a celebrated homeland served political, cultural, social, and aesthetic purposes.[43]

The debate over naming the organization that would serve as the umbrella entity for hundreds of black women's clubs across the United States occurred within the context of a broader conversation on the meaning of African American womanhood as blacks approached the end of the century. At its 1895 convention, the National Federation of Afro-American Women declared its number one objective to be "the concentration of the dormant energies of the women of the Afro-American race into one broad band of sisterhood" and secondarily to guide women in "the divinely imposed duties of motherhood" both for the purpose of advancing and "ennobling" the race.[44] This concept of a politicized womanhood bolstered by enfranchisement but not divorced entirely from ideologies of a women's sphere informed nascent black feminist theory and reflected the broader contours of the New Woman movement. Like their white counterparts, who merged in 1889 to form the General Federation of Women's Clubs, the NACW championed civic activism, humanitarianism, and social reform, as well as women's rights and suffrage. However, racial uplift and gender unity, as expressed in their motto, "Lifting as We Climb," marked the uniqueness of black women's club activities, which had to address the double burdens of racial and sex oppression in America; this meant that African American women could not totally ignore their African ancestry.[45]

As seen, in the last decades of the nineteenth century, when African Americans increasingly faced political repression, labor exploitation, social discrimination, and racial violence in a white supremacist society, conversations over the meaning of Africa to African Americans became more pronounced in black political and social thought. Running the gamut from discourses that reinforced Africa as the Dark Continent (from whose darkness the "Negro" in America supposedly escaped) to pronouncements of Africa as a place of return and/or celebrated ancestry, Africa as a cultural signifier operated to construct new forms of manhood and womanhood, as well as new definitions of blackness. For Pan-Africanists, particularly after the turn of the century, Africa evoked not only a sense of identity and religious mission, but also political purpose.

Reflections on the significance of Africa to African Americans took place both inside and outside the black community, as white Americans engaged Africa in their own political and intellectual thought. Somewhat ironically, Pan-Africanist thinkers, self-proclaimed white philanthropists in "sympathy with the Negro," and white supremacists began contemplating back-to-Africa movements with intensity, as lynching, racial violence, and political unrest escalated in the last two decades of the century. Whiteness as a racial identity and symbol of Americanness continued to function primarily in contradistinction to self-inscribed and imposed black identities, often predicated on the idea that the American Negro was more African than American. For many white Americans, African Americans were an enigmatic foreign element (despite whites' own immigrant origins) in the U.S. body politic.

Africa and the Inscribing of American Whiteness

In 1889, the *New York Times* reported on the *Montgomery Advertiser*'s recent article on the "movement to deport negroes." The Montgomery paper argued that the white people of Montgomery County, Alabama, did not advocate revolutionary steps to obtain a more favorable population balance between whites and blacks. Because Montgomery was a black majority county, residents in sympathy with the newspaper's position held that wide-scale deportation was impracticable and would cost taxpayers enormously. However, they believed that if deportation could remove "loafing" African Americans and criminals "living off those who work," then the entire United States would benefit. The article closed by warning that as long as blacks concentrated in one locale, they posed a danger to whites and to the prosperity of America.[46] Whites' consideration of exporting African Americans to Africa illuminated the functionality of race—and place—in constructing America as a white man's country. Blackness alone could not legitimize removing African Americans from their birthplace. However, reinventing Africa—a continent whose inhabitants made no conscious effort to colonize America—as the fatherland of American blacks rendered African Americans foreigners, descendants of aliens who never intended to help develop the nation.

While white Montgomerians feared a mass exodus of industrious black laborers to Africa, other whites in support of emigration and deportation of African Americans held that ultimately blacks and whites could not coexist peaceably in the United States. In an 1891 letter to the editor of *Science* magazine, R. W. Shufeldt explained why he supported the "transporting of the Negro back to Africa." Referring to arguments put forth by the "far-seeing thinker," palaeontologist, and comparative anatomist E. D. Cope, he agreed that African Americans could not be assimilated into the American body politic. Cope, who considered himself a convert to evolutionism, published

The Origin of the Fittest: Essays on Evolution (1886), in which he explained two variations of evolution, "progressive" and "retrogressive," which he also termed "acceleration" and "retardation." According to his revision of Darwinism, which his contemporaries labeled Neo-Lamarckism or American evolutionism, any character that a parent possesses during procreation will pass to the offspring, and any trait that the parent loses before or during breeding will be lost to future generations.[47]

According to the letter to the editor, Cope applied his theory of human evolution to call attention to the dangers he saw in interracial reproduction between blacks and whites in America, as well as to "the constantly disturbing element the negro is in our national organization." Arguably, Shufeldt reached this conclusion after reading Cope's description of blacks as possessing "a predominance of the quadrumanous features which are retarded in man"—including the nose and the beard—whereas Indo-Europeans as the "highest" race possessed such accelerated markers of growth as a "well-developed" nose and beard.[48] Shufeldt urged swift action to be taken, beginning with a successful expedition to Africa, noting that America's last expedition to the continent was a "puerile failure." This future trip, he said, should be undertaken by scientists with the aid of American battleships in order to discover the best conditions for the return of African Americans to "their proper home." Subsequently, he suggested, America should construct reasonably comfortable steamships to begin the long work of removing "every negro" to "Darkest Africa," where he could spread the lessons he learned from "the most highly civilized race upon the face of the globe." The author assured the editor that America does not need the "negro vote... his labor... [or] the injection of his lowly blood into our veins."[49]

The article "The Negro's Proper Home" (1892) published in the *New York Times* reiterated the belief that "the existence of the colored man in the South is a menace to the whites." The reporter interviewed a member of the Southern Associated Press, J. C. Hemphill, editor of the Charleston, South Carolina, *News and Courier*, on the race question. Hemphill accused the northern press of printing only one side to the question, which amounted to propaganda against southern interests. Referring to the lectures of Blyden, Hemphill stated that the only solution to the race problem was deportation of African Americans to "the home of [their] fathers." The article also cited several professors and intellectuals, both black and white, who advocated government sponsorship of a back-to-Africa program.[50]

These three white opinions, published during the migration of southern African Americans northward and westward to urban centers, articulated a fear held by many white racist Americans that America would succumb to its "African" population through natural increase or "hybridization" and cease to be "their" country. The use of the possessive pronoun "our" throughout these articles should not go unnoticed, as most European Americans who constructed their whiteness in opposition to the blackness of African Americans viewed the United States as a white man's country. Moreover, although the white racist proponents of "Negro removal" often shrewdly cited the opinions of black emigrationists, their use of the terms "deportation" and "their home" further enhanced the racialist discourses underlying their position. These pundits did not conceive of Europe as their true home, but they perceived blacks as interlopers, foreigners, visitors, despite their own acknowledgment that blacks and whites had arrived together in America roughly at the same time. On a more rudimentary level, although *deportation* can carry two different meanings—the expulsion of someone from his or her native land or the removal of unwanted aliens from a country—it was clear that these whites believed that African Americans were aliens living on U.S. soil. Where black emigrationists lobbied for voluntary emigration or repatriation, white advocates of deportation predominantly promoted forced removal of black citizens to Africa or someplace in the United States or its territories where they would not outnumber whites. In the wake of America's quest for empire and acquisition of the Philippines, some whites suggested black removal to the Pacific island territories, as it would place another ocean between blacks and whites.[51] Yet it was Africa that served as foil to America, inscribing whiteness onto the United States and framing the presence of blacks in America as a courtesy bestowed on them by a benevolent civilization.

Whites who championed the removal of blacks to Africa supported continued efforts to construct the United States as a white man's country. Darwinism, Social Darwinism, eugenics, and the cult of primitivism also instantiated white identities based on new theories of racial difference. Darwin's theory of survival of the fittest bolstered claims to white superiority and exceptionality, fueling social Darwinist and eugenicist thought. American social Darwinists believed that the laws that governed the natural world applied to the social world. Thus, if white Americans possessed more wealth, education, opportunity, and so forth, then social competition scientifically explained their privileged status, not systemic, institutionalized racism. In contrast, eugenicists viewed social status as the result of biological phenomena, the replication and transfer of superior genes almost exclusive to Anglo-Saxons.

Contrary to these doctrines that justified white supremacy and privilege based on pseudoscience and chauvinist politics, the cult of primitivism operated as a sort of apologia or critique for modernity by simultaneously projecting primitiveness onto nonwhites (in this case Africans and their descendants) and celebrating the lost primitive within as a space for white regeneration. Some scholars associate the American cult of primitivism with American modernism in the 1920s and 1930s, particularly in the context of the Harlem Renaissance and the Jazz Age, when white and black Americans alike idealized the primitive in understanding themselves as moderns.[52] However, white fetishization of the African primitive predates this period. The late nineteenth century ushered in a new fascination with African cultures associated with ethnography, anthropology, and folklore studies. Intellectually and culturally, the work of naturalists interested in Africa related closest to these scientists and men and women of letters, as they often worked in the same institutions, namely museums, and constructed much of their information about Africa based on personal journeys to the continent. Their work reveals the discursive relationship between American whiteness and blackness as mediated through the ethnographic subject.

The American Folklore Society (AFS) was founded in Cambridge, Massachusetts, in 1888 by "humanities scholars, museum anthropologists, men and women of letters and affairs" interested in studying traditional cultures and vernacular traditions. Appearing ten years after the founding of the Folklore Society in the United Kingdom, the AFS began publishing its periodical, *Journal of American Folklore*, that same year. In the second issue of the first volume, the journal's first entry on African American folklore appeared: a review of Charles C. Jones Jr.'s anthology *Negro Myths from the Georgia Coast* (1888). Review author W. W. N. agreed with Jones's argument that the folktales had part of their origins in Africa; however, he asserted that they are not African in "scenery ... morality ... [and] sentiment." In the review he asks where are "the mythological furniture ... the cruelty, the cannibalism ... the dwarfs and the monsters of savage fantasy." He concludes: "The survival of African mythology in the mind of American negroes seems to be no more extensive than the survival of languages, limited in very few words." Perhaps inspired by this review, Hanns Oertel, a professor of linguistics and comparative philology, began researching these stories. His "Notes on Six Negro Myths from the Georgia Coast" contends that the folktales "How Buh Cooter Fool Buh Deer," "Buh Rabbit, Buh Fox, and de Fisherman," and others "were borrowed" from German, Laplander, and French traditions. For W. W. N. the fact that "cruelty" seemed to be absent from the Sea Islands folktales negated their African origins, whereas Oertel reasoned implicitly that African folktales could not have survived unchanged across the Atlantic, and thus, cultural borrowing must have occurred.[53] As recent scholarship has established the syncretic nature of African American folktales, the accuracy of these arguments is less important than the ways in which they relied on assumptions that African folk traditions and storytelling either embody savagery or require mimicry or adaptation of European forms. Both interpretations reified and indeed celebrated images of authentic African cultures as static and homogenous, embodying primitiveness regardless of time and space.

The AFS limited its early interest in African folk traditions to exploring their relationship to African American culture, perhaps logically as the journal's title indicated a focus on American folklore. However, beginning in 1891, the AFS commenced regular publication of articles on African cultures, perhaps to compete with the *Folk-Lore Journal*, published in the United Kingdom, whose contributors often enjoyed unfettered access to British colonial possessions in the continent. The AFS published over two hundred articles that discussed African folk traditions or explored the connection between African cultures and diaspora black cultures in the Americas and the Caribbean. Many of the articles on Africa alone were short in length, averaging anywhere from one to seven pages, and took the form of reviews of texts published by noted European ethnologists, with the exception of articles written by explorer and missionary Heli Chatelain. Chatelain founded the Philafrican Liberator's League dedicated to the eradication of slavery in Africa and participated in the 1895 Congress on Africa. In 1894, he published "African Races," in which he explained the role that imperialists, explorers, and missionaries played in fostering ethnological and anthropological study of Africa.

> As distinct branches of science, ethnology and anthropology are barely out of their teens. In our own generation has the African continent, in its most populous and characteristic part, been explored and roughly mapped out. Many important tribes and languages we do not yet know, and even in the case of the best known tribes the information we possess is rarely of a scientific character. As com-pared [sic] with the past, no doubt, knowledge is progressing with gigantic strides; but every new ray of light only makes us more palpably feel how dense is the darkness which still covers the greater portion of the continent. No one should therefore suppose that ethnol-

ogy, which must be preceded by geography and philology, has mastered the subject of African races and tribes, or even come thoroughly to understand a few tribes. Governments have been breaking down the barriers; explorers and missionaries are preparing the ground; now is the time for ethnologists to collect and collate facts: as to final conclusions, these must be left to future generations.[54]

Chatelain's contention that imperialism contributed to scientific knowledge of the Other was not novel. Nevertheless, his theories on African races, as well as his publications on African fetishism, progress (more precisely "retardation"), and folk life exemplified Victorian ideas about racial backwardness, civilization, and heathenism. More important, they bridged Victorian images of Darkest Africa with modernist primitivism.

Chatelain endeavoured to prove the following: that there were several races that inhabit Africa; that there was no difference between the Bantu or Negro races—that they were in fact one and the same; that the typical black person was not the intermediary figure between man and ape; and that African Americans were descended from both Guineas and Bantus, with whom they were "physically and mentally on par." Somewhat similarly to votaries of the cult of primitivism of the early twentieth century, Chatelain viewed "the African Negro race" as ruled by emotion. He argued that this race's unity was evidenced in the "predominance of the emotional over the intellectual and moral side of human nature ... the love of ease and pleasure, of trade, of music, of rhetoric, style, ceremony, and of emotional religion." Additionally, he lamented the destruction that imperialism would work on the authenticity of African cultures in the process of uplifting the continent. He writes: "In Central Africa, the Kongo, Teke, Luba, Lolo, Fan, Ganda, and Nyam-Nyam languages may blossom into national literatures; and these will form the nuclei of regenerated African states built after the best models of modern Christendom. It would indeed be a great pity if all those grand Bantu languages should disappear, and all the African mind and sentiment be forced into the strait-jackets of European forms of speech."[55]

Chatelain's ambivalence about the forces of imperialist modernity—Christianization, commerce, and civilization—resonated with other contemporary white folklorists whose interests in African costumes, burial rites, divination, sacrifice, "witch-doctors," demon possession, and other cultural traditions jarred with their desire to see Africa redeemed or regenerated according to Western values.[56] In their writings on Africa, their fashioning of the white self permeates the text, as the native informant serves as the embodiment of "superstition" and irrationality juxtaposed to the religiosity and rationality of the Western writer (often a white missionary, traveler, or amateur ethnographer). Thus the authors' ability to demonstrate to the reader the cultural gulf between the West, in this case white America, and Africa authenticated their texts. Yet, arguably, these studies of Africa laid the foundation for less Eurocentric writings on African cultures, particularly those of African Americans who later joined the AFS (for example, Zora Neale Hurston) and white ethnographers and anthropologists who embraced the cultural relativism paradigm—the principle that the study of an individual's belief system and traditions should be governed by the terms of that person's own culture. In this context, American anthropological and folklore studies of Africa transformed into discourses that reimagined Africa against the trope of Darkest Africa. Interestingly, as discussed later in this chapter, both naturalists and Pan-Africanists expressed uncertainties about such studies, which despite their epistemological rejection of value judgments on cultures seemed to focus on the undesirable elements of Darkest African cultures—for example, studies of cannibalism.

In the fields of ethnology and anthropology, two major organizations formed in the nineteenth century, the American Ethnological Society (AES) in 1842 and the Anthropological Society of Washington (ASW) in 1879. (The American Anthropological Association formed in 1902.) The differences between the two organizations prove important for understanding their methodological and theoretical approaches to Africa that influenced their contributions to the journal *American Anthropologist*, which issued its first volume in 1888. Swiss-born Albert Gallatin and American-born John Russell Bartlett founded the AES with the goal of fostering "inquiries generally connected with the human race." The ASW organized to promote "the study of the natural history of man, especially with reference to America." Ethnologists and anthropologists alike displayed interest in so-called primitive cultures, revealing their oftentimes overlapping identities; however, the former employed a comparative approach to human cultures and the latter (an extension of ethnography) focused on studying individual societies.[57] For the first time, under professional anthropology and ethnology studies, Africa factored significantly in American social sciences.

Until 1900, *American Anthropologist* did not publish any articles on Africa based on original research conducted by members of the American organizations. Perhaps reflecting the interests of regular contributors, such as John Wesley Powell, first director of the U.S. Bureau of Ethnology, articles on aboriginal cultures in the Americas, Asia, and the Pacific Islands featured prominently in the journal. Discussions of Africa, however, did appear in comparative analyses of aboriginal rites and African practices or as extensively quoted and translated material from European journals (mostly from France, England, and Germany) with no accompanying editorial commentary. For example, "Human Sacrifices in Dahomey" (1891) quoted the work of former missionary Father Chautard from the *Bulletin de la Sociéte de Géograhie de Lyon*, and "Worship of Prehistoric Stone Implements in Yoruba, West Coast of Africa" (1891) quoted from the *Proceedings of the Royal Geographical Society* in London.[58] Clearly, American anthropologists during this period relied heavily on a transatlantic one-way transfer of knowledge about Africa to America, as many of the renowned anthropologists were trained in Europe and belonged to nations with colonies in Africa and, therefore, enjoyed more opportunities to observe Africans. Thus, the early institutional identity of both the AES and ASW reflected a focus on the Western Hemisphere, specifically on Native Americans, who in many ways were colonial subjects in the Americas. Africa as a subject of independent American social scientific inquiry became important in the context of European imperialism in Africa and as Pan-Africanism entered public discourse.

A noted exception to American scientists' reliance on European intellectual production to establish a corpus of knowledge on Africa was their references to American travel narratives. As mentioned, very few Americans had traveled to Africa before the European partition of the continent, but in the last two decades of the nineteenth century, black and white Americans increasingly traveled to Africa, predominantly as missionaries, but some as "gentleman" and "gentlewoman" travelers. Scholar James T. Campbell offers a compelling discussion of African American journeys to Africa in this period in *Middle Passages* (2006) in the context of missionary activities, emigrationism, and modern Pan-Africanism.[59] The white American public rarely noticed these African American journeys, while in contrast they followed those taken by whites, who subsequently published articles and books on their travels. One American traveler—other than Stanley—stands out in this period: May French Sheldon. According to one of her eulogizers she was "the first white woman to undertake an independent exploration of Central Africa." She was a quintessential modern New Woman—independent, intellectual, and daring—yet she also straddled Victorian sensibilities—she was "refined" and married (she was often referred to as Mrs. French Sheldon).[60] The *New York Times* described her thusly: "She has a clear, dark complexion, dark hair and eyes, her features are strong without masculinity, and her voice is pleasantly low in quality." In her performances as intrepid adventure she contributed to imperialist discourses on Africa, emerging as an expert Africanist recognized by the American Geographical Society and the Royal Geographical Society. She delivered papers at the International Congress of Anthropology (1893 and 1894) and the Chicago Folklore Congress (1893) and contributed to the *Journal of American Folklore*, the *American Anthropologist*, and the *Journal of the Anthropological Institute of Great Britain and Ireland*.[61]

Scholars and the reading public considered Sheldon's book *Sultan to Sultan: Adventures among the Masai and Other Tribes of East Africa* (1892) and essay "Customs among the Natives of East Africa" (1892) as critical analyses of, in her own words, "people who had never come into contact with whites, and were in a comparatively primitive state of existence." Sheldon discussed rites of passage, rituals, family relations, polygamy, the condition of women and children, marriage, religion and superstition, ornamentation, tattooing, and more cultural practices that she observed among the natives, admitting at times feeling a "strong prejudice" against some of the peoples she encountered. Her descriptions of Africans' faces and bodies, which often complemented her discussion of their advanced cultures, exuded her preference for features that were "anything but negroid, but . . . more Egyptian." However, to read Sheldon's work as simply ethnological and ethnographic description limits our understanding of the cultural, intellectual, and even political significance of her writings. The conclusion to "Customs" is one such example. She writes:

> the evidences that I have brought of the gentleness and intelligence of these natives certainly bears an indisputable proof in their own lineaments, and if a spirit is aroused among so-called humanitarians or those who have interests involved in East Africa to such an extent that they study the practical employment of these people in arts and crafts, which they may conduct within the limits of their own territory, and some movement is put abroad to make proper roads and substitute for human beasts of burden mechanical methods of transportation, there is a brilliant future for East Africa.

Sheldon warns against "zealous philanthropy" and urges treating the Africans "as the children they are," pledging to be a friend of Africa in promoting the interests of its people along these lines.[62] Sheldon was not interested in subverting the imperialist rule that made her trip successful, but rather she wished to work toward assuring Africans a bright future under colonial rule. She restated this position at the Congress on Africa. Like white American New Women explorers, particularly Mary Jobe Akeley, who came after her, Sheldon envisioned Brightest Africa as a land controlled by white men who allowed some native autonomy. The ways in which whites like Sheldon approached Africa as a recipient of philanthropy and object of their intellectual curiosity signaled the beginning of a new era when Africa no longer would remain a mysterious, remote continent to Americans but rather would become a site for scientific inquiry and political action.

On the Threshold of a New Era

When Americans confronted the Dark Continent in the late nineteenth century, they were on the cusp of a new era defined by imperial conquest, expanding capital, the color line, and the emergence of new identities and politics. Influenced by Stanley's celebrated conquest of Africa, a wider American public demonstrated interest in a continent many had forgotten or relegated to the dustbins of the history of the slave trade. Americans watched as Europeans scrambled in Africa to establish protectorates, colonies, and spheres of influence, as Africans mounted what seemed futile resistance to European invasion. Some Americans observed with admiration for the Europeans' supposed intrepidness, calling for the United States to embark on its own imperial ventures—to take up what Rudyard Kipling would later term in 1899 the "White Man's burden." Others looked on in dismay as a continent was ravaged to serve the interests of European metropoles. Yet Africa's significance was not confined to its rendering as colonialist plunder.

For many African Americans, Africa took on new meaning in a time when political repression, social ostracism, and economic exploitation revealed how circumscribed their lives were in the context of white supremacy. While not solely intrinsic to constellations of race manhood and womanhood, identification with Africa gave shape to New Negro identities. African American leaders, intellectuals, clergymen, and clubwomen alike theorized Africa to their own political, cultural, and intellectual ends, finding in the continent a homeland, a site for providential mission, a respite from American racism, a place for self-determination, an inspiration for a new name (Afro-American), and a cause célèbre. African Americans heard various cries from Africa urging them to emigrate, repatriate, proselytize, and unite against colonialist domination in their fatherland. Overwhelmingly, these calls came from inside the minds of blacks themselves—voices that negotiated what Africa meant to them, not so much what black Americans meant to the continent.

White Americans who exhibited interest in Africa also looked at the continent from a myriad of perspectives. Some saw Africa as the solution to the "Negro problem"—a place to relocate African Americans and preserve the whiteness of the American body politic. Others approached Africa as a site for intellectual inquiry, where scientists could study its primitivism and, in the process, ascribe new meaning to whiteness. Under the auspices of fledgling scientific societies, whites (and some blacks) reinvented Africa as a primitive paradise for a new generation of Americans. Primarily concerned with the habits and customs of Africans, this vision of the continent reconciled American fascination with Darkest Africa with emerging interests in race science. Africa was a tableau depicting the hierarchy and functionality of race.

The roles that white American ethnologists, anthropologists, folklorists, naturalists, and travelers, as well as African American missionaries, emigrationists, and Pan-Africanists played in shaping American imaginings of Africa established the intellectual, political, and cultural boundaries in which Brightest Africa narratives emerged in the United States at the turn of the century. Their work revealed how the competing narratives of "Brightest" and "Darkest" Africa were refracted through the politics of imperialism, specifically the Berlin Conference's partition of Africa. Inaugurating the first truly international discussion of the future of Africans, the results of the conference served as a tocsin for "anti-colonial Pan-Africanists" and white anti-imperialists, as well as an invitation for missionaries and scientists interested in Africa.[63] The Congo question that convened the conference as a dispute over King Leopold of Belgium's claims to the Congo and his establishment of the Congo Free State (1879–1890) erupted into a full-blown scandal in the first decade of the twentieth century. Charges of slavery, genocide, and atrocities associated with Belgium's imperial project surfaced. The Belgian Congo became the first African colony that would capture Americans' imagination since the founding of Liberia. The political work of U.S. ambassadors, the scientific work of American anthropologists, and the political and cultural work of white and black intellectuals and anti-imperial activists combined to provide Americans with a detailed and complex image of the region that became known as the Congo.

TWO

To Bunco a Yankee
America and the Congo Question

On May 15, 1883, American Minister Resident Consul General to Portugal, John M. Francis, wrote to the Secretary of State, Frederick Frelinghuysen Jr., to inform him of the recent fracas involving Portugal and France. Unlike previous disputes between the two nations regarding disputed territory in Europe, this disagreement involved land and access to trade on the River Congo in Africa. A year earlier, the French had ratified a treaty signed in 1880 between the Tio monarch at Lake Malebo (on the river) and French explorer Pierre Savorgnan de Brazza. According to the agreement, the king gave over his hereditary rights to the territory to de Brazza. Portugal protested strenuously, claiming ancient rights to trade and residence in the area dating back to the 1480s, when the first Portuguese sailors arrived at the mouth of the Congo River in West Central Africa. Shortly thereafter, the King of Kongo established diplomatic relations with Portugal. The Portuguese noted that the result of that encounter was a booming sugar trade with plantations based on the islands of São Tomé and Príncipe, as well as exclusive trading rights with that region of the Congo. (Incidentally, the Portuguese also began slave-trading in that area, which the crown downplayed.) In 1506, Afonso I took possession of the Kongo throne as a staunch ally of Portugal and a Christian convert, supposedly solidifying Portuguese commercial hegemony in his kingdom and outlying areas—including Tio.[1] Portugal held that neither the Tio ruler nor the French had a legitimate right to disrupt the four-centuries-long relationship between the Portuguese traders and residents and the Congolese people.

Detailing a standoff between French occupiers and Portuguese residents of Loango and Ponta Negra (cities in current-day Republic of Congo, formerly Congo-Brazzaville) and referring to "pending treaty negotiations between Portugal and Britain on the Congo Question," Francis urged the secretary to consider the ramifications of "the establishment of a *great* power on the banks of the river Congo." Declaring that "this question of the Congo . . . is becoming one of the most interesting and important international question of the times," the diplomat outlined three possible settlements that would favor the commercial development of the region, as well as aid in the "progress of civilization." First, the declaration of the region as independent or neutral, he argued, would incite anarchy, as no foreign power would be able to maintain its presence there. Francis found most troubling the prospect of "the white element" disgracing themselves "in the minds of the blacks," and thus destroying European influence over the native population. Second, he held that an exclusive sovereignty over the region exercised by one European nation would lead to "war and devastation." Lastly, he advocated the loyal acceptance from European powers of Portuguese control over the Congo, based on Portugal's centuries-long historic connection with the people of that region.[2]

A copy of Francis's letter to Frelinghuysen accompanied several documents submitted to the House of Representatives on the Congo question following an annual message to Congress from President Arthur on foreign relations. In the 1883 message, President Arthur highlighted Henry Morton Stanley's position as chief executive officer of the International African Association (IAA) and his status as a U.S. citizen. Assuring Congress of the IAA's philanthropic nature as an organization that promoted freedom of trade and repudiated slave-trading, Arthur argued that "the United States cannot be indifferent to this work nor to the interests of their citizens involved in it." Moreover, unlike Francis, the president saw no advantage in supporting exclusive rights of trade or residence in the Congo River valley to "any one nation." Although he did not mention Portugal outright, it was clear that the president's position on the Congo question favored the dominance of the IAA in the region as opposed to Portugal's near monopoly on trade. He reasoned that as long as the IAA continued to establish trading entrepôts along the river valley, American merchants would enjoy access to commerce in an area rich with natural resources.[3] Although Francis and Arthur differed as to the best solution to the Congo question, both men saw in the Congo potential for expanding American trade with Africa—achieved either through partnership with the IAA or reciprocal trade agreements with Portugal.

The Congo Question

The government's assessment of the relevance of the Congo question to U.S. foreign policy and trade marked the nation's first serious engagement in African affairs since its proactive role in establishing the colony of Liberia, which it recognized diplomatically as an independent nation in 1862. When President Arthur addressed Congress regarding the European presence in the Congo, America had been experiencing a decline in legitimate trade (that is, trade that did not include slaves) with Africa since the 1870s. After the abolition of the slave trade in 1807, American businessmen—some who had reaped the benefits of slave trading—turned to legitimate trade with the continent, focusing primarily on West Africa. The French, British, and Portuguese dominated the trade along the Windward and Leeward Coasts—present-day Sierra Leone, Senegal, Liberia, Guinea, Gambia, Guinea-Bissau, the Cape Verde Islands, Côte d'Ivoire, Ghana, Benin, Gabon, Nigeria, and Angola. American businessmen wishing to engage in unrestricted free trade in these regions had to establish working agreements with the local European traders. After the War of 1812, New York and New England businessmen began trading tobacco and rum in exchange for peanuts, ginger, hides, palm oil, ivory, and gold dust, among other commodities. In some instances American traders were able to trade directly with the various African traders and middlemen—what the British derided as "floating trade" that undermined the sale of British goods at a fair price. American commerce peaked with the Gold Coast (Ghana) and the Windward Coast in the 1850s and 1860s, respectively. Trade with Togo, Dahomey (Benin), and Nigeria increased in the 1870s and 1880s, but not enough to reverse an overall decline in American trade on the Leeward Coast. Overwhelmingly, American merchants suffered from protective tariffs on African goods imposed by the United States beginning in the 1840s, as well as from fees paid to European middlemen.[4]

As Europeans scrambled for Africa, unrestricted free trade on the West Coast began to diminish, so much so that by the 1870s, American trade with West Africa was restricted to Senegal, Sierra Leone, and the Gold Coast. Within two decades American trade in the region would be insignificant.

George Brooks argues: "American trade in the 1880s was increasingly circumscribed by the economic developments which accompanied European colony-building, notably the growth in size and influence of European mercantile and shipping interests and the higher tariffs enacted by colonial governments in their unremitting search for revenues." Perhaps to forestall further contraction in American trade with West Africa, the United States appointed a trader, Peter Strickland, as first U.S. consular representative to Senegal in 1883. By 1891, Strickland would complain of the English, French, and German firms through which he had to purchase goods; he could no longer buy commodities directly from American merchants, as was possible nearly twenty years earlier.[5] It is in this context of the United States being shut out of the West African trade, as well as the nation's desire to expand its overall foreign trade, that Francis and President Arthur responded to the events unfolding in the Congo. The prospect that an American (Stanley) could open up the Congo to benefit American commerce removed Africa temporarily from the periphery of American diplomacy.

Stanley's place in what Felix Driver terms "the popular mythology of imperialism" is crucial to understanding the official U.S. reaction to the establishment of the IAA (also known as the Association Internationale Africaine) in 1876 and the Congo Free State subsequently in 1885. Stanley's status as a naturalized American citizen and his active participation in the development of commerce in Congo territory proved important to American claims to financial and political interests in the region. Stanley epitomized the new imperialist, a conglomerate of the American colonial frontiersman and the shrewd businessman; he was an adherent of the "strenuous life" and a carrier of "civilization" who promoted trade and commerce for the benefit of "savages." Overall, many Americans (including President Arthur) revered Stanley, viewing him as a benevolent imperialist and philanthropist. It was Stanley's reputation, American identity, and close friendship with King Leopold II that made the monarch's venture in the Congo palatable to the United States. Essentially, the U.S. government's decision to officially recognize the flag of the IAA as a friendly government on April 22, 1884, reflected American confidence in Stanley. Thus, when the Berlin Conference convened in November of that year, the United States had already taken a position on the question of the Congo.[6]

Americans would not remain enamored of Stanley's imperialism or King Leopold's Congo Free State for long. In the 1890s accusations surfaced that, while on expedition to find the Emin Pasha, Stanley had whipped servants and enslaved workers and had sanctioned the raping of women and pillaging of villages by his porters. Although some Americans dismissed the charges as malicious gossip or baseless rumors, public opinion of his heroic role in the exploration of Africa began to shift. Much of the criticism launched at Stanley came from British dailies and philanthropic societies and gained some traction in the United States. Distrust of Stanley worsened when American and British missionaries and travelers reported on the atrocities meted out on the Congolese by King Leopold and his rubber agents. The Congo Free State stood accused of rape, pillage, mutilation, and murder, and some argued that Stanley had paved the way for the monarch's scheme to establish total sovereignty over the Congolese people.[7]

Biographer Tim Jeal argues that Stanley was "a pawn in great power politics"—a "great explorer" who was ignorant of King Leopold's real motivations and secret agreements to consolidate power of the Congo.[8] According to what Jeal terms the "putty in his hands theory," Stanley's guilt in the court of public opinion was based solely on his association with King Leopold and not his own actions. Jeal holds that archival research exonerates Stanley from any complicity in the crimes committed in the Congo. The monarch used Stanley's celebrity to his own ends, deceiving him throughout their entire friendship and allowing him to be tainted by the scandal of the Congo. Nevertheless, other scholars have arrived at different conclusions regarding Stanley's complicity in "creating the moral atmosphere in which crimes against humanity were likely to be committed" in the Congo.[9] Whether or not Stanley was involved in the depredations associated with Leopold's rubber-collecting enterprise, the fact that he attested to the king's integrity discredited him. By the end of the century, it became clear to many interested in the philanthropic and commercial exploitation of the Congo that something was amiss.

Some Americans, chiefly anti-imperialists, attacked Belgian colonialism in the Congo, joining the U.S. branch of the Congo Reform Association (the other branch was in the United Kingdom) or other humanitarian movements targeting King Leopold's rule in the region. However, their sustained critique of imperialism in the Congo emerged only after the publication of the Casement Report in 1904 by the British Diplomat Roger Casement at the behest of the House of Commons. Although members of the British press, most notably H. R. Fox Bourne of the *Times*, and missionaries (both American and British) had reported in the 1890s on the atrocities occurring in the Congo Free State, most white American anti-imperialists demonstrated little concern for the realities of colonial rule in Africa. The

Spanish-American War and the subsequent U.S. occupation of the Philippines dominated American anti-imperialist thought outside black political and intellectual circles until the Congo scandal erupted. Mark Twain, one-time vice president of the American Congo Reform Association and the Anti-Imperialist League, exemplified those few white Americans who merged their condemnation of Belgian colonialism in Africa with their anti-imperialist stance on the American occupation of the Philippines after the Spanish-American War. In the words of the league, "the subjugation of any people is 'criminal aggression' and open disloyalty to the distinctive principles of our Government." For these men and other like-minded Americans, imperialism—whether practiced by the United States or the Belgians—was an evil that deprived individuals of liberty.[10]

Events in the Congo interested not only American anti-imperialists, missionaries, and self-styled humanitarian philanthropists but also explorers and naturalists—mainly anthropologists and zoologists—who gained access to the Congo under Leopold's rule. Joining the ranks of the Liverpool School of Tropical Medicine, Italian explorer Prince Luigi Amedeo of Savoy, Duke of the Abruzzi; German ethnologist-ethnographer Leo Frobenius; British anthropologists Emil Torday, Melville W. Hilton-Simpson, and Norman H. Hardy; and Belgian geologist Jules Cornet, Americans began conducting expeditions in the Congo financed by major museums and/or private patrons. The American Museum of Natural History emerged as one of the leading institutions actively engaged in scientific research in the Congo. Many scientists placed the political and humanitarian question of the Congo in a subordinate position to inquiries into the cultures of the Congolese. Focusing on art, artifacts, cannibalism, cicatrization, and dance, American naturalists joined the collecting frenzy in the Congo hoping to unearth mysteries about the people who inhabited the heart of Africa.

From 1884 to 1919, American interest in Africa coalesced around commercial ventures, Christian propagation, and scientific expeditions. Heightened by the Berlin Conference of 1884, American curiosity about the Congo dominated public popular and intellectual discourses about Africa for over two decades. During that time, American images of Africa—informed strongly by the events taking place in the Congo—dislocated the established narrative of Darkest Africa. From those who saw the Congo as an African bonanza to those who exhibited primitivist fascination with the art and cultures of the Congolese peoples, the American people found that Africa ceased to be a dark, unknowable place. Their configurations of brightest Africa found expression in travel journals, museum exhibits, and scientific texts. While these did not debunk the Darkest Africa trope, they operated as strong counternarratives. Similarly, textual denunciations of the rubber trade and its attendant imperialist labor practices inverted the colonialist narrative, rewriting the Europeans as the savages in need of redemption.

America and the Kongokonferenz

The congressional discussion of IAA interests in the Congo beginning in 1883 in many ways anticipated the conference that would be called in Berlin in 1884. When the Senate issued its Joint Resolution 68 in 1884, Senator John Tyler Morgan of the Committee on Foreign Relations had amassed several official documents and supporting miscellany to draft his report, "Occupation of the Congo Country in Africa." Citing legation papers, State Department correspondences, testimonials from members of the IAA, scholarly law articles, chamber of commerce resolutions, as well as British North American colonial treaties with Native Americans, existent international trade treaties, and American Colonization Society documents relating to the founding of Liberia, the report recommended the passage of the resolution, which recognized IAA sovereignty in the region over the "Free States of the Congo." Morgan, a segregationist senator from Alabama and former Confederate soldier, would emerge as a prominent expansionist during the last two decades of the nineteenth century, favoring the annexation of Hawaii and serving on the Committee on Interoceanic Canals. While scholars have not traditionally linked American imperialism to any overt interest in gaining territory in Africa, Morgan and the committee's rather jingoistic support of the IAA and American investment in the Congo suggests that U.S. expansionist rhetoric of the 1890s owed as much to an earlier American-styled imperialist hunger for Africa as to the doctrine of hemispheric hegemony and the search for new markets in Asia. Revealingly, the report sought to convince the Senate and American people of the legitimacy of the IAA's occupation of the Congo based on two historical precedents: first, the founding of Liberia, and second, treaties signed between white colonists and Native Americans in the colonial period in the seventeenth century.[11]

Morgan's chronicle of the founding of Liberia credits "the people of the United States" with establishing "a free republic in Liberia, with a constitution modeled after [their] own, and under the control of the negro race." Ironically, the United States had withheld recognition of the independence of Liberia fearing agitation of the slavery question at home. Nevertheless, Morgan commends the people for achieving republicanism "with but little assistance" from the U.S. government. Praising the American Colonization Society, Morgan highlights the actions of private citizens motivated by a sense of humanity not only to return enslaved Africans rescued on the high seas after the abolition of the slave trade but also to provide a "congenial asylum and home for negroes who were emancipated in the United States." True to his segregationist leanings, Morgan extolled the "success of the Liberian colony" for its ability to answer "a social question, which is, to the people of the United States of the highest importance." Essentially, Liberia existed as a panacea to the so-called Negro problem. Convinced that whites and blacks could not live as equals in the United States, Morgan supported emigration to Liberia—the "restoration of the emancipated Africans to their own country"—if they so chose to "return to it." Perhaps more relevant to the IAA claims in the Congo, Liberia had "established a recognized precedent in favor of the right of untitled individuals to found states in the interests of civilization in barbarous countries, through the consent of the local authorities." Morgan ignored the well-documented resistance that the local leaders mounted against American attempts to purchase land, as well as the coercive tactics used by naval lieutenant Robert Stockton to purchase land for the African American settlers. Indigenous Africans continued to attack the settlement until the colonists fortified it. Nevertheless, Morgan held up Liberia as an example of the "pleasing history of progress," as the nation was now ensconced "firmly ... in the family of nations."[12]

After transposing the myth of the founding of America onto Liberia, Morgan made a more explicit comparison between colonial North America and the IAA in the Congo. Calling forth the memory of English settlers who negotiated with Native Americans to eke out an existence for their families, Morgan disentangled IAA motives from those of European nations engaged in what appeared to be an outright landgrab in the heart of Africa. The report provided excerpts from George Bancroft's ten-volume *History of the United States* (1834–1874) to argue that the United States owed its very existence to doctrines that recognized the right of private persons to enter into treaties with "chiefs of savage tribes," and thereby establish sovereignty over a region. Bancroft's account of the settlements of Massachusetts, the Providence Plantations and Rhode Island, Connecticut, New Hampshire, and North Carolina supposedly demonstrated that Americans owed their country's very existence to the principle that "the occupants of a country, at the time of discovery by other and more powerful nations, have the right to make ... treaties for its disposal, and that private persons, when associated in such country, for self-protection or self-government, may treat with the inhabitants for any purpose that does not violate the laws of nations."[13]

For Morgan, the Peace Treaty of 1621 (the infamous Thanksgiving treaty), which created an alliance between the Wampanoag and the Pilgrims against the Narragansett, was one among several colonial agreements that set precedent for the actions of America's countryman Stanley in the Congo. According to Bancroft, the 1621 treaty constituted the "oldest act of diplomacy recorded in New England." He also noted: "The men of Plymouth exercised self government without the sanction of a royal charter, which it was ever impossible for them to obtain." Similarly, Roger Williams's establishment of Providence Plantation in 1638 after purchasing land from Canonicus and the subsequent gift of Rhode Island from Miantonomoh of the Narragansett demonstrated individual ingenuity in securing land not for one's personal gain. Here Bancroft emphasized that the land patent from England was necessary for the colonists' security. The treaties signed between Kilcacenen, King of Yeopim, and George Durant to found Cape Fear Colony; Theopilus Eaton and Momauquin to establish New Haven colony; and the colonists and the Pennacook at Concord, New Hampshire, all supported the legal capacity of the IAA to make treaties with "native chiefs and government."[14] Morgan's selection of Bancroft quotes and accompanying interpretation of them left no doubt as to overarching questions that his report seemed to ask and answer. Did Stanley have a right to sign treaties with the Congolese that gave him control over parts of the Congo Basin? Was it possible that the IAA could bring brightness and progress to Africa in much the same way that British settlers had established a "city upon a hill" in North America? Morgan answered with a resounding "YES."

Not content with supporting Stanley's position based on the law of nations and colonial precedent, Morgan returned to the subject of the United States' special relationship to Africa via its African American population. "Our attitude towards [the Congo] is exceptional, and our interest in its people greatly enhanced by the fact that more than one-tenth of our population is descended from the negro races in Africa." Morgan held that Stanley's position in the IAA offered the United States a unique opportunity not only to secure a future homeland for its African American citizens but also to reap the benefits of free trade in the Congo.[15] Providing a revisionist interpretation of the origins of America's "Negro problem," the report stated:

> We owe it as a duty to our African population that we should endeavor to secure them the right to freely return to their fatherland, and as freely to agree with their kindred people upon any concessions they may choose to make to them as individuals or as associated colonists, looking to their re-establishment in their own country. The deportation of their ancestors from Africa in slavery was contrary to the now accepted canons of the law of nations and now they may return under those laws to their natural inheritance. In exercising this right they should not be obstructed by a power that had more to do with their enslavement and expulsion, in bondage, from their own country than any other, and that never held a claim upon that country for any purpose of advantage to the people there, but held it chiefly, if not entirely, for the mere purpose of enslaving them.[16]

Absolving the United States from an active or systematic role in enslaving Africans and waving its own version of the bloody shirt, the report couched its resistance to Portuguese control in the region in terms of both a moral and legal opposition to the slave trade. At once affirming America to be a "white man's country" and Africa to be the black man's "own country," the committee offered African Americans the chance to colonize the Congo and to liberate their "kindred" from the oppressive rule of Portugal. Morgan warned his readers not to be fooled by the benevolence of the Portuguese. He writes: "It is stated, with the support of strong testimony that Portugal is still protecting the slave trade on the west coast of Africa under a thin guise of the voluntary emigration of the negroes to other countries. . . . This violation of the slave-trade renders the occupancy by Portugal of any African territory at the mouth of the Congo dangerous to all the tribes of the interior, and cannot be sanctioned by the treaty powers while it is attended with such incidents without an abandonment of all treaty obligations and duties relating to the slave trade."[17]

In Morgan's estimation, the United States should object to Portugal's claim to exclusive trading rights in the Congo based on that nation's failure to suppress the slave trade, as well as its attempts to monopolize legitimate trade in the region. The report asserted that: "The merchants of Europe and America insist upon . . . equal and universal right of free trade with that country, and their chambers of commerce have earnestly pressed upon their respective governments the duty and necessity of such international agreements as would secure these blessings to the people of Africa and of the entire commercial world." Morgan praised the "enlightened" King Leopold for using his private purse to inaugurate "civilization in the Congo country under the authority of its native rulers." The report emphasized that Leopold had no personal designs to extend Belgian sovereignty over the people. Citing an 1882 article from the *Pall Mall Gazette*, he explained the progress that the IAA made in the Congo after Stanley's discovery, while the French (apparently another suspect nation) with de Brazza at the helm schemed to "gird the continent with the tricolor." Morgan ended his plea, which was followed by several appendices, assuring his readers that the people of the Congo blossomed under the "benevolent enterprise" of the IAA and would continue to thrive and civilize under the tutelage of "their benefactors."[18]

Morgan's lengthy discussion of the Congo proved significant to understanding the discourses against which Pan-Africanists argued in their opposition to European imperialism, as well as how Pan-African emigrationists distinguished repatriation from colonization. Where Morgan tried to draw a direct parallel between English colonization of North America and Stanley's activities in the Congo, emigrationists used the settler model as a tool to disrupt and prevent further European (and potential American) penetration of the continent. Under the guise of righting the wrong of slavery, Morgan advocated African American settlement in the Congo not to promote black liberation but to advance potential U.S. economic interests. Thus, Pan-Africanists in favor of emigration had to articulate a platform for black repatriation that did not play into the hands of white segregationists and proponents of black removal from America.

For the naturalists, Morgan's use of the American frontier paradigm to support the IAA would prove problematic. They articulated their own version of the frontier myth to argue for the preservation of wildlife in Africa. However, they did not want to see scores of white Americans and Europeans settling the Congo region and disrupting the pristine landscapes they imagined. Full-scale white settlement of Africa analogous to that of the American colonies would inevitably deplete African faunal species on the same scale as penetration of the American West decimated the buffalo.

Once the Berlin Conference convened in November 1884, the U.S. position on the Congo question became clearer. The Congo should be a neutral territory under the flag of the IAA, where American citizens could enjoy "freedom from custom dues, the right to trade, to reside and acquire property, whether as traders or missionaries, freedom of religious belief, and freedom from the slave trade."[19] Mainstream American press coverage of the conference deviated little from the party line. Yet the *Washington Post*, the *New York Times*, *Harper's Weekly*, and the *Chicago Daily Tribune* exercised their editorial license referring to "shrewd Americans," "a Yankee scheme," and "the American project for territorial neutrality." Extensive reporting on the conference by the *Chicago Daily Tribune* appeared throughout the month of December under the heading "THE DARK CONTINENT." Collectively, these newspapers played up the international context of the conference: European nations jockeying for power and Germany's attempt to establish an empire abroad, while Stanley and other American attendees—businessman Henry S. Sanford, diplomat John A. Kasson, and missionary-explorer Samuel Verner—inserted their agenda into the proceedings. The *Chicago Daily Tribune* predicted that "indications are that shrewd Americans at the back of Mr. Stanley will get the most of the substantial benefits, and that England or Portugal will get few of them."[20] American press coverage of the conference brought into question the validity of the argument put forth by John Tyler Morgan that the United States had a vested interest in the Congo due to either its African American population or Stanley's involvement in the IAA.

The American dailies and weeklies focused on the actions of the Americans at the conference, implying that Stanley and his cohorts either withheld important information about the true state of the natives in an effort to enrich their coffers or simply made sure they shared disproportionately in the commercial exploitation of the Congo. In an interesting turn away from the conference proceedings, the *Washington Post* and *New York Times* reported that a Belgian resident at Stanley Falls penned a letter to a Belgian newspaper claiming that the natives in the Congo were dangerous and plotted to "poison Europeans at Leopoldville." The informant accused the IAA of refusing to hire African porters to ensure the safe travel of Europeans in the Free State, leaving them to the mercies of "hostile" natives. The letter insinuated that Stanley concealed the "truth concerning the state of things on the Congo" from the conference attendees—that "a state of open war" existed between the IAA and the Manyanga and Lutib. The IAA did not enjoy peaceful relations with the objects of their benevolence.[21]

On a related matter concerning the inhabitants of the Free State, the *Chicago Daily Tribune* reported on the continued existence of slavery in the region, apparently with the IAA's blessing. The paper quoted Stanley as addressing calls to end the slave trade with this statement: "It would be impossible to abolish the traditional system of employing slave servants." Slave servants occupied a space in the social hierarchy that placed them between chattel slaves and domestic servants. Stanley appears to deflect the question by pointing out that the indigenous labor system practiced in the region was not that of the chattel slavery associated with either the transatlantic slave trade or internal slavery in Africa. This argument would come to haunt Stanley as philanthropists, Pan-Africanists, and anti-imperialists would later accuse the Congo Free State of using slaves to extract rubber and perform other arduous jobs.[22]

Adding to the charges that the Africans in the Congo desired to murder innocent Europeans or fell into the clutches of crafty slave traders, the *Tribune* also reported rumors of plans to foster widespread drunkenness among the African workers. The newspaper informed its readers that the German delegates intended to import spirits into the region, an issue that would claim the attention of missionaries and other Pan-Africanists who viewed the rum jug as one of many tools used by Europeans to subjugate Africans spiritually and morally. The articles covering this "scheme" implied that the Germans' actions would undermine the mobilization of labor in the region. However, Italy led the charge to prohibit the sale of alcohol in the Congo, citing moral reasons, although the image of drunken Africans refusing to work tirelessly for the Europeans appeared to disturb the delegates most.[23]

The coverage of these controversies surrounding the conference served various agendas to dissuade the United States from ratifying the Berlin Act. Despite statements by the American delegates avowing that the United States would not be "responsible for the execution of the resolutions" on account of their participation in the deliberations, the press and other commentators questioned Stanley, Sanford, Kasson, and Verner's intentions. These men's disclaimer did little to assuage American fears that the nation would be implicated in the imperialist conquest of Africa or become embroiled in European rivalries on the continent. These cleverly planted seeds of doubt served to influence American opinions about the wisdom of sending American delegates to the conference.

On the closing day of the conference, the *New York Times* quoted a thank-you letter from King Leopold to Prince Bismarck that praised the German chancellor for "the great services rendered to African civilization" in making the conference a success.[24] Unlike the black press, which would later discuss the impact of the Berlin Conference on "the colored people of this country," the white press did not link the American Negro question to the African questions.[25] Although the mainstream press declared the conference an achievement due to its issuance of the General Act and the establishment of the Congo Free State, members of Congress had already begun reconsidering U.S. involvement in European affairs, even if it meant abandoning their image of the Congo as a new commercial frontier.

The House of Representatives passed a resolution while the conference was in session requiring the president to supply it with all documents pertaining to U.S. participation in the Congo conference. This included copies of all correspondence between the U.S. government and the governments attending the conference, copies of exchanges between the U.S. government and Americans at the conference acting as either plenipotentiaries or delegates, copies of the credentials of said persons, and any records that indicated that other governments in attendance objected to the U.S. position on the Congo question. Elaborating on the latter demand, the House demanded to know which governments resisted the U.S. position on the "territorial neutrality" of the Congo and why. The House also insisted that the president provide an explanation as to why the United States found it necessary to be represented at the conference. What lay at the heart of these inquiries was the House's conviction that U.S. representation at the conference might initiate "a new departure in the foreign policy of the United States," specifically the Monroe Doctrine's dictum that the government steer clear of "entangling alliances with the nations of the Old World." Although the House comprehended the commercial and entrepreneurial advantages available to American businessmen once the Congo question was settled, many members felt uneasy about capitalism influencing foreign policy. Despite Kasson's assurance to Secretary Frelinghuysen that he made clear "with absolute certainty that the United States would not embark in the eager struggle among European powers for African colonial possessions," the House resolution revealed its doubts about the importance of Africa to American commerce and foreign policy.[26]

Members of the House of Representatives were not alone in questioning American entanglement in the Congo question and ultimately whether America should establish an economic presence in Africa. The Curaçao-born American Socialist Daniel De Leon published his assessment of the Congo conference in 1886 in the *Political Science Quarterly*. Maintaining that the gathering constituted "an event unique in the history of political science," De Leon argued that rather than address matters of "international jurisprudence," the conference, under the mask of diplomacy, simultaneously satisfied Germany's quest for empire in Africa and solved its peculiar "social problems," including preventing increased German emigration abroad. De Leon interpreted the conference as both a German mission to gain equal footing with its European neighbors in the broader imperial world and a mechanism for nation-building. Essentially, Prince Otto von Bismarck sought to weld "into one self-reliant and stable nation the

German-speaking peoples" from the Rhine to the Danube by creating a German empire overseas—a symbol of the strength and unity of the German people. De Leon's appraisal of Germany's motivations and harsh criticism of the outcome of the conference reflected his ideological commitment to Marxism that placed that "treaty" (there was debate as to whether the General Act constituted a treaty) within a materialist framework, which implicated not only European nations, but the United States as well.[27]

De Leon's interpretation of the conference as a tool for promoting capitalist expansion lay rooted in his analysis of the opposition to Portuguese claims to sovereignty in the region, as well as disputes over King Leopold and Stanley's claims to occupation rights in Central Africa. Partially under the guise of promoting civilization and eradicating the slave trade, plenipotentiaries representing various European nations, as well as Russia, Turkey, and the United States, gathered at Berlin to protest Portugal's claim to control over the western coast of Africa and thereby the Congo River, whose delta emptied out into the Atlantic Ocean.[28] Although conference attendees agreed that Portugal was the first "civilized" nation to establish contact with West Africa and to chart its coastline and many rivers, many held that Portuguese rights of ownership in the region based on that "ancient" history proved "inchoate" at best. They argued that in the intervening years (approximately 1448 to 1884), Portugal did little to solidify its rule in the area by either promoting legitimate trade, Christianizing the natives, or stamping out barbarism—namely cannibalism. Opponents of the Portuguese cataloged a list of violations of the British 1807 Abolition of the Slave Trade Act and wielded the rhetoric of Latin incompetence and mismanagement in favor of a more fair policy in the region—free trade and territorial neutrality. Additionally, attendees sought to definitively settle the question of whether an association with its own flag could exercise the rights of nations by entering into treaties with African rulers who ceded land and inheritance rights to it. The legal intricacies of the Congo question were not lost on De Leon, who ultimately determined that "diplomacy became subservient to an economic and social question" as the European-sanctioned Congo Free State amounted to a mercantile organization.[29] In his estimation, the free state increased the power of the Belgian monarch by creating a trade monopoly.

With regard to the United States, De Leon maintained that "the grossest political blunders" of American representatives at the Berlin Conference were threefold. First, like members of the House of Representatives, he contended that the mere presence of the United States at the conference marked a departure "from its time-honoured policy" of nonintervention in European affairs. He claimed that the Berlin Conference marked the first time in history that a U.S. delegation sat alongside the most powerful European states at a diplomatic conference held in Europe. Second, he argued that the U. S. representatives' decision to dispute Portuguese sovereignty over Angola and "assist at the carving of a new state on the Congo" went contrary to American principles that upheld the right of first discovery and occupation by authorized agents of a sovereign nation. (This argument challenged Senator Morgan's support of the IAA based on similar reasoning.) Thus, supporting the aims of the IAA promulgated commercial interests at the expense of the "law of nations." Third, unwittingly aiding the German chancellor's nation-building project checked German immigration to the United States. De Leon asserted that "of all the ethnic alloys" to reach American shores "that which proceeds from Germany is the most valuable." American support of the conference would stem the flow of "desirable" industrious European immigrants into the United States. Although he disapproved of the United States' move away from isolationism, De Leon took comfort in the Cleveland administration's decision not to present the General Act to the Senate for ratification.[30]

Despite the opposition launched by the House to any official U.S. recognition of the conclusions of the conference, Americans continued to demonstrate interest in King Leopold's state. Other African affairs claimed headlines in major newspapers, such as the Second Boer War in South Africa. However, American interest in Africa piqued as it had in 1884, when the once celebrated IAA became the subject of international controversy beginning in the 1890s, facing allegations that its officers exploited, enslaved, and mutilated the Congolese people to coerce them into working in the rubber plantations. One critic of the Congo Free State revealed that when such tactics failed, the company imported laborers from eastern and western Africa (Zanzibar, Lagos, Accra, Sierra Leone, and Liberia) and underpaid them for their services. That critic, George Washington Williams, wrote the first exposé on the atrocities committed in the Congo Free State. The son of former slaves, a Civil War veteran, a missionary, and a self-trained historian, Williams was initially convinced that the IAA was a "rising star of hope for the Dark Continent."[31] However, when he visited the colony in 1890, under the patronage of railroad robber baron Collis P. Huntington, Williams witnessed conditions in the Congo that led him to pen *An Open Letter to His Serene Majesty Leopold II, King of the Belgians and Sovereign of the Independent State of Congo*.[32] Williams's manifesto, which leveled twelve charges at Leopold, laid the foundation for a more systematic critique of the Congo Free State among missionaries, anti-imperialists, reformers, and humanitarians alike. Moreover, his letter contributed to growing concerns among those African Americans interested in Africa that the new era in European imperialism spelled doom for the continent that they sought to redeem.

The Crime of the Congo

Williams's open letter to King Leopold and his *Report on the Proposed Congo Railway* circulated in Europe and the United States in 1890, and the Belgian government took his charges seriously. His first accusation, that Leopold's rule was "deficient in the moral, military, and financial strength necessary to govern" a territory as vast as the Congo, prefaced more serious allegations that His Majesty's government violated contracts, abused prisoners, fostered unjust court procedures, trafficked in women, suppressed free trade, waged unjust wars against the Congolese, and engaged in the slave trade. Williams felt betrayed by Leopold, his "Good and Great Friend," because like many Americans who followed the Berlin Conference, he supported the formation of the Independent State of the Congo believing that the Belgians would bring "humane sentiments and the work of Christian civilization for Africa." Instead, his trip to the Congo left him "disenchanted, disappointed, and disheartened." Foremost, according to Williams, the IAA defrauded African chiefs in treaty negotiations. Recounting "sleight-of-hand tricks" and alluding to other means "too silly and disgusting to mention," he accused Stanley of manipulating Western technology to convince African rulers that the white man had superhuman strength, enjoyed an "intimate relation to the sun," and possessed immortality. These mythologies coupled with "a few boxes of gin" resulted in the secession of whole villages to the IAA. William also argued that under the cloak of "benevolent enterprise," Leopold convinced the United States that his altruism toward the Africans would govern his commercial endeavors. Yet, when the Congolese refused to be exploited by the IAA's arbitrary labor practices, the company resorted to cruel coercive measures to force them to work. Citing workers' testimonies depicting Belgians and their "black soldiers" burning towns, stealing property, enslaving women and children, and committing "other crimes too numerous to mention in detail," Williams hoped that an international commission would be formed to verify the evidence and investigate conditions in the Congo Free State. Interestingly, although Williams was an American citizen, he chose to furnish the British Parliament's Secretary of

State of Foreign Affairs with a copy of the letter and all supporting documents rather than the U.S. Secretary of State James Blaine.[33]

In order perhaps to understand Williams's reticence toward full disclosure to the U.S. government, as well as comprehend the initial American reaction to Williams's letter, a glimpse of popular and public opinion about King Leopold's Congo state after the Berlin Conference is warranted. Seven months before Williams wrote his letter to Leopold, *Harper's Weekly* featured an article on Western knowledge of the Congo obtained since the signing of the Berlin Act. In "Recent Discoveries in the Congo Basin: The Geographical Surprises and New-Found Peoples of the Past Five Years," its author, C. C. Adams, sketches a hagiography of explorers who traversed the Congo, beginning with the "ill-fated" 1816 trip of James Kingston Tuckey on the HMS *Congo* and ending with that of Belgian A. Van Gele in 1888. Adams wanted to demonstrate how in "the light of our present knowledge of the Congo, the wild speculations and beliefs of earlier decades in this century appear almost grotesque." Although he credited Stanley with opening the "gateway to the Congo Valley" and, thus, advancing knowledge of the region through his account of his work for the Congo Free State, Adams argued that the true importance of the Congo River and its tributaries remained undiscovered. Only after more European explorers navigated the riparian zones did "a series of revelations which astonished the geographers and anthropologists" unfold. Adams identified several important topographical finds that required geographers to revise the Congo map five times but declared the information concerning the human inhabitants of the region "even more interesting and unexpected." Adams recited several explorers' accounts of seeing "remarkable ... dwarfs" and witnessing "the greatest hot-bed of cannibalism of which the world ever heard." These tales whetted the appetites of Americans hungry for more news of Stanley's Dark Continent.[34]

The article reads as a vindication of colonialism as Adams rhapsodizes explorers' experiences with "these boisterous and sometimes dangerous children of nature." Fixating on cannibalism, Adams cites sources showing that over one-third of the peoples of the Congo Basin ate human flesh. Cannibal tribes were purported to be superior in appearance, intellect, and artistic sensibilities to those Africans who loathed the "atrocious practice." Thus, habitual cannibals reportedly used chicanery to conceal from whites their insatiability for human flesh. According to one explorer, who claimed to have lived among cannibals and observed three "cannibal feasts," a Hausa solider in the employ of the Congo Free State supposedly escaped from cannibals and lived on roots and raw manioc in the forest. After regaling his readers with anthropophagic anecdotes, Adams stated: "Though it will undoubtedly be a very slow process, there is reason to believe that as the influence of the white men extends, cannibalism in the Congo Basin will gradually disappear, as it has from many Pacific islands."[35] For him and many Americans, stamping out cannibalism in the Congo Basin justified any violent measures taken by authorities to protect white men from molestation and natives from anthropophagic aggression.

Adams's discussion of "dwarfs" departs little from the gruesomeness of his cannibal narrative, as he describes groups like the Batwa (Twa) and Akka as "cunning," "curious" cannibals who swing from trees like monkeys, kill with poisonous arrows, and attack their enemies at night, instilling deadly fear in neighboring tribes. He relays that anthropologists are working hard at ascertaining the origins of these peoples as they may be the aboriginal inhabitants of inner Africa. Adams ethnographic description of the Congo continues with stories of human sacrifice, slave-trading African rulers (including the notorious Tippu Tib), tattooing rituals, frenzied dances, and rare "progressive tribes." He concludes: "The good days is coming when this terrible custom [human sacrifice] and other savage enormities will be abolished in the Congo State. King Leopold's government is rooting them out as far as its influence extends.... Nearly a hundred chiefs in the past year have agreed to abolish human sacrifices to help enforce the regulations of the State for preserving peace and protecting human life." Adams then declared the Congo Free State the "greatest philanthropic project of the century." If the numerous accounts of King Leopold's "betrayal" that surfaced after 1904 are any indication of American support for the imperialist, Adams seems to have captured the sentiment of most Americans—that the Congo Free State engaged in good works, redeeming savages from their backward culture.[36]

In some black American political circles, the benevolence of Stanley and Leopold was not as clear. Although Blyden's 1890 speech on the solution to the African problem painted European imperialists as misguided, it did not accuse the Congo Free State of immorality. He did not dispute that Central Africa was "darker than ever"; rather, he questioned imperialists' convictions that they should be the emissaries of enlightenment for the continent. Nevertheless, the General Act of the Brussels Conference, which sought to "put an end to Negro Slave Trade by land as well as by sea, and to improve the moral and material conditions of existence of the native races," seemed to have alleviated many political concerns that African Americans might have had about Leopold's rule. Unfortunately, Williams's untimely death in 1891 prevented his fledgling campaign against Leopold from gaining momentum. The numerous eulogies to Williams made no mention of his quarrel with the monarch, focusing instead on his historical writings, military service, travels, and ministry.[37]

Twelve years after Williams's death, in 1903, British Consul Roger Casement wrote his report on the administration of the Congo Free State for Parliament. His description of the brutality meted out to the Congolese exceeded that depicted in Williams's letter. It is doubtful that Williams held back any information to appease Leopold. More likely, conditions in the Congo Free State deteriorated to such a degree that the plight of the Congolese might have been unfathomable to Williams had he lived. Casement himself expressed surprise when contrasting the state of the Congo to what he had encountered there sixteen years earlier. Wistfully recalling the time when "natives loved their own savage lives in anarchic and disorderly communities," he despaired at the depopulation evident in the villages. Casement explained how those communities that had not been burned harbored refugees escaping government soldiers who killed individuals who failed to make their rubber quotas. Furthermore, soldiers prevented foodstuffs from reaching towns, leading to death from starvation and bad health. They employed these and other punitive measures, including floggings, beatings, imprisonment, and amputation of hands and penises to force the Congolese to cultivate "India-rubber."[38] To Casement's chagrin, the Foreign Office rushed to censor the more graphic descriptions of torture before publishing his report. He responded by granting interviews to various newspapers in order to prevent the government from suppressing the evidence he collected. When the report came out in February 1904, Belgian journalists questioned the integrity of his sources and witness statements. Casement wanted to protect his informants and, thus, refused to divulge their identities, exposing himself to charges of fabricating testimonials. Shortly thereafter, he established a friendship with E. D. Morel, who founded the Congo Reform Association in March, which soon led to the chartering of an American branch.[39]

Harper's Weekly reversed its position on the Congo Free State in a 1904 article titled "Worse Than the Sixteenth Century," postulating that the crimes committed against the Congolese surpassed those of the Spanish and Portuguese against the indigenous peoples of the Americas, which included forcing them to work and then almost exterminating the entire native population. The article did not mention Williams's open letter but referred to the book *The Curse of Central Africa* (1903) written by Captain Guy Burrows, who included a report on cannibalism by Edgar Canisius. Admitting that it was "easier to believe that the two authors . . . had been guilty of gross exaggeration than that a thousand Belgian officials" committed atrocities against the Congolese, the author explained that it was impossible to discount the Casement report. The Congo Committee of the Massachusetts Commission for International Justice concurred, urging the United States to join the international investigation led by Great Britain. The committee wanted to contribute to the "education of public opinion in America upon the whole issue." More important, they argued that because the United States did not have "territorial ambitions" in Africa their intervention in the Congo affair would not be "ascribed to interested motives."[40]

By 1905, Consul General of the Congo Free State, James Gustavus Whiteley, could declare in the *New York Times*: "If anybody thirsts after knowledge about the Congo in these days it's his own fault if he doesn't get it. He can get true stories or false ones, just as he pleases, the latter. Like false diamonds, being much cheaper and more numerous." In a spirited defense of his sovereign's rule in the Congo, Whiteley reviewed American painter and lawyer Henry Wellington Wack's book *The Story of the Congo Free State: Social, Political, and Economic Aspects of the Belgian System of Government in Central Africa* (1905). Whiteley declared Wack's book a help to Americans who wished to know the truth about the Congo in light of the "combined forces of missionaries and British merchants [who] began a siege on American public opinion." Whiteley also censured the Americans who "up to a few years ago . . . got along very well without knowing anything at all about the Congo." He claimed that the United States as the largest rubber-using country and consumer of Congo rubber was content with allowing the Rubber Trust to worry about what "was going on in Central Africa." In essence, Americans were "ignorant, but . . . very blissful" as long as the rubber kept coming into the country at fair prices. Whiteley claimed that Wack's book provided an uncompromising account of the anti-Congo campaign in the United States and England.[41]

Wack, a member of the New York Bar, had resided in England for several years when he observed a "small *clique* of Liverpool merchants" manipulate religious organizations to attack the Free State. However, he was hesitant to get involved in English affairs until "the campaign of calumny against the Congo Free State was being extended to the United States." He believed that as an American he could not stand passively by as the group aided by misguided missionaries sought to "deceive" his countrymen. Wack's book includes 125 illustrations and maps that demonstrate the economic, cultural, and political "improvement" of the region under the Belgian regime, as well as provides ethnographic data on the various African peoples inhabiting the Congo. Pictures of "native boys" in Western garb, a post office, a public library, a rations station for native employees, African laborers engaged in a myriad of tasks, and a tribunal sentencing a man to death for cannibalism all served to support Wack's underlying thesis that the Congo Free State brought civilization to the Congo and that partisanship, and not truth, guided the Congo reform campaign. He opines:

> The results of only twenty years' guidance in this direction are manifest to-day. They have placed the Negro in the midst of the uncovered wealth of a vast and fertile country; of waterways teeming with traffic; of a magnificent forest stored with rubber; timber of great variety, ivory, oil, and fruit; of promising fields of coffee, cotton, cocoa, tea, and sugar; deposits of gold, copper, coal, and iron.... In the midst of it all the black man's hands and acquired energy have provided him with new value to himself and to the State ... learning the uses of the white man's implements of labour, and imitating his enlightened ways. Industry and order, Christianity, civilization, and material progress have succeeded tribal wars, cannibalism, and the horrible atrocities of the slave chase. This has been achieved by the brawny men of Belgium in less than twenty years.[42]

Wack's book was among several published since Casement submitted his report, but his stood out for its unapologetic support of King Leopold's administration over the Congo. Despite Whiteley's endorsement of Wack's tome, Mark Twain's *King Leopold's Soliloquy: A Defense of His Congo Rule* (published that same year) contributed to the body of recently printed material condemning King Leopold and the rubber trade.

Twain's book depicts King Leopold as a greedy potentate, preening in self-indulgent piety as he reflects on his establishment of the Congo Free State. The monarch recalls his once congenial relationship with the United States when the nation "wept in sympathy" with him as he embarked on a mission to "lift ... twenty-five millions of gentle and harmless blacks out of darkness into light." Leopold recounts the role that the United States played in the recognition of the IAA flag and the attendance of Americans at the Berlin Conference, proclaiming: "Yes, I certainly did bunco a Yankee—as those people phrase it. Pirate flag? Let them call it so—perhaps it is. All the same, *they were the first to salute it.*" The king accuses "meddlesome American missionaries," "frank British consuls," and Belgian traitors for revealing details of his labor and economic policies within the state. The soliloquy enumerates the charges leveled at Leopold: barring all foreign traders from the region, imposing burdensome taxes on the Africans, employing African soldiers to burn villages and butcher workers who do not meet their rubber quota, raping women, and murdering and mutilating men, women, and children. Twain calls attention to the cutting off of hands, especially of children.[43]

Twain mocks King Leopold's piety and the constant refrain from his supporters that the Congo Free State has "spread the Gospel" to the benighted Africans. Twain's Leopold is an "absolute sovereign" whose desire for personal wealth and admiration from great European powers guides his every calculated move. Leopold relishes his ability to shame America for its initial support of his colony. Twain's book not only condemned King Leopold but also reproached the United States for being buncoed or swindled into setting up an "absolute monarchy." Twain goes beyond implicating President Arthur in Leopold's scheme. He accuses the U.S. government outright with lending their power and influence to establishing the colony.[44]

As Twain, Wack, and other writers engaged in a war of words in addressing the Congo controversy, African American newspapers, leaders, and writers also responded to the Congo crimes. The *New York Age* showed interest in the Congo, but the editor Fortune's apprehensions about African "barbarism" contextualized the paper's discussions of the atrocities. Reprinting a 1905 article from the *New York Sun*, the *Age*'s headline read: "Redeeming Africa: Ancient Barbarism 'Losing Its Foothold in Widening Areas'—Up from Cannibalism." The subheading indicated that the article would discuss the "industrial training" of the "fiercest of savages," the Congolese ruled by "the Government." Fortune's friendship with Booker T. Washington may explain his decision to rename the article and highlight the content on industrial education. "Up from Cannibalism" was an obvious play on the title of Washington's biography *Up from Slavery* (1901). The *Sun*'s reporter claimed that "every white settlement throughout the Congo State shows the new arts the natives are learning." Including many photographs of "tropical Africa," the reporter downplayed reports of colonial mismanagement and cruelty. A year later, the *Age* reprinted an article by Washington calling for industrial education in Africa. Washington proposed forming an international council comprised of scientists, missionaries, explorers, and others doing "constructive work in Africa" to assert a

Image of King Leopold clutching treasure while Africans labor from Mark Twain's *King Leopold's Soliloquy*, 1905.

"wise and liberal influence" on the European colonial powers governing the continent. Washington dismissed criticism of colonial rule that offered no remedy for the harm done to Africans. Referring to the "atrocities in the French Kongo" and pleas for American intercession in the Congo Free State, Washington called on "friends of Africa" to unite and promote "positive improvement for the people" via industrial education and missionary work.[45] He envisioned a reformed Africa inhabited by industrious African Christians.

William H. Sheppard, the first black missionary in the Congo under the Presbyterian Church, beginning in 1890, documented the atrocities committed by the Compagnie du Kasai (the Kasai Rubber Company) in photographs, speeches, and print. During his travels in the Congo, Sheppard uncovered proof that the Belgian rubber firm exploited, killed, and mutilated workers. In 1908 he published his findings after forming a friendship with another American missionary, William Morrison. The Kasai Rubber Company accused both men of libel, demanding twenty thousand dollars in damages from each man for "calumnious denunciation." The men stood trial in 1909, but they were acquitted.[46]

Although the sensationalism surrounding the Congo scandal led many Americans to see the Congo primarily in political and humanitarian terms, the region known for its wild rubber vines and rumored cannibalism also fascinated scientists. As controversy increased regarding King Leopold's rule, naturalists and ethnographers nevertheless sought access to the region for collecting expeditions. During these tumultuous times, a number of scientific institutions expressed interest in financing expeditions into the Congo, seeking confirmation of the existence of "little people," okapis (a rare faunal species), and cannibals. However, not until King Leopold surrendered possession of the Congo Free State to the Belgian government in 1908 did scientific research in the region truly escalate. With the cooperation of the Belgian colonial authorities, the American Museum of Natural History (AMNH) sponsored its first expedition to the Congo under the leadership of German-born zoologist Herbert Lang and ornithologist James Chapin. Although the AMNH financed this trip as a zoological survey—whose specimens would later contribute to Akeley's exhibit of Brightest Africa—Lang's interest in the Congolese peoples facilitated the museum's first systematic attempt to construct an anthropology of the region. More important, the AMNH expedition reflected the influence of international politics on American scientific study of Africa. As an experiment in both zoological and anthropological knowledge production, the expedition placed the Congo under a scientific gaze, and in so doing, provided one model for American naturalist discourses on Africa.

Toward an Anthropology of the Congo

In 1907, President Morris K. Jesup expressed his desire for the museum to carry out an expedition in the Congo. After presenting preliminary plans for the expedition to the Belgian dignitaries in New York and Baltimore, the museum sent its director, H. C. Bumpus, to Brussels to solicit patronage from the Belgian authorities and King Leopold. As an expression of his support for the endeavor, the sovereign presented the museum with "an ethnological collection from the Congo" of over three thousand artifacts, which became part of the permanent exhibits in the African Hall of ethnology. Scholars have pointed out the calculation behind the donation, as key American businessmen, such as J. P. Morgan, sat on the museum's board of trustees. Gossip circulated that Leopold was trying to secure additional American investors for his colony. Sometime in the interim a copy of Twain's *King Leopold's Soliloquy* was given to the AMNH along with a letter from the Congo Reform Association urging conscientious readers to write their congressmen to demand immediate action from the government in the interest of the Congolese people. It is unclear whether the book was meant to discourage the AMNH from pursuing research in the Congo or to question the motives behind Leopold's gift. Whichever the case, the collection later became the subject of intense ethnographic analysis in the AMNH from 1910 to 1911 by Robert H. Lowie during his tenure as assistant curator of anthropology. Simultaneously, self-fashioned ethnographer Lang embarked on his own anthropological investigation, exhibiting and publishing his findings four years after Lowie. Interestingly, both men—Lowie, an anthropologist trained under Franz Boas, and Lang, a German-trained mammologist—reached radically different conclusions about the cultural achievements of the Congolese and, by extension, whether or not the peoples in the region deserved the designation "savage."[47]

In 1908, when noted eugenicist Henry Fairfield Osborn became museum president, he took up Jesup's cause, appointing the six-man Special Committee on the Congo Expedition, with Bumpus serving as chairman and Whiteley as a member-at-large. Through the efforts of the committee, "the [Congo] project became a reality." The Belgians contributed funds to subsidize the fieldwork, and the AMNH promised to share the scientific results of the expedition with the Musée de Congo in Tervuren, Belguim.[48] When Lang and Chapin left New York in 1909, they departed with instructions from President Osborn to "proceed without delay to the most promising zoological regions" in the Belgian Congo. The two men traveled thousands of miles inland to reach the northeastern region of the colony, where they hoped to secure the necessary material for the construction of okapi and "square-lipped" rhinoceros habitat dioramas.[49]

While Lang and Chapin were collecting in Africa, the African Hall of ethnology at the AMNH opened in 1910. According to Lowie, "the great preponderance of material from the Congo as compared with other regions of Africa made necessary the allotment of an apparently disproportionate amount of space" in the hall to Congolese cultures. The museum designed the hall so that each side of the rectangular space would represent a division of the continent (northern Africa, southern Africa, eastern Africa, and western Africa) around "the great heart of Africa, the Congo." The architects intended for the patrons to walk "the length of the hall along the right, and back along the left ... as if actually traveling north from the Cape of Good Hope to the Mediterranean, east of the Congo, and south again, west of the Congo." In doing so, the viewer would encounter material culture representing peoples from the Nile regions, the Sahara, and so forth. The exhibition illustrated "phases of native life" by converting photographs of African cultures into colored glass transparencies that sat in the lower window frames of the hall. The museum hoped that these transparencies would "convey to the public a clearer and more impressive picture of aboriginal African culture than could otherwise be hoped for."[50]

When Lowie decided to analyze the contents of the hall for a scholarly article, he wanted to do more than simply catalog the material culture specimens. He desired to dispel public myths and challenge accepted scientific truths about the supposed inferiority of Africans and African Americans. His 1911 article "Industry and Art of the Negro Race" declared that the African exhibition "enforces new ideas as to the capacities of the negro race and reveals the ground on which are based some new theories regarding the negro's relation to civilization."[51] In explaining the importance of the Congo to these latest hypotheses, Lowie wrote: "The Congo embraces within its boundaries tribes representing with special clearness the development of negro culture as uninfluenced by external causes; it includes not only divisions of the Pygmy race representing perhaps the lowest of cultural stages to be found in Africa, but also a number of Bantu-speaking negroes whose artistic work may be fairly taken as representative of the capacities of African natives."[52] He argued that the only way to truly evaluate "Negro" culture was to examine a group of indigenous Africans reasonably uninfluenced by outsiders (that is, Arabs, Europeans, or Americans). For Lowie, the Congo represented a cultural river at a standstill, a static portal to the past in the present, despite recent European penetration into the area. Thus, its peoples and their cultural forms were unbiased barometers of the "Negro's" capacity for civilization.

Lowie intimated that past studies of black and African cultures failed to accurately assess their artistic and industrial capabilities. Tainted by Social Darwinism, eugenics, and theories of biological racial hierarchy or influenced by political considerations (for example, imperialist agendas), much of the accepted research on Africans maintained that "Negroes" were incapable of distinguishing themselves in the arts or in any way culturally. Some scholars went so far as to state unequivocally that Africans possessed no culture. Lowie referenced layman opinions that would "not likely associate" "certain broad features" with African people, but assured the reader that these features were indeed aboriginal to African culture. Symptomatic of his training under Boas, Lowie sought to interrogate both scientific and popular understandings of African cultural production by focusing on physical objects and using them as evidence of both the cultural forms and achievements of Africans.

Once Lowie established that the uniqueness of the Congo allowed anthropologists to ascertain the promise of black culture, he argued that metallurgy used to make "spears, battle-axes, throwing-knives and scimitars" best exemplified the cultural achievements of a race. Indeed, among anthropologists—including those at the AMNH—the debate over whether or not metallurgy could reliably gauge cultural progress and achievement was often fraught. In curator Clark Wissler's 1907 discussion of the Douglas African Collection, which was later incorporated into the ethnology hall, he noted: "Study of Africa proves that an 'iron age' is not itself to be regarded as a guarantee of an advance order of civilization. The effect of the use of iron implements is but one of the many interesting problems arising from the study of the Dark Continent, all of which render an ethnological collection from any of her people a matter of great educational value." Despite the possibility that "while the savages of the Stone Age were hacking each other to pieces in primeval Europe, the peoples of the Dark Continent were smelting and forging iron," as Lowie argued, Wissler would not concede that metallurgy proved that "civilization" existed in Africa before it did in Europe.[53]

During the decade before the opening of Lowie's hall, anthropologists in England debated each other over similar issues, most notably the origins of Benin Bronzes seized by British forces during a punitive expedition in 1897.[54] The disagreement over the classification of the Benin Bronzes utilized racialist discourses to explain the aesthetic quality of the material culture of Benin as well as the metallurgic processes used to produce the art. The most prominent thinkers involved in this discussion were anthropologists and museum curators. They found it difficult to ascribe the aesthetically pleasing nature of the art to a "savage" people and, thus, sought an origin thesis that would not contradict their belief in racial hierarchies.[55] In his work *Antique Works of Art from Benin*, Augustus Pitt-Rivers wrote that the Benin artworks' "real value consists in their representing" an art of "rather an advanced stage—of which there is no doubt actual record, although no doubt we cannot to be far wrong in attributing it to European influence, probably that of the Portuguese some time in the sixteenth century."[56] Lowie refused to emulate this reductio ad absurdum.

Lowie compared the Congolese favorably to "highly developed tribes in Polynesia" and "inhabitants of ancient Mexico and Peru" who "had not learned to smelt iron from the ore," affirming that "all the tribes of Africa have in historical times practised the iron technique, some having attained a high degree of perfection in this industry." Instead of developing theories about mysterious Caucasian travelers who brought metallurgy to the Congo, Lowie boldly defied conventional thought about the dissemination of culture, explaining to his readers that "scientific travelers of the highest rank, such as Dr. Schweinfurth and Professor Von Luschan, have advanced the theory that the African negroes were the originators of the technique and transmitted it through the intermediation of other peoples to the ancestors of our civilized nations of to-day. Should this theory prove tenable, it is obvious that a complete revision of popular beliefs as to the negro's relation to modern civilization would be a necessary consequence." Schweinfurth, a German botanist, and Von Luschan, an Austrian-born anthropologist who worked for the Royal Museum of Ethnology in Berlin, believed that Bantu Africans introduced iron smelting to the Egyptians, and thus, Europe owed its metallurgical development to Africa. Lowie held that art was not foreign to "the African race," and he described musical instruments, woodcarvings, pile cloth, and ironwork—all which he viewed as substantiation of "a strong development of the aesthetic sense." In his final analysis of the African exhibits, Lowie conjectured that they would "temper current misunderstandings as to the capacities of the negro race" and expose the "wider public" to the "most fundamental and now firmly established conceptions of ethnological science."[57]

Lowie's assessment of the importance of the material displayed in the African ethnology hall did not attempt to link cultural phenomena to racial hierarchy. Nor did Lowie assume that evaluation and classification of the Congolese material depended on some abstract comparison of it to other material from outside its cultural sphere. However, it is clear that Lowie did not view the artifacts simply within the context of Africa. In his efforts to "redeem" images of Africans from public misconceptions, he employed comparative methodology, which contrasted the development of metallurgy in Africa to that in both Western and non-Western lands. Essentially, because smelting techniques emerged in Africa *before* they did in Europe, blacks' relationship to civilization had to be reconsidered, as the metanarrative of civilization assumed unidirectional cultural diffusion from whites to Others.

It is unlikely that Lowie anticipated that Lang and Chapin's expedition in the Congo would amass more ethnographic material for the African hall of ethnology. Nor could he have imagined that Lang would return a self-trained ethnographer. By 1910, Lang and Chapin had secured the requisite materials for the Okapi Group, along with general collections including mammals, birds, reptiles, fish, and invertebrates. From 1911 to 1913, they obtained a bull and female for the rhinoceros habitat group and unexpectedly collected a giant eland for another diorama during a hunting sojourn into Anglo-Egyptian Sudan with the "kind permission" of the sirdar (the British commander in chief of the army). The expedition party also collected some 1,900 ethnographic specimens. By the end of the trip in 1915, the total collections included 3,800 anthropological specimens and 5,461 anthropological photographs, the latter which filled three "ethnological albums."[58]

Lang's travel writings and journal articles reveal that his views on Belgian imperialism and the "white man's burden" stirred his interest in ethnography. In his 1915 article "An Explorer's View of the Congo," he writes: "It was well that some power should undertake the civilization of the natives even though difficulties and misunderstandings might ensue." Lang claimed that misguided "reformers" in their humanitarian efforts obscured the real nature of the native, believing that they were "rendering a service to humanity" in taking up the cause of the native and condemning the authorities. He credited the Belgian government with destroying the barbaric practices of cannibalism of which "internecine warfare" was "the inevitable sequel." In his judgment, the civilizing hand of the Belgians not only eradicated cannibalism but also brought order to a people predisposed to tribal warfare. He conceded that the "stories of the horrors connected" with rubber extraction seemed credible, as the trade "netted some very handsome financial gains" for rubber dealers; however, he attributed these atrocities to a few officers who became overzealous in their mission and began to rule the regions as little kingdoms. Instead of attacking these would-be potentates, the agitators tainted the "remarkable advance" of the Belgians. Lang lamented:

> The impetuosity of the unfortunate campaign of the reformers is responsible for producing a number of laws of such great leniency that the strong and successfully guiding hand is often stayed by inappropriate measures, which positively injure the general welfare of the natives. Some of these laws actually seem systematically to encourage degradation by openly encouraging idleness, although the negro would be perfectly willing to contribute his share to the progress and elevation of his race, which will probably never be attained except by giving him a fair chance for useful work and by establishing correct compensation.

Only after this lengthy elegy to Belgian rule did Lang launch into his ethnographic commentary decrying the reformers' description of the natives of the Congo as "poor defenseless children."[59]

Lang divulged that the Congo peoples love meat and "enjoy a marvelous digestion." Contrary to being frail, these men and women (some eleven million) pioneered applied eugenics as they cannibalistically eliminated the weak adults and crippled children from society. Purportedly, the Congolese sold those individuals deceased from natural causes to satisfy the hunger of their neighbors. Lang remarked that the flourishing of cannibalism kept the natives protected from invaders and incidentally created a hunting ground of abundant game, as men and women feared traveling in the forest alone. This in part explained the expedition's success in securing zoological specimens from the region. Lang concluded his article with an ethnographic analysis of a group of portrait-style photographs of Congolese peoples.[60]

In 1919, Lang penned "Nomad Dwarfs and Civilization," wherein he stated: "For centuries Africa's black sons have struggled with the horrors of famine, cannibalism, war, and slavery, while the white man has slowly evolved civilization.... White man's impetus must be the motive to progress, whereas the Negro will supply the activity to bring final order from chaos." Justifying imperialism as a necessary measure to civilize the continent, Lang recounted the Belgians' occupation of the basin when "practically all of its inhabitants were cannibals" or had been "laid waste by Arab slave-traders and by the Mahdists." He described how prior to the arrival of the Belgians and Stanley, the Muslim marauders—who killed General Charles "Chinese" Gordon in 1886—fostered savagery in the "swampy regions of darkest Africa." The Arabs' alleged rapacious desires for slaves left the land underdeveloped and the natural resources untapped. Although many European nations navigated the region, most notably the stereotyped inefficient Portuguese, they failed to bring civilization and progress to the natives—that is until the Belgians established commercial stations in 1876 and later the lucrative rubber trade.[61] Lang's retelling of the events leading up to the founding of the Congo Free State seemed to address Western uncertainties about the future of colonialism in Africa in the aftermath of World War I. As if to assure those with misgivings about the beneficence of empire, he reminded his readers that if not for the Belgians, Arabs and cannibals would have overrun the Congo.

The only sympathy Lang displayed for the Congolese under Belgian rule was toward the so-called Pygmies. What he viewed as the mystery surrounding the "Origin, Distribution, and Classification of Pygmies" intrigued him. In his article "Nomad Dwarfs and Civilization," he summed up the enigma as follows: "The question arises whether the Pygmies are merely degenerate types of Negroes and therefore of relatively recent origin, or the earliest type from which all taller African races have evolved, or one entirely distinct and as old as any living race."[62] Disclosing a eugenicist preoccupation with degeneration, Lang noted his failure to discover a "pure" Pygmy racial characteristic in the Pygmy body. Despite this shortcoming, Lang resolved to create a habitat group for the AMNH so that patrons might get a sense of what Pygmies looked like and where they lived. Under the direction of Lang and museum director F. A. Lucas, sculptor Frederick Blaschke (later known for his four life-sized Neanderthal sculptures at the Field Museum of Natural History) designed and completed the diorama in 1915. The group depicted a Pygmy camp in the rainforest, where a hunter is returning from the hunt with his "faithful companion, [a] hunting dog." Members of his family, including his wife, two children, and mother, greet the hunter and the dog. Lang claimed that the group provided "to the public always eager for information about primitive types of man, an opportunity to become better acquainted with the Belgian dwarfs."[63]

For Lang, the Pygmies represented bright spots in a precolonial Congo otherwise debased by the darkness of cannibalism, slavery, and superstition. Moreover, the Pygmies were specimens of African "wildlife" facing extinction through misguided "interbreeding," not the activities of white men.

Herbert Lang's Pygmy group. Neg./Transparency no. 33305, courtesy the Library, American Museum of Natural History.

Lang reasoned that the Pygmy type, as it existed since antiquity, might disappear as "tall Negroes" overtook the Ituri, physically and racially. In contrast to those Americans who exhibited Pygmies at expositions or in zoos—as was done to Ota Benga at the St. Louis World's Fair and the Bronx Zoo—or advocated creating preserves for the Ituri, Lang put his faith in the habitat diorama and photography to capture the essence of the Pygmies for perpetuity.

Lang's decision to wear the mantle of ethnographer produced the rather eclectic collection of photographs of Africans from the Congo region. Notwithstanding Lang's accreditation as a mammalogist, museum officials considered his photographs and descriptions of native life authoritative because they were "based on six-years intimate acquaintance with natives of many tribes."[64] His proximity to Africans while on expedition rendered him an expert on their behaviors, movements, intellect, and culture. Yet, the photographs could not stand alone as ethnographic evidence of the nature of Africans; the textual accompaniment to the photos—Lang's articles and published excerpts of his diary entries—legitimized his interpretations of the photographs. Lang's visual and written descriptions of ornamentation, ritual, performance, and tradition among the peoples of the Congo reflected ethnography's broader preoccupation with classifying races in the early twentieth century. His account of the Mangbetu emphasized the aesthetic sensibilities of "untutored savages" who abandoned cannibalism for "higher civilization." In contrast, his description of "nomad dwarfs" revealed a refuge in the "steaming equatorial forests," a "stronghold for the 'Negro race,'" where the white man's civilization had not yet penetrated." Lang's treatment of other Africans in the region served as a discourse on the "great progress" in "the civilization of the natives," fashioning an ethnographer's tale of man's cultural and racial evolution in Africa.[65]

King Leopold's Soliloquy

Mark Twain's accusation in *King Leopold's Soliloquy* that Americans led by President Arthur had been buncoed, swindled into supporting the Congo Free State, and then stood by complacently as thousands of Congolese were killed, raped, and mutilated by King Leopold's administrators, expressed the sentiments of many Americans whose interest in Africa piqued after the Berlin Conference. Many of the same Americans who applauded the IAA and King Leopold for bringing civilization and commerce to the Congo found themselves sickened by stories of the systematic rape of women, the amputation of children's hands, and the pogromlike burning of villages whose men refused to work tirelessly for the "free state." The popularity of the Congo reform campaign in the United States attests to the sense of betrayal felt by many Americans who idolized Stanley and believed in his benevolence toward the natives and supported the outcome of the Berlin Conference. It also points to a nascent anti-imperialist movement that would find deeper and longer-lasting roots in the African American community.

While the Congo Reform Movement sought to improve the treatment of the Congolese peoples, it proved unsuccessful in convincing mainstream Americans that the region and its inhabitants were not "dark." Americans who read Joseph Conrad's *Heart of Darkness*, despite the author's intent to critique imperialism in the Congo, demonstrated an inability to simultaneously reject imperialism on the continent and abandon negative tropes of Africa and Africans. Oftentimes their castigations of King Leopold's rule employed language that depicted the Congolese as "savage children" victimized by superior, yet crafty Europeans. Nevertheless, literary reactions to the Congo controversy like Twain's *Soliloquy* operated as forums for not only interrogating imperialism but also challenging the myth of Darkest Africa. Contrarily, those Americans who sided with Wack and other apologists for the Congo Free State found themselves clinging ever tighter to images of African savagery.

The cultural work of American museums and anthropologists interested in the Congo question further illuminates the contrasting images Americans held of the Congo and Africa in general. Lowie's work with the Congolese artifacts at the AMNH pointed to a desire among some anthropologists to reject the racist assumptions held by their peers, especially many members of the American Anthropological Association who espoused African cultural inferiority. Although this racism had its origins in America's historical contact with Africans via the transatlantic slave trade, late nineteenth- and early twentieth-century imperialist narratives of savagery in Africa—specifically, tales of cannibalism and human sacrifice in the Congo—confirmed anthropology's basic mythologies about race, culture, and progress. In this context, Lowie's explication of "Negro" art and industry represented an epistemological break with old ethnographical discourses and thus resonated with diverse cultural agendas to confront images of Darkest Africa and savage Africans. The anthropological trajectory in reimagining Africa, however, faced limitations in romanticizing the continent for the broader American public, as seen in Lang's articles. Arguably, Lang had been "buncoed" by King Leopold as well, allowing his fidelity to the sovereign's colony to influence his ethnographic analysis of various Congolese cultures. The antiracist politics of Lowie and the pro-imperialist position of Lang mirrored the stances articulated by Twain and Wack respectively on the Congo question.

Twain's leadership in the Congo Reform Association was short-lived, as was much of the anti-imperialist sentiment embraced by white Americans during the height of the controversy. In contrast, Pan-Africanist thinkers and black emigration proponents stepped up their critiques of imperialism in their quest to foster the continent's autonomous political and economic move into modernity. For them, the crime of the Congo offered further confirmation that Europeans had no desire to see a bright Africa emerge on its own terms. Africa would remain the Dark Continent as long as imperialist ventures went uncontested. The Congo served as a referential point for Pan-Africanist critiques of imperialism, becoming synonymous with white misrule and greed in Africa and the most heinous mistreatment of blacks. Interestingly, W. E. B. Du Bois would refer to the American South as the "American Congo," comparing the "horrors of the Belgian Congo" to the treatments of blacks in the South.[66] By and large, Pan-Africanists felt apprehension about the future of Africa as Europeans demonstrated little restraint in their desire to rule the continent and prevent the emergence of African self-determination.

The Congo conference of 1884–1885 hastened African Americans interested in the redemption of Africa to take an active role in opposing white imperial rule on the continent. The question of the Congo that emerged in the late nineteenth century and the subsequent Congo controversy of the early twentieth century convinced many black leaders, grassroots activists, and intellectuals that Africa had to be reformed from within, preferably with the aid of her dispersed descendants. Galvanized by the imperial politics they watched unfold not only around the Congo Free State but also across the continent, these men and women gathered together to imagine and work toward a free Africa comprised of modern republics or one vast empire that could stand up to the Europeans and expel them from the continent.

THREE

Written on the Wall
Pan-African Dreams of African Empires and Republics

In 1887, two years after the signing of the General Act of the Berlin Conference of West Africa, an editorial titled "An African Empire" appeared in the *New York Freeman*. The author explained how European exploration of the continent, beginning with Mungo Park's expeditions (1794–1797) and culminating in the journeys of Stanley (1871–1877) and de Brazza (1874–1882) had "completely revolutionized accepted opinions of the geography and people" of Africa. While the article did not explain how those views were altered, it predicted that the "'Dark Continent' will soon hold within its grasp no secret as to its people ... climate ... exhaustless and priceless resources."[1] The author accounted for the "modern explorations and discoveries" in Africa by addressing problems facing the "Occident"—overcrowding, population increase, and immigration from the "hungry millions of Europe." Postulating that Atlantic seaboard nations would need to close their borders to European immigrants, as the U.S. had closed the Pacific Coast to the Chinese and Japanese via the U.S. Chinese Exclusion Act of 1882 and immigration quotas, the author predicted that Africa would become the next "objective point of the surplus population of Europe," as

"Africa is the newest find." Systematic colonization of Africa would ensue as "European robbers" set their sights on the Grain and Gold Coasts (Liberia and Ghana). The article cited the "corrupt" Portuguese presence in Africa, the British colonization of Sierra Leone, the formation of the Congo Free State, the Dutch establishment of the Transvaal Republic, and the colonial ambitions of France, Germany, and Italy as evidence that Europeans intended to subject Africans to their rule. The author further explained: "The railroad, the steamboat, the missionary and the rum jug have begun in earnest the conquest of the riches of Africa. The iron heel of the military despot and the oily cunning of the commercial Shylock have already shown the inborn spirit that ever propels them in the bloody wars necessary to break the independence of the people" of Africa. He prophesied that "the white race" would use whatever means ("bloodshed and usurpation") and tools ("the rum jug and the Bible") necessary to render the entire African continent prostrate to European powers for the next one hundred years. Painting an ominous picture of tyrannical European colonial officials, unscrupulous Jewish merchants, and fanatical white missionaries run amuck in Africa, the author interpreted the scramble for Africa as one episode in the long history of the European quest for empire.[2]

Despite the article's rather pessimistic view of Africa's immediate political future, its author expressed faith in the resilience of the African character. Recalling the settlement of the Americas and "Australasia," the editorial predicted that, unlike the aborigines of those continents, Africans would launch successful revolutions against their foreign occupiers, stating: "In the course of time, the people will become educated not only in the grasping and cruel nature of the white man, but in the knowledge of their power, their priority of ownership in the soil, and the desperation which tyranny and greed never fail to breed for their own destruction. Out of the convolutions which are sure to come an African Confederation . . . So out of toil and privation and long agony good will eventually come to the swarthy millions of our Fatherland." Accordingly, the only thing that could prevent the inevitable, the redemption of Africa from its European usurpers, was "Omnipotent interposition." The article declared: "It is written on the wall that there will one day be an African Empire whose extent and power will be inferior to that of no government now denominated as a first-class power. All the indications point to this fact as one of the certainties of the future." In an interesting political exegesis infused with black liberation theology, the author imagined an Africa as an empire or confederation free from colonial rule.[3]

Although the article did not detail the specific nature of either form of political consolidation, in the context of the late nineteenth-century Western political culture, two assumptions can be made. As an empire, various African nations, kingdoms, or territories would fall under the control of one single authority; as a confederation, sovereign African states would enter a permanent union (similar to the United States under the Articles of Confederation) to ensure common political purpose. Most black political thinkers who imagined a confederation pointed to Liberia, the only African republic, as an example on which Africans should model their political formation. In contrast, those envisioning an empire to rival Britain did not oppose monarchical rule on principle but rather desired to see African kingdoms, chieftaincies, and other allied groups retain their historical political culture yet submit perhaps to one ruler or leader.[4] The article signaled the inauguration of a new Pan-Africanism that differed from the emigrationist version (what some scholars call Pan-Negro Nationalism) that preceded the Berlin Conference. While acknowledging the role that European explorers played in shaping present knowledge about Africa, the author held that their achievements would advance the subjugation of Africa by whites, out of which a revolutionary spirit would emerge among Africans to take back their freedom.

The editorial "The Negro's 'Peculiar Work,'" which appeared alongside "An African Empire" in the *Freeman*, offered a response to the *New York Sun*'s coverage of Rev. J. C. (Joseph Charles) Price's Emancipation Day address and attests to how some African Americans reacted to the aftermath of the Berlin Conference with either their own imperial eyes or a call for sobriety. The article opened with a direct quote from Price, a faculty member of the Zion Wesley Institute of the AME Zion Church, who the church considered "the most popular and eloquent Negro of the present generation."[5] Price stated: "The whites found gold, diamonds, and other riches in Africa. Why should not the Negro? Africa is their country. They should claim it: they should go to Africa, civilize those Negroes, raise them morally, and by education show them how to obtain the wealth which is in their own country, and take that grand continent as their own." Unlike the author of "An African Empire," Price offered a counterpoint to the "white man's burden"—the "American Negro's burden" or the black man's burden to uplift his racial brethren and, in so doing, help them take Africa back from the colonizers. This Pan-Africanist vision circulated commonly among black missionaries and clergymen who inextricably linked proselytizing in Africa to the continent's political and economic independence.

The white-owned and -controlled *Sun* echoed Price, arguing that the "civilization of the native Africans by American Africans" might be the best method for developing the continent. Moreover, the newspaper urged African Americans to take up their burden immediately as "a tremendous stream of Europeans" poured into the continent to exploit its natural resources "for their own benefit." The *Sun* speculated that whether African Americans or Europeans "civilized" Africa, "perhaps some day there may be there a Negro State that will rank with the great nations of the world." The *New York Freeman*'s editorialist, Fortune, conceded that "colored people all over the world" held a vested interest in the development of Africa as it might one day provide a site for their own liberation, believing that it might take centuries for African Americans to achieve equality in the United States. Nevertheless, Fortune stated that African Americans were "here and must make the very best of the situation as we find it," assuring his readers that in the interim "thoughtful" African Americans would pay close attention to occurrences in Africa, as these events would determine both the continent's and their own futures.[6] Although Fortune did not reject Pan-Africanist sentiment outright, clearly the political issues confronting African Americans subordinated any concerns about African independence.

V. Y. Mudimbe argues that the Pan-Africanist "invention of Africa" in the late nineteenth century involved an intricate melding of Christian values, Western political theory, racial myths of "blackness" and "Negro personality," and anthropological readings of "primitive" cultures projected onto Africa as a promised land for African Americans and West Indians in search of political enfranchisement. Indeed, African Americans and West Indians—predominantly from Trinidad, Jamaica, and the Francophone Caribbean—exhibited increasing interest in Africa during the latter half of the nineteenth century, often looking to it as a panacea for the economic and political marginalization that they endured in the Western Hemisphere. Mudimbe identifies Edward W. Blyden as the preeminent Pan-African intellectual of the period who fashioned diaspora blacks as "agents for the [cultural and political] modernization of Africa." Blyden, along with African American leaders Alexander Crummell, Henry Highland Garnet, Bishop James Holly, Martin Delany, and Bishop Henry McNeal Turner imagined an Africa uplifted through black-styled Christianity and Western civilization. As David Levering Lewis states, these men were "forerunners of the Pan-Africanism and black nationalism that would expand early in the next century."[7]

African American anticolonialist and emigrationist interests in Africa at the dawn of the twentieth century were part of black internationalism discussed by Brent Hayes Edwards, Kate A. Baldwin, Robin D. G. Kelley, and other scholars. While Edwards's focus is on black internationalist initiatives in the early twentieth century (particularly during the interwar years) and the significance of Paris to Pan-African, literary, and anticolonial enterprises, he acknowledges that the linking of blacks in the diaspora began before the 1900 Pan-African Conference. However, 1900 signaled a new era in African American politics and engagement with Africa as a physical, geographical, and intellectual construct. Brenda Gayle Plummer notes that the Pan-African Conference constituted an international response to the new imperialism of the late nineteenth century, the disenfranchisement of African Americans, the political unrest in the Caribbean colonies, and the declining status of persons of African descent in Latin America. Although Pan-Africanism involved a good deal of myth-making and the reimagining of Africa as a New Canaan, real political commitments to anticolonialism and black self-determination stimulated rural, working-class, and elite African Americans alike. Stirred by W. E. B. Du Bois's proclamation that "the problem of the twentieth century is the problem of the colour line," which he first articulated at the 1900 conference and then in *The Souls of Black Folk* in 1903, elite American Pan-Africanists embarked on what Lewis describes as "an inherently revolutionary Pan-African idea" that was "bound to take on a life of its own." Yet, as Robert Hill, Barbara Bair, Tony Martin, Judith Stein, Mary Rolinson, and Ibrahim Sundiata (among others) have well established, it was Marcus Garvey who amassed the largest Pan-Africanist following that moved beyond elite circles.[8]

The transnational scope of the Pan-African Congresses and the Universal Negro Improvement Association (UNIA) helped blacks renegotiate the significance of Africa to African American identity and liberation. As Plummer argues, "Pan-Africanism expanded Afro-American consciousness by rescaling questions of racial justice to global dimensions." Du Bois's and Garvey's movements effectively placed African American enfranchisement and African independence (or a least self-determination) in a discursive relationship with global and foreign policy issues such as Liberia's loan readjustment, World War I, and the redistribution of German colonies. Pan-Africanism evaded the seemingly parochial politics of the American

"Negro problem" by insisting on a global solution and perspective to localized black struggles. This internationalist framework for addressing racial injustice drew consternation from many white Americans and European imperialists reluctant to concede that blacks could function in a Western body politic or that Africans could exercise self-rule.[9]

Somewhat ironic, if not paradoxical, many Pan-Africanists sought to bring Western values and governance to Africa, envisioning what Plummer calls a Victorian Africa.[10] As expressed by Rev. J. C. Price, the idea that white men could better govern, rule, and uplift Africans than African Americans was ludicrous. However, Price believed that only the introduction of Western values to Africans by their black brethren could redeem the continent. Similarly, Blyden's confidence in republicanism and democracy as antecedents to the regeneration of Africa reflected a dominant theme in Pan-Africanist discourses on black nationhood. Many Pan-Africanists demonstrated faith in the transformative and liberatory power of Western democracy. What Garvey referred to as a "bright star" among modern nation-states—an African empire or confederation—would work to secure the political autonomy of not only the continent but also of all persons of African descent. For Pan-Africanists, reimagining Africa as "bright" in political terms entailed inventing a usable African past, foreshadowing African modernity and inventing a Pan-Africanist black identity. This vast cultural, economic, and political project, however, was not without its contradictions and did not go uncontested, as a significant number of Pan-Africanists moved further to the left on the political spectrum. Political philosophies such as socialism and communism appeared more reconcilable with African communalism than Western-style capitalist-democracy.[11]

For some African American thinkers, leftist political philosophies could potentially break down indigenous social hierarchies associated with chieftaincies and monarchies and reject tribalism in favor of Pan-African universalism. They posited that African precolonial history was replete with examples of communalistic ethos, for example those stateless, semistateless, or decentralized societies where there existed no apparent ruler or leader (or one with nominal power) or which embraced a tradition of common ownership of land. Supposedly tapping into these uncorrupted values offered the best opportunity for Pan-Africanists to unite a continent divided according to European spheres of influence. Moreover, developing the continent economically did not necessarily translate into importing capitalism wholesale to Africa. Many of these Pan-Africanists expressed skepticism that the very economic system that exploited black labor in America and colonized Africa could benefit Africans in the long term. The African Blood Brotherhood emerged as one of the most significant Pan-Africanist-leaning organizations that rejected capitalist solutions to Africa's plight. Not incidentally, they became a leading opponent of Garvey's UNIA.[12]

From the Pan-African Conference of 1900 to the peak of Garveyism in the 1920s to the Italian invasion of Ethiopia in 1936, Pan-Africanism's multivocality assumed a dynamism that traversed the Black Atlantic. The process of theorizing Pan-African politics began with inventing a modern blackness based not only on shared identity and struggle but also on a sense of mission. In the era of the New Negro, which for certain black thinkers began at the turn of the twentieth century, the political imperatives of Pan-Africanism began to influence black artists and writers, most notably—but not limited to—those residing in New York and Chicago during their respective renaissances. In addition, many working-class blacks began to interpret their political and labor struggles within a broader transatlantic framework, finding common cause with their brethren in Africa.[13] As a process of imagining an independent, modern Africa, Pan-Africanism began dismantling images of Africa as a Dark Continent at multiple sites of knowledge production.

"Brethren across the Deep"

In an 1888 letter to the editor of the *New York Age*, William A. Peete, a resident of Tyler, Texas, addressed the "problem of Liberia"—the alleged inability of the Liberians to transform the country into a leading state on the continent or to "civilize" the indigenous peoples. Rejecting arguments based on the law of association that African American immigrants were the cause of the country's downfall, Peete dismissed observers who generally regarded Liberia as a failure, and placed the blame on the inefficiency of black self-government and "enterprise . . . in civilizing and developing a country." He blamed Liberia's failure on Christianity, which he argued had a long history of standing aside while blacks fought against prejudice and political persecution. At best, Christians remained content with joining the battle after it had already begun, or they "led the assault" in "Quixotic skirmishes against the devil." Peete argued that the increase in the African Muslim population in West Central Africa suggested that the providential mission of Christianity was not a foregone conclusion. Unless missionary efforts in Liberia worked toward the benefit of the Africans by investing capital instead of Bibles and hymnals, he saw no immediate resolution to the "Liberia problem."[14]

In another letter to the editor, B. Bowser of Hartford, Connecticut, commented on his fifteen-year (1860–1875) residence in Liberia, in light of the "considerable interest manifested of late about the condition of that country, its people, and climate." Bowser dismissed common mythologies that the African climate was fit for neither African American immigrants nor white missionaries, stating that the temperature proved equally burdensome to white and black (including native Africans) alike. As for assertions that Liberians (of American origins) prospered and Liberia College thrived, he argued that the "aborigines" stood between the immigrant and starvation and that the university boasted no significant student body. Bowser painted a less flattering picture of black immigration to Liberia, noting that the average Liberian demonstrated little initiative and patience in cultivating the land.[15]

As both letters reveal, Liberia became contested ground for African Americans interested in promoting republicanism and commerce in Africa. That same year, Price declined President Grover Cleveland's appointment as Minister Resident and Consul General of the United States at Liberia. Price explained that he needed to dedicate his energies to the "work of Negro education in the South." However, he offered this caveat: "My interest, however, in Africa must not be measured by my refusal to this position; for while my work here has for its primary object the education of the Negroes, and the bringing about of a better state of things in the South generally, still it also has in view, as an ultimate object, the enlightenment of Africa and the final redemption of the Dark Continent, which will be greatly advanced by the Christian education and the industrial development of the Negroes in this country." Price made explicit the connection between the uplift of African Americans and the redemption of Africa. He believed that only Christian, educated American blacks could go to Africa and enlighten its masses.[16]

Late nineteenth-century Pan-Africanists waivered on how best to redeem Liberia in the court of public opinion, as the nation seemed to confirm the stereotype of African backwardness, particularly when Europeans argued that Africa needed guidance from white civilization. Paradoxically, a contingent of early Pan-Africanists, while safeguarding the independence of Liberia, argued that white imperialism benefited other parts of Africa. Blyden at one point stated that European imperialism was "for the good" of Africa. However, by 1890 the tenor of his rhetoric had shifted. In the speech "The African Problem and the Method of Its Solution," delivered before the American Colonization Society during his lecture tour across the United States, Blyden addressed the "African problem" and its relationship to the American "Negro question." He stated that the former was "no new problem" and was "nearly as old as recorded history." The African problem was the inability of the ancients to penetrate the interior of Africa and thus control the source of the Nile. In lengthy prose citing ancient and biblical texts, he explained how the ancients imagined Central Africa as a region where Africans lived in isolation from the rest of the continent, worshipping unknown gods and living off the fruits of the fertile soil. He held that even in 1890: "The mystery still remains. The problem continues unsolved. The conquering races of the world stand perplexed and worried before the difficulties which beset their enterprise of reducing the continent to subjection."[17]

Despite Europeans' success in discovering the Nile's source and occupying the Congo Basin, Blyden claimed that media reports exaggerated Europeans' successful penetration and establishment of "vast 'spheres of influence'" in Africa. He argued that in reality white-occupied Africa could be charted on a map with "microscopic dots," mostly due to climatic reasons, but primarily because Europeans were ill-equipped morally and biologically to conquer Africa. This ran contrary to their victory in other continents in subjugating or exterminating their inhabitants. As European nations consolidated their power in the continent via commercial stations and failed missionary activities, Africans converted to Islam and joined forces with their one-time Arab conquerors to create harmonious societies. Blyden predicted that Europeans would never gain a strong foothold on the continent as they offered no alternative to the fraternity of Islam. Yet, he did not expect Islam alone to bring about change, and consequently, he called on African Americans to join the effort to regenerate Africa.[18]

Blyden argued that black immigration to countries like Liberia would divest Europe of the notion that "she can take and utilize Africa for her own purposes" as she had the Americas and parts of Asia. With the aid of "brethren across the deep," Africans would not "share the fate of some other dark races who have come in contact with the aggressive European." Rather, they would make Europe see that "Africa is to be for the African or for nobody." Blyden forecasted that King Leopold and other European imperialists would "see that for Africa's redemption the Negro is the chosen instrument." He remarked that, coincidentally, as the Belgians expended great sums of money in opening the Congo, the U.S. Senate debated the Butler Bill. Seeing the "Almighty's" hand in all of these events, Blyden prophesied that as the "Negro emigrant" heeded his brethren's call to "come over and help us," he would feel himself "lifted into manhood," no longer the abject victim of the history of the peculiar institution. Blyden diagnosed the African problem as the result of the contentious history between Africa and Europe, in which Europeans attempted to oppress Africans first via the slave trade and later through imperialism. Furthermore, the problem existed between "two distinct races," defined not simply by color but rather by racial affinity or "instinct"—the ability to recognize a kindred "mental and moral constitution." Thus, only "distinct race perception and entire race devotion" could stave off further European colonization of the continent. Blyden's racialist vision of an Africa united according to ancestry and a strong sense of race consciousness began with Liberia, which he declared to be both "inspiring and uplifting" and proof of intraracial cooperation. Hoping to dispel recent rumors of the failure of the Liberia experiment, Blyden painted a portrait of the republic as "the garden spot of West Africa" brought into "a glorious light" both morally and politically. Describing the black "settler" in Liberia as "independent and productive ... on the continent of his fathers" and "the glories of a changeless and unchanging nature" of the landscape, he encapsulated the beginnings of modern Pan-Africanist rhetoric in which Liberia functioned as the sine qua non topic for political discussion.[19]

Reaching a consensus definition of the African problem and finding methods for its solution proved difficult. That the first major conference on Africa convened to discuss the continent's redemption was organized under the auspices of the Stewart Missionary Foundation for Africa reveals the theological origins of early Pan-Africanist thinking. The 1895 Congress on Africa held in Atlanta, Georgia, was not a Pan-Africanist conference, as Henry Sylvester Williams or Du Bois would later define such a gathering. It brought together an interracial and international delegation to discuss the Christianization of Africa as a white and "pan-African" mission involving Africans in the diaspora. Nevertheless, in the face of European imperialism, the congress served as an early site for African Americans to participate in the production and dissemination of knowledge about Africa. The gathering also provided a public space for attendees to reimagine Africa as a bright continent, its darkness extinguished by the light of Christianity. In this context, the congress reflected the orientation of many African Americans who first articulated their Pan-Africanism in religious terms.

In his opening remarks for the conference, white clergyman Wilbur Thirkield, president of the congress, spoke of the Dark Continent stretching its hand in vain toward God. He opined: "While light is breaking in upon its darkness, the hand that blights and curses is not yet lifted. In other centuries the curse was the *stealing of Africans from Africa*. Now, it is the game among European nations of 'shut your eyes and grab' in their efforts to *steal Africa from the Africans*. But God is yet in that world. Not in vain has its two hundred millions stretched forth their hands to Him. He causeth the wrath of man to praise Him. Even through the greed and wars of nations, in their selfish partition of Africa, He shall yet 'save many people alive.'" Thirkield's remarks mixed theology with anti-imperialist criticism, yet fell short of rejecting the image of Darkest Africa. For him, Africa would remain dark until its people united under Christianity. He made clear to the African American attendees that the purpose of the conference was to arm them with facts about Africa necessary to the success of their ordained mission.[20] He informed them:

> We aim ... to give the public clearer views of Africa and of the African movement. From a survey of the knowledge and experience gained in the last twenty-five years we should be able to deduce general principles and definite plans that may influence future work in the line of commercial, industrial, civilizing, and redeeming effort.... You shall have presented to you the latest and most accurate information on Africa; you shall have set forth clearly by word, by maps, and by illustrative slides, the land and people as they are; the life, character, customs of the natives; their tribal relations, and languages; the progress of discovery and occupation; the latest work of geographers; the march of civilization; the partition of Africa; the achievements of missions; the difficulties and drawbacks of missionary efforts, and the outlook of missions for the nineteenth century.[21]

The contention that the public had little access to knowledge about Africa produced by "heroic missionaries," "Africanists of world-wide fame," travelers, and "natives," supposedly explained their reluctance to embrace their duty to redeem the continent. As was made perfectly clear throughout the proceedings, the "public" was the African American populace.

The nature of the information presented at the conference attests to the early work of ethnologists, anthropologists, folklorists, philologists, linguists, and geographers, as well as journalists and clergy, in reeducating the American public about African life under imperialism. Zealous in its rhetoric of Christian redemption, what Wilson Jeremiah Moses termed "missionary Pan-Africanism" simultaneously denounced European imperialism as motivated by avarice and reconciled its place in the divine plan to redeem Africa.²² Although white participants utilized the same rhetorical strategies as their black counterparts, they rejected or acted ambivalently toward the political agenda of Pan-Africanism. Offering a racial interpretation of the history of nation-state building through conquest, several African American speakers argued that the "white minority" seizing control of the continent would either be absorbed by the African majority or lose its foothold on the continent. Employing the metaphors of dark, light, and bright to contrast the Africa that was to emerge under the tutelage of Christian missionaries and their helpers, these spokespersons for "the race" dreamt of bright Africa as part of Christendom.

Fortune, who would later become the editor for Garvey's *Negro World*, attended the conference and offered his analysis of the colonization of Africa. In his address, "The Nationalization of Africa," he referred to the coming of railroads, steamboats, and electricity, as well as the colonial extraction of natural resources and precious minerals, as evidence of the civilization of the continent under European control, but he observed that these achievements were obtained with "human blood and tears." Noting the heroism of the Ashanti and Zulu in fighting the British, Fortune claimed that Africans with their primitive weapons could not withstand the "conquering forces" of steam, electricity, and gunpowder. He declared that might makes right in the spread of Western civilization, no matter how much theorists denied it as foundational to their political ethos, arguing: "In this, as in many other of the Christian virtues, our precept and our example are radically at war." As if conceding to the inevitable, he envisioned a united Africa.²³

> If the conquest of Africa shall proceed in the next seventy-five years as it has done in the past twenty-five, the whole continent will be as completely under European control, after the lapse of a century, physically and mentally and morally, as it is possible for conquerors to impose their conditions upon the conquered. The vast population of Africa will be brought under Christian influences in new forms of government and habits of thought and of conduct. The whole life of the people will be revolutionized. Ancient beliefs and superstitions and tribal relations and dissimilarity of vernaculars will, in the course of time, be transformed entirely. The demoralizing heterogeneousness which now prevails over the whole continent will give place to a pervading homogeneity in language, in religion, and in government.²⁴

Fortune envisioned a United States of Africa, Anglophone in language, Christian in religion, and politically aligned with the English system of civil government. He argued that Africa would follow the example of the United States when it broke away from the British Empire, projecting that "the nationalization of the African confederation ... will be the first step toward bringing the whole continent under one system of government."[25] Thus, uniting Africa linguistically, religiously, and culturally became a prerequisite for effective independent nation-building.

M. C. B. Mason, Assistant Corresponding Secretary of the Freedmen's Aid and Southern Education Society, offered a similar view of Africa's future, calling for African Americans to evangelize in Africa and not emigrate there. Emphasizing that African Americans were citizens of the United States by birth and constitutional amendment, he claimed America as their "home," "land," and "country." Yet, he argued, "the obligation, my brethren, for African evangelization is nevertheless upon us—the obligation by racial affinity, by providential preparation, by special adaptation, by divine command, is upon us." For Mason, *race* operated as an organizing principle for black unity in America and informed blacks' duty to redeem Africa. Declaring that a new era was upon African Americans, Mason called forth to Africa: "A new day will dawn upon us; a new day for Africa in America and for Africa beyond the seas; a new day of moral, vigorous activity; a new day whose morn shall ever be bright, and whose sun shall never set. Africa, there is hope for thee. All the world is turning toward thee and thy children from the four corners of the earth have come to bring thee light." In return, Africa would become a haven for the world's oppressed people and "feed the famished nations."[26] Mason like Fortune, imagined an enlightened Africa brought into modernity by technology and commercialized agriculture; however, for him the continent's future political organization ranked below its religious redemption.

Alexander Camphor, born to former slaves in Louisiana, submitted a hymn that echoed Mason's Christian-centered Pan-Africanist vision.

> Far across the mighty ocean
> Is a land of palmy plains,
> But that land is not enlightened;
> It is one where darkness reigns,
> There the heathen in his blindness,
> Knoweth not the blessed word,
> Nor of Jesus Christ, the Savior,
> Precious Lord, our only Lord.

> Africa, 'tis named, that country,
> Far away from this bright shore,
> Far removed from light and knowledge,
> Far remote from Christian lore;
> There, for many, many ages,
> Ling'ring still in blackest night,
> Africa, dark land of hist'ry,
> Void of light, is void of light.

Playing on the image of Africa as the Dark Continent, Camphor opens "A Hymn of Sympathy and Prayer for Africa" contrasting the beauty or brightness of the African plains to the dark condition of its people. The song asks African Americans if they can remain content while their "brother gropes in darkness." They respond no, pledging both work and prayer toward realizing Africa's freedom "from degradation." Here Camphor's religiosity eclipsed any concrete discussion of political independence compared to Fortune's speech. Spiritual freedom defined as conversion to Christianity was central to missionary Pan-Africanists' images of a bright Africa.

African American and white males did not opine alone on the spiritual redemption of Africa. The congress featured two female speakers—white traveler May French Sheldon and a Bassa woman from West Africa, Etna Holderness. Holderness recounted her childhood as an orphan who endured abuse at the hands of her caretakers. After several unsuccessful attempts at running away, she eventually found refuge in the home of "good missionaries" who raised her to "love Jesus" while she worked in the gardens and attended school as a pupil of one of Blyden's protégés. Holderness, who took her adopted family's name, came to America as a nursemaid for a child she had been entrusted to deliver to its deceased mother's family in North Carolina. Through a series of introductions that led to financial patronage, she attended a university. In her speech she stated that she wanted to return to Liberia to open up a school for girls and help "civilize" the people of Bumley Town who engaged in "heathen feasts, devil's dance and grigra [sic] bush." Holderness used her conversion experience to argue not for the political liberation of Africa but for an increase in missionary activity in her country.[27]

Collectively, the Pan-Africanist views expressed by African Americans at the conference elucidated the centrality of religion to their reimagining of Africa. Yet, as the conference speeches made apparent, the future task for Pan-Africanists would be mediating between the various political and religious agendas informing African redemption narratives circulating in black communities. For Pan-Africanists like Peete, Christian missions in Africa subordinated the political interests of Africans to a faulty sense of religious piety and, thus, contributed to the oppression of the continent. In contrast, Islam united men regardless of race, with both their spiritual and political welfare in mind. This line of argumentation would inform Blyden's conversion to Islam and the emergence of African American Muslim Pan-Africanism during the early twentieth century as a counternarrative to Christian missionary Pan-Africanism. Politically, Pan-Africanists continued to envision republicanism as the solution to the African problem, although the model on which this wholesale political reorientation would take place remained somewhat murky. The public image of Haiti and Liberia as examples of black republicanism suffered in the last decade of the nineteenth century, leading some Pan-Africanists to conjecture that independent African nations stood a better chance at longevity under a confederation. At the turn of the century these issues continued to fragment an already decentralized, amorphous Pan-Africanism. Nevertheless, African Americans joined diaspora Africans in Pan-Africanist organizations to challenge white imperialism on the continent and imagine a brightest Africa. In so doing, they conceived of New Negro identities relevant to their anti-imperialist politics and desire to redeem Africa.

"A New Era for the Colored Race throughout the World"

In 1900, Booker T. Washington published the book *A New Negro for a New Century* (coauthored by Norman Barton Wood and Fannie Barrier Williams), which cataloged the struggles of African Americans and their most important achievements made since slavery. The text included several portraits of distinguished men and women who exemplified the qualities of the New Negro for the twentieth century: educated, refined, business savvy, and proud of their heritage. The essays in the volume discussed the roles that black men and women should play in uplifting "the race." Fannie Barrier Williams addressed "the colored woman and her part in race regeneration," contributing to ongoing conversations among African American women about the meanings of womanhood and femininity in the modern era. Overall, the book took a historical look at the African American experience, cataloging black industrial achievement and educational progress and projecting a future when blacks would enjoy financial prosperity and all the rights of citizenship.[28] Although some critics of Washington viewed his New Negro as apolitical, they agreed that the turn of the century marked a sort of coming out for the African American who adopted new strategies for self-determination. Despite the high profile of the Congress on Africa, Washington's book, while praising the work of African American missionaries, did not systematically factor Africa into the future of the New Negro. By 1912, Washington would envision a changing future for his New Negro with regard to Africa by convening the International Conference on the Negro.

The intersections of New Negro identities and Pan-Africanism emerging at the turn of the century manifested not only in missionary activities and political thought but also in cultural expression and identity. Using Camphor's hymn as an evidentiary starting point, Africa and African Americans' relationship to the continent would feature more in black musical traditions, literature, art, and poetry. Similarly, as discussed in chapter 1, Victoria Mathews's assertion at the National Association of Colored Women convention that she was "Afro-American" and not "Negro" reflected the sentiments of an emerging generation of blacks in America who would reclaim their African past not only as a Pan-Africanist political posture but also as a statement of identity. Perhaps taking the lead from their missionary forerunners, Pan-Africanists convened a conference in 1900 that would merge the African and Negro questions, setting one of the main trajectories for black political thought in the twentieth century.

S. E. F. C. C. Hamedoe, writing for the *Colored American Magazine*, declared that "a new era for the colored race throughout the world" began on July 23, 1900, when people from all over the African diaspora convened the first Pan-African Conference in London "with the object of discussing and improving the condition of the colored race." Organized by Trinidadian H. Sylvester Williams and AME Zion bishop Alexander Walters, the conference was attended by several African Americans—including Du Bois, Anna Julia Cooper, Mrs. Jones of Kansas, former slave Henry "Box" Brown, and author D. Tobias. The participants discussed the global black population's deservedness and worthiness for freedom. They called attention to the lack of equal rights granted African Americans, the political and social discrimination faced by blacks in the British Empire, and the harsh labor conditions for black workers in South Africa, among other topics, arguing that the "future of the race must be in the hands of the race itself." Instead of looking to whites to lead the way, the attendees argued that blacks should take additional initiatives to secure freedom and equality for all people of African descent. Nevertheless, they petitioned Queen Victoria and the British Colonial Office to take up their resolutions, which ideological collusion in colonialism." The conservatism of many of the participants evidenced by their refusal to issue an outright call for the immediate dismantling of colonialism undermined their political agenda. Like those who attended the 1895 congress, many conference delegates believed that adoption of Western values and Christianity would prepare Africans for "eventual self-rule" and modernity.[32]

The next major international gathering of Pan-Africanists would not assemble until 1919, under the leadership of Du Bois; however, by then, Garvey's UNIA had already formed in Jamaica (1914) and a chapter had opened in New York (1917). In the intervening years, Africa featured prominently in black newspapers and periodicals, including the *New York Age* under Fortune's editorship, the *Chicago Defender*, the *Colored American Magazine*, and the *AME Church Review*. In the absence of a mass gathering or formal association, Pan-Africanist thought could be located in these papers, sometimes as a syndicated article (often from a mainstream white periodical), an editorial, a letter to the editor, or a featured story. Some black periodicals penetrated borders, forging transnational anti-imperialist and Pan-Africanist alliances throughout the Black Atlantic. Many of these articles appeared during the height of the Congo controversy, encapsulating a moment of crisis in European imperialism in Africa.[33]

The article "Hostility to Europeans: Feeling May Spread over the Entire African Continent," published in a 1906 issue of the *New York Age*, addressed imperialism in Africa as "the Congo question ... passed from the stage of sentimental discussion into a serious international issue." Reprinted from the *New York Sun*, the article summarizes the *London Spectator*'s news story about the race question in Africa. According to the reporter, accounts of colonial officials abusing Africans in German and British colonies began to surface, many of which rivaled the accusations leveled against the administrators of the Congo Free State. The German socialist leader August Bebel claimed that German troops "massacred" entire villages in South Africa, murdered adults, and drowned children in nearby rivers. While the German government maintained that many of these reports exaggerated the confrontations between troops and natives, the article made clear that such stories pointed to a larger problem—the mistreatment of Africans under the rule of Christian nations. The London daily warned that "the whole native population of Africa" would soon "become penetrated with dread and hatred of white men" if matters did not improve. Claiming that "the African" did not object to being ruled by "his white superior" but abhorred "unreasonable cruelty," the reporter feared that the natives would resort to included allowing Africans access to education and participation in the colonial government, and called for the end of racial discrimination and labo[r] exploitation in the colonies.[29]

Tobias's presentation went beyond the immediate political goals [of] the conference to address misperceptions about Africa and Africans. H[is] speech "claimed and proved that civilization has been commenced by bla[ck] men," establishing a historical basis for fashioning a Pan-African identi[ty] that rejected the idea of Africa as the Dark Continent.[30] This celebrati[on] of the civilized African past informed Pan-Africanist thought that posit[ed] the restoration of African independence as a continuation of a bright p[re]colonial historical tradition of progress and cultural refinement. For Tobi[as,] acknowledging the glories of the African past legitimated the conferen[ce] platform that depicted Africans as capable of functioning in Weste[rn] styled governments.

The conference closed with H. F. Downing stating that the "black ra[ce]" sought freedom by "deserving it" and not by violent means. The ne[wly] formed Pan-African Association planned to convene a conference in [the] United States in 1902 and one in Haiti in 1904. As Hamedoe noted, ne[ver] before had that many people of African descent from around the wo[rld] gathered together to discuss their political and social status as citizen[s of] democratic republics or as imperial subjects. Convened on the basis of bl[ack] brotherhood, the conference added to existent conversations among A[fri]can Americans about the political significance of Africa to their lives. E[m]bracing Pan-Africanism as a political position meant first acknowledg[ing] the collective plight of diaspora Africans as they encountered the "c[olor] line" and, second, working with other blacks to actualize self-determinat[ion.] As a basis for constructing a New Negro identity, Pan-Africanism off[ered] blacks a chance to reinvent themselves both domestically and internat[ion]ally, as people of African descent invested in their "brethren's" lives.[31]

The initial fervor that surrounded the 1900 conference did not sus[tain] itself, as the 1902 conference did not successfully convene. The fact that [no] high-profile African Americans attended the conference or held top p[osi]tions in the Pan-African Association may explain the lack of momen[tum] behind the fledgling movement that officially declared itself to be [Pan-] African. Plummer explains: "Pan-Africanists faced overwhelming od[ds;] they organized a conference in the midst of a bloody, global assaul[t on] black people. Coordinators had to assemble participants from territ[ories] controlled by powers inimical to their views. Conference goals were fu[rther] confounded by attendees' partial acceptance of imperialist ideas and

Written on the Wa[ll]

violence as a means for "deliverance." In spite of these potentially dangerous circumstances, the article declared that Europeans were determined to rule Africa and would do it without resorting to the tactics employed in the Congo Free State.[34]

A month later, another article appeared in the *Age* detailing more "colonial abuses." "Leopold's European Rivals in African Atrocities," syndicated from the *New York Press*, covered a paper delivered by Louis L. Seaman at the National Geographic Society. Seaman lambasted the actions of "Christian nations of Europe ... in the so-called 'civilization' of the Dark Continent," through "disastrous" means. Based on firsthand observations, Seaman's work drew explicit analogies between the "butchery" of women and children in the Congo and the mistreatment of Africans in German East Africa. However, he pointed out that the Reichstag "refused to underwrite the atrocities upon the natives." As if echoing the reporter for the *Spectator*, Seaman stated: "A continuance of the policy of cruelty by the invaders is rapidly creating a dread and hatred of the white man throughout the entire native population of Africa."[35] Fortune's decision to publish these two articles written by white reporters expressing concern about Africans' potential hatred for "the white man" revealed his political and tactical motivations. Such testimonies from whites confirmed what he stated at the Congress on Africa—that white rule in Africa benefited European coffers at the expense of Africans, who would one day throw off colonial rule. These articles contextualized Pan-Africanists convictions that colonialism in Africa would collapse—and with it the last vestiges of Darkest Africa.

Overwhelmingly, the black press safeguarded and policed Pan-Africanist politics within their pages, often printing articles that reflected black middle-class and elite doctrines of racial uplift and self-help. Although the entire continent was of general interest to readers, South Africa and Liberia made headlines, as their African populations hosted black missionaries and favored Washington's industrial education model. Black South Africans came under increasing scrutiny by Europeans who feared that independent black institutions would undermine their justification of white rule as a "civilizing mission." Liberia faced "threatening encroachments" by European powers, which African Americans and Liberians alike interpreted as a conspiracy to destroy the only black republic on the continent. These two controversies unfolded as the Congo atrocities came to American public attention; yet, the black press's coverage of these two countries proved equally important to the emergence of more radical critiques of imperialism that fostered dreams of Pan-African republicanism.

The publication of AME bishop Charles Smith's 1906 address to the Negro Young People's Christian and Educational Congress in the *Age* provided the newspaper's readers with an extensive description of conditions in South Africa, with special emphases on British governance and the presence of African Americans in the country. While Smith framed his paper as a discussion of the status of native South Africans, it at times reads like a testimonial to the successes of missionary activity and industrial education. However, his address aimed to highlight the suppression of African freedom and political rights in the colony. After providing a historical sketch of the British presence in South Africa, Smith furnished examples of "the well defined and inflexible purpose of the European element to make South Africa a white man's country." In a witticism, he claimed that the term "white man's country" was "as much in vogue in South Africa as it is in Georgia or Mississippi." Smith wanted to elicit more than laughter from his audience, as the remainder of the speech makes both implicit and explicit comparisons between the situation of blacks in America and indigenous South Africans with regard to land tenure, suffrage, education, and religion. Incidentally, Smith refused to refer to South Africans as "Negroes," arguing that the indigenous South Africans did not like the term *Negro* and that the term did not exist in South African literature.[36]

According to Smith, Africans could not purchase or sell land in South Africa without restrictions, noting that in some colonies they could only sell land with the government's consent or purchase land with the title registered in the name of the Commissioner of Native Affairs. Thus, private land ownership was practically nonexistent among the indigenous population. With regard to voting rights, he explained that "equal suffrage" in Cape Colony and Rhodesia meant that Africans had to meet education and property qualifications. In addition to being required to write their name, address, and occupation, potential voters had to provide proof of a yearly wage of at least three hundred dollars or "occupation" of a building or land equivalent in worth. As for education, missionary and government schools offered the only opportunities for instruction. Smith criticized the government for using only 10 percent of African taxes to educate their youth. In contrast, he praised the mission schools "as a most potent and valuable factor in awakening the native mind of South Africa." He discussed the Lovedale Industrial Institute established in Cape Colony in 1841 as preceding Hampton and Tuskegee and demonstrating as much success in producing missionaries, evangelists, teachers, clerks, interpreters, and other entry-level office workers. Smith claimed that despite these advances in education,

"South Africa has not yet produced any great native intellectual luminaries," reasoning that the opportunity for such distinction had yet to arrive.[37]

Smith ended his address by commenting on the presence of African Americans in South Africa. As he relayed, the South African government mistrusted American blacks not because they "incited the natives to sedition, disloyalty, or rebellion" but because they supported the natives in their independent church movement. Moreover, he charged African American presence with being "a source of positive helpfulness to the native," which "awakened within him a spirit of laudable aspiration and ambition that cannot now be effectually suppressed." Smith credited African Americans with instilling racial pride and manhood in the Africans, which "caused the scales of servility and self-recognized inferiority to fall off." Effusively praising African Americans as the most "advanced" descendants of Africans and as beacons for all Africans wishing to uplift themselves, Smith held that the source of white suspicion and fear of American blacks was not only their "unparallel advancement" but their adherence to republican values. As African Americans did not reside in a monarchy, Smith argued that European imperialists feared African Americans would "instill into the minds of the native that love of liberty and independence so characteristic of a republican form of government." For Smith, the possibility that native South Africans could form an independent republic held out hope for the rest of the continent under white rule. However, as his speech made clear, the liberation of Africa required a Pan-African effort, where African Americans brought their "acumen," energy, and knowledge of republicanism to the aid of Africans. He briefly mentioned Liberia as an "inviting field" for African Americans to exercise similar energies in uplifting both themselves and Africans. Smith's pointing to Liberia as a place where American blacks could help preserve black democracy came as international speculation arose that Europeans had designs on Liberia.[38]

In 1907, a reporter for the *New York Age* quoted Arthur Barclay, president of Liberia, asking his House of Representatives to "consider what our success or failure will mean for our race" around the world, as their "petty factional fight" disenchanted "the masses." Such disunity could prove useful to Europeans looking to invade Liberia. Some months later, the special correspondent to the *Age* reported on rumors circulating in London that the British would cede Sierra Leone to French control. Supplying the readers with a brief history of Sierra Leone as a haven for freed slaves and those captured during the illegal slave trade, the reporter explained the colony's similarity to Liberia. The article blamed the European partition and exploitation of

Africa for the present situation in Sierra Leone, forecasting similar "high jinks" would ensue among European nations wishing to control the entire continent. In the reporter's analysis of the situation, Liberia stood as an obstacle to this goal, specifically France's desire to expand its sphere of influence in West Africa. The reporter anticipated that African Americans would show little interest in European machinations in Africa and urged them to recognize their intertwining fate with Africans, especially Liberians. He wrote, "Though the Afro-American displays but little concern as to the fate of Liberia, the truth is that the West African Republic is an asset to the whole African race which that race cannot well afford to lightly lose." The reporter called attention to the role that the "effective classes" of African Americans supposedly played in bringing "civilization" to Liberia. Like Smith, he argued that "the presence of a civilized Negro sovereignty in West Africa is not approved of, or favored, by either Great Britain or France; in fact, by none of the European land-grabbing states."[39]

In 1908, Liberian officials confirmed Pan-Africanists' fears that the rapid European colonization of West Africa threatened their sovereignty when they appealed to the United States for arbitration in a border dispute with France and Germany. In the 1907 Franco-Liberian Agreement, the two nations agreed to use "natural topographical lines" to determine the boundaries between French West Africa and Liberia to "prevent all possible contestations in the future." The Liberians would police the "frontier," establishing garrisons to which the French would enjoy unfettered access. According to a *New York Age* article, James J. Dossen, the Liberian vice president, arrived in Washington, D.C., to explain how the French violated the agreement and to alert the United States to German encroachment on "undisputed" Liberian territory. He explained that his nation petitioned the United States as an "independent government" and not a protectorate, believing that "no other nation" would be as sympathetic to Liberia's interest as America, which had played a role in founding the nation and populating it with "energetic colonists." Dossen accused Europeans of "coveting" the natural resources found in his country and desiring to exploit Liberian laborers. The newspaper implied that the "ties of fraternity" between Liberia and the United States would aid in checking the "menacing attitude" of the imperialists. The United States responded by guaranteeing the "territorial and political integrity of Liberia," with several agreed upon conditions for change within the African country.[40]

President Roosevelt and President-elect William Howard Taft agreed to investigate matters via the Commission on Liberia. Edward O. Erhagbe points to the "pivotal role" that Booker T. Washington played in "suggesting members for the commission." Washington's correspondences with the president, key senators, and secretaries of state fostered U.S. interest in Liberia when Africa was otherwise invisible in American foreign affairs. Clearly Washington's interest in Africa did not end with the 1895 congress and was not confined to missionary work and industrial education. Washington wanted to protect Liberia's symbolic example of black republicanism and self-determination.[41]

By 1909, Secretary of State Elihu Root declared: "The condition of Liberia is serious." In a letter to President Roosevelt, he detailed the history of the founding of Liberia, noting that its "civilized negroes" descended primarily from African Americans, the "original colonists." Root declared that the United States' duty to the "unfortunate victims of the slave trade" did not end with the establishment of Liberia and, thus, America had "the highest obligation" to support the African nation in maintaining a "free, orderly, and prosperous civil society." Additionally, Root argued, as had Blyden, that the interests of African Americans demanded that Liberia retain its freedom. He stated: "The interest of the people of the United States in the welfare and progress of the millions of American citizens of the black race in the United States also furnishes a strong reason for helping to maintain this colony, whose success in self-government will give hope and courage, and whose failure would bring discouragement to the entire race."[42] Root suggested that African Americans found inspiration in Liberia as an independent black republic. Moreover, he intimated that European colonization of Liberia could negatively impact domestic race relations within the United States. He proposed sending commissioners to the country to investigate conditions there and compile a report suggesting solutions to the "Liberia problem."

Upon the return of the commissioners to the United States, the State Department recommended protecting Liberia's "sovereign statehood" by signing a treaty to guarantee its territorial integrity, extending it a loan for debt repayment (as America had recently done for the Dominican Republic), sending troops to train a frontier police force, establishing an American research station, and building a naval coaling station. This decision furthered Taft's "dollar diplomacy," although the targeted nation was not in Latin America or Asia. As U.S. foreign relations reports on Africa revealed, the Roosevelt and Taft administrations limited their interest in African independence to Liberia, reasoning that only there did American citizens have a direct relationship with the continent. While they held up Liberia as a black republic modeled after the United States that could maintain its sovereignty with U.S. help, they simultaneously praised Belgium for being "among the foremost in the great work of uplifting the uncivilized regions of Africa and urging the extension of the benefits of civilization, education, and fruitful open commerce to that vast domain." Referencing the Congo scandal and the "sympathy" of American citizens toward the Congolese, the Taft administration approached the issue with "benevolent encouragement" for the Belgians to initiate reforms.[43] In a marked departure from the Cleveland administration's earlier argument that U.S. interests in the Congo stemmed from a direct consanguine relationship between African Americans and Congolese, the Progressive Era presidents did not acknowledge such a connection, which arguably could have been exploited to endorse African independence from Belgium. As seen, despite the United States' affinity for Liberia, African American Pan-Africanists expanded their politics beyond the republic, slowly abandoning juxtapositions between "civilized" Liberians and "savage" Africans under white rule. This break evidenced a new emerging strategy in defending Africa as articulated by Tobias at the Congress on Africa—emphasizing Africa as a country fighting to regain its brightness.

By and large, many early Pan-Africanist thinkers who endorsed some form of "pan-African" cooperation held steadfast to images of Africa as dark in order to reimagine it as bright. Rhetorically, this reflected a sense of divine purpose in the redemption of Africa tied either to the Christian mission or political undertaking of bringing modernity to the continent. However, on the eve of the Pan-African Congress of 1919 and the issuance of the UNIA's "Declaration of Rights of the Negro People of the World" in 1920, more radical images of independent Africa emerged as discursive ruptures in Pan-Africanism thought dominated by ideals of Christian and Western civilization. Although what David Levering Lewis calls the "two Pan-Africas" (that of Du Bois and Garvey) did not reject in toto the idea of racialized African uplift based on Western economic models and republicanism, both tended to abandon the more polemical and ethnocentric language of African "savagery" and "heathenism." Redeeming Africa as expressed in the Pan-Africanist philosophies of both Garvey and Du Bois was foremost a political imperative—a commitment to aid Africans who suffered under white imperialism. For Garvey, the UNIA's mission was not purely to bring "civilization" to the "savages," but to restore African manhood and womanhood by preserving "Africa for Africans." In contrast, Du Bois did not initially advocate for African independence, but rather pushed for "internationalization" under the guidance of an elite Pan-African vanguard. During this new era of Pan-Africanism, the importance of Liberia would continue as Garvey, Du Bois, and other activists reassessed the symbolic and practical value of the sole African republic to black liberation.[44]

Brightest Africa for Bright Africans

When the International Conference on the Negro convened at the Tuskegee Institute in April 1912, Liberia and Abyssinia (Ethiopia) remained the only independent African states, as Morocco had signed the Treaty of Fes in March, making it an official French protectorate. According to the *Chicago Defender*, Washington called the conference to "bring about an exchange of ideas among those who are working for the uplift of the black race throughout the world." Attended by representatives from missionary societies; several countries from the Western Hemisphere, including Jamaica, Puerto Rico, the Danish West Indies, and Venezuela; Europe; and eight "states or provinces" from Africa, including Liberia and South Africa, the conference represented the first pan-Africanist gathering of the new century held on American soil. Washington demonstrated a marked consistency in his promotion of industrial education. As expressed in his 1906 article "Industrial Education in Africa," he wanted to ascertain whether or not the curricula embraced at Tuskegee and Hampton could aid in the uplift of Africans, particularly those under colonial rule.[45] Washington sought not only an international venue to promote his politics of black self-determination but also a space to shape African American ideas about Africa. In many ways, this conference foreshadowed a changing of the political guard in the black community, as well as in the Pan-Africanist rank and file. The Victorian values that infused the Congress of Africa and Washington's International Conference on the Negro faded as Pan-Africanists assumed a more aggressive stance, which downplayed the role of white philanthropists and missionaries in the redemption of Africa. This transformation from accommodationist politics, which emphasized cooperation between peoples of African descent and "white well-wishers of the race" to save Africa (not to end colonial rule), to a more radical and revolutionary activism, which celebrated blackness and demanded African independence, mirrored the shift in Pan-Africanist images of Africa from a Dark Continent to a land of enlightenment.[46]

It can be debated to what extent the International Conference of the Negro was Pan-Africanist in orientation. As Washington stated in his official announcement for the conference in 1911, his goal was to foster dialogue among not only blacks but also government representatives of African colonies to discuss methods for educating and "upbuilding Negro peoples." Like Pan-Africanists, he viewed the situation of African Americans and West Indians as related to "the problems of Africa." While he did not call for deliberations on African independence, he invited the participation of missionaries, workers, and anyone who could bring empirical knowledge of the African diaspora to bear on the conference proceedings. Indeed, Washington received enthusiastic responses from members of the Ethiopian Church in South Africa planning to attend the conference, who praised him as a "race man." Tellingly, in his opening address, Washington mentioned Africa once, to urge African students attending Tuskegee to return to and uplift their communities. The proceedings of the conference included several notable contributions from white "experts" on Africa—Maurice S. Evans's "Education among the Bantu of South-East Africa" and a speech delivered by Cornelius Patton, Secretary of the American Board of Foreign Missions. Patton warned the participants that the spread of Islam in West Africa threatened advances in Christianizing Africans since the partition. Evans argued against the "Europeanising of the African peoples," citing the opinions of Blyden and cofounder of the Congo Reform Association E. D. Morel, who in "The Future of Tropical Africa" advised against educating blacks with curricula designed for white students.[47]

In his report to the Royal African Society on the conference, Evans recounted the highlights of his lecture in which he claimed that African Americans were "more white than black" in "racial traits and characteristics," and thus the affinities between their position in the United States and that of natives in South Africa was not entirely comparable. Moreover, he held that educating black South Africans en masse in industrial education would foment labor conflict with white workers and lead to "racial trouble." In the end, he argued for "a measure of separation of the races" in South Africa, eliciting several favorable responses from the audience. Evans remarked that he expected a different response as members of the "militant Radical School" claimed that African Americans desired equality through integration and not segregation. Evans expressed relief that Washington declined an invitation from black missionaries to visit South Africa, as through the AME Church's affiliation with the Ethiopian Church they preached doctrines considered "subversive to the constituted political authority ... which [were] likely to cause mischief." He noted that a scheduled paper on the Ethiopian Church was never presented. (The paper was most likely written by Isaiah Sishuba, a representative of the congregation who corresponded with Washington.) Evans informed the Royal African Society that African Americans wishing to work toward the redemption of Africa should focus their energies in tropical Africa and not South Africa.[48]

The conference issued several declarations emphasizing the need for cooperation and establishing a committee to work on the second conference, scheduled for 1915 (the year that Washington died). Noting the urgent need to address the "Negro race and its problems," the document claimed the meeting's importance was "obvious" as Europeans had colonized tropical regions with considerable black populations. Even as the participants acknowledged the impact of imperialism on "native races," they did not critique it as the source of "Negro" degradation in Africa. The declarations neither mentioned African republicanism as a panacea for the problems of Africa nor imagined a united African continent under black leadership. Black missionaries continued to refer to the "redemption of the Dark Continent."[49] Although vestiges of the missionary Pan-Africanism associated with the 1895 Congress on Africa remained, blacks attending the conference incorporated Washington's message of industrial education into their dream of a new Africa.

Washington's ideology of racial uplift and industrial education philosophy wedded to his own brand of Pan-Africanism resonated with many blacks, including Marcus Garvey. That Garvey, who was committed uncompromisingly to African independence, claimed inspiration from an "accommodationist" speaks to the multiplicity of texts, voices, and ideologies from which Pan-Africanists could draw. Garvey revered Washington but rejected accommodating white imperialist sensibilities, fashioning a separatist Pan-Africanism purportedly based on blacks' terms and militant in its denunciation of imperialism in Africa. Garveyism idealized Africa as "the Motherland of all Negroes," a "vast continent" whose treasures were stolen by unscrupulous Europeans. As Mary G. Rolinson argues, "Garvey undoubtedly shared a romanticized image of Africa with many African Americans, who like the UNIA leader, had never been there." In reinventing Africa as "Ethiopia, Thou Land of Our Fathers" (the title of the organization's Negro anthem), the UNIA discursively extracted the continent from the annals of Darkest Africa.[50]

When Garvey formed the UNIA in Jamaica in 1914, he hoped to mobilize West Indians to fight for self-determination and freedom from British rule. For him, the quest for his native Jamaica's independence was part of broader struggles for black autonomy around the globe. Garvey believed that a sense of race pride and a "Universal Confraternity among the race" had to serve as the foundation of any collective action to dismantle white rule over people of African descent. Unable to establish a large following in the West Indies, Garvey came to Harlem (known as the Negro capital of the World) in 1917 to open up a chapter of his organization. As Du Bois claimed, and scholars have argued, Garvey's popularity in America increased after a wave of immigration from the West Indies to Harlem during and after World War I. The upper echelons of his organization reflected his West Indian roots, as he rewarded Afro-Caribbeans with high offices, while rural and working-class African Americans composed the rank and file membership. Despite Judith Stein's contention that Garveyism failed because it was an elite response to "material existence" of working-class blacks and eventually proved "irrelevant to the lives of most blacks," the complex class dimensions of the UNIA seemed to bolster rather than splinter the organization, as working-class people came out to fete Garvey's "First Lady," cabinet, and army in parades that resembled the procession of European monarchs to their palaces.[51]

By the time Du Bois organized the 1919 Pan-African Congress in Paris, Garvey had amassed such a following in the states outside of New York that other Pan-Africanists (including Du Bois) had to contend with his charismatic style and ability to get ordinary folk excited about Africa. Du Bois once remarked: "Garvey is an extraordinary leader of men. Thousands of people believe in him. He is able to stir them with singular eloquence and the general run of his thought is of a high plane. He has become to thousands of people a sort of religion." Tony Martin reads the Du Bois–Garvey struggle as "a continuation of the Washington–Du Bois debate," emphasizing that Garvey was a disciple of Washington, whose attraction to the masses Du Bois also viewed suspiciously. Du Bois's overall portrait of Garvey was not flattering, as he essentially accused him of leading a cult and basking in the "personal adulation" of his followers. Du Bois found it incredulous that working-class blacks invested their money in the Black Star Line, in what amounted to a pyramid scheme, on the promise that they would one day leave behind their life of toil for commercial independence and wealth in Africa. Indeed, Garvey struck many of his admirers and critics as messianic in his message of black deliverance. Yet, while the financial appeal of Garvey's message was critical, the imagery he evoked of black men waging battle to liberate Africa, of a "new negro race" asserting its manhood and womanhood around the globe, and of African republicanism captivated and emboldened his followers to dream of a bright Africa.[52]

In several speeches monitored by U.S. intelligence agencies, Garvey warned "man and nation" not to stand in the way of diaspora Africans as they strove to "make Africa a republic." Identifying the white man as "the barrier" to African republicanism and democracy, Garvey emphasized that members of the UNIA were "not Bolshevik, I.W.W. Democratic, Republican, or Socialists," but unwaveringly "pro-negro." He disavowed any connection to political parties and labor unions dominated by whites, but he did not discard the idea that republican government and democratic political processes could best uplift Africa. Garvey believed that blacks in the West would emerge as formal political leaders in Africa. Prophesying a judgment day, when the world would have to account for its treatment of peoples of African descent, he prefigured a "new Toussaint L'Ouverture" carrying "the sword and banner of the new African Republic" to the court of judgment. He believed bloodshed would prove necessary for the New Negro bent on claiming his Motherland, as the imperial powers would never willingly surrender control over their African colonies. When Garvey called for a black government, he emphasized that Africa once had its own government and that what the UNIA demanded is the restoration of black political autonomy. Garvey bolstered this political discourse of militaristic nation-building with images of Africa as a continent of riches.[53]

Garvey justified the Black Star Line venture as essential to building African republicanism by describing Africa as a land where blacks could prosper according to prescribed gender roles. Fanning the flames of lost manhood and in the process relegating black women to the home, he informed a Philadelphia crowd: "you can leave the white man's job as a porter and go into the Negro factory as a clerk, you can leave the white man's kitchen and go into your home as a wife of a big Negro banker or a corporation manager" in Africa. In Garvey's African republic, black men asserted their manhood as sole breadwinners, while black women returned to the home, a privilege they were deprived of toiling as domestic workers in the "greatest democracy of the world for white men." Garvey explained how the Black Star Line would carry blacks to their Canaan, once again calling on black men to wrest control of the continent from European "parasites" living off the blood of their children. He proclaimed: "Today the richest people of the world are the Negro peoples of Africa. Their minerals, their diamonds, their gold and their silver and their iron have built up the great English, French, German and Belgian Empires." Garvey intentionally rejected images of Africa as poverty ridden or savage, reminding his audience that the wealth of the European superpowers derived from natural resources that belonged rightfully to Africans. Africa could reclaim its riches upon the ousting of the Europeans from power. Garvey used this imagery to rally blacks to contribute to the UNIA's African Redemption and Colonization funds.[54]

When the UNIA issued its "Declaration of Rights of the Negro Peoples of the World," it demanded "Africa for the Africans at home and abroad." Its members enumerated several complaints and demands with respect to Africa, foremost among them their objection to the European partition of the continent and colonial policies that treated Africans as slaves. In a bold statement on race solidarity, the organization declared all persons of African descent to be free citizens who enjoyed the right to claim Africa as their nation and to "reclaim the treasures" and land seized by "open aggression or secret schemes." The convention attendees adopted red, black, and green as "the colors of the Negro race" and a national anthem. The song referred to Africa as "Ethiopia" based on the biblical verse Psalm 68:31, "Princes shall come out of Egypt. Ethiopia shall soon stretch forth her hands unto God." Infused with images of black armies carrying swords advancing into battle, the song pledged to "smite" the "tyrants" that conquered the continent and with the help of Jehovah bring freedom and victory to "Ethiopia." At the Second UNIA Convention in 1921, Garvey echoed his call to arms, protesting the League of Nations' decision to divide the former German African colonies between France and England without asking "the civilized Negroes of the world" how to dispose of their homeland. Declaring that "the handwriting is on the wall," he announced that the UNIA members would return to their communities resolved that Africa would become free at whatever cost. Garvey foresaw race conflict and war, where people of African descent would bring destruction to Western civilization and subsequently build a "new civilization founded upon mercy, justice, and equality." In the interim, he advised his followers to preach "the doctrine of universal emancipation for Negroes, the doctrine of a free and a redeemed Africa." In contrast to missionary Pan-Africanists, who spoke of redeeming Africa from its own "savagery" and "superstition," Garvey used the term *redeem* to mean the rescue of Africans from European "unrighteousness." In this sense, Europeans were guilty of "inhuman, unchristian, and uncivilized" behavior in Africa, becoming the source of the darkness emanating from the continent.[55] Garvey's rewriting of the white man's burden as the white man's iniquity appealed to black audiences who felt victimized by white injustice.

Garvey's appeal to the masses continued even after his arrest for mail fraud in connection with the financing of the Black Star Line. In his 1923

Marcus Garvey delivering the Constitution for Negro Rights, 1920. Library of Congress, Prints & Photographs Division, NYWT&S Collection, [reproduction number, LC-USZ62-109628].

essay, "The Negro's Greatest Enemy," he explained his long journey toward Pan-Africanism and an epiphany that revealed that he was "doomed" to be a "race leader." Garvey's recollection of that passage reemphasized his commitment to black self-government and his dream of a unified Africa as an unchallenged political power among "the nations of the world." He recalled that while traveling through Europe he found himself reflecting on the disenfranchisement of black peoples worldwide. He asked: "Where is the black man's Government? Where is his King and his kingdom? Where is his President, his country, and his ambassador, his army, his navy, his men of big affairs?" Finding none (he appeared to have discounted Liberia, Haiti, and Ethiopia as significant republics and empires), he pledged to "help make them" as he commenced "advancing the race." Garvey dreamed of "a new world of black men ... a nation of sturdy men making their impress upon civilization and causing new light to dawn upon the human race." In a reversal of European imperialist rhetoric, he envisioned self-governing black men bringing lightness to shine on the entire world, supplanting conquering whites who pretended to spread civilization, commerce, and Christianity to the "weaker races of the world."[56]

For members of the UNIA, many of whom aligned themselves with Washington's philosophy of racial uplift through entrepreneurship and the accumulation of wealth and assets, black capitalism seemed the perfect tool to wrest Africa from European control. Their vision of Africa as a wealthy continent protected by a strong leader commanding a powerful military manifested in UNIA rituals and pageantry that in many ways symbolically summoned the precolonial African past that boasted of powerful kingdoms and empires and warriors. The organization's members expressed a penchant for monarchical imagery, referring to Garvey as "His Excellency" or "His Majesty," despite his official title as "Provisional President of Africa." UNIA parades displayed the military prowess and manhood of black men, contrasted to the womanhood of black women based on nurturing and caregiving. These performances of manhood and womanhood, bolstered by the political act of electing a black man as president of the organization, represented more than rhetoric and ceremony. They represented the dream of Africans united under one president, a world power with which whites would have to contend. Until Africa gained its independence, Garvey and his followers would safeguard the Africans' birthright to freedom and self-determination.

Garvey's faith in the African capacity for instant self-government under the counsel of enlightened blacks from America, the West Indies, and

Europe and nonnegotiable stance on European imperialism distinguished his Pan-Africanism from that of Du Bois, the Pan-Africanist thinker to whom he is often compared. Unlike Garvey, Du Bois's search for a brightest Africa entailed not the immediate dismantling of the European colonial system in Africa but rather a gradual movement toward "Africa... ruled by the consent of Africans." In his 1915 essay, "The African Roots of War," Du Bois argued that the Dark Continent was "in a very real sense... a prime cause of this terrible overturning of civilization which we have lived to see." The Great War was a contest between European imperialist nations whose antagonism toward each other continued to build after the partition of Africa. Rewriting "this most marvelous of continents" back into "world-history," he explained that since ancient times, nearly every "material and spiritual" empire of consequence had "found some of its greatest crises" in Africa. Du Bois reclaimed Africa as the birthplace of the earliest civilizations and the nesting place of world religions. He claimed that Europeans from the Renaissance to the Berlin Conference of 1884 sought African commerce in precious minerals and human bodies to enrich their coffers. He argued that this legacy of "greed" led to the partition of Africa—"the undisguised robbery of the land of seven million natives" by "contemptible and dishonest" methods that rivaled the slave trade. Du Bois used uncompromising language to compare the Congo scandal that degenerated into "murder, mutilation, and downright robbery" and other imperialist ventures in Africa with its predecessor, the transatlantic slave trade—"that sinister traffic" that built the British Empire and the United States. Du Bois posited a causal connection between the two, suggesting that the slave trade left Africa helpless and ripe for European "aggression and exploitation." He argued that over four hundred years of slave trading led to the new European imperialism, which left Africa powerless as the "conquering Philistines of Europe" sought world domination. The Great War, he averred, was one more episode in this saga, a result of the rivalries among European "trade-empires" seeking to exploit the world's wealth.[57]

Du Bois identified three needs for imperial subjects that would have to be satisfied if the war was to end—land, training in "modern civilization," and home rule. Like Garvey, he predicted that Africans would one day rise up and demand their freedom from foreign authority and that the "War of the Color Line" (what Garvey called the "conflict between the races") would ensue, causing more death and destruction than the Great War had seen thus far. However, he believed that this could be forestalled, if not prevented entirely, if Europeans gave up their monopoly on African land,

Africans sought to become "modern men," and colonial powers allowed Africans to participate in the political process. Du Bois envisioned an Africa where educated and modern Africans participated in democracy and held high positions in state governments. Summoning the figure of Queen Nefertari as a black woman who became Pharaoh and protected her people from outside invaders, Du Bois called for a "new peace and new democracy" that would defend the equality of all peoples and end the despotic reign of imperialism. Thus, when he organized the Pan-African Congress in 1919, he believed (like Garvey) that the Versailles Conference's deliberations on the status of Germany's African colonies offered a forum for European nations and America to reject the imperialism that, he argued, impelled the West into the Great War.[58]

A U.S. report on the Pan-African Congress reveals the degree to which the American government monitored Pan-Africanist politics espoused by African Americans and resident black aliens abroad during the peace negotiations. In a letter to William A. Phillips, Third Assistant Secretary of State under President Wilson, Harry F. Worley, the Financial Adviser to the Republic of Liberia, reported his observations on the Pan-African Congress being held in Paris at the same time as the Versailles Conference. As one U.S. representative among many attending Versailles, Worley was expected to contribute to the discussions on Africa, specifically anything that would impact Liberia and U.S. financial custodianship over the country. Worley thought it prudent that he make inquiries about the speeches delivered at the congress, particularly those made by U.S. citizens, many of whom narrowly escaped being denied passports to France. (The State Department summarily denied passports to members of the UNIA with U.S. citizenship and to William Monroe Trotter, editor of the *Boston Guardian*.) He claimed that African Americans delivered "inflammatory and condemnatory" speeches that lambasted the United States for its treatment of black citizens. Worley speculated that this characterization might be the result of the difficulty that African Americans faced obtaining passports, which allowed other diasporic Africans to attend the conference. He noted the attendance of Haitian-born Eliezer Cadet, a representative of the UNIA and the *Negro World*, who distributed literature from the organization and "prophesied" a "day of judgment and retribution for the American people" for its injustice toward African Americans. Worley identified Blaise Diagne, Senegalese representative to the French Chamber of Deputies, as a main source of criticism of the United States. He described how Diagne feted the Liberian delegation, explaining that in France black men could marry white women, enjoy political and social equality with whites, and hold important positions in the government. These were freedoms denied African American men.[59] Worley appeared convinced that the congress did not impress the Liberians, intimating that Pan-Africanists would not disrupt U.S. relations with the country. Overall, his report depicted Du Boisian Pan-Africanists as nuisances to be monitored, but he foresaw no immediate impact of their platform on American politics, a noteworthy contrast to the perception of U.S. surveillance that the UNIA was a subversive organization.

Although Worley's assessment was rather dismissive, a great deal was accomplished at the conference. Du Bois proposed the creation of an independent African state—a republic comprised of the former German colonies and the Belgian Congo. This would be the stage for the development of African modernity, with black elites at the helm. In this sense, Du Bois proved equally as convinced as Garvey that the redemption of Africa required leadership from peoples of African descent living in the West. Demonstrating his leftist politics, Du Bois called for the common ownership of land and "the socialization of income"—for the latter the state would provide social services, establish wages, and convert private wealth into public wealth to ensure the economic stability of the nation. When he convened the congress of 1921 promoting similar policies, Du Bois faced opposition from French delegates opposed to communism. The 1919 conference was timely, but the momentum for Du Bois's brand of Pan-Africanism came from the 1921 conference, which met in Paris, London, and Brussels, with forty-one African participants among over one hundred white and black delegates from Europe and other continents, including writer Jessie Fauset. The "Statuts" issued by the Pan-African Association reflected Du Bois's commitment to cooperative action in fostering the economic and political development of Africa. Open to persons of African descent, "colored" organizations, and anyone interested in the "progress of the Race," the association favored "the spread of culture, the creation of an 'elite' in large numbers and the development of leaders with high ideals," who would usher Africa into political and economic modernity. As an intellectual vanguard, these leaders would conduct investigations, seek public opinion, meet with "responsible authorities," and collect information pertinent to the "Black Race" without disrupting the "political affairs of any state."[60] Although the Pan-African Association embraced a public position of noninterference in colonial African affairs, its members, like those of the UNIA, believed that black elites occupied the best position for negotiating with colonial authorities and the League of Nations on behalf of the

Pan-African Congress, Belgium, 1921. Courtesy of the Department of Special Collections and University Archives, W. E. B. Du Bois Library, University of Massachusetts Amherst.

African masses. As Du Bois had argued in his 1915 essay, those leading the revolution would come from outside of Africa. He asked: "Who better than the twenty-five million grandchildren of the European slave trade, spread through the Americas and now writhing desperately for freedom and a place in the world? And of these millions, first of all the ten million black folk of the United States, now a problem, then a world salvation." Like Garvey, he saw the destiny of Africa in the hands of Africans in the Americas, as they took on the metaphorical role of Queen Nefertari to bring redemption to her people.[61]

Pan-Africanism, particularly the variants advocated by Du Bois and Garvey, spread throughout black America as more African Americans and black organizations and newspapers embraced the idea that their fate intertwined with that of Africans denied freedom under imperialist rule. Although Garvey claimed to have the most followers of any race movement in America, other organizations emerged with Pan-Africanist leanings during World War I and the interwar period. The African Blood Brotherhood (ABB), founded in 1918 (the year of the armistice) by Cyril Briggs, while not exclusively a Pan-Africanist organization, drew parallels between the oppression of blacks in America and Africans under colonial regimes. In 1922, the ABB issued its most comprehensive Pan-Africanist program, in which it committed itself to defending Africans from imperialist aggression. This platform would later inform its reaction to the Italian invasion of Ethiopia in 1935. The National Association for the Advancement of Colored People (NAACP) offered support for Pan-Africanists, especially for its cofounder Du Bois; however, as Du Bois embraced a more separatist/nationalist approach to black liberation and Pan-Africanism, he found himself alienated from the organization's leadership and readership. He resigned from the board and the *Crisis* in 1934 after publishing his essay "Pan-Africa and the New Racial Philosophy" (1933). The *Pittsburg Courier* (edited by Robert Lee Vann) and the *New York Amsterdam News* (under Briggs's editorship) began publishing more articles with a decisively Pan-Africanist bent, while black artists began "mining the African past" for inspiration and black historians unearthed the "glorious" African past. Collectively, the anti-imperialist activism of these individuals, organizations, and media contributed to Pan-Africanists' reimagining Africa as a free, modern "Motherland" to all "Negroes."[62]

"Our Motherland, Africa"

In 1922, the ABB published its program in the *Communist Review*, the organ of the Communist Party of Great Britain, "for the consideration of other Negro organizations and of the race in general." Declaring that "a race without a program is like a ship at sea without a rudder," the ABB outlined a plan for the liberation of all people of African descent based on the premise that their struggle was primarily economic, the result of white capitalist exploitation of black labor around the world. The ABB asserted that the problem with the black race in the past and present was its inability to ascertain "what it was seeking" and, on the rare occasions that it did, to devise "any intelligent and workable plan" to achieve its goals. Accordingly, the ABB called for a "powerful world movement for Negro liberation" that addressed the circumstances of race in Africa and the New World, principally the United States. The organization claimed that the starting point for this global mobilization was a clear identification of "our enemies." The ABB explained that it looked toward Soviet Russia for inspiration not solely because of its political system but also because it opposed "the imperialist robbers who have portioned our motherland and subjugated our kindred."

Briggs and his followers maintained that the Soviets instilled fear in capitalists and imperialists alike, and thus communism offered the best solution for liberating blacks.[63]

The Pan-Africanist platform of the ABB offered a counterpoint to Pan-Africanist rhetoric that emphasized the necessity for Africans to unite to form a republic or confederation based on democratic values and capitalism. While democratic-republicanism remained the dominant philosophy behind Pan-Africanist visions of a redeemed Africa, the communist ideas of the ABB presented an alternative to this narrative. Many members of the ABB were former constituents of the UNIA whose leftist politics were anathema to the latter organization. Tony Martin argues that the ABB attempted to "infiltrate" the UNIA and "made an unsuccessful bid to capture [Garvey's] following" at the 1921 convention. Subsequently, ABB members went on to repudiate and harass Garvey and his supporters. Africa became a contested battleground both physically and ideologically for Pan-Africanist thinkers dedicated to remaking Africa in their image. Accordingly, their visions of postcolonial Africa represented radically different political futures for the continent even as they conceded that blacks in America possessed the unique qualities to liberate their "kindred."[64]

The first item on the ABB platform was "Our Motherland, Africa," giving the continent a prominence that contrasted the platforms of other mainstream organizations that ranked the American Negro problem above all other race considerations. The ABB referred to the European nations controlling Africa as "Big Capitalist Powers" that established colonies under the management of planters and capitalist merchants who expropriated African lands, exploited the continent's natural resources, and forced Africans to work for "starvation wages." In narrating the "covetous and murderous inhumanity" of capitalism and imperialism in Africa, the ABB overturned the colonial myth that Africans acquiesced to this domination via faithfully negotiated treaties and military alliances. The organization explained that Africans "rebelled and fought the invader in an unequal struggle," where their "primitive and old weapons" offered no match for the modern technologies and weaponry of the Europeans. In insisting that Africans fought to the death, taking many "a British square" (a combat formation of troops), the ABB reclaimed African manhood and warned that the spirit of rebellion festered in Africans, who would one day secure their freedom and take back their motherland. In the intervening period, Europeans continued to squelch the militant spirit of Africans with Christianity and whiskey while they introduced material improvements to the land. According to the ABB, the latter would prove the imperialists' undoing as Africans mastered European technology, including guns, with the goal of one day overthrowing white rule.[65]

The ABB called for a "Negro Federation" led by "the more able and developed Negroes" on the coasts of Africa and by existent African organizations in the colonies to work with Africans in the interior "barely touched by predatory Capitalism." This federation would ally with Arabs, Egyptians, and revolutionary groups in Europe and America to organize African workers, create a secret Pan-African army, smuggle modern arms onto the continent, and map the geography of the interior. Reemphasizing their contempt for "the white man's religion," the ABB suggested that comrades travel to Africa in the "guise of missionaries," as the colonial authorities appeared to favor their presence as a civilizing force. (The ABB's reading of the status of missionaries was somewhat faulty, as the South African government and other colonial powers distrusted many black missionaries as race agitators.) Like Garvey and Du Bois, the ABB viewed blacks in America as the saviors of the race worldwide. The program stated that "the Negroes resident in America—whether native or foreign born—... are destined to assume the leadership of our people in a powerful world movement for Negro liberation," as they lived in a "great empire" with access to modern technology, warfare, and industry. The ABB called for an end to rhetoric, public performances of Africanism, and "other tomfoolery" and for the adoption of "proper tactics" to defeat capitalists and imperialists oppressing African peoples. The program called for an alliance with the Third International, offering what was surely criticism of the tactics of the UNIA and Pan-African Congresses.[66]

> To pledge loyalty to the flags of our murderers and oppressors, to speak of alliances with the servants and representatives of our enemies, to prate about first hearing our proven enemies before endorsing our proven friends is nothing less than cowardice and the blackest treason to the Negro race and our sacred cause of liberation....
>
> To be kidded along with the idea that because a few hundreds of us assemble once in a while in a convention that therefore we are free to legislate for ourselves, to fall for the bunk that before having made any serious effort to free our country, before having crossed swords on the field of battle with the oppressors, we can have a government of our own, with presidents, potentates, royalties, and other queer mixtures; to speak about wasting our energies and money on propositions like Bureaus of Passports

and Identification, diplomatic representatives, etc., is to indulge in pure moonshine, and supply free amusement for our enemies.[67]

The ABB rejected the position taken by the Pan-African Congresses of 1919 and 1921 that its leaders would refrain from interfering with European governance in the colonies and would instead enter into dialogue with the imperialists concerning their native subjects. The organization most likely disparaged the Afro-French delegates, particularly Diagne, who pledged loyalty to the French flag, claiming in 1921 that he was foremost a Frenchman and secondly a black African. Extending this argument, the delegates who rejected Du Bois's socialist agenda in favor of prestige and status in French government and society served the imperialist enemy. When the ABB spoke of "vain indulgence in mock-heroics, empty phrases, unearned decorations, and titles," it clearly targeted Garvey, who called for "Africa for Africans" as he carried the title of First Provisional President of Africa and often referred to himself as the "elected spokesman of the Negro peoples of the world" when corresponding with American and European officials. The ABB insinuated that the parades of officers, nurses, and other UNIA officials added to Garvey's Pan-African extravagances and delusions of grandeur. Moreover, in the organization's analysis, Garvey's and Du Bois's conferences amounted to posturing, not effective political action.[68] Yet, despite the ABB's critique of existent Pan-African platforms, masses of African Americans found inspiration in performative Pan-Africanism—whether as participants in organized street pageants, rallies, conventions, or conferences—and in the slogan "Africa for Africans." Their attendance at these public sites of protest enhanced their sense of race pride and commitment to African emancipation.

In 1924, a delegation of the UNIA returned from Europe and Liberia after meeting with colonial officials and the heads of the Liberian state to "negotiate for the repatriation of Negroes" to a homeland in Africa. The trip proved unsuccessful, as the Europeans and Liberians summarily dismissed their proposal for colonization. To celebrate the delegation, Garvey delivered a speech at Madison Square Garden wherein he declared that blacks' desire to establish a nation in their "motherland" was "no joke." As had become customary, he recalled the long history of African Americans in agriculturally developing the United States, building its cities, and sacrificing themselves in wars that "laid the foundation" for American imperialism. In return, African Americans only asked an opportunity for self-governance and self-determination, to "re-establish a culture and civilization exclusively ours." Garvey drew a portrait of historical Africa that "boasted of a wonderful civilization on the banks of the Nile, when others were still groping in darkness" and called for a return, this time to the "banks of the Niger," where repatriated Africans would "sing hymns to the God of Ethiopia." Assuaging fears that blacks sought social equality with whites and the right to intermarry, Garvey reemphasized the separatist agenda of his organization—"a black Africa" for the "black race." He drew analogies between blacks' aspiration for a homeland and nationalist movements in Europe that led to the breakup of the German empire, Armenian independence from the Ottomans and Russians, the Irish liberation movement, and Zionism. He called on America to help blacks as it had these peoples and nations. Garvey's speech—delivered the year before his incarceration—marked a turning point in mainstream Pan-Africanist thought, as self-proclaimed militant anti-imperialism replaced calls for repatriation/colonization. Although black critics of Garvey credited him with bringing Africa to the consciousness of African Americans, particularly those in Harlem, they broke with his "false doctrine" that Africa was, and should be, the homeland of all blacks to the exclusion of other races.[69]

During the 1920s and 1930s, as if taking a cue from the ABB, American Pan-Africanists allied themselves increasingly with labor organizations, anti-imperialist activists, and international associations dedicated to aiding oppressed people. In 1926, a mass meeting was held at Unity Hall in Chicago (the headquarters of the People's Movement Club established by black congressman Oscar De Priest in 1917) to protest race discrimination against peoples in the African diaspora. The *New York Amsterdam News*' interview with the meeting's secretary, Walter Anderson, revealed that a discussion of Liberian and Haitian affairs would be part of a "formal protest" against imperialism. Anderson remarked that the "Harvey Firestone scheme . . . marks the definite participation of American imperialism in the partition of Africa" and he imagined an American "military dictatorship" ruling Liberia similar to the one established in Haiti. In 1915, the United States' military had occupied Haiti, establishing a puppet government and taking control of the customhouses. President Wilson's "moral diplomacy" operated much like Taft's "dollar diplomacy" had in the Caribbean. The occupation would last until 1940. In 1917, the Finance Corporation of America extended a five-million-dollar loan to Liberia that would ensure the Firestone Rubber and Tire Company the right to cultivate rubber on a million acres of Liberian land. Sources have revealed that Liberians' decision to reject Garvey's colonization plan stemmed from their negotiations with

Firestone, which began as early as 1923, and which would have allowed them to repay a 1912 loan from the French and British. Sidney De la Rue, the General Receiver of Customs under the United States' loan to Liberia, advised gaining African American support for the Firestone proposal by promising jobs to black graduates of technical schools and manipulating "the radical press controlled by Du Bois." Apparently, Garvey's plan posed a threat to mollifying "the negro element." Anderson declared: "Imperialism is the universal exploiter of the Negro people in this country and abroad, just as it is the exploiter of all other oppressed races and nationalities. All the oppressed must unite against this monster."[70] In an interesting rhetorical shift reminiscent of Twain's accusations against the American government in the Congo controversy, the United States became complicit in the scramble for Africa by endorsing capitalist ventures in Liberia.

Although earlier Pan-Africanists suggested that America stood to gain from the imperial exploitation of Africa, more often than not, they appealed to the United States to intervene in Africa, to promote democracy and republicanism as alternatives to colonial regimes. By the 1920s and 1930s, such illusions began to fade quickly, as the Firestone investment made clear that free markets and profit trumped personal liberty and workers' rights. In 1934, the Comintern expelled leader George Padmore, a Trinidadian Pan-Africanist resident in America, for his "collaboration with the American imperialists for the exploitation of Liberia." According to ABB founder and the Communist Party USA member Briggs, the Firestone agreement was forced on Liberia. Additionally, Briggs asserted that Padmore's "Liberian-American Plan of Co-Operation" empowered upper-class Liberian overseers who suppressed "the revolutionary struggles of the Liberian masses." Although not all Pan-Africanists embraced the Marxist rhetoric of the ABB, they began to emphasize everyday labor exploitation in Africa instead of focusing solely on accounts of murder, rape, and mutilation, such as those that had roused philanthropic concern about the Congo. Moreover, they strengthened their internationalist framework, working with other organizations interested in Africa but not self-defined as Pan-African.[71]

When Cameroonian immigrants formed the League against Cruelties and Oppression in the Colonies (later the League against Imperialism) in Berlin, they protested the Allied trusteeship over the former German colonies and the exploitation of African workers to "pay off the war debt." The organization called a conference in Brussels in 1927, which caught the attention of American Pan-Africanists and activists "from the intellectual down to the workers," including members of the UNIA, the NAACP, and the

American Negro Labor Congress (ANLC). In 1929, the league called for another conference, the Congress of Oppressed People, to be held in Paris from June 25 to 29. The All-America Anti-Imperialist League met earlier that month in New York City to elect delegates to represent the workers of the United States and other nations at the conference. A group of African American workers attended the New York meeting to ensure black representation in Paris.[72] Pan-Africanism transformed from a strictly racialist movement emphasizing the shared fate of all persons of African descent and the duty of Africans in the Americas to uplift the "Motherland" to a movement including a broader crusade against imperialism and discrimination affecting all "colonial people" and "the darker races on the globe."

Du Bois's seminal 1933 essay, "Pan-Africa and the New Racial Philosophy," and subsequent writings on the "theory of colonial imperialism" encapsulated this new marriage of traditional Pan-Africanism, anti-imperialism (in a global context), and workers' rights. In "Pan-Africa," Du Bois argued that the so-called Negro problem had to be approached not from a "narrow, provincial, or even national background, but in relation to the great problem of the colored races of the world and particularly those of African descent." Although he had made a similar argument in *The Souls of Black Folk*, that the problem of the twentieth century would be the "problem of the color-line," Du Bois had yet to articulate that concept in the framework of a radical Pan-Africanism influenced by leftist philosophies. Du Bois implored African Americans to cease thinking of themselves "as belonging to the white race," from reacting as white Americans did to "Asiatics ... Jews ... Mexicans and West Indians." He argued that despite the fact that by birth African Americans were "American," in reality their experiences resonated more with those of "the dark people outside of America than to his white fellow citizens." Citing "color caste," discrimination, and labor exploitation as experiential links between African Americans and the "colored peoples" of Latin America, the Caribbean, Africa, and Asia, he called for "spiritual sympathy and intellectual cooperation" in working toward the "freedom of the human spirit ... incased in dark skin." Du Bois stated that this was the idea behind his organizing the Pan-African Congresses, which the European powers perceived as attempts to provoke violent revolution in their colonial possessions. Yet he speculated that "in the end nothing but force" would be able to destroy the color line. In lieu of that day, Du Bois advised African Americans to begin the work to dismantle the economic and political systems that deprived "darker peoples" of their humanity.[73]

Du Bois believed that people of African descent had to take the lead in addressing the problems of "the colored peoples of the world" first by embracing Pan-Africanism. He defined "Pan-Africa" as "intellectual understanding and co-operation among all groups of Negro descent in order to bring about at the earliest possible time the industrial and spiritual emancipation of the Negro peoples." Du Bois's definition did not differ substantially from that of Garvey and other radical Pan-Africanists, such as the ABB, except that he did not call for the immediate political emancipation of peoples of African descent. In explaining the new racial philosophy for Pan-Africanists, he returned to the idea of black self-governance and the need to reject stereotypes of Africans. He asked African Americans to reject the images that the white media had fashioned of other "Negroes" "for us" in what he called a "spiritual housecleaning." He demanded that blacks "cease to think of Liberia and Haiti as failures in government; of American Negroes as being engaged principally in frequenting Harlem cabarets and Southern lynching parties; of West Indians as ineffective talkers; and of West Africans as parading around in breech-clouts."[74] His emphasis on race pride, not to be confused with race chauvinism, served as a rallying cry for African Americans to move beyond their color and nationalist prejudices (supposedly inherited from white Americans) to embrace their mission to help emancipate the colored peoples of the world. Du Bois postulated that the championing of Africa required not only political action but a reimagining of the black self as proud descendants of Africa, the motherland.

African Empires and Black Republics

The development of Pan-Africanism in America from 1890 to 1936 embodied not only feelings of political frustration, social displacement, and cultural and intellectual marginality among African Americans but also a desire to see a bright future for blacks imprinted on the African continent. In this context, what became known as the "African problem" or "African question" in the immediate years after the Berlin Conference meant something radically different for Pan-Africanists and white imperialists. The former questioned the relationship of diasporic Africans to the future of the continent, while the latter sought the most effective methods of maintaining white rule over Africa. Edward W. Blyden played a pivotal role in defining the African problem in the last decade of the nineteenth century, and in the process he laid the foundation for early twentieth-century Pan-Africanism. In articulating the problem and suggesting methods for its solution, Blyden envisioned an African utopia, where Africa's "sons and daughters" would return to the land of their "forefathers" and assist in "modernizing" the continent politically, culturally, intellectually, economically, and spiritually.

The Pan-Africanisms formulated after the 1895 Congress on Africa and the 1900 Pan-African Conference demonstrated the integral relationship between African Americans' perceptions of Africa and their personal and political attitude toward the continent. African Americans who by and large conceived of Africans as heathens and Africa as the Dark Continent, limited their Pan-Africanism to advocating the "civilization" and Christianization of the continent, often arguing that African American emigration to and missionary work in Africa proved the best methods for "redeeming" Africa. They promoted Liberia as an example of black republicanism and "Negro Christendom" in Africa on which to build their efforts. As blacks began to question these dominant Western images of Africa as benighted, particularly as scholars uncovered the forgotten precolonial and pretransatlantic slave trade history of Africa, they articulated new Pan-Africanisms that dismissed European imperialist rhetoric of the "white man's burden." Concomitant with this new awareness of what Garvey called the "glories" of Africa was a desire to see a bright Africa re-emerge; some Pan-Africanists sought an empire, and others envisioned a confederation of republican states. Africa became reinvented not only as motherland or fatherland but also as the battleground for the redemption of blacks around the world.

The interwar years saw further radicalization of Pan-African politics and representations of Africa in the face of popular cultural assaults on Africa's image and unrelenting European imperialism. Expressing feelings of betrayal by the Versailles Conference, which preferred ceding German territories in Africa to European nations rather than granting Africans their freedom, many American Pan-Africanists broke ranks with integrationist organizations whose internationalism did not include an explicit anticolonialist platform. They formed, joined, and affiliated with new organizations committed to anticolonial Pan-Africanism, promoting more aggressive transatlantic alliances. The Italian invasion of Ethiopia in 1935 altered the face of radical Pan-Africanism as groups such a the Harlem-based Provisional Committee for the Defense of Ethiopia and the American League against War and Fascism joined together in the "Hands off Ethiopia Campaign." Their efforts mirrored those undertook across the Atlantic by the London-based International African Friends of Ethiopia and the Parisian Comité de Défense d'Ethiopie. Brenda Gayle Plummer argues that "the

Italo-Ethiopian War significantly elicited unprecedented mass involvement of Afro-Americans in a single foreign policy issue ... [revitalizing] black nationalist organizations." William R. Scott expounds: "African-American identification with the Abyssinians' cause was widespread. It extended throughout the nation, including the most lynch-ridden states in the South's 'Tar and Feather Belt,' where nearly twelve million blacks still resided in the Depression era." However, the North became the focal point for black activism in response to the invasion of Ethiopia.[75]

In a 1936 response to the Italian incursion, Du Bois explained how colonial imperialism "succeeded the slave trade," and instead of transporting labor to colonies inhabited by white men, imperialists dominated areas inhabited by persons of color. He argued that although this subjugation was political, it was primarily economic—the European empire, based on financial investment, capitalism, and labor exploitation, justified its actions as "carrying civilization to the natives." Du Bois made plain the propaganda depicting Africans as lazy and inferior to legitimate their serfdom under colonial rule. He interpreted Italy's aggression on Ethiopia as based on this "colonial theory of the domination of the colored races" but foresaw its "breakdown." Du Bois stated: "One remembers the indictment against the Belgian Congo."[76]

During the years that American Pan-Africanists fought to redeem Africa from "heathenism," "savagery," and ultimately imperialism, first looking toward the Congo and then the rest of the continent, American museums began constructing elaborate African exhibits for the public. These displays would mirror and at times rival those found in European colonial metropoles. Reflecting on her visit to the Musée de Congo Belge during her participation in the 1921 Pan-African Congress session in Brussels, Jesse Fauset noted the "treasures" and "illimitable riches" and the museum's significance to the colonial project. While American museums did not operate from an overtly imperialist framework with regards to Africa, the narratives of white supremacy and Social Darwinism that propped up colonialism were (and still are) reflected in the composition of many of their African exhibits. Taking the form of either ethnographic or zoological displays from the turn of the century, these installments intrigued the American public. As discussed, men like Robert Lowie and Herbert Lang were among the leading scientists interpreting African material culture and artifacts. However, white zoologists and naturalist-environmentalists took the lead in creating an image of Brightest Africa in the American museum.[77]

Although African Americans tended to eschew the self-serving white supremacist narratives embodied by museum exhibits on Africa, some appropriated ethnographic, naturalist, and environmentalist arguments concerning the uniqueness of Africans and Africa. Attuned to the Darwinian discourses traversing the Atlantic, some sought to include Africans in the evolutionary paradigm in meaningful ways. In 1895, African Americans and white Americans came to Piedmont Park near Atlanta, Georgia, to view the exhibit of the Dahomey village as part of the Cotton States and International Exposition. As race leaders, missionaries, and businessmen gathered to discuss the economic future of the South, particularly its agricultural exports and the redemption of Africa, men, women, and children entered the building showcasing "40 Cannibals and 15 Amazon Warriors." The exhibit, like the Dahomey village featured at the 1893 World's Columbian Village in the White City, played on American desires to see "savages" in their natural state. The exhibit's explicit claim to authenticity ensured the success and popularity of the village. That some African Americans found these exhibits credible speaks to the power of the Darkest Africa narrative. However, by and large, blacks protested the fair not because of its portrayal of Africans but because although they were allowed admittance they could not purchase refreshments except in the Negro Building and had to sit in segregated sections in the auditorium.[78]

When the 1901 Pan-American Exposition in Buffalo, New York, featured another African exhibit, Xavier Pene's "Darkest Africa," African Americans protested their exclusion from the planning stages of the fair. There was no organized protest against Pene, although some spectators questioned the authenticity of the Africans in the exhibit. Indeed, it was later revealed that black vaudeville actors often played Africans at fairs to supplement their work on the "chittlin' circuit." The fairs' own naturalist version of Africa, fashioned primarily by anthropologists and show men, made Africa real to the average American fairgoer.[79]

African Americans like sculptor Meta Warrick Fuller understood the role that such exhibits played in reemphasizing racial hierarchy. Under the guise of science, these naturalistic displays confirmed the "savagery" of Africans. By placing African American exhibits alongside those of Africans, the fair planners erased blacks and other nonwhite colonial subjects. Fuller sculpted an African American series for the 1907 tercentennial celebration of the founding of Jamestown that showed the history of black advancement in America since 1619, when twenty-two Africans were sold to the settlers. W. Fitzhugh Brundage argues that this work helped "destabilize

Dahomey village, Cotton States and International Exhibition. Kenan Research Center at the Atlanta History Center.

the binary classification of civilization and 'the other,' of modernity and primitiveness."That Fuller did not imagine Africans as they may have lived before landing in Jamestown is noteworthy, as arguably such an inclusion could support existing narratives of African primitivism. Renée Ater points to the Pan-African ideals embodied in Fuller's series *Ethiopia* sculpted for the 1921 America's Making Exposition, explaining how Fuller sought to use her work to discredit the racialist assumptions of Anglo-Saxon supremacy informing expositions and world's fairs. Yet as Nell Irvin Painter argues, the aesthetics of *Ethiopia Awakening*—specifically Fuller's homage to Egyptian ancient art—reflects New Negro conflations of ancient Egypt, Ethiopia, and Kush in constructing new models of black womanhood and identity. West Africa was not looked to as a source of African historical and future glory. As noted, for Pan-Africanists the image of Ethiopia countered any claims that Africans were incapable of achieving civilization.[80]

Fuller's sculptures contextualized in a broader history of African American engagement with naturalist and ethnographic discourses reveal that

African Americans were interested in the cultural and scientific as well as political meanings of Africa. Black intellectuals, like their white counterparts, began to celebrate primitivism in the 1910s and 1920s. Although ethnographic and primitive images of Africa continued to enthrall Americans, African wildlife dominated America's fascination with the Dark Continent. Some blacks joined in the naturalist-environmental chorus proclaiming the tragedy of the disappearance of African wildlife as Europeans ravaged the continent via their various modernity projects. American naturalist-environmentalists waged their own campaign to save Africa. While they were not ignorant of the politics of imperialism in Africa, they concentrated their endeavors on the natural environment. They looked to colonial Africa, not as evidence of the horrors of colonialism but as proof of the vanishing natural wonders of Africa. They would rescue the "vanishing continent" by means of scientific expedition, museum exhibition, and nature preservation.

FOUR

To Capture a Vanishing World
Naturalist-Environmentalist Discourses and Displays of Africa

In 1900, *Science* magazine, the official organ of the American Association for the Advancement of Science (founded in 1848), published an article entitled "Protection of Wild Animals in Africa," a reprint of a letter sent to the London *Times* by one of its correspondents in East Africa. According to the missive, the district of Beria, "which formerly teemed with game, [would] be denuded of all game through indiscriminate shooting." The reporter identified three sources of depletion: the native and white hunters who hunted for canteens, seasonal hunting parties that shot young antelope, and the Rinderpest epidemic of 1898. Recognizing the latter as an act of nature, the report outlined several steps that the government should take to curtail hunting activities, including supervising hunting parties, limiting the number of animals to be shot by Europeans, employing gamekeepers, establishing a closed season, declaring certain animals to be royal game, and preventing Africans from shooting game for food. The letter concluded with the author deploring the "slaughter" of "these beautiful animals" and urging the cessation of profligate hunting.[1]

The reporter's apocalyptic portents about the future of game in East Africa came nearly four years after American naturalist D. G. Elliot returned from British Somaliland and informed his employer, the Field Museum of Natural History in Chicago, of "the gradual disappearing of large animals, which [had] been going on in the African continent for a considerable period," resulting "in the complete extinction of some of the finest species."[2] If Elliot's report was accurate, the "indiscriminate slaughter" spoken of in the *Times* commenced sometime after the British established its sphere of influence in East Africa (present-day Kenya, Somalia, and Uganda). The building of railroad systems utilizing African laborers required the shooting of game "for the pot." However, the opening up of the colonies as a tourist destination for Western travels often meant the arrival of white hunters in Africa who hunted for sport and not for subsistence, food, or science. Elliot and naturalist-environmentalists excused the shooting of game by men and women of science as advancing Western knowledge of Africa and expressed heightened dismay about the actions of white hunting parties reminiscent of the United States' regrettable past in nearly killing off the buffalo and other rare North American fauna. Although reporters and travelers made imperial and other public officials aware of the likelihood of faunal species extinction in Africa, naturalists and environmentalists created their own discourse for protecting African wildlife.

The naturalist-environmentalists' myth of Africa as the "disappearing continent" informed their crusade to save Brightest Africa for future generations of humanity. In order for Americans—and the rest of the Western world—to comprehend the severity of game depletion and the endangerment of species in Africa, naturalist-environmentalists argued for the continent's uniqueness as a natural history laboratory caught in time. Reinventing Africa as an "ageless continent" proved integral to this reimagining, as well as to rhetoric that emphasized the primordial nature of the land. Due to the supposed simplicity or, for some naturalists, the inferiority of Africans, the continent remained locked in stasis, shielded from the ravages of human civilization and industrialization. Thus, unwittingly, by not mastering the land and asserting dominion over the animals, Africans allowed the continent's natural environment to flourish. Animals roamed relatively untroubled (unless killed to feed the hungry), tracks of jungle remained unexplored, and flora grew in abundance. Naturalists wanted the world to see that had not the white man intruded upon this Eden—this natural paradise,—the continent would have continued to be the "Africa of the Age of

Mammals." On one thing the naturalists agreed with Pan-Africanists: Africa did not menace the white man; the white man threatened Africa. However, naturalists concluded that it was, therefore, the white man who bore the responsibility for saving it and not the sons and daughters of Africa.[3]

American naturalist-environmentalists reasoned that neither making public speeches, penning articles for scientific journals, nor publishing travel narratives alone could convince their countrymen that Africa was bright and, thus, worthy of saving. They argued that forward- and scientifically thinking men and women had to bring Brightest Africa to the people, displayed visually so that Americans could see with both the mind's eye and the physical eye that Africa was something to behold with reverence. These naturalists privileged two mediums above all others to promote environmentalist awareness of African wildlife: films and museum exhibits (specifically, the diorama). They believed that the popularity of cinema and museums in the early decades of the twentieth century if properly exploited could ensure that their cause would capture the attention of their fellow countrymen. Specifically, the foremost architects of the American naturalist-environmentalist image of Brightest Africa—zoologists, taxidermists, and filmmakers affiliated with the American Museum of Natural History (AMNH)—embarked on a mission to renovate museological techniques and produce wildlife films as vehicles for capturing the wonders of Africa. The political, social, and cultural realities that surrounded their ambitious undertaking revealed the intransigence of a public all too comfortable with stereotypes of Africa and Africans. Thus, naturalists' reinvention of Africa, intended to highlight the natural environment, became fraught with contradictions as they attempted to incorporate images of Africans into their project.

In the intricate processes of constructing their version of Africa for the museum, naturalists found themselves grappling with the incongruities of their work. Simultaneously, while professing to save Africa, they killed the very objects of their supposed philanthropy. This realization, although explained by them as a necessary evil to serve science, led to their participation in modern conservationism in Africa. Although some American naturalists argued that they originated the movement in Africa, specifically in the Belgian Congo, the historical record shows that arguments for conservation in Africa had nineteenth-century roots. While the question of who deserves credit for initiating conservation in Africa remained important for American naturalists, the relationship between their museum work and travel narratives illuminates their national park advocacy.

The game preserve operated as a living museum. Instead of viewing dead, stuffed animals in glass cases, visitors to the preserve could view Brightest Africa *in* Africa. Thus, for the AMNH naturalists, their fight for a gorilla sanctuary, which the Belgians responded to by chartering Parc National Albert, could not be extricated from their work in America. As limited finances and other practicalities prevented many Americans from visiting Africa, the habitat diorama could not be abandoned in favor of the preserve. The two museums, if you will, had to coexist on both sides of the Atlantic. Once again, the presence of Africans in this extension of the Brightest Africa dream revealed the tensions inherent in conservation "savior" discourses that favored the rights of animals over those of humans. As Roderick P. Neumann has argued with regard to contemporary conservation debates, the alienation of Africans from their traditional lands and, thus, from securing their livelihood through hunting and agriculture resulted from many of these environmentalist initiatives.[4] In the case of the Belgian Congo, the AMNH naturalists (and others affiliated with the gorilla sanctuary) took a more moderate position on native hunting rights than their European counterparts. For example, members of the British Society for the Preservation of Fauna of the Empire who rejected the argument that game and natural resources were the "property of the indigenous natives" agreed with the *Times* correspondent who approved of divesting Africans entirely of their hunting rights.[5] Despite these differences, however, Americans and European conservationists aligned with one another in one important aspect: they agreed that Westerners should decide the fate of the African environment and prescribe the role of Africans therein. Saving Africa via museum display and conservationism was the white man's burden, a performance of white masculinity, a new physical womanhood, and white superiority.

Akeley of Africa

Carl Akeley, the man credited with coining the phrase "Brightest Africa" and the architect behind African Hall at the AMNH, emerged as the preeminent American naturalist-environmentalist who rejected stereotypes of Darkest Africa by pointing to the continent's rich faunal heritage. In his campaign to present a positive image of the continent to the public and to save African wildlife, he utilized his training as a taxidermist, in the process becoming a self-trained naturalist and environmentalist. His journey to becoming a taxidermist involved affiliations with several public and private intellectual and scientific institutions that took him across his native New

York State, to Milwaukee, to Chicago, and finally back to New York City. This odyssey to the AMNH not only accredited him professionally but also introduced him to Africa.

Carl Ethan Akeley was born to Daniel Webster Akeley and Julia Akeley née Glidden on May 16, 1864, in Clarendon, New York. At the age of nineteen, Akeley began training as a taxidermist as an employee of Henry Augustus Ward's Natural Science Establishment in nearby Rochester. Despite Ward's extensive patronage, reflecting on his tenure there, Akeley lamented that "the profession [he] had chosen as the most satisfying and stimulating to a man's soul turned out at that time to have very little science and no art at all." Akeley did not concede that there should be a firm distinction between taxidermy as art and taxidermy as science in crafting natural history displays. He complained of the simplicity of the taxidermy practiced at the establishment.[6]

Akeley was offered his first major taxidermy job in 1885. Jumbo, P. T. Barnum's East African circus elephant, died in a collision with a Canadian locomotive on September 14 of that year. Barnum commissioned Ward to stuff the elephant, whose body was in bad condition, so that Jumbo could be "carted around the country with the circus." The process of mounting Jumbo—which Akeley recalled as his first contact with an African specimen—reflected his aesthetics, which combined sculpture with taxidermy. The Jumbo mounting gained Akeley public notoriety, yet despite his success, Akeley left Ward's in 1886 for a part-time job in the Milwaukee Public Museum (MPM).[7]

In Milwaukee, Akeley immersed himself in taxidermy literature and trained under John P. Taylor and Swedish-born and -trained Thure Kumlien, graduate of Uppsala University. Akeley completed his first habitat diorama, *The Muskrat Group*, for the MPM in 1890. In 1892, he opened a private taxidermy studio in DeKalb, Illinois, where he employed two assistants— his future wife, Delia Julia Reiss née Denning, and his brother Thomas. That year Akeley received a commission for Chicago's World's Columbian Exposition to be held the following year. William Henry Holmes, curator of the Bureau of Ethnology of the U.S. National Museum (the Smithsonian Institution) in Washington, D.C., asked Akeley to mount a mannequin of a Native American warrior astride a stuffed mustang.[8]

With hopes of paying off his debts, Akeley set out to leave Milwaukee for the famous British Museum. In 1894, when Akeley was en route to London through Chicago, he decided to visit the Field Museum of Natural History. There he met the curator of zoology, Elliot, who gave him a guided tour. Akeley offered his professional opinion on many of the animal displays and Elliot immediately offered him several taxidermy commissions. Akeley aborted his trip to London and returned to DeKalb.[9]

Akeley's decision to accept a post at the Field Museum reflected his increasing interest in the museum world. Unlike the British Museum, the Field was young, undeveloped, and thus could offer a measure of freedom that Akeley probably would not have enjoyed at the older and more prestigious British Museum. Moreover, at the Field, Akeley could make a name for himself in the rapidly growing world of American natural history museums. Coincidentally, the museum had developed from the 1893 Columbian Exposition, for which Akeley provided a taxidermy specimen. The fair's exhibits comprised mainly anthropological (or ethnographic) objects from selected world cultures and included several ethnological villages, including one from Africa. Frederic Ward Putnam—a former student of Louis Agassiz at Harvard University and one of the fair's directors—persuaded retail entrepreneur Marshall Field to build a new museum in Chicago that would house much of the fair's material. However, despite the museum's initial orientation as an anthropological museum, it opened a taxidermy department. The Field eventually offered Akeley a permanent position in that department in 1896.[10] Akeley's tenure at Field allowed him to merge his years of taxidermy experience with both his artistic approach to museum exhibition and what would become his image of Brightest Africa.

When Akeley arrived in Chicago in 1896 to take up his position as taxidermist at the Field Museum of Natural History, he craved a project that would allow him to showcase his artistic and aesthetic sensibilities. Having recently won acclaim for his dioramas constructed for Ward's Natural Science Establishment in Rochester, New York, and his muskrat group installed in the MPM, he hoped his new job at the Field would not set him backward as a taxidermist. His prior conversations with Elliot centered on the need for him to improve existing zoological exhibits, install new dioramas, and innovate taxidermy techniques at the Field. Elliot also invited Akeley to join him on safari in Africa, an opportunity that Akeley believed would allow him to transcend the seemingly confined boundaries of his craft.[11] Akeley arrived in Chicago to go on his first African adventure. This safari not only introduced Akeley to Africa but also inspired him to use his taxidermy skills to create evidence of African wildlife supposedly doomed to extinction.

When the two men departed Chicago for New York to await passage to London, Elliot had yet to pinpoint the exact location of the expedition.

Finding a safe place to hunt and travel in Africa involved navigating complex cultural, social, political, and physical landscapes, especially given the recent uprisings in the British possessions. In fact, Elliot changed the intended site for the prospective safari three times because of environmental conditions and the colonial political atmosphere. In a letter addressed to F. J. V. Skiff, director of the FMNH, Elliot expressed his confidence in British rule in Africa. Elliot, the letter informed Skiff, would receive a note introducing him to the British minister of the colonies, Joseph Chamberlain. Elliot believed that the "influential letter" would afford him assistance from the Crown should he visit "*any* British possession" (emphasis added). Elliot went on to assure Skiff that he would "go [to England] with strong letters to persons in authority that [would] be of great assistance," which included the legal advisor of the sultan of Zanzibar and the consul general. Elliot also claimed that the American ambassador F. F. Bayard would "do all he [could] to further [Elliot's] wishes." As if to alleviate Skiff's concerns that the Shona would continue their rebellion against the British in Rhodesia, Elliot requested money to buy presents for Mashona chiefs, so that he could "pass through, or hunt in their territories" unmolested. Although Elliot had some idea of the volatile political climate in British-controlled Africa, he sought comfort in British governance and ability to put down any rebellion.[12]

While awaiting passage to England, Elliot decided to take a quick trip to Philadelphia to visit Arthur Donaldson Smith, explorer and honorary member of the Academy of Natural Sciences. Smith had just returned from Somaliland and discussed matters of outfitting a safari with Elliot. Smith relayed to Elliot how during his recent expedition he had to arm "his men with 75 Snyder rifles ... as he pitched battles with the Natives and whipped them until they sued for peace." Implicitly, he suggested that Elliot travel to East Africa well armed. Smith ended the meeting by furnishing Elliot with memoranda to refer to while in Africa. As Elliot and Akeley boarded a ship for England, Elliot still remained unsure of his safari site. Disturbed by portents of battling hostile natives, he sought counsel from the South African Chartered Company (based in London). Yet, after several meetings with company officials, Elliot claimed to have abandoned all intentions of traveling to "Mashonaland" for financial reasons and not fears of the Ndebele (Mashona) revolt engulfing Rhodesia.[13]

Not to be deterred from obtaining his trophies, Elliot sought another site for the expedition. This time, he relied on his "long residence in England and ... membership in ... various scientific societies," which brought him "in touch with many persons of influences, as well as travelers all of whom" were anxious to make his trip a success. After making numerous inquiries, he learned from his informants that in Zanzibar and "the Masai country," war ensued. However, the resourceful British "Government [had] sent for a contingent of Indian troops to wipe out the Masai," and Elliot did not falter in his conviction that the British would be victorious. If "warring natives" could not spoil his plans, however, the "Murrain," or Rinderpest epidemic, that decimated cattle herds and potentially threatened wild game would. Elliot conjectured that this latest disease constituted just "one more and new method to cause the extinction of African wild creatures."[14]

As Elliot's connections were limited to the British colonies, Somaliland represented his last hope. After consulting with a "brother-naturalist" and Joseph Edward Dodson (Smith's companion on his expedition) and hearing reports of an abundance of animals in the area, Elliot decided to travel to the region, despite becoming aware of possible impediments to the expedition. First, because the faunal species he sought did not congregate in one part of the colony, the hunting party would need to travel long distances to secure taxidermy specimens. Second, it was not "the proper season" to travel to the area. Third, as revealed in his official report to the Executive Committee of the Field, the India Office (a branch of the Foreign Office) warned him that "the Tribes if not actually at war, were in a state of unrest, and the Government was quite unable to afford [him] any assistance in case [he] got into trouble." Ignoring these warnings, Elliot secured the necessary traveling papers and hunting permits and set sail with Akeley and Dodson for the Gulf of Aden.[15]

The expedition proved a success, despite agonizing heat and torrential rains. The party obtained specimens of warthog, wild ass, lion, antelope, kudu, gazelle, dik-dik, oryx, hartebeest, hyena, jackal, cheetah, gnu, bongo, aardvark, monkey, nyala, buffalo, and leopard. Akeley and Elliot returned to London in October, where Elliot remained to conduct research while Akeley set sail for New York en route to Chicago. In the African expedition report submitted to the Field, Elliot credited Akeley with recognizing the severity of the situation for African wildlife and having the foresight to purchase a camera for the expedition. Akeley initially procured the camera to take pictures of the faunal specimens, so that the taxidermy performed on their skins would be first-rate. Commenting on the number of specimens collected for the Field, Akeley wrote that he preferred "photographing animals to shooting them. However, in order to obtain specimens for our museums it is necessary to do so." Akeley revealed that he had no tolerance for "mindless" killing, criticizing the Masai for their "savage hunts" to obtain the skull of the bull oryx for shield coverings, which served no scientific end. For Akeley, his over five hundred photographs of people, landscapes, and fauna would serve as archival evidence of the Africa that was disappearing. Akeley exemplifies the naturalist dilemma in constructing Brightest Africa—preserving the wilderness while simultaneously shooting specimens for the museum, and thereby contributing to the depletion of wildlife. Also, he demonstrates the dismissive attitude that many naturalists had toward Africans and their cultural traditions.[16]

For Elliot, taking pictures alone could not rescue the last vestiges of African wildlife. Rather, he argued that the acquisition of skins for taxidermy supplied "the only proper way to secure collections for the Museum" and to ensure that "those that come after us" would have records of the existence of these fauna, inevitably fated to extinction. As proof of his convictions, Elliot and Akeley exported to America 205 skins from 27 species and 129 antelope horns. Despite this bounty, Elliot remained dissatisfied. In the report, he wrote: "Of all the existing wild creatures, those of the African continent are disappearing the most rapidly, and although the Field Museum by its recent acquisitions is ahead of all its sister institutions in the United States as regards the large quadrupeds of Africa, yet there are large numbers not yet represented, and no opportunity should be allowed to pass without securing them. At present in most cases, it is merely a question of money; in the near future money will be of no avail." Elliot's plea for the museum to sponsor another expedition to Africa to secure specimens or large mammals and his ominous portrait of barren African landscapes captured Akeley's imagination, and he began crafting a proposal for his own safari to the continent.[17]

During the next decade since Akeley and Elliot's British Somaliland Expedition, Akeley worked diligently preparing animal skins for taxidermy. All the while, he harbored feelings that the African specimens that they collected did not adequately represent the diversity of African zoology, as the collection did not include many of the continent's megafauna. He questioned whether one could render an accurate picture of Africa without including some of the largest and rarest fauna in the continent, and indeed, in the world. Consequently, Akeley drafted and submitted his own prospectus for an expedition to British East Africa (BEA) in search of large mammals, with the elephant as top priority. When Elliot declined Akeley's invitation to accompany him, the museum placed the young taxidermist in charge of the safari, and his wife, Delia Akeley, served as his companion and assistant.[18]

While Akeley viewed this expedition as an opportunity to create a lasting record of the wildlife of Africa, other members of the museum viewed the trip from another vantage, reminding him of the disciplinary origins of its institution. Although the Field was a natural history museum, defined as a museum interested in studying all living things with special focus on their origins, evolution, and relationships to one another, the sciences of zoology, mineralogy, geology, and paleontology did not eclipse that of anthropology and ethnography. The curator of anthropology, W. A. Dorsey, expressed concern about the Field's African ethnology collection. The Elliot expedition had brought back over 140 ethnographic specimens, including weapons, utensils, and ornaments, all "being a fair representation of the materials in use among the tribes" they encountered, which were "apparently unique among savage people." Those objects only added to the meager numbers of artifacts from the African village constructed at Chicago's world fair. In a letter to Skiff, Dorsey remarked: "you will realize that our collections representing the ethnology of Africa are considerable in extent and represent certain regions of that continent fairly well." However, he went on to note, the collection did not cover the entire continent and in all likelihood it would remain incomplete due to the museum's insufficient funding for ethnological expeditions and acquisitions. He encouraged Skiff to view Akeley's expedition as a chance "to secure certain classes of material which must soon disappear from Africa owing to its desirability from the museum [in general] standpoint." Moreover, he posited that in terms of ethnology, Africa remained the "least known" to the ethnologist and "the poorest represented" in Western museums. Dorsey agreed that the entire natural history of Africa stood on the precipice of extinction; however, according to him the ethnology of the continent (and not so much the zoology) would most likely vanish as "civilization" marched across the Dark Continent.[19] This marked the first time that Akeley confronted an alternative discourse to Africa as a "disappearing continent" that had little interest in African zoology.

Although relatively few American anthropologists in the early twentieth century dedicated their individual research to Africa, those affiliated with museums argued that recording the cultures of the African peoples demanded as much (if not more) importance as securing specimens of mammals. Such sentiments were commonplace among European anthropologists who viewed their science as invaluable to the imperial project in Africa, as it could help foster commerce and civilization in the region. They argued that imperialists armed with anthropological knowledge of Africans possessed an advantage over the ignorant colonial in convincing Africans to abandon their "primitive" lifestyles in favor of jobs in colonial industries. Moreover, these anthropologists reasoned that their work could help colonial officials understand the peculiarities of African customs and traditions and reconcile those cultural traits with colonial rule. American anthropologists, less invested in African imperialism, more often viewed colonialism as potentially destructive to "pristine" African culture. Regardless of their position on colonialism, Western anthropologists often approached "primitive" cultures as a part of nature. Dorsey, through Skiff, encouraged Akeley to broaden his understanding of the significance of Africa in the discipline of natural history. Although no one at the Field challenged Akeley's prophecy that African wildlife (at least its rare species) would soon be extinct, not everyone agreed that wildlife depletion would be the only casualty of modernity on the continent. Akeley viewed Dorsey's request with equanimity, agreeing to do what lay in his power to secure skulls, skeletons, and carvings from the areas he visited.[20]

Akeley learned one valuable lesson from the Elliot expedition, which was to know your destination before setting sail for Africa. Through a series of correspondences between Secretary of State John Hay's office and H. N. Higinbotham, president of the museum, Akeley secured the requisite permission to enter and collect in the British East Africa Protectorate, the German East Africa Protectorate, and the Congo Free State. In the letter to Hay, Higinbotham sought passports and permits for the Akeleys and their companions. He assured Hay that "it [was] their purpose to secure only a limited number of specimens of the different species of animals and birds, and they [would] not, in the common acceptation of the term, be hunters having a right to kill for the sake of killing, but they [would] only take specimens in the interest of science." Higinbotham wanted to assure the colonial authorities that Akeley intended to help the West create a tangible record of endangered African wildlife—not to contribute to its decimation.[21]

Akeley's numerous requests for additional funding while on expedition revealed the precision with which he constructed Africa as a vanishing wilderness. Not content with amassing a modest collection, by November 1905, a mere three weeks into camp, Akeley requested five thousand dollars for additional expenses. In a letter to Skiff, Akeley gave a progress report.

His party secured 49 large mammals, 109 small mammals, 90 birds, and numerous "reptiles, insects, etc." Although Akeley expressed a fascination for large mammals, he explained that many of the smaller mammals would go to other departments in the museum to complement dioramas featuring larger specimens. Despite this glowing report, Akeley cautioned that the safari was just "getting started" in the collection process. The scope of the exhibit that Akeley planned to mount for the museum required more specimens and, therefore, more funding. He justified these expenditures by reminding Skiff that "the country is enormously rich in zoological material of great interest," just enough to "make a noteworthy collection." The urgency of the letter reflected the gravity of the situation for Akeley—the inevitable depletion of these zoological specimens in the modern age.[22]

The Akeley safari party returned to Chicago in 1907 (it left Africa in late December 1906) with thirteen faunal genera and various curiosities. The "curios" collected included miscellaneous shields, spears, "native mats," skeletons, skulls, and Maasai, Wandorobo, Wakamba, and Wateita artifacts. Akeley also took photographs of the fauna, flora, and Africans that filled several albums. The majority of the natural history collection was zoological, in accordance with the primary goal of the expedition—to secure specimens of vanishing wildlife. The contents of the inventory in many ways mirrored the changes occurring in the museum when the Akeleys returned. The Field, now under new directorship, moved to a new location, and the compartmentalization of natural history became more distinct; the museum appointed directors who hired specialized teams for each department. This loss of disciplinary fluidity within the museum meant that Akeley would find his activities limited to taxidermy. Although he had collected ethnographic objects from Africa, Akeley would have little say in how the Department of Anthropology exhibited and interpreted them. Although he found himself "turned away from taxidermy" in this new environment, he dedicated himself to completing the elephant diorama, *The Fighting Bulls*. Simultaneously, he started looking for a new job and further developed his dioramic and mounting techniques. Over the next two years Akeley delivered lectures on his African travels, slowly establishing himself as an expert on African zoology.[23]

In Africa with Teddy

Although the Field Museum launched one of the first American museum collecting expeditions to Africa, many prominent Americans aspired to safari in Africa in hopes of securing the rarest animal species for both private and public consumption. Like the Field Museum, the Smithsonian Institution in Washington, D.C., expressed interest in developing an African zoological collection, but it did not rank it as top priority until the whims of Teddy Roosevelt reoriented the museum plans. Whirling from the success of his progressive domestic agenda and "big stick" diplomacy, Teddy Roosevelt decided to take a trip to "the Jungles of Africa, inhabited by the wildest of wild beasts [gorilla] and wild men." In 1908, President Roosevelt confided in his friend Lyman Abbott that, after his term ended, he planned to take a year-long African hunting trip to collect game. His private letter to Abbott conveyed his desire to hunt where Winston Churchill, Joseph Chamberlain, the Duke of Abruzzi, the Duke of Connaught, and the Duke of Mecklenburg, among others, had recently traveled. After hearing of Carl Akeley's pending expedition to BEA, Roosevelt made arrangements to meet with the taxidermist to discuss preparations for his "great adventure." According to museum lore, Akeley made his decision to leave the Field Museum *after* having dinner with the president.[24] Akeley's meeting and later rendezvous with Roosevelt in Africa are important for understanding the origins of African Hall as embodying not only the doctrine of the "strenuous life" and new white manhood but also a messianic environmentalist version of the "white man's burden."

Roosevelt publicly announced his trip on December 6, 1908, to great fanfare. On the Smithsonian African Expedition of 1909–1910, the president would prove his mettle by conducting a safari in a continent reputed to be dark and dangerous. At last, Roosevelt would perform the ultimate feat of manhood—leading an expedition through the "heart of Africa" at the age of fifty. The humorist poet Thomas R. Ybarra mockingly hailed Roosevelt as "the nearest human approach to perpetual motion." Akeley praised the president for his bravery and encouraged his efforts. In contrast, New York Senator Thomas Platt remarked that the president "may be very strenuous and he may be physically strong, but he is taking a long chance." Professor Starr of the University of Chicago predicted that the president would return to America in a casket because of his temperament and advanced age. Friends like Cecil Spring Rice worried for Roosevelt's safety. Despite such reservations, Roosevelt determined to set sail for Africa and prove his manhood.[25]

Roosevelt and Akeley rendezvoused in BEA to search for a bull elephant and agreed to meet in Londiani, about eighty miles outside Victoria Nyanza. After starting their trek toward the Uasin Gishu Plateau in BEA, Roosevelt's expedition united with Akeley's party. Roosevelt credited a member of his party, famed Australian hunter Leslie Tarlton, with hearing the sound of the elephant trumpet. When the men from the hunting party proceeded on foot, they encountered a grazing herd—six cows and two calves (one male, one female) some sixty yards from an anthill. Roosevelt, to Akeley's surprise, stepped forward to take the shot. Akeley had expected Roosevelt to shoot from behind the safety of an anthill, because he "wanted him to shoot her, not take her alive." The president shot one female in her lungs and heart with his double-barreled Holland rifle. The elephants responded by heading in the direction of the hunters. Roosevelt shot another cow, this time in the forehead. Tarlton, Akeley, and Kermit Roosevelt opened fire, the latter two felling another cow. Kermit Roosevelt then shot the bull calf with his Winchester. Four elephants had been killed, but not a full-grown bull.[26]

The frenzy that surrounded the shooting continued as Akeley and Tarlton pitched camp and began preparing the skins for shipment back to the museum. Roosevelt went in search of dinner, sorry that he had unnecessarily shot the second cow, since Akeley did not need it for the AMNH exhibit. Hyenas circled the camp, fighting over the elephant carcasses, while Akeley and Tarlton worked on the skins well into the next day. That morning, they headed back to the Roosevelt camp for breakfast not completely satisfied with their trophies. The Roosevelts and Tarlton departed with Delia Akeley, Stevenson, and McCutcheon to hunt for lunch, while Akeley remained with taxidermist James Clark to continue preparing the skins.[27]

The search for the bull continued after the two groups parted. The Akeley expedition then crossed the Nzoia River headed to Mount Elgon on the border of Uganda and BEA. The Akeleys entered Uganda and hired a new group of porters to aid them in traveling between Masindi and Foweira, a region reputed to have numerous male elephants. Yet the search proved unfruitful, and the Akeleys returned to Uasin Gishu to renew their search. En route, Carl Akeley went out to hunt "alone" (without his wife). Supposedly suffering from malaria, Blackwater fever, and dysentery, Akeley refused to abandon his quest. When he had just finished inspecting the guns of the bearers, he recalled: "I was suddenly conscious that an elephant was on top of me.... My next mental record is of a tusk at my chest. I grabbed it with my left hand, and the other with my right hand, and swinging in between them went to the ground on my back.... He drove his tusks into the ground on either side of me.... I had the realization that I was being crushed.... I heard a wheezy grunt as he plunged down and then—oblivion. Delia Akeley remembered hearing the shout *"Tembo piga bwana"* (The elephant has the master) from a runner. When she arrived on the scene, her husband had three broken ribs and a split cheek, opened to the jawbone. The elephant had mauled Akeley.[28]

Despite his near-death experience, Akeley continued his hunt for the bull and succeeded. The particulars of this event are somewhat confusing, as the narratives differ from author to author. What is known is that a bull was shot. According to Roosevelt, "Mrs. Akeley had to her credit a fine maned lion and a bull elephant with enormous tusks."[29] Delia Akeley, in her book *Jungle Portraits*, hedges about who shot the bull, while Carl Akeley's *In Brightest Africa* evades the issue. However, a series of pictures of Delia Akeley and R. J. Cunninghame reveals that she did indeed shoot the bull. One shows Delia Akeley with the blood of the elephant smeared on her forehead—a hunting ritual restricted to honoring the slayer.[30]

Witnesses to the elephant attack recounted the hunt not only for its sensationalism but also for its symbolism. The hunt itself was an exercise in the strenuous life and masculinity for its male participants, as hunting experts considered elephants one of the most difficult creatures to hunt in Africa. Many hunters deemed the bagging of an elephant prestigious; thus, they argued that only the most vigorous and experienced *male* hunters could secure the animal as a trophy. It follows that only those men could capture the most evasive of elephants, the bull. This view of the bull elephant as a man's trophy in part explains the adrenaline that accompanied the Akeley hunt, as well as the men's dejection each day at not capturing the bull. Moreover, the relative silence about the securing of the bull by a woman—Delia Akeley—is consistent with the view of the hunt as a male rite.

Yet the narrative of the hunt represents more than a reification of masculine prowess; it symbolizes Akeley's image of Africa. More concretely, the bull elephant stood as an icon of Brightest Africa—an emblem of a fast-vanishing continent and a link to the earth's primordial past. Akeley articulated this sentiment best when discussing the elephant group that would occupy center stage in the African Hall: "In this, which we hope will be an everlasting monument to the Africa that was, the Africa that is now fast disappearing, I hope to place the elephant group on a pedestal in the centre of the hall—the rightful place for the first animal of them all.... As civilization advances in Africa, the extinction of the elephant is being accomplished slowly but quite as surely as that of the American buffalo two generations ago."[31] Here Akeley indicated that he saw Africa as disappearing in the midst of European colonialism. Drawing analogies between the

Delia Akeley with the bull elephant she killed, 1909. Neg./Transparency no. 211518, courtesy the Library, American Museum of Natural History.

buffalo and the elephant, Akeley prophesied that untouched Africa would go the way of the mastodon.

Akeley, like Roosevelt, experienced the American frontier and its official closing by the Census Bureau in 1890. Perhaps both men saw in Africa a place to find the elusive frontier, to shed civilization, to reject an American culture debased by vestiges of European traditions, or to engage in manly pursuits. In speaking of Africa and "golden joys," Roosevelt remarked: "There are not words that can tell the hidden spirit of the wilderness, that can reveal its mystery, its melancholy, and its charm. There is delight in the hardy life of the open, in long rides rifle in hand, in the thrill of the fight with dangerous game. Apart from this, yet mingled with it, is the strong attraction of the silent places, of the large tropic moons, and the splendor of the new stars; where the wanderer sees the awful glory of sunrise and sunset in the wide spaces of the earth, *unworn of man*, and changed only by the slow change of the ages through time everlasting" (emphasis added). Using poetic imagery, Roosevelt clearly articulated what attracted him to

Africa, the "greatest of the world's great hunting grounds." As he conjured up vistas of the East African region, he wistfully alluded to his engagement in the strenuous life as he moved from camp to camp. His rides were long, yet enjoyable. They allowed him to encounter nature up close and uninterrupted, as a wanderer in a foreign land, armed only with his rifle and his imagination. The last phrase in this musing is most telling, as Roosevelt attributed the splendor of the African wilderness to the absence of man. By this he did not mean the want of human life, but rather a lack of human settlement. Though similar conditions existed in America (despite the closing of the frontier), in Roosevelt's estimation, it was rare to encounter nature in such a state and to revel in it unabashedly. His point is implicit as he distinguished Africa from all other "hunting-grounds": Africa was unique, a place where one could indulge in "primitive passions" and manly pursuits without the cloying strictures of social convention.[32]

In commenting on Africa's suitability as a place for escape and adventure, Roosevelt compared the continent to Pleistocene Europe because "the low culture of many of the savage tribes . . . substantially reproduced the conditions of life in Europe as it was led by our ancestors ages before the dawn of anything that could be called civilization." Going to Africa would put the Anglo-Saxon man in touch with his primordial roots. Instead of "blacking up" or watching vaudeville sketches of cannibal tribes or participating in Masonic rituals—all in the safety of American venues—white men could experience the primitive up close. However, perhaps more enticing than traipsing through a land devoid of civilization filled with "dark-skinned races" lay the promise of traveling to a land teeming "with beasts of the chase, infinite in number and incredible in variety." According to both Akeley and Roosevelt, Africa intrigued Americans nostalgic for their own frontier because the continent remained a hunter's paradise—an "animal kingdom."[33]

Roosevelt's declaration that the continent teemed with beasts that had no likeness elsewhere echoed Akeley's image of Africa as an animal kingdom. Roosevelt wrote:

> It [Africa] holds the fiercest beasts of ravin [sic], and the fleetest and most timid of those beings that live in undying fear of talon and fang. It holds the largest and smallest of hoofed animals. It holds the mightiest creatures that tread the earth or swim in its rivers; it also holds distant kinsfolk of these same creatures. . . . There are creatures which are the embodiments of grace; and others whose huge ungainliness is like that of a shape in a nightmare.

> The plains are alive with droves of strange and beautiful animals whose like is not known elsewhere; and with others even stranger that show both in form and temper something of the fantastic and the grotesque.[34]

Yet, both men found their image of Africa as a faunal paradise constantly tested and threatened by the realities of safari and imperialism. It had become increasingly clear that this utopian world would soon disappear under the onslaught of colonialism.

Akeley and Roosevelt both elegized the abundant fauna, eventual game depletion, and the lost "charm of Africa." They argued that natural history museums had to become the primary custodians of the "real" history of Africa. Akeley himself mused that "it may not be many years before such museum exhibits [of elephants] are the only remaining records" of his "jungle friends."[35] Thus, Akeley resolved to build a monument to the continent after his return to America. Similarly, Roosevelt agreed to further his commitment to institutions responsible for documenting the natural history of the world. When Akeley set sail for America in 1910, he dreamed of creating a permanent and unparalleled record of African fauna, the most unique and endangered of wildlife. When he returned to the AMNH, however, he found himself having to convince the board of trustees of the exigency of his work, as the museum had its own ideas about the development of African exhibits in its halls. The initial hesitancy with which the museum accepted his proposal but then championed his vision reflected the disciplinary compartmentalization of the museum staff, as well as the institutions' somewhat desultory approach to African natural history.

An American Museum's Africa

Carl Akeley's dire predictions of game depletion in Africa underscored his affiliation with the AMNH and served to shape the museum's primary mission in Africa. With three major expeditions to his credit, Akeley began to view himself as a preeminent spokesman on African zoology. No one could doubt that he had in fact experienced more of Africa than many of his peers working in either museum exhibition or taxidermy. Despite Akeley's familiarity with the continent, the museum world considered him an upstart. When Akeley submitted his plan for an African Hall to the AMNH, the museum had only recently emerged as a major intellectual institution in America. It boasted some rare collections, but it had not yet reached the status of its European counterparts. Opened in 1869, the museum obtained its earliest acquisitions by purchasing established collections from European nobility. Slowly, the museum began to sponsor its own expeditions, primarily in North America and Asia. Not until 1908, under the presidency of Henry Fairfield Osborn, did the museum begin expanding its horizons through expeditions to Africa and South America. However, at the same time that the museum broadened its vision of the world, North American acquisitions took precedence as Franz Boas, noted anthropologist and assistant curator of anthropology, continued his quest to enlarge the museum's Native American collections.[36]

Akeley faced the difficult task of convincing a somewhat intractable board of trustees that Africa approximated (if not rivaled) North America in its importance to natural history. This was not an easy undertaking, as the closing of the frontier had renewed American interests in "noble savages" at home. It was evident that the Department of Anthropology (established in 1873) represented the future of the novice museum seeking to fix its place in the hierarchy of scientific institutions around the world. Akeley did not have to sell Africa to the trustees, as the museum had in its possession several African anthropological collections. Rather, he needed to persuade the board that the appropriate African natural history should focus primarily on zoology.[37]

Akeley resolved to secure the museum's commitment to creating "a great museum exhibit, artistically conceived, which should perpetuate the animal life, the native customs, and the scenic beauties of Africa." Although he had returned from Africa extolling the glories of African wildlife, he did not exclude anthropological matters in his initial plans for African Hall. What accounts for the museum's openness to refocusing its gaze on Africa principally through Akeley's zoological lens? Why did the museum gravitate toward Akeley's vision of a Brightest Africa, so much so that by 1911 it became the "chief aim of the Museum" to prepare and exhibit faunal specimens for his African Hall?[38]

An examination of the early history of the AMNH reveals that the museum had no comprehensive approach to representing Africa before 1911. The museum did not envision an African project to parallel the North American wing (the halls of North American mammals and cultures). In 1911, Robert Lowie remarked on the museum's recent acquisition of large ethnographic collections from the Congo: "a few years ago all the Museum's ethnological material from Africa could have been conveniently placed in a few cases." Lowie's quote read alongside Akeley's hall plans reveals that Africa had not been a priority for his department, nor had it been for the Department of Zoology. Lowie, with the help of Director Bumpus, had developed a small African Hall devoted to "African industry, art and tribal customs" in 1910. However, this hall did not expand as "the Museum entered the period in which its major exhibition efforts were directed towards the creation of large mammal dioramas," which included Akeley's project.[39] The events surrounding the proposal for Akeley's African Hall expose the tensions between the roles of zoology and anthropology in the museum's image of Africa. What emerged was a conviction held by both the museum and Akeley that public and popular images of Darkest Africa could foremost be challenged and dismissed by a hall where exhibits of wildlife would occupy center stage.

The founding of the AMNH coincided with tremendous transformations in American intellectual and cultural life. Officially, the museum opened in 1869, when the study of nature began branching out beyond the literate elite. As naturalism and natural history collecting became more popular, its practitioners sought a site that would both enhance and disseminate naturalist study. The old "cabinet of curios" style of natural history exhibit approximated hiding a treasure in a closet, undemocratically confining nature to a select group of viewers. Thus, the natural history museum in America emerged out of a desire to bring natural history to the people. However, the promulgation of natural history required funding and a place to house exhibits. Reflecting the Victorian impulse for order and the Gilded Age obsession with consumption, philanthropists began funding natural history museums as monuments for the urban landscape. The museums would contain every conceivable natural and cultural object, classified and exhibited in glass cases.[40]

The establishment of an urban natural history museum in the 1870s, however, required a careful navigation of the cultural and intellectual scene. Foremost, the museum had to establish its purpose and authority within the worlds of science and popular culture. At a time when universities grew at a rapid pace due to the Morrill Act of 1862, which increased the amount of state-funded colleges, museums vied for authority as spaces of intellectual production. They had to prove that the production of knowledge could occur in a public, civic-minded institution, just as it did in an Ivy League or land-grant college. Many museum advocates went so far as to claim the museum as the only true site for scientific research and production. Simultaneously, museum professionals targeted a public that they could mold into their image of modern enlightened Americans. The founders of the AMNH, to a great extent, adhered to this belief in the transformative power of the museum.[41]

The AMNH reflected founder Albert Bickmore's exposure to the Museum of Comparative Zoology at Harvard as a student of Louis Agassiz from 1861 to 1865. Bickmore marveled at the breadth of Agassiz's museum, but at the same time he imagined a museum broader in scope and, more important, accessible to the public. He, like many naturalists of the period, embraced the popularization of natural history as a means to detach it from the confines of the university and elite parlors. Bickmore arrived in New York in 1865 as part of an expeditionary staff bound for the Far East and Siberia. During his stay in the city, he met with Wall Street financier William Earl Dodge Jr., to whom he divulged his plans for building a great urban museum. First, however, he had to commit three years of his life to the expedition.[42]

Upon his return to New York in 1868, Bickmore met again with Dodge, whose commitment to the project had waned since their first meeting. Still interested in Bickmore's proposal, Dodge sent him to meet with Theodore Roosevelt Sr., who subsequently introduced him to the men who would comprise part of the first Board of Trustees of the AMNH. The list of the founders and board is a testament to New York urban culture. For example, soap magnate Robert Colgate and department store entrepreneur Alexander T. Steward reflected the culture of consumption in the city that centered on the preoccupation with health and beauty and the convenience of purchasing ready-made items. In terms of the financial district, bankers Morris K. Jesup and J. P. Morton Choate mirrored the growth of big business in urban America. Lawyer Joseph H. Choate was part of the expanding white middle class composed of white-collar workers and professionals who lived in the suburbs and wealthier sections of the city. The only man who stood out on this roster was Robert L. Stuart, a sugar refiner, who listed his interests as natural history and "illustrated travel." The remaining members of the museum's administration were well-known socialites—wealthy men who viewed themselves as custodians of the growing metropolis. A fledgling institution, the AMNH developed into one of the most important natural history institutions in the United States, in part because of the tenacity of the board of trustees.[43]

In many ways the acquisitions of the museum reflected the interests of the trustees. They allocated funding for exhibits and expeditions according to their desires. In some cases they even donated their personal collections, which served as the bases for developing a particular department. For example, D. Jackson Steward donated his collection of shells, described as "one of the rarest and largest... in the world," to the AMNH during his tenure as the museum's second vice president.⁴⁴ Many of the trustees had no or few African collections, thus (in part) explaining the relative absence of African objects in the museum's early history when compared to North American accessions.

When Akeley proposed the elephant-collecting expedition to BEA, the museum's African collection contained limited ethnographic specimens. The earliest African acquisitions dated back to 1869, the founding year of the museum. However, the materials amassed in subsequent years lacked cohesion. In 1894, the museum combined the departments of archeology and ethnology under the already established Department of Anthropology. In 1895, the museum appointed Frederick Ward Putnam (a specialist in North American archeology) administrator, and he rather arbitrarily began incorporating existent and newly acquired African accessions into this new conglomerate.⁴⁵

In 1902, the museum received several woodcarvings, which constituted the Western African Raff Collection. The following year, the museum acquired the Bowdoin Collection, composed of "implements of warfare, idols, fetiches [sic], and masks, clothing, baskets, and musical instruments, household utensils of bamboo, ornaments of beads, shell, and brass, and seven carved ivory tusks." In 1907, the Belgian government presented the museum with similar items from the Congo Free State. That same year, Percy R. Pyne, Cleveland H. Dodge, and Arthur Curtiss James donated five thousand ethnographic specimens, collected by Richard Douglas from the British South African region. Also in that year, Richard Tjäder collected two hundred specimens from BEA. Bronzes (actually brass), carved ivory tusks, and ornaments from the Benin Kingdom (acquired during the British punitive expedition of 1896) presented by Archer M. Huntington rounded out the African acquisitions. Among them, only two resulted from organized expeditions. African archeology collections included "flaked material" from Mediterranean Africa, flints from the Fayum Desert, and Stone-Aged implements from Somaliland. Patrons donated the remaining African collections, reflecting the fact that the museum had neither a curator of African ethnography nor showed any interest in the systematic development of a major African collection. The curators, nevertheless, seemed to display a keen interest in African material culture, particularly those relating to technological advancements.⁴⁶

The museum considered the Douglas African Collection of "particular importance" not only because of the variety and amount of material it contained but also because, until the collection's acquisition, the museum had in its possession "few and only isolated specimens from the Dark Continent." The ethnological collection came mainly from south central Africa. Douglas, himself a resident of South Africa for twenty years, collected the material primarily from Barotseland (or the Barotse kingdom). The kingdom, ruled by King Lewanika, was a protectorate of the British Empire. Supposedly, Douglas enjoyed a special relationship with the ruler and the British government, which allowed him to secure artifacts from the region rather easily. The Douglas collection included hoes, baskets, pottery, gourds, "wooden ware," stools, and "knob-sticks." According to museum official Clark Wissler, the collection was "a good beginning toward an African hall in which will be shown the original culture of the great Negro branch of the human family."[47] However, that beginning was stunted by the museum's overwhelming support for Akeley's project.

Akeley's first safari for the AMNH was among four expeditions that embodied the museum's first financial commitment to natural history collecting in Africa. The trustees appropriated $55,000 for the collection of specimens that would "secure the fast vanishing forms of that continent before it becomes too late." Of the four expeditions, three began before Akeley's proposal for African Hall. The museum later incorporated the Tjäder Expedition (begun in 1906), the Fayum Expedition (also begun in 1906), and the Congo Expedition into the collecting activities for the "new African Hall" in 1911. While naturalists and hunters conducted these expeditions, the museum purchased or contemplated buying "several valuable ethnological and zoölogical collections."[48]

The Tjäder Expedition (also called the Tjäder East Africa Expedition), conducted by hunter Richard Tjäder with the help of Herbert Lang, aimed to collect "fine specimens of large mammals." Philanthropist Samuel Thorne principally funded the trip. This safari marked the museum's first commitment to secure African mammal skins directly from Africa. Those African fauna specimens already in the museum vaults were trophies donated to the museum by a patron, purchased from a natural history dealer, or obtained through the exchange system from another natural history museum. For the first time, the museum approached its natural history inquiry of Africa to zoology in a more empirical manner. The Tjäder collection numbered 205 specimens, representing 56 species, predominantly mammalian, including the much-in-demand antelopes and giraffes. The museum determined that the material collected by Tjäder supplied "exceptionally fine material of species which [had] hitherto been wholly lacking in the Museum collections." This statement is revealing since the preponderance of the zoological specimens at the institution came from the Americas.[49]

Despite the zoological focus of the expedition, Tjäder collected some "ethnological material." Although the museum's published report of the expedition did not say much about the value of the materials, some listed items are worth mentioning as they reflect interest in the everyday life of Africans—and not solely their relationship to the animal kingdom. The ethnographic items included "charms, ornaments, weapons, cooking utensils" and "long battle spears, ugly arrows bearing rows of jagged points and slender clubs with egg-shaped stone heads" illustrating "how the tribesmen contend with their enemies or attack wild animals." More than likely, the museum housed these items in the African Hall of ethnology.[50]

Unlike the Tjäder and Congo expeditions, the Fayum Expedition did not focus on zoological collecting or engage in ethnographic gathering. This trip was in effect a fossil hunt. Paleontology at the museum had become a focal point of collecting, especially after the appointment of the paleontologist Osborn. Yet, like most of the collecting engaged in by museum personnel, excavations in the Americas assumed priority. However, a series of paleontology discoveries in northern Egypt by Hugh J. L. Beadnell of the Egyptian Geological Survey and Charles W. Andrews of the British Museum between 1902 and 1905 shifted the inquiry of many paleontologists to the Fayum. The Fayum is an ancient depression near the Nile River transformed into a lake during the Pleistocene. Andrews and Beadnell posited the region as the key to the origin and evolution of four groups of mammals whose early history remained obscure. Osborn theorized in 1900 that antecedents of the forms that existed in North America would be discovered in Africa. The animals were of a "peculiar interest" for the department of vertebrate paleontology, rich in specimens from the American "phases" as it "was obviously desirable to trace the ancestry [of them] back to the earliest known stages."[51] Osborn's hypothesis reflected scientific discourses that posited Africa as the lasting remnant of earth's primordial past. In many ways the interest in African paleontology further served to present Africa as an unpopulated region. Excluding humans from the image of Africa coincided with Osborn's scientific agenda.

With the blessings of the museum's president, Morris K. Jesup, and President Teddy Roosevelt, Osborn traveled to Egypt with his assistants Walter Granger and George Olsen. For the first time, the Fayum—previously dominated by European scientists and museum collectors—opened to American researchers. Yet as Osborn and his team excavated in the area, he lamented, "The halcyon days of easy collecting have passed, just as they have passed in our western tertiaries [*sic*]." Nevertheless, he hoped that "not only a representative collections of these very important mammals may be secured, but considerable additions may be made to our knowledge, especially of the smaller mammals of the Upper Eocene period in Northern Africa." The Osborn collection consisted of about 500 to 550 specimens of more or less complete remains of prehistoric fauna.[52]

Like Akeley, Osborn viewed parts of the African continent as keys to a lost past of faunal life, as evidenced by his conviction that the Fayum depression held the key to the zoological origins of North American mammals. Both men also realized that collecting in Africa would become increasingly difficult as more explorers traversed the continent and as "civilization" encroached on research areas. However, Osborn and Akeley differed in their views of Africa, in their respective work, and in their positioning of Africa in the overall scope of their fields. For Akeley, Africa possessed the key to unlocking the secrets of zoology, because the rarest species of animals dwelled there. In contrast, Africa was a mere footnote in Osborn's paleontology research. Osborn devoted most of his time to excavations in North America.[53]

The expeditions conducted under Osborn, Tjäder, and Lang examined together reveal that the museum approached African research from three major disciplines or directions—ethnology or anthropology, paleontology, and zoology. Yet it is clear that ethnological research was most central to the museum's image of Africa, despite its at times sporadic and unsystematic presentation. The creation of the African Hall of ethnology constituted a watershed in focusing the museum's research agenda on Africa. Despite the existence of a substantial Congo collection and pleas from Lowie to expand African accessions, the museum pushed African anthropology into the background behind Akeley's African Hall. Images of large mammals on exhibit beyond what would become the Roosevelt Rotunda captured the imagination and coffers of the museum, as Akeley presented to the board of trustees his monument to a dying continent.

Akeley's tumultuous years in Africa trying to secure specimens for the elephant group left him unnerved. His ordeal of hunting the bull elephant convinced him that Africa's large mammals faced imminent annihilation. As he returned to America in 1911 with elephant skins in hand, he pondered the relative scarcity of fauna he encountered in comparison to his earlier trips to Africa. Akeley found little comfort in his animal trophies, even though his wife secured a much coveted male elephant. The elephant group alone was not a substantial monument to a fading continent. He remained "aware of the rapid and disconcerting disappearance of African wildlife." This awareness coupled with the slow progress of museum taxidermy "gave rise to the vision of the culmination of [his] work in a great museum exhibit."[54]

Akeley began "dreaming of African Hall" in 1911 as "a great museum exhibit, artistically conceived" that would "perpetuate the animal life, the native customs, and scenic beauties of Africa." He wrote: "When I got back from Africa in 1911 I was dreaming of a great African Hall which would combine all the advances that had been made in taxidermy and the arts of museum exhibition and at the same time would make a permanent record of the fast-disappearing wildlife of that most interesting animal kingdom, Africa."[55] In 1912, Akeley presented his preliminary plans for the hall to Osborn. Attempting to convince the museum of the urgency and timeliness of his project, Akeley stated: "I feel that immediate and aggressive action is necessary. Africa has changed rapidly in the past twenty-five years and is changing even more rapidly as time goes on. The men who knew Africa twenty-five years ago have a good conception of Africa before the invasion of modern civilization; and those men are growing old and few. The men who can do the African Hall as originally planned are here now—but ten years from now it will be too late." Akeley's prospectus impressed Osborn, who subsequently requested that it be submitted to the board of trustees. Several trustees financially supported Akeley's Elephant Group Exhibition and thus appeared predisposed to approving his project. Moreover, ethnological and zoological acquisitions from Africa had increased over the years due to the Fayum, Tjäder, and Lang-Chapin (Congo) expeditions, which signaled an increased dedication to African research, as well as to the existent African Hall. Akeley assured the trustees that nothing on the scale of his proposed hall and organized according to his methodology had yet been attempted by premier museums throughout the Western world. Yet funding concerned the trustees, as well as the lack of qualified personnel required to carry out Akeley's ambitious plan. Akeley initially estimated that the project would cost half a million dollars; he revised that estimate to one million dollars after World War I. However, the trustees enthusiastically received Akeley's plans, hoping to secure the AMNH's place in the museum world with an unprecedented African exhibit. They approved Akeley's plan that same year.[56]

In 1913, the museum loaned Akeley a hall, which had previously been the North American mammals' hall, to serve as his "elephant studio." There he continued the mounting of the elephant group. While in the studio, Akeley constructed a model of the African Hall. His prospectus included "sketch models of the proposed groups ... models of cases ... methods of lighting exhibits," and a system for regulating the humidity of the hall. Akeley recommended that the museum make no attempts to secure further African material "except such as may be secured without cost or under especially advantageous conditions or material that because of rarity or danger of exterminating may be lost through delay." Akeley feared that the museum would begin to accept gifts from donors or sponsor expeditions without regard to the enormous amount of time required to preserve specimens. His worst fears appeared to be that skins would deteriorate or that the museum would pay a hefty sum to acquire already mounted specimens. Clearly, Akeley saw the hall as his project, and he assured President Osborn that once the trustees officially adopted the plans for the hall and secured funding for the expeditions, he would "assume full authority and responsibility" for the exhibit. Moreover, Akeley promised that at the point of adoption he would "devote all [his] time and energy to the vigorous prosecution of the work."[57]

The four elephants that Akeley so diligently worked on that year would sit in the center of the African Hall, with rhinoceros groups—one black, one white—at each end (north and south). The ground floor and the gallery would have various African faunal groups, complete with painted landscapes and "typical accessories." In his proposal to the trustees, Akeley emphasized that the hall would be "devoted entirely to Africa" and would contain exhibits of "fast-disappearing fauna and give a comprehensive view of the topography of the continent." This would be achieved through the construction of habitat groups using "the best museum technique."[58]

In sketching out the plan for the hall, Akeley did not limit his commentary to floor dimensions and museum displays. He related every corner of the future hall to a certain vision or impression that he intended the viewer to receive of Africa. He also discussed the role of museum personnel (at home and abroad) in furthering the mission of the project. Akeley reasoned that it would be through the eyes of the director and his personnel that the visitor would see Africa. Forty groups in total—twenty large "panoramic" mammal groups—would occupy the main floor, and twenty smaller groups would compose the gallery. Artists would paint forty canvases to serve as backgrounds for each group. The treasured elephants would form the centerpiece of the hall and would be flanked by other mammal groups. Two life-size bronze figures of Africans would be on either side of the elephant group, near the rhino groups. Nothing else would crowd the 60 x 120 foot space of the main room "except comfortable seats where the visitor may sit and look out as through a window onto a scene in Africa, a scene showing a group of one or more of the animals of the continent in their natural environment of forest, plain, river or mountain surroundings."[59]

The forty canvases would depict the topography of Africa from the Cape to Cairo and from the Atlantic to the Indian Ocean. These paintings of "artistic beauty" were to be "an accurate study of a definitive type of African scenery usually showing features of importance" (for example, Mount Kenya, Table Top Mountain, the pyramids of Egypt, and so forth). Four of the forty canvases were meant to "present the four important physical features of African game country." One canvas would correspond to the habitat group devoted to the Tana River region in equatorial Africa. Flora and fauna would be equally represented, with hippopotamuses, impala, monkeys, crocodiles, turtles, birds, and trees filling the landscape "consistent with scientific fact." A second group and canvas would depict a plains scene, with klipspringer, hyrax, reedbuck, and baboons. A third would represent the Congo forest, featuring okapi and chimpanzees. A fourth would represent the desert with a water hole scene. A giraffe would drink at the hole, while other animals stood by, waiting for their turn.[60]

The hall would be decorated with bronze panels showing "the relationship between the natives of Africa and the animal life." Again, although the plans called for both zoological and ethnological study, it was clear that "telling a story of the lives of the people" meant telling narratives of Africans in their encounters with wildlife. Akeley's conceptualization of the relevance of Africans to his monument to disappearing Africa was a radical departure from that of ethnographic collections and the emerging "social anthropology."[61] Africans would not be shown preparing meals, weaving, dancing, or participating in religious ceremonies. Nor would African material culture (artifacts and arts) emblematic of old-style ethnography be displayed in the hall. In a manner reminiscent of Lang's *Pygmy Group*, Africans would be shown interacting with animals. However, that is where the similarity ended. Akeley's panels would not illustrate family life and structure or discuss racial characteristics; rather, they would show Africans as extensions of the animal kingdom.

The highlighted elephant group would be accompanied by "correlated bronze miniature groups," which would illustrate "the massing of the animals in herds and other features of the story of the African elephant and its relation to the country and to the natives." The two life-size sculptures flanking the elephant group and the six-by-eleven-foot panels would be the only representations of human life on the continent. The panels themselves would serve as the actual frieze of the hall. The proposed panels included a Dorobo family, featuring the father skinning an antelope while his wife and children waited with two hunting dogs; Somalis at a water hole with their domesticated animals; and Migdans engaging in a hunt. Akeley emphasized that although these panels would be accurate from the standpoint of ethnography, "the theme running through the whole series should be the relationship of people to animal life." A systematic ethnological analysis of African cultures had no place in Akeley's hall. Unlike the old African Hall, the new African Hall would be primarily a zoological project, as evidenced by Akeley's descriptions. The old ethnology hall contained faunal mountings, and ethnographic collections stood as the focal point of the exhibit; Akeley's hall would exhibit the reverse. However, achieving the balance that Akeley sought in his hall required dedicated fieldwork, which he anticipated would last some ten years in Africa.[62]

Akeley's vision of the African Hall reveals how naturalist-environmentalist perceptions of the continent often subordinated human life to the wildlife and flora. That the depictions of Africans would be peripheral to the animal exhibits indicates that Akeley did not want to exclude people but saw the true beauty of the continent in its nature. Arguably, as a zoological exhibit, African Hall and the dioramas had no place for Africans. However, Akeley's decision to include Africans and subsequent struggle over where to insert them in his narrative reveal the complicated terrain on which naturalists imagined a bright Africa.

The fieldwork for the hall would essentially be a "survey of the continent" from four major directions. Thus, the director of the hall would "be practically resident in Africa," where he would direct the fieldwork, plan the groups, select the locations depicted in the dioramas, and study the life histories of the fauna to be exhibited. A "small force of men" including a painter and a sculptor taxidermist would travel with the director to the research site to "make studies of the background" and "secure and prepare the specimens and accessories." After completing these tasks, the men would return to New York with the material for the exhibits and work on them "while the material [was] fresh and their minds clear as to the results" to be achieved in the dioramas. A second team, similar to the first, would join the director at another safari site in Africa and repeat the process. Because of the enormity of the tasks before them, Akeley argued that the men chosen to accompany him would have to possess "energy, common sense, a special ability, and a great love for the duties at hand." In essence, they had to have a "faultless knowledge of taxidermy, landscape painting," and the techniques of the "new zoological exhibits." More important, they had to know how to shoot in cases of emergency. Thus, most men "carefully chosen" had to be both taxidermist or painter and hunter.[63]

Overwhelmingly, those people chosen to lead or participate in the African Hall expeditions were transplanted country folk—men and women who grew up in rural areas and migrated to the cities during the later decades of the nineteenth century. Although Akeley viewed his "force" as male, in reality over six women and one "girl child" would travel to Africa to help secure specimens for the African Hall. Others members of the expedition parties emigrated from Europe to New York to take part in the intellectual culture of the times. Still others grew up in New York City, connected to many of the metropolis's prominent middle-class and upper-class families. These city dwellers—men and women who navigated the intellectual and culture life of the metropolis—included the hall's directors, curators, associates, and a forty-five-member staff. However, the bulk of their work could not begin until the war's end.[64] The faunal specimens procured by Lang, Chapin, and Akeley from 1905 to 1910 represented a significant portion of the Congo and East African landscapes. However, to achieve Akeley's panoramic continental view of Africa, the museum had to secure zoological samples from southern, northern, and eastern Africa, areas colonized by European powers at war that could not spare Africans to serve as safari porters and *askaris*.

Akeley and his staff resumed work on the hall in 1920. In the interim, on January 6, 1919, Teddy Roosevelt had died of heart failure. The AMNH trustees and personnel responded to Roosevelt's death with private and public lamentations. Akeley wrote a brief article in the museum's journal *Natural History* in which he recalled the elephant hunt in BEA. He professed his love for the former president and hailed his influence beyond the grave. Akeley asserted, "Perhaps no man in modern times has gotten so much out of the Dark Continent as did Roosevelt." In the article, he quoted extensively from the foreword of Roosevelt's *African Game Trails* and expressed his wish to build the hall as a memorial to Roosevelt. The entrance to the newly named Roosevelt African Hall would have a bronze tablet engraved with the foreword of *African Game Trails*.[65]

The death of Roosevelt renewed Akeley's commitment to complete the hall as well as his sense of a vanishing Africa. He warned the museum that the African Hall could not be delayed and must "become a reality." He noted several obstacles to successfully completing the hall despite postwar innovations in taxidermy and museum exhibition techniques. First, Akeley claimed that the "innumerable specimens" of mammals that hunters could find on the continent twenty-five years before the war were disappearing. Second, men who had at least a quarter-century of experience with Africa were also scarce. Relying on untried men to travel to Africa would never do. Third, European colonialism continued to "civilize" the continent, so that "modern Africa, the Africa of the Age of Man" was slowly destroying "Africa of the Age of Mammals."[66]

The commitment to create the African Hall brought many people from diverse backgrounds together under the auspices of the AMNH. These men and women would travel to Africa and secure specimens with gun, camera, paint, and easel. Children of the Gilded Age, these individuals grew up listening to Roosevelt's doctrine of the "strenuous life," his pleas against race suicide, and his castigation of "nature fakers." They embraced naturalism and all the glories associated with a communion with nature, as their former president had. Thus, traveling to Africa for the museum was not only scientific work but also an adventure of renewal—an escape from the cloying atmosphere of city life and a return to nature. Characterizing this work that would serve as a tribute to "Teddy," Akeley wrote: "I have dreamt many dreams. Some of them have been forgotten. Others have taken concrete shape and become pleasing or hateful to me in varying degree. But one especially has dwelt with me through the years, gradually shaping itself into a commanding plan. It has become the inspiration and the unifying purpose of my work; all my efforts during recent years have bent toward the accomplishment of this single objective—the creation of a great African Hall which shall be called Roosevelt African Hall."[67]

For Akeley, achieving his dream demanded extensive expeditions in Africa, several which would continue or commence after his death. The Eastman-Pomeroy-Akeley Expedition (1926) acquired the waterhole, buffalo, klipspringer, Serengeti Plain, greater kudu, and bongo groups and allowed the museum's landscape artists to complete the background paintings for the hall. The Sanford-Legendre Abyssinia Expedition (1929) secured the *Nyala Group*, the Vernay-Lang Kalahari Expedition (1930) the giant sable and gemsbok groups, and the O'Donnell-Clark African Expedition (1931) various smaller groups. While these expeditions proved invaluable to the completion of African Hall, the Akeley African Expedition to the Belgian Congo (1921–1922) to obtain specimens for the *Gorilla Group* proved unique, as it completed Akeley's and his colleagues' transformation from zoologists and taxidermists to naturalist-environmentalists. This safari led to the establishment of Parc National Albert and in the process provided a living site for the preservation of Akeley's Brightest Africa, inspiring other Americans to support conservationism in Africa. Moreover, the gorilla hunt and sanctuary became symbols of Africa's importance to uncovering the evolution of man.

Gorilla Trails in Paradise

In July 1921, the AMNH approved the expedition to the Belgian Congo to collect gorillas. According to Akeley, the trip from Cape Town to Kivu would take six weeks and leave the party at "the cloud-wrapped peaks of Mikeno and Karisimbi," the "distant gorilla heights." In his recollections of the journey, Akeley noted that he did not see "a single head of game" on the entire railroad journey from to Bukama, the last railroad stop before continuing on to Kivu. "So rapidly," he remarked "has African wild life disappeared in the south." After securing a barge at Bukama, Akeley was relieved to see bird life "in great profusion," a "few crocodiles," and occasionally a hippopotamus or elephant. These sightings, however, did not dissuade his conviction that Africa was disappearing.[68]

Upon arrival at the White Friars' Mission, a Catholic outpost in Usumbura (present-day Bujumbura in Burundi), Akeley heard tales of a gorilla killed nearby. Apparently, the animal had ravaged a banana grove owned by the regional chief, who subsequently sent men after it. Unfortunately, one of his trusty subjects fell victim to the gorilla. Enraged, the chief ordered the men to kill the gorilla with their spears. In his recollection of this story, Akeley questioned the "veracity of this tale" of men armed with sticks chasing a gorilla and discounted the ferocity of the animal offender. He also showed little concern for the life of the African man, as he remarked that the chief underestimated the ape's harmlessness. More important, the tale signaled that the safari party was "getting into the real gorilla country" and this pleased Akeley tremendously. The knowledge that they were getting close to the animal "quickened the blood," as this mission represented "that last word in African adventure."[69]

At Gisenyi, the Akeley party met the wife of T. Alexander Barnes, a hunter collecting gorillas for the British Museum. There, the men left the women as they "push[ed] on into gorilla country." Akeley left with 30 of the 170 porters to secure the first moving pictures of gorillas in their natural habitat. En route, Akeley came upon another mission in Lulenga (present-day Bena-Lulenga in the Democratic Republic of Congo), where he learned that the prince of Sweden had used that very area as a base for his gorilla expedition. Akeley was both "nervous and anxious" about the prospect of seeing a gorilla as he traversed the landscape that reminded him of past adventures on Mount Kenya. Monotonous treks across walking paths and game trails gave way to the moment of splendor when Akeley saw his first gorilla track. He remembered:

> I'll never forget it. In that mud hole were the marks of four great knuckles where the gorilla had placed his hand on the ground. There is no other track like this on earth—there is no other hand in the world so large. . . . As I looked at that track I lost the faith on which I had brought my party to Africa. Instinctively I took my gun from the boy. I knew then the feeling Du Chaillu described in his quaint phrase, "My feelings were really excited to a painful degree." I had more thrill from the sight of this first track than from anything that happened later.

Akeley's companions, Mary and Herbert Bradley, similarly recollected their first sight of gorilla prints. On this occasion, Mary Bradley joined her husband in the hunt. Upon hearing their guide refer to the prints as "big, big," she called the news "stirring" and set out to follow the tracks. She wrote: "We followed with a feeling of tremendous exhilaration. It was the actual mark of the great beast we had come so far to see; he was there somewhere ahead of us, hidden in a turning of the green thicket—any moment a parting of the leaves might show us his black, twitching face and sparkling eyes."[70]

Akeley's fervor dampened as the realities of safari returned full force. He had no knowledge of the area that he desired to explore and, thus, was at the mercy of guides. At one point, Akeley offered the "useless" and "lackadaisical" guides "a king's ransom" to take him to see the "old Boy" before dark. Akeley found himself engaging a sultan, who sent "two splendid fellows" to guide him into Mount Mikeno. Despite his enthusiasm at finding two reliable scouts, Akeley remained restless and impatient. When the guides appeared before him the next day, he forced himself to trust them as they led him to the gorilla.[71]

Akeley's recollection of his first sighting of a wild gorilla (he had seen one in captivity at a London zoological garden) echoed the euphoria that surrounded his first encounter with wild elephants. Culminating years of effort to secure specimens of vanishing Africa, this event seemed to transport Akeley into a trancelike state, even as he reached for the gun (or camera) to shoot the object of his adoration. In poetic and reverent language he described his first glimpse of a wild gorilla. He wrote: "It has left an everlasting impression, for it was so totally different from anything I had expected. In a solid wall of vivid green a great scraggly black head rose slowly into view where it remained motionless for perhaps half a minute, giving me time to view it with field glasses so that I was able to make out the features. I was actually seeing a live wild gorilla. At the end of a long journey I was face to face with the creature I sought. I took the gun."[72]

Akeley's gorilla hunt was arduous. At first glance, his narrative of the gorilla killings seems straightforward. A great white hunter surrounded by "forty odd" hands and guides endured unseen dangers to secure specimens for a museum. However, it bears noting that Akeley began his narrative by reviewing all the false notions people held about the gorilla, particularly its viciousness. He observed that "this reputation is so firmly established in the popular mind" that his and Herbert Bradley's decision to take women and a female child to Central Africa "was looked upon as madness." To rid his mind of these popular myths, Akeley fashioned a mantra to recite before he set out on the hunt: "I believe that the gorilla is normally a perfectly amiable creature. I believe that if he attacks man it is because he is being attacked or thinks he is being attacked. I believe that he will fight in self-defense and probably in defense of his family."[73] According to Akeley, the male gorilla behaves like any human male would. In evolutionary terms, he believed the human male inherited the gorilla's masculine impulse to protect.

Akeley's audience did not necessarily understand or know the emotive qualities of gorillas. More important, Akeley offered no scientific evidence of the complex emotional lives of primates as evinced in his reliance on safarilike encounters with the animals to describe their behaviors. Akeley had yet to observe systematically the gorilla outside the hunt—that is, as anything other than prey. Thus, his description of gorilla behavior in his creed was a well-crafted fiction, a deliberate equating of gorilla with man to illicit sympathy and a sense of familiarity from his readers. Yet it is not simply the stated creed or the detached descriptions of evisceration that unmask Akeley's revisioning of the image of the gorilla. Rather, the humanlike characteristics that he imparted to the primates as he stalked them, killed them, and prepared their death masks disclosed his desire to solidify the humanness of the gorillas.

In "Adventures on Mt. Mikeno," Akeley humanized the gorillas he shot, particularly "the old black female" and her son. By referring to the female gorilla as an "old black female," Akeley may have been playing on images of the "mammy" that popular culture often troped in precisely those terms. Also, for the first time in his recollection of gorilla hunting, Akeley designated his guides "Negroes" (an American term for blacks) instead of boys or Africans. Akeley employed a more precise language to avoid confusing the reader, suggesting a confluence of his earlier descriptions of Africans and gorillas. In this retelling, Akeley also put on the mantle of "savage" and "aggressor" as he recalled shooting the female and her offspring. The latter ran away, only to be located thirty minutes later, running about until speared by a guide. As Akeley looked down upon the infant gorilla's dying face he saw "a heartbreaking expression of piteous pleading" and reasoned that had the infant been able, he would have "come to [his human] arms for comfort." Here the prey ceased to be an object of science but rather a mother and a son brutally killed by savage men (Akeley and the guide). Akeley reaffirmed the remorse clearly shown here after he shot another female gorilla mistaken for an immature male. However, he consoled himself by reverting to scientific jargon to avoid guilt. The knowledge that the female was a "splendid large specimen" absolved him of murder despite his observation that the mother gorilla left a baby "crying piteously" but unscathed.[74] In his description of his gorilla encounters, Akeley endowed the gorillas with features and emotions reminiscent of human family interactions to reinforce notions of human-gorilla similarity.

The making of the death masks for the gorillas also contributed to the humanization of the gorilla family. Dating back to antiquity, death masks were literally impressions taken of the faces of the deceased, often in an attempt to secure the appearance at the last breath. The death mask had mystical qualities, capturing for posterity the imprint of death upon one's countenance. Cultures designed this ritual for humans as part of the rite of passage of dying and transition. Akeley's decision to create death masks of the gorillas symbolized an initiation of them into the human family and into a cultural practice that had been reserved for man. While the death masks may have been used for scientific research in comparative anatomy, there is little evidence to suggest that this was Akeley's purpose; he did not make masks of any other faunal specimens collected while on safari.

After completing the masks, Akeley sojourned in the forests of Mount Mikeno, where he secured four more gorilla specimens and shot some three hundred feet of motion pictures of lone gorillas and gorilla bands. Traveling up the slopes of Mount Karisimbi, the entire safari party came upon "a magic spot" where the group spotted "a male gorilla in his savage haunts." The lone male did not afford Akeley and Herbert Bradley the opportunity to "defend the ladies heroically from threatened death," to perform feats of masculine prowess. Rather, as if to confirm Akeley's creed, the animal with "huge, uncouth, slouching shoulders" remained motionless as Bradley shot him in the neck. But when the gorilla proved still to be alive and ran off, Bradley shot him again, killing him.[75]

Akeley's recounting of Bradley's killing of the ape upheld the image of the gorilla as the noble king of the jungle. Akeley commented that the animal had shown no sign of aggression; it just sought to escape and made no sound as the men gunned it down. He lamented that "it took all one's scientific ardour to keep from feeling like a murderer."[76] Akeley's use of the term "murder" is important here, as only humans could be victims of murder, as understood by Americans. Great white hunters customarily did not refer to the killing of animals or faunal specimens while on safari as murder. Yet, Akeley viewed the act of slaying a gorilla in these terms, even as he took solace in knowing that they killed for science rather than sport.

Mary Bradley also remembered seeing the gorilla being shot and it subsequently "plunging down the slope." She stated that she would "never forget the humanness of that black, upturned face." The gorilla's face concealed no ferocity, as its "normal expression was of a curiously mild and patriarchal dignity." The animal only seemed vicious when its mouth was open. Decrying any sentimentality, Bradley wrote, "You could see in that face a gleam of patient and tragic surmise, as if the old fellow had a prescience that something was happening in the world against which his strength was of no avail—as if he knew the security of his high place was gone." She mused that the animal had "been indeed the King of the African forests," capable of crushing or strangling a lion or capturing an elephant. Unlike Akeley, Bradley indulged in flights of fancy, seeing the gorilla as it had been in the public mind—a beast capable of unfathomable violence.[77] More noteworthy, not only did she anthropomorphize the ape, but Bradley also bolstered the image of the gorilla as the masculine progenitor who knew he must step aside for man to assume his right/rite of having dominion over the animals.

The lone male gorilla shot for the exhibit, dubbed Uncle Africanus.
Neg./Transparency no. 315078, courtesy the Library, American Museum of Natural History.

During the day, the men worked on preserving the gorilla for the museum. Later that evening, in a moment of curiosity, the *wazungu* (whites) of the safari party sought communion with the dead gorilla. In an exercise of quasi-cannibalism—for in their minds the gorilla was a long lost relative, or at best a cousin to the "savage" African—they cooked the meat and ate a little, finding it "firm and sweet." Mary Bradley noted that she "couldn't get over the family feeling of sampling grand-uncle Africanus" as they feasted in ritual over the body of their "primitive cousin," the evolutionary father figure.[78] It is worth noting that they did not sample the mother, as in the Freudian family romance, it is the body of the father/male figure that is cannibalized. Interestingly, the African porters refused to eat the meat. (As many of the porters were Muslims, it is possible that they refused to eat the meat on religious grounds.) In her narrative, Bradley reveals that the racial assignments had been reversed. The stereotypical cannibalistic Africans—images of whom propped up the colonial project and legitimized Belgian empire building in the Congo—expressed repulsion at the prospect of eating the ape, while the civilized whites appeared nonplussed.

As if taking in the enormity of eating Uncle Africanus, members of the safari party contemplated their role in hunting gorillas. Reminiscent of the colonial/imperial enterprise, they justified their shooting of five gorillas for science as destruction in the name of improvement. As Europeans destroyed the Congo rainforests to ship rubber to the West to support industrialization, they killed apes to produce scientific knowledge about the gorilla and its relationship to human evolution. These were necessary evils. Yet Akeley rejoiced at seeing other gorillas escape, "none the worse for having met with white men." And Mary Bradley proclaimed, "There is no reason for keeping the gorilla on the game lists." She argued that it was too "valuable" and "rare" to be hunted and killed. She called for the creation of gorilla preserves and official (that is, colonial) protection of the gorilla, so that it would not "go the way that so many great beasts have gone—the way that all are going fast now in Africa." After estimating that Mounts Mikeno and Karisimbi might contain seventy-five to one hundred gorillas, Akeley, like Bradley, imagined a vanishing Africa. The gorilla had become a symbol of a bygone age in Africa, a tangible link to man's primordial past. With a heavy heart and a full bag of specimens, the group departed for the White Friar's Mission, knowing that the taxidermy performed on these skins could neither capture the true beauty of the gorilla and Africa nor preserve them for future generations.[79]

The meditations of Akeley and the Bradleys while on safari underscored Akeley's campaign to create a gorilla sanctuary in the Lake Kivu district. However, Akeley was not the first explorer to lobby the Belgians to create a national park in the Congo. In 1888, English explorer Major von Wissmann promoted the creation of a game reserve in equatorial Africa. At the turn of the century, like-minded preservationists convened in London at the International Conference for the Protection of Wild African Animals, where they took up Wissmann's idea. When Akeley returned to the states, he appointed himself the protector/savior of the vanishing gorilla. Through lectures and literary output, he cautioned a complacent America that the gorilla in Africa would go the way of the buffalo that once roamed the plains. He attempted to mobilize as many followers as possible by corresponding with noted scientists, intellectuals, and foreign dignitaries, employing the politics of preservation to reinforce imperialist rhetoric that presented the empire as benevolent protector.[80]

Akeley's terminology used to describe the place where his simian friends would thrive reflects the importance he assigned to the project. In one of his earliest correspondences regarding the gorilla sanctuary, Akeley termed the area a "reservation." While the British tended to use the term "animal preserves" and the Belgians "les réserves de chasse" (game reserve), Akeley's terminology betrayed his American sensibilities. During his lifetime, a reservation defined a place where the government placed Native Americans in an attempt to "protect" them from the onslaught of civilization. The reservation system rhetoric attempted to downplay the real politics behind its inception—to appropriate fertile land from native peoples under eminent domain and visions of Manifest Destiny. However, some white advocates of the reservation system did indeed view it as the only vehicle through which the dying cultures of Native Americans could be preserved and where tribes could live with some autonomy. In paternalist rhetoric, white Americans construed Native Americans as an endangered species, much like the buffalo of the Great Plains. Similarly, some Europeans in the early twentieth century argued for creating reserves for endangered tribes in Africa. Members of the Royal African Society and the Congo Reform Association advocated for the protection of the so-called Pygmies as deforestation in the rubber regions of the Congo River Basin and other imperial projects threatened to undermine their lifestyles.[81] In calling the gorilla preserve a reservation, Akeley made the American Indian tribe and the gorilla band interchangeable. His implications were clear. On a reservation, the primitive, be it man or animal, would be protected from and by the white man.

Akeley considered the reservation a sacred place, as he romanticized the refuge as the gorillas' "sanctuary for all times." The reservation would be a place of worship, where a biological research station would attract would-be congregants. The gorilla would be safe from white hunters. However, Akeley realized that such a place could not exist unless the colonial government of the region saw the imperative for protecting the gorilla. For millennia the gorilla endured, but now it faced extinction, according to Akeley. Ironically, he sought cooperation from the same government that issued thousands of hunting licenses to Europeans and Americans to hunt the gorilla and, thus, helped facilitate its threatened disappearance in less than a century.[82]

The Belgian government sympathized with Akeley's plan, for as early as 1901, it had issued a decree to regulate hunting in its African territories. King Leopold II began envisioning the creation of a national park modeled after Yellowstone National Park. However, only after the death of the king and the transfer of ownership of the Congo to the Belgian State did King Albert (after traveling to the Congo in 1909) recognize the necessity for creating reserves to protect flora and fauna. Unfortunately, the Great War prevented the prince from realizing his dream. After a trip to the United States in 1919 to visit American national parks, King Albert revived Leopold's plan to create a wildlife refuge in the Congo.[83] Thus, Akeley's desire to protect the gorillas of Kivu corresponded with a long-held desire of the Belgian royals—a desire that cast the monarchs (alive and postmortem) as benevolent imperialists in the eyes of the Western world.

Akeley still faced obstacles even after securing additional support from scientists, scientific institutions, and plenipotentiaries, including the AMNH, the National Geographic Society, Yale psychologist and National Research Council affiliate Robert Means Yerkes, Belgian Ambassador to the United States Baron de Cartier de Marchienne, and Belgium Consul James G. Whiteley. Setting aside valuable land in a colonial territory would require support from the Belgian elite and business community. Whiteley sent copies of Akeley's articles on the gorilla to government officials and personal friends. These men had to be convinced that it would be in the best interest of the empire to save the gorilla. As a result, Akeley's narratives of the gorilla expedition began to appear in more print media, including *The World's Work*, which claimed a wide readership in America and Europe. Eventually, his gorilla tales would be published in his book, *In Brightest Africa*. Revelations of slaughtering safaris (of course, not conducted by Akeley) and dire predictions of the disappearance of teeming bands of gorillas culminated in images of vulnerable, docile, family oriented primates preyed on by man. The haunting idea of seeing man's distant relative, a key to the missing link, obliterated by civilization validated the expensive undertaking to create a gorilla preserve.[84]

The frenzy to obtain a firm commitment to the gorilla sanctuary (as it was being called in late 1922) left a bitter taste in the mouths of many hunters and governments. Akeley's descriptions of indiscriminate killings of gorillas were met with acrimony and suspicion. In order for Akeley to advance his cause he had to furnish indisputable proof that the number of gorillas in the Kivu district was rapidly depleting and that greedy white hunters were at fault. In his plea for the primates, Akeley casually noted: "If being molested by man would make gorillas ferocious and aggressive, these animals should have been excessively dangerous, for within a very short time the Prince of Sweden had shot fourteen of them, and Barnes had killed several more. The very animals that I followed had probably heard the guns of these other men."[85] Noted popular magazines and science journals quoted Akeley's statements in articles, as well as his estimation that fifty to a hundred gorillas were left in the region. These publications elicited harsh retorts.

For example, the Swedish charged Akeley with being a hypocrite for criticizing the Swedes for collecting fourteen specimens and Barnes's shooting "several more" when he himself had shot five gorillas. Wils Glydenstople of the Royal Natural History Museum in Stockholm went to great pains to list the specimens collected and their subsequent use in the museum, as well as the Swedes' securing of the requisite rights and permissions to hunt in the Congo. He disparaged Akeley's statements as inaccurate and motivated by jealousy. Furthermore, he emphasized that they did not shoot in the same place as Akeley, Bradley, or Barnes. Therefore, if the number of gorillas dwindled, it was not on account of the prince—who, he added, incidentally shot only one of the fourteen specimens. This letter was the first of several to question the data on which Akeley built his case for a gorilla sanctuary. Never in the letter did Glydenstople dismiss the need for a reserve; rather, he refuted the claim that the prince participated in "slaughtering safaris" endangering African wildlife.[86]

Glydenstople's accusations of ulterior motives behind Akeley's comments on the prince did not appear to be far-fetched. In a confidential missive between Herbert Bradley and Akeley discussing selecting R. van Saceghem as a member of the commission to create the sanctuary, Bradley revealed his concern about a proposed gorilla expedition led by Edmund Heller and Alfred Collins for the Field Museum of Chicago. Bradley wrote:

> I haven't any complaint about museums obtaining gorillas and I don't think anything else in the world would ever compete with your group. I do however object to anybody getting any more gorillas from our sanctuary but the one thing that especially troubles me is the fact that this man Collins financing the expedition wants a gorilla for himself. Why in heavens name he should want a gorilla is beyond me, and personal[l]y, I would do anything I can to oppose his getting one for his private collection.

Bradley proposed "tipping off" Van Saceghem to deny Collins and Heller private permits for securing Congo gorillas for any private collection. He stated this before revealing that his own personal collection was complete in order to reassure Akeley that he would not be seeking any trophies should they return to Africa in 1924.[87] Whether or not jealousy motivated Bradley's concerns is debatable. Clearly, however, Bradley (and by implication Akeley) believed their gorilla group procured for the AMNH diorama was authoritative and unparalleled. Indeed, Akeley did not seek to secure a moratorium on the hunting of all gorillas, just those on Mounts Mikeno and Karisimbi.

As the Belgian government's decision to create a gorilla preserve gained international coverage, other nations seized on the opportunity to promote preservation of rare African fauna. The London *Times* published an article on the disappearance of the rare game in Africa and praised the British government and such groups as the Society for the Preservation of Fauna of the Empire for furthering game preservation. The paper also credited the British for initiating the movement to protect the gorilla. Upon reading the article, Akeley requested that Whiteley write a letter to the *Times* "so that the Englishmen will have the facts and not run away with the idea that they have done the whole trick," pledging to arm him with "a lot of facts" to include in the letter. This matter was crucial as the Belgian government had yet to state exactly what actions they would take on behalf of the gorilla sanctuary. Nevertheless, in a letter to the editor of the *Times*, Whiteley pictured the "sanctuary" as "a sort of Garden of Eden where animals [would] live in peace, amid their natural surroundings, without fear of man." More important, he confirmed that the idea for the sanctuary was first suggested by Akeley and that the plans for the preserve would be carried out in accordance with Akeley's wishes.[88]

Despite Whiteley's corrective letter, some hunters remained unconvinced by Akeley's prophecies of the probable extinction of the gorilla. In an article in the *African World*, Barnes called into question Akeley's "misstatements" about the numbers of gorillas on the Kivu district mountains. He disparaged Akeley's numbers as "nonsense" easily refuted by discussions with the White Friars at the French Mission. He argued that there were thousands of gorillas in the area and accused Akeley of "making a mountain out of a molehill in his campaign for the preservation of the gorillas." He stated that the Central African gorilla could be found in nearby Tanganyika and on the east bank of the Congo River. Yet Barnes carefully affirmed his agreement with the Belgian government to create a sanctuary, although he disagreed that shooting gorillas should be forbidden in the eastern Congo; he urged the government to allow hunters to shoot one or two gorillas per license.[89]

In a letter to de Cartier de Marchienne, Akeley denounced Barnes's statement as "absurd," citing his own sources on the scarcity of gorillas. He also weighed in on the Heller-Collins gorilla expedition, for which Barnes served as guide. According to the expedition's own findings, there were very few gorillas to secure. In fact, Barnes gave up and left the party, and Collins and Heller killed only two. For Akeley, this sufficiently proved the inaccuracy of Barnes's declarations of seeing thousands of gorillas. More important, Akeley conjectured that those statements covered up his aspirations to secure financiers for the Alexander Barnes Adventure Tours in the Kivu district and the rest of equatorial Africa. Apparently, Barnes promised his prospective patrons the opportunity to see many bands of gorillas.[90] If Barnes could deliver on this promise, it would be hard to convince the Western world that brightest Africa was endangered.

By 1925, the Belgians had issued the royal decree to establish the park. It named the preserve Parc National Albert (Albert National Park), which comprised the mountains Mikeno, Karisimbi, and Visoke. In the zone, the colonial government outlawed the "killing, capture or pursuit," and hunting of the gorillas, as well as that of any other wild animal, unless killed in "legitimate self-defense." Although the creation of the first official gorilla sanctuary succeeded, some scientists felt that the decree to create the park "proved to be insufficient for allowing for the perfect scientific development of the institution," which would be dedicated to studying and protecting the gorilla. Thus, Akeley and Belgian J. M. Derscheid, naturalist and professor of science at L'Université Coloniale D'Anvers, would conduct a reconnaissance of the volcanoes within the park and study the life and customs of the Kivu gorillas. In 1925, the party set out for Africa, this time with a team of landscape artists and taxidermists. Armed with funding from film magnate George Eastman, AMNH trustee Daniel E. Pomeroy, and Colonel Daniel B. Wentz of Philadelphia, Akeley planned to devote six weeks to studying Mounts Mikeno, Karisimbi, and Visoke and to film gorillas on the top of Mount Karisimbi.[91]

Visions of an Ageless Continent

The urgency and sincerity with which AMNH naturalists approached their display projects, as well as their endorsement of conservationist movements in Africa, signified both their rhetorical and real commitment to the image of Africa as a disappearing "ageless continent." For them, the term Brightest Africa suggested not only a place filled with natural wonders but also an unchanging landscape, which could be replicated in diorama or captured for posterity in a wildlife sanctuary. Brightest Africa was primeval, existing before Darwin's "descent of man," and because "primitive" humans inhabited it, the continent could have remained so, had imperialism not threatened to undermine its brightness. These naturalist-environmentalists did not admonish the imperialist hand that supposedly improved the material and cultural situation of Africans; rather, they decried the destruction of the environment that accompanied the civilizing mission.

Locating the brightness of Africa in its environmental natural history, naturalists demanded that displays of the timeless beauty of the continent achieve verisimilitude so that their viewers felt as if they were seeing Africa. Without question this would happen in the wildlife sanctuary, but outside the venerated forests of the Congo, capturing Africa's eternal essence could prove elusive. Yet AMNH naturalists stood firm in their belief that Africa had to be brought to America as scientific display and not popular spectacle. While they desired to attract the American public to the splendor of Africa, they refused to pander to base stereotypes and perpetuate mythology—or so they argued. Essentially, the AMNH naturalists created their own mythological image of Africa as an animal kingdom devoid of any "civilized" human presence. Their Africa obscured the human element, rendering Africans into the background, not as shadows cast by its brightness, but as minutia. Mary Akeley came closest to acknowledging that African Hall itself was spectacle, an exhibit intended to seize the imagination. However, she urged viewers to understand its "underlying significance" as "a vision of this ageless continent."[92]

AMNH naturalists considered African Hall and Parc National Albert to be crowing achievements in the campaign to save Brightest Africa.

However, they realized the limited American audience for such venues, especially a national park thousands of miles across the ocean. The average working-class American had little time to spend in a museum during its opening hours and did not possess the funds to go on safari. As museum officials and naturalists interpreted their work as not only scientific but educational, they launched projects that would reach the masses by tapping into the new consumer culture and the popularity of cinema. Thus the filmic campaign to provide the movie-going public with images of Brightest Africa developed alongside the construction of habitat dioramas and the lobbying for a nature preserve in the Congo.

Stirred by the Congo question and the 1884 Berlin Conference, naturalist-environmentalists and Pan-Africanists began charting out separate defenses for Africa—one premised on the preservation of wildlife and the other on the redemption of the continent from European domination. Pan-Africanists saw the scramble for Africa, which began in the Congo, as a harbinger of the continuing subordination of blacks by whites. Naturalists shared Pan-African anxieties over European penetration into the Congo and the remainder of Africa. For them, the opening of the continent brought unscrupulous hunters unguided by scientific principles to Africa, spelling the demise of allegedly the last pristine landscape on earth.

Interestingly, in film culture is where Pan-Africanists and naturalists found common ground in critiquing films that propagated the myth of Darkest Africa. The Pan-Africanists' goal was to combat "anti-Negro" movies that showed Africans to be savages or lackeys for white imperialists, whereas the naturalists focused on films that distorted the African jungles and savannahs as filled with dangerous beasts and that made white men out to be heroes as they killed animals and traversed the landscape. Inevitably, both groups critiqued many of the same films, particularly the endless array of jungle movies, although no coordination occurred among them to take on the film industry.

FIVE
Reel Africa
American Filmmaking and Criticism in Defense of Africa

In 1920, members of African American and African diaspora communities assembled at Liberty Hall in New York City, the site of the UNIA convention, "to protest the wrongs and injustices" that they were "suffering at the hands of their white brethren, and state what they deem[ed] their fair and just rights." Presided over by Marcus Garvey, the convention drafted and adopted the Declaration of the Rights of the Negro Peoples of the World, wherein the organization enumerated twelve complaints about the treatment of people of African descent. The declaration also listed fifty-four demands and objections, including the following: "We hereby protest against the publication of scandalous and inflammatory articles by an alien press tending to create racial strife and the exhibition of picture films showing the Negro as a cannibal." In this one sentence, the UNIA condemned not only newspaper articles that defamed the black character (most likely those that described black men as rapists and fanned the race riots of 1919) but also films that showed Africans as savages who engaged in cannibal feasts. The self-proclaimed "duly elected representatives of the Negro people of the world" believed that white-controlled popular media provided forums for the dissemination of propaganda that contributed to the subjugation of all persons of African descent.[1]

Three years after the UNIA issued its declaration, the AMNH hired wildlife filmmakers Martin and Osa Johnson to produce three commercial films about Africa that would provide "a sincere representation of the life of Africa in all its phases." Although the museum originally conceived of the film project as a fund-raiser for the completion of African Hall, it also became a crusade to discredit films made by "nature fakers" and those featuring "fake heroes of 'darkest Africa.'"[2] Like the UNIA, the AMNH believed that the American and British film industries since their inception produced films about Africa that fueled images of the continent as dark. However, the UNIA interpreted such films as performing political work—justifying the dehumanization of Africans and their descendants by depicting them as cannibals. Such films legitimized white imperialism in Africa as a civilizing mission to rid the continent of its most objectionable cultural practice. In contrast, the AMNH focused on the cultural work carried out by such films, uncovering how these movies distorted the African rainforest, presenting it as a savage jungle and a place where white heroes triumphed over nature.

An analysis of how African Americans critiqued commercial films about Africa alongside white Americans' critiques of films that misrepresented African wildlife speaks to the intersections of both Pan-Africanist and naturalist-environmentalist film criticism. Both groups found themselves independently objecting to the same films, albeit from different perspectives. In some instances, they shared the same language, describing filmic obsessions with cannibals and savages as detracting from the magnificence of the continent and its people. Paradoxically, actors and filmmakers who sought to defend Africa against cinematic slander often replicated the very Darkest Africa discourses they opposed in an attempt to stay relevant in an increasingly commercialized film industry. Exploring Pan-Africanist Paul Robeson's role in *Sanders of the River* and naturalists Martin and Osa Johnson's production of *Simba, The King of Beasts* (1928), *Congorilla* (1932), and *Baboona* (1935) explicates the processes through which these films, actors, and producers mediated among ethnographic, wildlife, and jungle film genres in depicting Africa and Africans.

As Anna Everett argues in *Returning the Gaze*, since 1909 "African Americans regularly returned the motion picture camera's often distorting gaze by scrutinizing the medium closely, vigilantly, and forcefully, and by publishing their criticisms and observations in the extensive network of publications that made up the black press." Everett uncovers a rich history of black film criticism, including L. D. Reddick's 1944 essay "Educational Programs for the Improvement of Race Relations: Motion Pictures, Radio, the Press, and Libraries," published in the *Journal of Negro Education*. As Everett acknowledges, Reddick articulated one of the most important readings of film's and other mass media's ability to act as cultural and political propaganda: "In a word, what the citizens of this nation think about any broad question is determined, largely, by what these citizens read about it in their newspapers and libraries, hear over the radio, or see and hear about it at the movie." Reddick repined for a day when individuals and organizations claiming to work toward better race relations recognized the power of mass communications, particularly the "immediate effects of motion pictures on their audiences," as did the wartime federal government and the propagandists of "race hatred." Of course, organizations like the NAACP and the UNIA participated in their own forms of film criticism and coordinated efforts within their constituencies to ban, boycott, or protest films that stereotyped blacks. Arguably, the NAACP, NACW, and other civil rights and racial uplift groups pioneered such tactics when they launched a campaign against the release of D. W. Griffith's *The Birth of a Nation* (1915). Black filmmaker Oscar Micheaux joined the fight in 1920 by producing the film *Within Our Gates* to challenge Griffith's portrayal of African Americans, slavery, and Reconstruction. Thus, there existed an established tradition of public civil disobedience and private remonstration against the misuses of film within the African American community on which Pan-Africanists could draw. Reddick acknowledged some of these historical moments, but he seemed to view such endeavors as sporadic.[3]

Although much of Reddick's criticism of the film industry focused on films depicting African American characters, he did mention several African-themed films, characterizing them also as "anti-Negro," as films wherein "the Negro elements ... are limited to the stereotyped conception of the Negro in the American mind." These films contrasted to "pro-Negro" films that cast African American actors as heroic, courageous, and dignified. In his essay, Reddick characterizes *Dark Rapture* (1938), a film about the Denis-Roosevelt expedition to the Belgian Congo, as "one of the few authentic films of Africa to reach the commercial theatre houses." He describes *Dark Sands* (1937) and *Sanders of the River* (1935), both produced in Britain starring African American actor Paul Robeson, as "justifications and apologies for colonial imperialism." He argues that *King Kong* (1931) and Martin and Osa Johnson's *Baboona* (1935) contribute to the "typical African films with the usual emphasis upon the naked, 'primitive,' black savages who consider every blonde a goddess and every trader or missionary a god." Reddick alludes to films that showed wild animals "absconding with a native woman," perhaps *Ingagi* (1930), and those showing animals eating Africans, such as *When Africa Speaks* (1930). The latter film (also titled *Africa Speaks!*) recounted explorer Paul Hoeffler's Belgian Congo expedition, a safari that followed his famed Denver African Expedition of 1925 under the auspices of the Denver Museum of Natural History. Reddick mentions *Trader Horn* (1931) as one of the African films that turned out to be "false and misleading."[4]

It must be remembered that Reddick's analysis of mass communications included radio, which he posited followed "the general pattern" as film. However, he argued, "Radio is less unfavourable to the Negro than motion pictures," and he cataloged several educational radio programs featured on NBC, CBS, WNYC, WMCA, and WEAF. Reddick focused his critique of radio on such programs as *Amos 'n' Andy*, which presented African Americans played by white comedians as buffoonish, lazy, and deprecating in their humor. Declaring that a PhD dissertation could be written on that program alone, the essay highlights the efforts of the *Pittsburgh Courier* to have the show banned from the airwaves. Reddick did not mention any African-themed radio serials, perhaps because most radio broadcasts that addressed African affairs or featured Africa in its programming took the form of news radio. There is little scholarship on American radio coverage of Africa before the 1950s, but since radio stations relied on the same wire services as the print media, most likely their reports on Africa differed little from that of the mainstream press. Indeed, radio coverage of African topics in the early twentieth century appeared intermittent and limited to European intervention in the continent.[5]

Naturalists seized on the popularity of radio to bring their tales of Brightest Africa to a broader audience beyond the halls of the museum. They expanded their promotional activities for the hall by scheduling appearances on local stations and lobbying for broadcasts of speeches and events about Africa. In 1929, WRNY in New York City hosted radio talks featuring James L. Clark, an AMNH zoologist working on the African Hall exhibit. Clark's talks, "Collecting for Museum Exhibition," described to his listeners the safari experience in BEA, which he described as "a white man's country." He relayed: "In this section are great grass lands, like our West—

and here are Africa's greatest game fields—where one can see thousands of head of wild game from the car window—while riding from Mombasa to Nairobi, the capitol town. Here is the happy hunting ground of the big game hunter and the museum collector. Here he collects his varied specimens from beautiful camps and in fine climate where the nights are almost cold and only the mid-day really hot."[6] Clark's Africa was a pristine wilderness where white men could observe, hunt, and collect big game.

In 1932, the Tarzan radio serial began and became a hit with listeners. Occasionally, however, radio stations would broadcast African material that did not satisfy American cravings for jungle thrills and safari adventures. In 1934, the Washington, D.C., NBC affiliate, WRC, broadcasted fifteen minutes of Asadata Dafora's "native African opera," *Kykunkor (Witch Woman)*. According to the *Washington Post*, the opera was "a folk legend of courtship and marriage in a Dark Continent village told in native chants and music." Dance scholar Brenda Dixon-Stowell has described the production as "a spectacle which marked the advent of authentic African dance in Black America and of Black concert dance [on] the American Stage." Like Pan-Africanists who sought to challenge stereotypical depictions of Africans in the media, Dafora used his choreography to defy the exoticized, eroticized, and inauthentic African dance sequences seen on the silver screen, on the stage, or in white entertainment venues like the Cotton Club. Unfortunately, the brief broadcast of *Kykunkor* represented a minority of radio segments that departed radically from the usual African fare.[7]

The success of Clark's talks and the popularity of the *Tarzan* serial supported the argument made in 1935 by Anne O'Hare McCormick that news about Africa "does not broadcast over the radio or attract the Argus-eyed movie camera save as a preserve of big game." McCormick, the first woman to win the Pulitzer Prize for journalism as a foreign correspondent for the *New York Times*, was covering the Italian invasion of Ethiopia and expressed frustration that Americans seemed uninterested in Africa unless they were listening to the Tarzan serial or watching an endless array of wildlife or jungle films.[8]

Exploring the corrective interventions of Pan-Africanists and naturalists-environmentalists in the film industry must begin with their critiques of the jungle film trend, primarily in the form of letters to newspaper editors and film reviews and secondarily in boycotting campaigns and independent filmmaking ventures. Their chief concern was the authenticity of the images of Africa presented to the American public on screen.

When Jungles Were En Vogue

In 1931, the American film critic for the *Washington Post*, Nelson B. Bell, offered his explanation for the popularity of wildlife and jungle films. In "The Jungles: A Vogue and a Tear for Some Old Friends," Bell remarked that with the recent success of *Ingagi*, *Africa Speaks*, and *Trader Horn* "the tide has set in" for similar pictures to appear on the American market. Attempting to explain their appeal to the American audience he states: "Each, to be sure, has had its human narrative, bound up more or less with romantic qualities that have been familiar from long usage and varied only by the peculiarities of locale in which they have been placed, but the fillip of novelty and the spur to our interest have sprung from the spectacle of strange wild beasts—and many not so strange—left to their own devices in their natural habitats." Essentially, Bell argued that the love story that served as the plot to a host of jungle movies held no interest for the moviegoer. Instead it was the sight of wild animals living in pristine landscapes that attracted American viewers. Bell's editorial appeared more than a decade after Hollywood's jungle film genre emerged with such films as *The Jungle Master* (1914), *Judgment of the Jungle* (1914), *The Jungle Lover* (1915), and *The Jungle Trail* (1919). Expeditionary films also contributed to American fascination with the jungle. Yet, it was not until the 1920s that the jungle film vogue took off in earnest. As Gregg Mitman reminds us, wildlife films became popular in America in the early twentieth century. Originating as expeditionary footage and presented at public lectures or scientific institutions, these films targeted a select audience—foremost middle- and upper-class white Americans. When Hollywood studios began producing wildlife films for commercial distribution, they popularized a genre initially restricted to scientific and learned audiences. Thus, the popularization of African wildlife movies overlapped with the proliferation of jungle films, and not coincidentally both genres featured great white hunters, cannibals, and gentlemen and -women travelers overcoming travails in the heart of Africa. Producers of jungle films would often purchase stock footage from expeditionary films to splice into their movie reels to give their films the illusion of reality.[9]

Film critics classified many jungle films as adventures, featuring a white hero searching for lost treasures, civilizations, and tribes in Darkest Africa, or as dramas or melodramas, which evoked the jungle as a place whose darkness illuminated the qualities of the white hero as he battled for survival and inevitably fell in love with a white woman. Several earlier popular silent jungle films reveal how the "savagery" of African characters served as foils to the "heroism" of whites and how surviving the jungle became a metaphor for their personal journeys to manhood. *The Jungle Trail* follows a lion-hunting trip to an unexpected encounter with a lost Egyptian city inhabited by cannibals. The hero, Robert (William Farnum), escapes becoming the main course and falls in love with Mary (Anna Luther), the heroine of the film, despite African Princess Wanada's (the Austrian actress Anna Lehr) obsession with him. The *Los Angeles Times* declared the silent film "a superb romantic story ... spoiled by the slush of sentimental subtitles." Although Wanada was not a blonde, Reddick's argument that the typical African film showed Africans worshipping white women holds true, as Wanada is an obviously white queen ruling over a fictitious cannibalistic kingdom inhabited by black Africans. *The Jungle Princess* (1920) further elucidates the thematic confluence of the savage jungle and white heroism. In this film, a Spanish girl who is kidnapped by Africans, a young American millionaire aviator, and an American prizefighter face life-threatening adventures in Africa while in search of a lost white race. *The Jungle Goddess* (1921), with the title role played by Elinor Field, initiated the director Colonel William Selig's twelve-chapter jungle goddess serial. A white princess, this time a blonde, rules over Africans bent on killing innocent white travelers.[10]

Many of the early jungle films featured original screenplays. Their producers relied on moviegoers to bring their literary and popular cultural images of the African jungle with them to the theater and hoped to capitalize on established stereotypes of Darkest Africa made popular by Stanley in the nineteenth century and by travelers in the early twentieth century. The Tarzan films proved an exception to this trend. Initially, Tarzan was a literary hero, appearing first in 1912 in Frank Munsey's *All-Story Magazine*. Sales of the novel *Tarzan of the Apes* by Edgar Rice Burroughs were modest until the release of the first Tarzan film. John Kasson describes how interest boomed: "A succession of film versions powered the Tarzan machine, beginning the release of the first *Tarzan of the Apes* in January 1918. With a coordinated publicity campaign of film distribution, newspaper serialization, and book sales, the movie proved one of the most profitable in the history of the nascent industry, and sales of Burroughs's Tarzan books soared." Tarzan became the archetype for the white American male hero. In this context, he embodied the "fake heroes" of Darkest Africa decried by both Pan-Africanists and naturalists alike.[11]

Nothing evoked the image of the African jungle more than the cry of Tarzan as he roamed the "mysterious haunts of the savage jungle."[12]

Burroughs had become famous in the early twentieth century for his serial novels depicting white male protagonists enduring hardships in the jungle and outer space. His character Tarzan became a popular culture icon, especially after his novel *Tarzan, the Ape Man* became a best seller. However, when his novel came to the big screen as a silent movie in 1918 it received mixed reviews. The *New York Times* critic found the "domestic narrative" that organized the jungle story to be "tedious at times," yet he held that this detraction was "more than compensated for ... by the stirring scenes of the jungle." The *Washington Post* also seemed impressed by the "jungles scenes ... [which] show wild life as it really is." In contrast, *Chicago Daily Tribune* film critic Mae Tinée called the film a "lemon" in a poem written to ridicule it. She declared that *Tarzan* is not a "pill," as they can be swallowed quickly, but rather a lemon, lasting a "LONG TIME" and "sour to the END." Making reference to veterinarians, Darwinists, and zoologists, Tinée argued that the film did not live up to the novel, which was "interesting if far fetched." Unlike the *Times* critic, she was not impressed by "the incredible amount of jungle and prowling on the part of everybody" and concluded that the film was "decidedly QUEER." In her review of the sequel, *The Romance of Tarzan*, Tinée unabashedly gave thanks that the film concluded the adventures of Tarzan. When a new talkie version of *Tarzan* appeared in 1933 starring Buster Crabbe, it became one of the top twenty grossing films of that year.[13] The success of and critical acclaim for *Tarzan of the Apes* speaks to the audience's investment in the white male body and the artificiality of African jungle realism.

As Kasson and Walt Morton have argued, the transmedia popularity of Tarzan stemmed from concerns about modernity and its effect on white manhood. As Kasson states, searching for the perfect man entailed constructing the perfect white male body, often in opposition to the imagined lesser bodies of nonwhites. The iconography deployed by both Burroughs and filmmakers to depict Tarzan adhered to racialized discourses on manhood and masculinity. Speaking of the casting of Elmo Lincoln as Tarzan in the silent film series, Tinée wrote that he was "the best person I know for the part, for he is a giant physically and has enough idea of acting values to carry him through." In selecting an actor for the role of Tarzan, the casting director had foremost to select a man whose physique proclaimed him king of the jungle. Lincoln, Crabbe, and later Johnny Weissmuller fit the archetype of the perfect white male body. Moreover, in their scenes with Africans, who were played by Brazilians and African Americans, they towered over these men and defeated them easily. Despite their supposed savagery, Africans on screen posed no match for Tarzan.[14]

The Tarzan movies played on the trope of Darkest Africa by attempting to capture the authentic dangerous African jungle on screen. The silent versions filmed the jungle sequences (over 200,000 feet of film) in the Amazon River basin in Brazil. The National Film Company transported lions, elephants, tigers, panthers, and wild boars, presumably from an American zoo or circus, to the region where the production crew constructed a cannibal village inhabited by Brazilian extras. Aerial acrobats in suits played the apes that raised Tarzan. Critics claimed that this counterfeit setting not only captured the reality of African jungles but also had "a touch of educational value." In the talkie versions, many of the jungle scenes were either shot on an MGM lot with circus animals or were clips from ethnographic films spliced into the main reels. In the Johnny Weissmuller version, the scene where Maureen O'Sullivan admires African dancers was shot with her standing in front of a screen projecting footage from a recent safari. MGM also purchased the scenes of the lion running across the plains from a safari film. It is a stuffed animal that attacks Tarzan. This type of "fakery," acceptable to popular audiences, fell under increasing scrutiny in the late 1920s and in the early 1930s.[15] Self-proclaimed experts on Africa, predominantly white naturalists and travelers, denounced such films for their outrageous depictions of the continent's wildlife and its people.

When Carl Akeley expressed his desire in 1922 to have "beautiful Africa come into its own," he envisioned a cinematic corrective to the dominant Darkest Africa themed movies. In a letter to Martin Johnson, he wrote: "The motion picture industry back here is in pretty punk condition, partly because of hard times and partly because the public is sick and tired of the junk that they have been fed. The public will pay for good stuff when the producers and distributors wake up to the fact that men like you are producing good stuff and there will be plenty of market. I really have great hope for the future of nature photography. It is just a question of getting it past the barrier of motion picture distributors and promoters. The public wants it." Akeley castigated the "fake heroes" featured in commercial jungle films and argued that Johnson's films lacked the contrivance found in many of the more popular wildlife documentaries. Writing to Gifford Pinchot, former chief of the United States Forest Service and then governor of Pennsylvania, he declared Johnson's film *Safari* (released as *Trailing*

African Wild Animals) superb "photographically ... from the standpoint of composition as well as skillful photography." He continued: "In it you will find not a hint of anything unsportsmanlike, or lack of consideration for the animals, except in such cases as where somebody must die, the animal is elected rather than the cameraman or woman. There is no 'bunk' to the end that the makers of the pictures shall appear as heroes, because of their having lived through great dangers and hardship. You will see from the pictures that they were having the time of their lives all the time. From a scientific and educational standpoint it is accurate and truthful, chock full of beauty and thrills." Akeley believed that the motion picture industry's investment in the jungle film craze prevented distributors and producers from taking a chance on reputable films about Africa that might not sell out the theaters.[16]

Akeley saved his harshest criticisms of jungle films for H. A. Snow, the producer of the film *Hunting Big Game in Africa with Gun and Camera* (1922). Capitalizing off the trope of the Dark Continent, the film follows the travels of Professor Snow and his son Sydney through South Africa under the auspices of the Oakland Museum of Natural History and includes footage of the Kimberly diamond mines, an extinct volcano, encounters with rhinoceros, giraffes, and elephants, dancing natives, and a tsetse fly invasion. The film received rave reviews. Tinée told her readers that "this animal picture is sure going to make a hit with you," noting the "marvelous scenery and footage of natives in their various haunts in various naïve exhibitions of home and social life." Another critic complimented the film as a documentary of "one of the most successful expeditions ever made in the Dark Continent." Drawing parallels between Snow, "red-blooded" Teddy Roosevelt, and the fictional Allan Quartermain of *King Solomon's Mines* on the pursuit of African game, the reviewer called it "a real treat." Other critics lauded *Hunting Big Game in Africa* as thrilling, noting the variety of animals featured in the movie, including the "vicious," "wild," and "untamable" African elephant, as well as Africans doing "the shimmy dance."[17]

On first glance it is difficult to ascertain why Akeley objected to the Snow film. Perhaps it was the "deadly rhinoceros charge" or the manner in which Snow obtained his footage. Faced with the difficulty of filming the "many fleet footed inhabitants" of South Africa, Snow decided to "run down" the animals in his flivver until they were tired out. Then he proceeded to "walk right up to them and crank at leisure." Akeley expressed his dislike for the Snow picture to Samuel Rothapfel, owner of the Roy Theatre, while simultaneously endorsing Johnson's films. Akeley deplored "any form of fake, misrepresentation or disagreeable feature or killing or torturing animals" as was common in many African films on the market. A series of correspondence among Akeley, Herbert Bradley, and George Eastman intimated that Snow's film fell into that category. Johnson's film had the misfortune of showing in Chicago at the same time as Snow's picture. Akeley had yet to be "convinced that the public [would] pay for straight stuff" despite the favorable reception of Johnson's film. In fact, Johnson and motion picture insiders informed him that there would not be a viable market for such films for two years, the expected run of the present releases. Moreover, in order for a wildlife film to "find a market through the distributors [it had to] be an extraordinary sensational thing to get a hearing at all." Indeed, one could follow the Snow Plan and invest $100,000 into promoting a picture and convincing a distributor of its potential popularity or emulate Flaherty's advertising strategy for *Nanook of the North*, in which "distributors could see nothing in it until the public was clamoring for it."[18]

Competition for audiences for these films remained extremely tight as rumors circulated that "Snow's crowd" offered Martin Johnson $50,000 to "keep his films off the market." Bradley heard this gossip straight from Snow, but because he distrusted him, he sought confirmation of the tale from more trustworthy sources. According to the head man of Pathe, the same distributor for *Nanook of the North*, Snow had lied—they had offered less than $50,000 for the film. The unnamed "head man" had little liking for Snow but supported him because his skillful marketing schemes put "African stuff on the market." Johnson's film was "almost a failure" because of the "lack of proper advertising, coupled with the failure to get it into a good house."[19]

To compete with Snow, Akeley—with AMNH president Henry Fairfield Osborn's approval—approached Kodak magnate George Eastman for financial backing. In a letter to Eastman, Akeley justified the museum's backing of Johnson's film projects in Africa. After describing Africa fauna as endangered due to the onslaught of civilization, he argued, "a motion picture record is one of the most important that can be made of the life histories of wild animals." However, for them to be of scientific value they had to be "free from misleading titles, staging, misinterpretation, or any form of faking or sensationalism." Akeley told Eastman that the Snow film represented the "last word in misrepresentation of fact in relation to Africa in general and its animal life in particular." He assured Eastman that although Johnson was "under great pressure" from the motion picture industry to sensationalize his films for commercial gain, Johnson refused to compromise his principles and, thus, gained the respect and backing of Osborn and the periodical *World's Work*.[20] Akeley assured him that Johnson's first films made under the auspices of the AMNH would distance his work from that of Snow and other "nature fakers." Akeley believed that the Johnson films made during the next five years in Africa (1923–1928) would make it "hard for any fakers to get away with things." The "campaign against Snow" commenced, as the Johnsons set out to film Brightest Africa.[21]

Africa as God Made It

According to Akeley's original African Hall plans, filmmakers would play the most important role—outside of those naturalists collecting faunal specimens—in the project dedicated to Teddy Roosevelt's memory. He envisioned a "motion picture maker" carrying the burden of securing additional funding for the hall through the production and marketing of commercially successful wildlife films. The director of photography and his crew would engage "in filming Africa in the broadest and most comprehensive sense," covering nine suggested fields—mammals, birds, reptiles, insects, scenery, natives (customs, dances, ceremonies, and so forth), history ("scenarios of historical events"), drama ("dramatization of native legends and so forth"), and industry ("industries of Natives and Whites"). Akeley stipulated: "This motion picture enterprize [*sic*] should be undertaken only on the basis of thoroughness which is to characterize the doing of the African Hall. The film must be of the best possible quality technically and contain nothing that can be criticized as to truthfulness. When a scenario is prepared to tell the story of a historical incident—native tradition, folk story, or any thing that is prepared and 'staged'—the facts must be frankly stated on the film." Despite the hall's zoological orientation, Akeley acknowledged that the public craved images of exotic Africans as popular culture barraged them with images of savage Africans. Thus, any financially successful cinematic portrayal of Africa could not ignore the human presence. The films, like the dioramas, would tell the truth about Africa. The filmmakers would shape that truth as they traveled the continent in search of the real Africa. However, before their mission could begin, a "preliminary investigation" had to be undertaken.[22]

The inquiry would include an assessment of the motion picture industry to determine "the probable financial success" of the films that the museum wished to produce. In essence, this required an analysis of both ethnographic and discovery films, as well as "the study of the receptions accorded similar films by the public, the interviewing of motion picture people—

distributors, producers of educational films, educators, and so forth, the preparation of 'blue prints' of the undertaking—a schedule of film possibilities based on the requirements of the public and educators." In order for the proposed films to generate the necessary revenue for the hall they had to compete with the most lucrative nature pictures, but they had to do so without resorting to the "fakery" associated with popular fictionalized safari movies. The films coupled with the dioramas would convey the true nature of the bright continent to the public and educational institutions of the Western world.[23]

Renowned French filmmaker Félix-Louis Regnault argued when commenting on the role of the motion picture in furthering scientific knowledge and endeavor, "film is superior to the best of descriptions" as it provides "exact and permanent documents to those who study movement." In a similar vein, Akeley explained the power of cinematography: "The perennial cry, 'The game must go: this is no longer the world's zoo but an agricultural country' is heard throughout Africa. There is just one relieving circumstance to this doleful prospect: what man seems bent on destroying with his gun can be rescued from complete oblivion and given the illusion of reality through the camera." Akeley criticized the shooting of game to make for imperialist commercial agriculture. More important, like Regnault, Akeley believed that the descriptions of Brightest Africa in his travel narrative alone could not capture the "exactness" of African nature. Instead he looked to film to capture what the printed page could not. To that end, he determined to meet Martin and Osa Johnson at their induction into the Explorer's Club in New York in 1918, seven years after the AMNH approved his plan. After the ceremony, he went to the Johnsons' apartment, where he informed them that Martin had "a very important mission"—"to perpetuate vanishing wild animal life" on film "available to millions of people all over the world." The AMNH subsequently hired the Johnsons to make films for African Hall, hoping to capitalize off their previous success in nationally marketing their films about Hawaii, Fiji, and the Solomon Islands. Their cinematic tales of headhunters, cannibals, and slave traders, as seen in *Cannibals of the South Seas*, enthralled audiences. However, the Johnsons' record with wildlife footage was not as laudable. Their film of animal life in Borneo, *Jungle Adventures* (1920), flopped as evidenced by its reception in theaters. However, the AMNH declared their first African film, *Trailing African Wild Animals* (shot during their 1921 expedition to Kenya), to be "*true* natural history." Akeley argued that Johnson "had no superior in wild-life cinematography."

Thus, in 1922 the AMNH entrusted the Johnsons with the delicate task of producing "sincere" pictures of Africa—educational and entertaining films true to the scientific spirit.[24]

According to a 1923 article in *World's Work*, Martin Johnson stated that his and Osa's

> prime purpose is to photograph Africa and the inhabitants of Africa—to photograph them as they normally exist—to photograph them in their wanderings, in their play, in their migrations and their congregations—in their natural relations to each other and to the world in which they live. Thrills in plenty we will have—and I hope we'll photograph many of them—but they are incidental to our main purpose, which is to secure a truthful, accurate, complete, and interesting picture of Africa as it is—not a picture of "The Adventures of Mr. and Mrs. Martin Johnson."

The Johnson's contract with the AMNH stipulated that the filming expedition would last five years in Africa and yield three full-length motion pictures, one of which was to explore native life. However, only one film resulted—*Simba, King of Beasts: A Saga of the African Veldt* (1928). Interestingly, the Johnsons released two African films after their museum expedition—*Congorilla: Adventures among the Big Apes and the Little People of Central Africa* (1932) and *Baboona: An Aerial Epic over Africa* (1935)—which the AMNH refused to officially endorse. The story behind the failure of the Johnsons to complete the other two films for the museum illuminates the tensions between showmanship and scientific inquiry in their quest to capture Brightest Africa on film. Osa Johnson once stated that editing the pictures taken in Africa was a "two-fold task, inasmuch as the camera studies which Martin [had] taken to meet the scientific needs of the Museum of Natural History required one type of assembling, while those to be released through the regular motion picture channels to defray the expenses of the *safari* and return money to the investors were of another type."[25] How did the assembling process dictate the images that the public would see of Africa through the lens of Martin and Osa Johnson?

To secure the footage that would provide the basis for one of the three proposed films, the Johnsons headed out for a region in East Africa they christened Lake Paradise. While on safari in 1921, Blaney Percival, game warden in BEA, shared a secret with the couple, which the Johnsons swore to "never confide ... to another living soul," with the exception of Carl Akeley. According to a book written by a Scottish traveler in the early nineteenth century, there existed a "phantom lake ... a crater lake which [was] on no map ever made of this country [BEA]." Martin Johnson marveled at the prospect of seeing thousands of animals in one location. Percival assured him that such an experience proved likely as the "hundreds of miles in every direction" from the lake the region served as "a sort of sanctuary, undisturbed by the white man and his gun." Percival explained that he divulged the location of the lake to the Johnsons because he wished them to capture on film "what animals are really like in their natural, undisturbed state."[26] Osa Johnson recalled their first site of "Paradise."

> The lake was shaped like a spoon, about a quarter of a mile wide and three-quarters of a mile long, and it clopped up into steep wooded banks two hundred feet high.... the tip of the spoon... was a high cliff, and opposite, a deep cleft served as the handle. It lay in the center of an extinct volcano, and the beach which ran back a hundred feet or so to the edge of the forest was of hard, washed lava. A tangle of water vines and lilies—great blue African lilies—grew in the shallows at the water's edge. Wild ducks, cranes, and egrets, circled and dipped. Animals, more than we could count, stood quietly knee-deep in the water and drank. "It's Paradise, Martin!"[27]

Similar to Akeley's first impressions of Brightest Africa, the Johnsons' descriptions told of animals roaming freely amid the startling beauties of African flora in Lake Paradise. Few white men had traveled to this place and Africans were near invisible. The Johnsons believed that any cinematic narrative of Africa had to begin here, a place they began to call home.

The Johnsons reached Lake Paradise again in 1924 and began the task of creating "a vivid portrayal of untouched Africa." Martin Johnson wanted to make a picture of Africa that would be different from what normally passed for films in Hollywood. This meant that staging and piecing together "haphazard scenes" would be shunned to guarantee that the film would be "the whole story of a country, its peoples and its animals, slowly unrolling against a background of magnificent scenery." Johnson hoped this picture would immortalize Africa as it existed before the coming of the white man.[28]

The film *Simba* opens with a title card proclaiming itself "the cinematographic record of adventure in Africa—the classic land of mystery, thrills, and darksome savage drama through all the days of history." The foreword introduces the spectator to Martin Johnson and his "companion and full partner," Osa, who throughout the film plays the role of the attentive wife who possesses both "courage and skill" to pick up a gun when called upon.

Reel Africa 191

However, Martin assures the viewers that Osa is no slaughtering sportsman, as she only shoots animals to feed the party or save the life of someone in danger. The film promises to show the audience "one of the most beautiful places on earth"—Lake Paradise—"so that [the viewer] may see the real Africa ... Africa as God Made it."²⁹ The Johnsons faced travails, including "thirst, storm, sickness, and savages," but emerge triumphant as they capture on film some of the rarest footage of animals and natives. The film pledges that the lion will be shown in "the unspoiled freedom of his native wild"—in "the blue" of BEA.³⁰

The opening scene establishes clearly the hierarchy of race and safari, in much the same manner as popular travel narratives. Osa Johnson is shown scolding a porter for dropping dinner (an animal carcass) on the ground, establishing herself as white mistress and the porter as black servant. In a pastiche of images, beginning with a map of Abyssinia, BEA, and Tanganyika, the film illustrates the relationship between the proverbial white hunter (Osa), the cinematographer (Martin), and African "boys." Hundreds of porters are shown as beasts of burden, carrying packages atop their heads. According to the Bureau of Native Affairs, those packages could not exceed sixty pounds; moreover, porters could not travel more than fifteen miles a day. However, the film did not reveal these regulations on the uses of porters, and they are shown to work without ceasing—driving mules, pushing Ford trucks up hill, and navigating vehicles through "crocodile-infested rivers," while the whites remain safe inside their vehicles. The intersplicing of scenes of elephants, crocodiles, porters, and hippos blurs the distinction between African and beast in the narrative. The distance shown between white man and wild animal equated that depicted between white man and "black boy." The amused glances directed toward the Africans as they trudge alongside the cars mirror that of the travelers as they watch camels carrying additional packages. Interestingly, the porters remain anonymous in the film, although in the written narrative of the expedition, Osa Johnson revealed that "old Boculy," Jerramani, and Ferraragi were 3 of the 110 individuals who made up the safari party. In the films, their names are unimportant, as they are part of the safari and not the "real" Africans that inhabited the continent.³¹

A scene of "half-wild" camels introduces the viewer to "the great wild"—"a scenic wonderland filled with the magic that is Africa." Despite Johnson's desire to avoid showing disorganized scenes, pictures of "wild neighbors," including "chattering profane baboons," immediately follow the camel series. Without warning, the film turns its attention to "trap cameras

The Martin Johnson African Expedition, 1924. Neg./Transparency no. 128755, courtesy the Library, American Museum of Natural History.

with flash lamps" set up by the Johnsons to capture lions on film during the night. The film crew resorted to using a zebra carcass for bait to attract a lioness. Almost as abruptly as the transition from camel to lion, the film shifts to "The Mad Elephant Stampede in the burning jungle."[32] It is in this sequence that the viewer is introduced to "Africa as God made it, never disturbed by civilized man." The viewer learns that the lion's "next door neighbors" are "Mama Tembo" and "Willie Tembo" (the "eldest" of the baby elephants). Here the Johnsons humanized the elephants, in much the same way Akeley had done for the gorillas he encountered on Mikeno. The film crew follows elephant trails through "blazing African days." While watching the filming process we are made privy to the crew's fear of an elephant charge. The elephants are shown going about their play, but some are clearly annoyed by the presence of the camera crew. A caption follows a frame of an elephant, asking: "Who's [sic] Africa is this anyway?" Here the cinematographers (including the one African shown working the camera) acknowledge themselves as outsiders in the elephant haven. Without warning, a bush fire is spotted and a "mad stampede" ensues. The crew runs toward the stampede to capture this "rare" occurrence on film and escapes

Reel Africa 193

unscathed. Osa Johnson is able to shoot a bull, whose carcass is shown lying on the ground as an African (possibly a Nandi or Maasai) leans against the animal wiping his spear clean. It is unclear whether the fire was started by a member of the safari party or if the crew benefited from a moment of serendipity. Whatever the source of the blaze, supposedly "the greatest natural scene" ever to be recorded by "human eye" was forever captured on celluloid.

While this scene was meant to represent the life and habits of the elephant, it ended oddly with the misplacement of an African into the frame, who, despite his motion of wiping the blade clean, did not deal the fatal blow to the elephant. The violent act ascribed to him was in actuality executed by Osa Johnson. Perhaps, the scene with the African amounted to a clever segue into a sequence on native life. However, there was something more insidious about his position in the film at this juncture. He represented a metaphorical time capsule where the camera would transport the audience "back to nature," where they would witness "the age-old story of Man emerging from savagery"—where the African killed with spear instead of gun.[33]

In the film's exploration of native life, Africans served as the punch line to jokes and not-so-clever witticisms. The Africans of this ambiguous region are described as "a pastoral race of half savage blacks." Their leaders' dress and mannerisms are ridiculed. The intertitle notes that Chief Galla Russ always dresses up to receive safari leaders; subsequently, he appears on screen wearing a top hat. Here the Johnsons deride the chief's traditional form of dress, conveying the inappropriateness of viewing the African chief as one would an esteemed Western leader. Similarly, when introducing the audience to the chief's son, Songa, the film mockingly declares him "an African gentleman" as he assumes an aggressive stance. The filmmakers' assessment of the two Africans is clear: Africans live in a natural state of belligerence, savagery, primitiveness, and seminakedness, and thus their royalty commands little respect. In contrast, in an encounter not captured on film but described later in Osa Johnson's travel narrative *I Married Adventure*, the Johnsons met with the Duke and Duchess of York while on safari. In anticipation, they prepared themselves with frenzy. Osa instructed Martin to put on his "best shirt" while she rushed to perform "a sketchy but much needed manicure." The meeting with the duke and duchess was absent any mockery as the two couples discussed the future of African wildlife in the empire. Clearly, Galla Russ and Songa could not match the future king of England.[34]

The ridicule of Africans did not end with this scene. The audience learns that drought and wild beasts of the desert and jungle are foes to the natives. In a scene clearly meant to elicit laughter, a brigade carries water to the village with an allegro version of "Dance of the Sugar Plum Fairies" from *The Nutcracker Suite* as background music. The lens moves from the water brigade to a panorama of Samburu jewelry worn by the villagers. This is the first time the film affiliates the Africans with a tribe, subjecting them to the ethnographic gaze. The camera examines these artifacts cursorily, as if they themselves supplied evidence of the "half-savage" state of Africans alluded to in the opening credits. Then the scene ends with a shot of George Eastman filming with his Kodak. Again, the correlation between the Samburu and Eastman is puzzling. Arguably this could be a subtle transition to the next scene. However, an implicit juxtaposition occurs here. This scene contrasts the Samburu's jewelry to Eastman's camera. The savage is to ornamentation as the civilized is to technology. The discourse of racial hierarchy is reinforced in two seemingly unrelated frames.

Yet another hodgepodge of scenes of animal life follows this sequence. The camera takes the viewer to "rhino country," where the "two-ton killer" runs amuck. Here again Osa emerges as the heroine, as she first baits the rhinos and then shoots one. The subsequent frames include footage of zebras, oryx, ostriches, Grant's gazelles, eland, hundreds of birds at a watering hole, and an impala and "his harem"—the gerenuk, giraffes, hyenas, and vultures. While watching the vultures and hyenas feed on carrion, the audience reads, "There is no waste in hungry, thirsty Africa." A rainstorm and a tribal "dance of thanksgiving" follow this proclamation. Once again, Africans reenter the lens as the object of the filmmaker's humor.

This lampoon features "the village soak," village dancers, Osa's maid, and several African women. The would-be drunkard is a constant in the sequence as scenes alternate between his drunken revelries and the actions of the other characters. While the tribe rejoices at the drought-ending rainstorm, the drunkard fumbles with a bottle opener while trying to drink a bottle of Guinness. As the drunkard struggles to become inebriated, Osa's maid plays with "the mistress's makeup." Like any popular vaudevillian sketch, racial bending is present, as the maid is shown covering her face with cold cream, as the camera focuses on her white visage. Here the audience is treated to a reversed minstrel scene, reminiscent of performances of *Uncle Tom's Cabin*, where Topsy similarly powders her face with the mistress's makeup.[35]

The Johnsons then splice scenes of the drunkard with the dancers. Next, the film introduces the viewer to African women wearing beaded necklaces.

The caption reads: "It only takes a few beads to glorify the African girl." An intertitle follows, stating, "The short skirt movement has gone about as far as possible," and the camera pans in on the loins of two African girls. Whether or not the Johnsons intended this up-close view of adolescent genital regions to titillate the audience is debatable. However, such shots proved the norm in "wildlife" films, which often contained scenes of topless women (some coaxed to open their shirts for the camera) and panoramic views of male and female buttocks. Wildlife filmmakers often treated African women's bodies as they would that of animals—that is, as natural history specimens. The Johnsons' reference to flappers and short skirts merges popular cultural views of the Jazz Age and its "jungle music" with the pornographic gaze of ethnography, analogizing a liberating fashion for American women to African primitivism. The sequence ends with a return to that resourceful drunkard, who had solved the riddle of the bottle opener and imbibed the beer. Instrumental versions of "How Dry I Am" and "He's a Jolly Good Fellow" accent these scenes. As in the first frames of "native life," the Africans narrated no story of their own. After over fifty-one minutes of disjointed sequences, perhaps the most cohesive part of the film begins.

Ndorobo hunters run to the camp with report of lions spotted in Tanganyika. The figure of "a wise, withered old savage" warns the ambitious white hunter that "Simba" may devour him. The climax of the film, "The Lion War of a Lumbwa Tribe," commences. For almost twenty-three minutes, the audience views a lion hunt, which pits "naked men against tooth and claw." "Simba, the killer" fights two other lions over the carcass of a zebra. The film exposes his "treacherous calm," but remarks that Simba is about "as gentle as a load of dynamite." Next, a vision claimed to be without parallel in the history of wildlife films appears—fourteen lions including cubs at play. However, this scene did not enchant the Lumbwa, as the lions had been menacing the village. The film introduces the "half-civilized tribe of herdsmen" at their "capital," a group of huts. The narrator informs the audience that the king is "dignified" at six feet and four inches but that the queen is a "great executive but no real beauty." In another evocation of the flapper, the intertitle divulges that she had worn her hair short for years, as the Johnsons offer her her "first smoke" of a cigar. Again, using Jazz Age symbolism, the Johnsons mock Lumbwa practices.

The king's "new wives" appear with veils to "keep their fatal beauty covered," as a "page boy" with the moniker "His Darksome Highness" brings news of the killing of livestock by a lion. The priests declare this "a time for prayers and incantations." The king then dismisses the dancing priests while the warriors declare war on Simba and dance for hours into a "frenzy." After seeing the lions run from the warriors, the narrator remarks, "It seems cruel." The high-powered rifles used to shoot lions appear humane compared to the spears of the Lumbwa. The warriors successfully kill one lion with several spears. While Martin Johnson tends to one fallen warrior in the battle, the men offer a prayer "to their black gods." After another spearing, Osa Johnson shoots a lion that charges the group. The Johnsons' sympathies lie with the lion and not the Lumbwa. Osa Johnson then reclaims her domesticity by baking an apple pie. "The drama of desperate realities" ends the "tale of the land of romance and magic and mystery."[36]

Simba debuted at New York at the Earl Carroll Theater and received rave reviews at its other showings. Film critic Edward Schallert dubbed the film the "Museum Opus" and noted that the AMNH declared it to be "an outstanding achievement in screen portrayal of authentic animal life and adventures in African deserts, plains, and jungles." Of the film's depiction of Africans and Africa, critic Ralph Flint wrote: "Here is a graphic and moving scene of African pomp and ceremony, the King and Queen of the Lumbwas being every inch what such regal folk should be. But it is primarily the animals that hold the center of this generous slice of Africana, and here one can enjoy their maneuverings to the limit." Tinée declared that "'Simba' shows jungle life in Africa as it is." She also noted that the Field Museum of Natural History endorsed the film.[37]

Before *Simba* could be released, Akeley and the museum had to approve of the film's content and narrative. That they did not find the material or the narrative objectionable is intriguing, since *Simba* offers a compelling example of how the trope of Darkest Africa infiltrated many Brightest Africa texts. The hackneyed scenes that the Johnsons, the AMNH, and Akeley deplored in films featuring the "fake heroes" of the Dark Continent are replicated in *Simba*. In the film, Martin and Osa emerge as heroes as they prevail over the animal kingdom, escaping elephant stampedes, rhino charges, and lion chases. The film subverts the image of Osa's bright Paradise to shock reviewers with frames of dark dangerous animals tramping through forests and savannas. Similarly, the film undermines the museum's directive to procure sincere pictures of Africans by inserting Africans into its narrative either as punch lines to jokes or to mock their culture and appearance. Superstitious Africans pray to pagan gods and venerate nature. Natives display their "half-savage," naked state, and fight with "primitive" weapons. In lighthearted fashion, the film propagates racist and sexist images of

Africans under the guise of scientific education. Thrills and adventures with "wild beasts" and "wild savages" keep the audience captivated. Far from providing images of the realities of native life, the film places Africans in scenes meant to pacify American audiences' cravings for adventure and simultaneously bolster their sense of superiority over "primitive" nonwhites.

While filming *Simba*, Martin Johnson explained his and Osa's inability to create a coherent narrative of African life in East Africa on film and his decision to focus on wildlife, particularly the elephant.

> It may seem queer that we started right out after elephants instead of the picture "Songa the Tale Bearer." But you see the elephants kept bothering me all the time. They seemed to beg to be photographed. As elephants interest me more than any other animal in the world, we could not help going right after them, and it would have meant traveling long distances to get the tribes necessary for "Songa the Tale Bearer."
>
> As a matter of fact, "Songa" has been in the back of my head all the time. I continually photograph natives whenever I find them but I have not succeeded in getting the proper sequence to make up the completed feature.[38]

The Johnsons never made a separate film on African native life, because Africans when viewed as natural history objects could be interwoven into a film about wildlife in Africa. As long as Africans appeared on screen as children unspoiled by civilization, then they fit into the discourse of Brightest Africa as a primitive continent.[39] Clearly, the Johnsons responded to the forces of commercialization in making *Simba*; however, they never conceded that they had faltered as scientists and naturalists in presenting the "real" Africa to the American public.

The Johnsons would adapt the formula used to write *Simba* to produce their later films, *Congorilla* and *Baboona*, which the AMNH refused to endorse officially as collaborative with the museum. Nevertheless, the museum noted that in the Johnson films there was "a commendable absence of the extraneous and the preposterous," deeming the pictures "natural and enlightening." The museum lamented, "So much misinformation exists regarding animal behavior" but rejoiced "to witness a series of films that far from perpetuating error, or more damaging still, swelling the total of untruths, succeeds in presenting unchangeable facts about animals." Johnson's fashioning of himself as Bwana Picture—"Master of Pictures" or "Mr. Picture" (as he was called by Swahili-speaking Africans)—and expert on Africa seemed to have gone unchallenged by many of his peers. Indeed, Martin and Osa "Memsahib Kidogo" Johnson established themselves as innovators in wildlife documentary and destroyers of myths about unknown Africa. According to Ernest Hemingway, the Johnsons had shattered all presumptions about Darkest Africa by bringing it to the "silver screen." Martin Johnson once assessed his and Osa's contribution to the film industry and science: "For twenty-seven years we devoted our lives to trying to capture a vanishing world. We have assembled a vast library of film of wild animals, savage human beings, and landmarks of natural beauty so that posterity might forever be able to recall it as it once existed in its last and greatest stronghold." Leaders in wildlife photography, naturalists who "bagged" with "camera rather than the gun," and crusaders in the fight against nature fakers, they did everything in their power to save a vanishing continent for coming generations.[40]

If the more than fifteen reviews of the film provide any significant gauge of public reception of *Simba*, then the movie, despite its supposedly uncompromising image of African animals and contribution to environmentalism, did more to buttress the stereotype of Darkest Africa than to deconstruct it. An examination of the production of the Johnsons' later films, *Congorilla* and *Baboona* (during the 1930s reprisal of the jungle movie "vogue"), against such films as *Ingagi*, *Trader Horn*, *Ubangi*, and *Sanders of the River* unveils the Johnsons' complicity in making "inauthentic" films of Africa. Additionally, it places the Johnsons' works alongside the very films that they themselves vehemently opposed. The overall criticism launched against jungle films centered on the notion of authenticity.

Making Africa Real

When *Ingagi* opened in theaters in April 1930, no one suspected that the film would become controversial and eventually be banned by Will H. Hays, president of the Motion Picture Producers and Distributors of America and architect of the Hays Motion Picture Code. Moreover, it seemed unlikely that independent movie houses would champion the film, earning its distributor Congo Pictures millions of dollars, over three times what it cost to make. The film's debut at the Orpheum Theatre in Los Angeles drew crowds. Initial reviews of the movie hailed it for its daring in presenting "weird tribal rites" that might lead scientists to the "missing link," echoing a display ad that asked: "Has the fabled Missing Link been found at last?" Critics claimed that the film surpassed "the wildest imaginings of H. Rider Haggard and Jules Verne." Producers stated that *Ingagi* was made from footage of Sir Hubert Winstead and Captain Daniel Swayne's Congo expedition to secure rare game specimens unique to the region. The safari party encounters wild beasts—buffaloes, elephants, leopards, lions, and crocodiles—before coming across an African tribe that has captured an "ingagi" (gorilla). Then the men filmed evidence of a practice previously dismissed as myth: African men sacrificing African women to gorillas, who carry them off to the jungle. Several reviewers, although disturbed by the scenes, never doubted their veracity, as critics and moviegoers alike seemed to believe that the film was a documentary, an assumption that Congo Pictures never corrected until the film was banned.[41]

Quoting several of these commentaries on the sacrifice and abduction scenes elucidates the power of the film to deceive even the most vigilant of critics. One reviewer wrote: "The apex is reached in the final scenes which shows [sic] an African tribe (believe it or not) making a human sacrifice to the Ingagi, or gorillas." Another stated: "It seems that amongst the more advanced thinkers of the Upper Congo there is, or was, a deep-seated conviction that it would be a smart thing every year to sacrifice some women folk to the gorillas. It is upon this spirit of altruism that at least part of the plot . . . is based." Yet another proclaimed "the discovery of what may easily be creatures that are half human, half ape." Another reviewer wrote: "Apparently also there is a tribe of natives lowest of all in the scale of humanity, scarcely as intelligent as the apes, who each year after an elaborate celebration which is hideously weird, give one of the women to the gorillas. That these women are taken as companions by the great apes is claimed and some of the pictorial evidence in 'Ingagi' . . . seems to bear out this belief." This same reviewer stated that the footage of wild animals indicated that African wildlife was not "rapidly disappearing." Lastly, one reviewer noted that the white men "encountered not only gorillas in plenty, but wild women, queer children, that seemed to be the offspring of some unholy alliance, and finally came upon a tribe very low in the scale of intelligence which had a yearly custom of giving a woman to the apes! Unbelievable as it seems, the record has been obtained." These critics recognized how incredible the "evidence" of ape-human mating and missing links may have appeared, especially as many of the scenes suffered from "graininess," which they attributed to the African climate.[42] Nevertheless, they did not waiver from their conviction that Africans were capable of the acts alleged in the movie. So what convinced them that the film was a fake?

The revelation that *Ingagi* was a hoax can be attributed to several factors. First, someone discovered that the African scenes were spliced from "a majority of all the jungle pictures ever made." Second, an African American actor, Hilton Phillips, filed a suit in court for unpaid wages for playing both a native and Ingagi. Third, the National Better Business Bureau made inquiries with British agencies, who could not verify the existence of Sir Winstead. Last, someone discovered that one of the African women featured in the film lived in Los Angeles's "black belt," where she attended school, and that the Pygmies were actually African American children from California. One article referred to "complaints from various organizations" about the film, requesting that it be banned. In a biting exposé, Mollie Merrick lambasted film critics who attested to the educational value of the film and the realness of the Africans. She wrote: "That some of the Negresses from this remote African locale—a locale so primitive that women were allowed to be sacrificed to 'Ingagi'—carried vaccination marks on their arms and legs, didn't seem to register with the savants who hailed it as a contribution to the world's general information." Critics like Merrick seemed less concerned with the splicing of wildlife footage in the film, as those scenes represented the "real" Africa. They objected to the role African American actors and extras played "in making Africa real" in *Ingagi*. Only after critics discovered that the gorillas and Africans were not "authentic" (a term used repeatedly) did white film critics (often for the same newspapers that praised film) dismiss the film as a fraud. It must be emphasized that they did not reject the idea that gorillas could successfully mate with African women or that African men callously and routinely engaged in rituals that abused women; rather, they expressed shock and offense at discovering that the scenes were shot in Los Angeles.[43] In stark contrast, African American critics objected to the film's depiction of gorillas carrying off African women to defile them, as such scenes debased black womanhood and portrayed African men as exploiters of black women. Ida B. Wells, who led the film committee for the Urban League, launched a campaign against the sequel *Song of Ingagi*.[44] Arguably, *Ingagi* was the most objectionable film depicting Africa as the Dark Continent produced up until 1930. However, film studios released more controversial "African" films well into the 1930s.

Nominated for Best Picture (Outstanding Production) in 1931 by the Academy of Motion Picture Arts and Sciences, *Trader Horn* was the first feature fiction film shot in Africa. It tells the story of real-life explorer Aloysius "Trader" Horn, who accompanies Edith Trent on a search for her long-lost daughter, Nina. When Trent enters a village alone, convinced that the natives will become violent if they see white men (Horn and his sidekick, Peru) with guns, Edith is murdered. Horn continues the journey in honor of Edith and encounters the White Goddess (actually Nina Trent), an evil "deity" ruling over the Africans, who worship her beauty. The goddess sentences the men to death but has a sudden change of heart and returns with them to "civilization." The film includes actual footage of African crewmen who had been killed by crocodiles and charging rhinos and other scenes of mayhem as the protagonists escape the dangerous forests with the aide of Pygmies. Tinée said of the film: this "is Africa." In a letter to the editor of the *Chicago Daily Tribune*, Carveth Wells, a member of the New York Explorer's Club, objected to Tinée's review, declaring: "As a faked motion picture it isn't in the same class as 'Ingagi'; it is so much more cleverly faked." He reprimanded Tinée for not informing her readers that the film "is not intended to present a true picture of Africa, but merely to give the public a pictorial version of a book of fiction," claiming that there existed more accurate pictures of Darkest Africa. Wells based his objection to the film on what he alleged were staged or fake scenes, not the location, which is how the editor interpreted his critique, stating: "Of course, it is possible that the company spent a year or two in Africa for their health and returned to Hollywood to make the picture."[45] Tellingly, Wells argued for a more "accurate," but no less dark picture of Africa. The Johnsons, fellow Explorer's Club members, criticized such films as inaccurate—not only as forgeries but also for failing to capture Brightest Africa on screen.

Fresh off their success with *Simba*, the Johnsons did not hesitate to critique other African films. Martin Johnson reviewed Paul Hoeffler's film *Africa Speaks* (1930), which was also inspired by an African expedition for a natural history museum. He criticized the film for showing Africans outside their "real situation." Contrary to Johnson's "expert" analysis, the *Chicago Daily Tribune* critic Roberta Nangle called the film "another star-winning jungle picture," jokingly adding, "[Yes, I remember 'Ingagi,' but this one looks authentic to my untutored eye.]" Johnson also reviewed the film *Ubangi*, produced by Louis Newman in 1931 at the request of the National Better Business Bureau, the same agency that initiated an investigation of *Ingagi*. Johnson reported that the film was a "mockery." He and other "scientific authorities" revealed that the film contained a significant amount of misinformation in the commentary that accompanied the film. This film also claimed to be a record of the Davenport-Quigley Expedition, an African safari to cannibal lands. The Better Business Bureau advised audiences not to see the film if "they wanted to see their knowledge of Africa and of natural history moved back several years."⁴⁶ Johnson's most consistent condemnation of these two films was that they misrepresented the natural history of Africa and African life. Ironically, he and Osa Johnson would exercise similar creative license in their final two African films, *Congorilla* and *Baboon*.

In *Congorilla*, the Johnsons declared the Congo to be "a land where man and beast still live as in the Garden of Eden." Once again they had captured Africa "as God made it." However, this Eden was far from paradise as "the Dark Continent is also a land of hardship—a land where Peril and Death stalk amid primitive savages and primeval monsters—a lure indeed to the adventurous spirit of the explorer." The content of this blatantly commercial film greatly resembled scenes in *Simba*. Once again "an animal paradise"—the Serengeti Plains—is presented on screen. Zebra, wildebeest, eland, ostrich, giraffe, oryx, and lion roam the plains. As in *Simba*, the Johnsons play up the sense of danger and death that lurks at the waterhole as animals stalked their prey. Scenes of a lake in Nakuru "such as might have existed in the days of the Dawn of Life" and other panoramas of landscapes display the beauty of Africa. This magnificence is then contrasted to the "tangled jungles" of the Ituri forests and its "weird tribes of Little People."⁴⁷

As in *Simba*, the Johnsons exploited Africans as comic relief; however, in *Congorilla* for the first time they began manipulating the environment in which they filmed Africans as children of nature awed by white technology. The Johnsons place the peoples of the Ituri forest, labeled "pygmies," into awkward situations. In one scene, Martin Johnson gives cigarettes to the "funny little savages" to smoke and says, "Now I hope you get sick." The Africans are shown choking and coughing on the smoke. Another group is given cigars to smoke, again with the hope that they would become ill. In yet another scene of mockery, Osa Johnson plays jazz for the Africans and teaches them to dance to "jungle music." Martin remarks, "Most savages are greatly puzzled by the phonograph, but the childlike pygmies accept it without curiosity, as just another wonder of the white man." He noted that although the African occasionally fell out of time it was "remarkable how quick they caught the rhythm of our modern music." At one point a native girl sings a song, which the Johnsons dub the "pygmy version" of "We Have No Bananas." Earlier, Osa had rendered her adaptation of the song after doling out bananas (that is, "monkey food") to the Africans. Perhaps equally disturbing as the debasing scenes of the Ituri peoples is the fantasy that passed for the Ituri village. Due to technical problems, the

Johnsons were unable to shoot lasting footage of the Ituri in the village. Therefore, they reconstructed a village in the plains, where five hundred villagers would live. In effect, the village was a controlled environment much like a Hollywood set. Instead of receiving the unyielding approval from the museum community and scientists, the film was criticized for its "showmanship."[48]

In *Baboona: An Aerial Epic over Africa*, the Johnsons blazed "a new trail of exploration and discovery" and took "to the air for their last African safari." The film included shots taken from the Johnsons' amphibians (seaplanes), *The Spirit of Africa* and *Osa's Ark*. The film claims to be "a new picture of the secrets of the Dark Continent" taken "in a real modern way." Comparable to *Simba* and *Congorilla*, the film focuses on the wildlife with some random scenes of native life. The Johnsons showed the film to the scientific staff of the AMNH before releasing it to the public. The museum president, F. Trubee Davison, praised the film for its "marvelous records of the wild life of Africa as well as [its] exquisite views of the deserts, plains, and mountains." However, he regretted that they used "dramatic license" in depicting a "fight between a leopard and wart hog." This scene was "superfluous in an otherwise superb picture."[49] Once again, the Johnsons succeeded in filming the wildlife and landscapes of Africa. However, their films did little to accurately represent the lives of various African peoples. *Simba, Congorilla*, and *Baboona* failed to meet the supposedly objective standards of Brightest Africa converts. Africans did not fit into their narrative unless they could be ridiculed or infantilized. With the exception of the Ituri, in the Johnsons' cinematic imagining of Brightest Africa, Africans were not disappearing and, thus, did not warrant further expenses and travels to document their lifestyles. Fortuitously, according to Johnson, the Pygmies, believed to be an "endangered species" by many Westerners, resided in the Congo forests.

The release of *Baboona* coincided with the debut of *Sanders of the River*. Although some film critics labeled the latter film one in a long succession of jungle pictures, for Pan-Africanists the film served as imperialist propaganda. Ironically, Pan-Africanist, anti-imperialist, internationalist, and communist Paul Robeson appeared in the film alongside Nina Mae McKinney. Both Robeson and McKinney were accomplished thespians of stage and screen respected in the black community and by the guardians of race pride. The film tells the story of Lord Sanders, a British colonial commissioner who comes to Africa to rule over a district in Nigeria. What he finds is fugitive Bosambo, played by Robeson, exiled from his village by warmongering Chief Mofolaba, played by Tony Wade. Bosambo helps "Lord Sandy" wrest power from Mofolaba and gladly assumes his place as chief, appointed by the colonial official. Under Sanders's rule, with the help of Bosambo, the region enjoys five years of peace and prosperity. When Sanders departs for London, the district falls once again into chaos as white gun dealers and liquor distributors foment chaos and drunkenness among the Africans. Mofolaba stages a coup and captures Bosambo's wife, Lilongo, played by McKinney. A white missionary priest with the aid of African drummers sends for Sanders, who returns to save the district and subsequently declares Bosambo king.[50]

African American war correspondent and author Roi Ottley assessed the film in his column "Hectic Harlem" for the *New York Amsterdam News*. An anti-imperialist who embraced Pan-Africanist demands for the self-determination of African peoples, Ottley wrote that the film "was a subtle bit of propaganda in favor of imperialism" that conveniently arrived "at a strategic moment when the Italian-Ethiopian fracas was on the lips of everyone." He declared that the film "as a story failed miserably," despite its "beautiful photographic shots" and an "adequate" performance by Robeson. Ottley went on to discuss the negative impact the film could have on "ofays" (Pig Latin for "foes" and an offensive slang word for whites) "witnessing such a film." Remarking that the director, Alexander Korda, seemed obsessed with producing films that glorified Britain and her empire, Ottley explained that *Sanders of the River* failed to reveal the true reason behind Sanders's (and British) brokering of peace among Africans—the exploitation of black labor for the Crown. He feared that white audiences would leave the theater believing that "Africa should be ruled by overlords . . . which would naturally color their opinions" on the Italian-Ethiopian crisis. Ottley said that the mood of the film could be summed up in one "classic line" from the movie that identifies the Africans as "Sanders's Black Children." Although the film was fictional, Ottley placed it in historical context to explain the political work performed by the movie.[51]

Ottley recounted the exile of King Jaja of Opobo to St. Vincent Island from 1888 to 1891 by the British government. In Ottley's rendition of the story, the king refused to submit to British rule, especially to white commercial exploitation of gold and other natural resources in his kingdom. The British lured him to England to visit his son, a student at Oxford University, only to place him in shackles aboard ship, which set sail for the Caribbean. After five years in exile, the king was allowed to return to Africa; however, he never reached its shores alive. Some claimed that he "dropped dead" at the sight of Africa, while others believed (including Ottley) that he was "murdered on the altar of British Imperialistic greed." However, the history of King Jaja's relations with the British was more complex, as he at one time traded slaves with them and sent military assistance to British forces as they invaded the lands of the Asantehene. However, when King Jaja objected to the provisions of the Berlin Act of 1885 that placed his kingdom in the British sphere, the British resorted to "trickery" to dethrone him. Ottley's intent was clear: to draw parallels between the filmic seizure of power from an African ruler (Mofolaba) and the installation of an imperialist lackey (Bosambo) to the throne and the tragic story of King Jaja. For him, the politics behind the film could not be dismissed on account of it being fictional. These subtle glorifications of white seizures of power from "dark" Africans troubled Pan-Africanists.

Ottley did not stand alone in his interpretation of *Sanders of the River* as an apologia for imperialism that distorted "English diplomacy at its peak" and sugarcoated a coup d'état with musical numbers sung by the talented Robeson and McKinney.[52] As scholar Stephen Bourne notes, Marcus Garvey criticized Robeson harshly for his acceptance of the role of Bosambo, especially in light of his Pan-Africanist politics and arguably his place among Du Bois's "Talented Tenth" of Harlem. Garvey accused Robeson of contributing to the "vile and vicious propaganda against the Negro" by accepting roles that depicted African Americans as subservient to whites or willing helpers in the subjugation of Africans. Garvey did not discredit Robeson's talent but marveled at what he considered his naivety in trusting white directors to portray Africans favorably. Black critics on the left, presumably members of the African Blood Brotherhood and the Communist Party USA, felt that Robeson's appearance in the film betrayed his pilgrimage to the Soviet Union the year before the film's release. Robeson defended himself by admitting that he had not seen the entire film, only the initial African footage, which impressed him with the scenes of African "folk-ways." Only after learning of these criticisms did he view the entire film and realize its political bent. He also explained how the financial success of *Sanders* allowed him to win the screen role of King Christophe and begin the production of a film about Ethiopian King Menelik II. Additionally, he stated that if African American actors "rejected every role with which he is not ideologically in agreement" they would find themselves unemployed or confined to the "Left Theatre." The ends justified the means. Robeson eventually denounced the film publicly, positioning himself as the victim of unscrupulous British filmmakers invested in their country's imperialist agenda.⁵³

Reel Africa

The film critic Nelson B. Bell in "A Hollywood Secret—Jungle License—A Pointed Analogy" (1931) addressed moviegoers' expectations of authenticity in jungle pictures, describing the film criticism of this genre as absurd and misguided. In many ways his criticism reveals the failure of Pan-Africanists and naturalists to successfully challenge and thereby transform cinematic portrayals of Africa. Wearied by what he viewed as endless complaints that African adventure films showed "indifference to the facts of nature and the habits of the beasts of the jungle ... from the textbook truths taught in the classroom," Bell asked: "What has become of the much vaunted 'Land of Make-Believe' that was supposed to be the theatre?" He argued that audiences should not hold the theater and the screen to "rigid limitations" so that the only African films that get produced are those that cease to entertain.⁵⁴ Bell's opinion in many ways explains the limited success of Pan-Africanists and naturalist-environmentalists in challenging the film industry. Although the lack of finances and access to film studios hampered Pan-Africanists seeking to rehabilitate Africans on screen, in contrast to naturalist filmmakers, the expectation of the audience dictated the formulaic content of screenplays. Bell represented the mainstream American moviegoer who sought escapism in cinema more than education. The American public was not ready to sacrifice its fantasies of African jungles, savages, white heroes, and mysterious white goddesses for the sake of racial understanding and scientific accuracy.

Recalling the *Ingagi* controversy, Bell conceded that the film was "an unconscionable piece of fakery" but reminded his viewers that neither Congo Pictures nor the other host of production companies that backed fictional African adventure films made any "pretense at historical and zoological accuracy." Looking back on all the jungle films he reviewed for the *Washington Post*, Bell claimed that the only unsuccessful ones were those that developed their plot from *Encyclopedia Britannica*. These "realistic dramas" bored audiences with their endless scenes of sunsets, immobile animals, and drifting clouds. Bell ended his discussion of the censorship campaigns against and negative film reviews of African jungle movies thusly:

> I view the jungle pictures in much the same light—and possibly there is more of an analogy than I have expressed, or cared to. It seems to me

of secondary importance whether the troupe of lions that makes its kill almost under the expedition's motor truck is half tame or ferociously wild; or whether the leopards and the lions fight savagely over their four-legged breakfast of baby hyena in northern Mexico or in the heart of darkest Africa, so long as they put on a good show. And assuredly, they have done that, almost without exception. Our lessons in natural history we can get out of a book.[55]

Bell targeted naturalists and members of scientific institutions who disapproved of filmmakers shooting African scenes on Hollywood lots or in the rainforests of Brazil or Mexico. He may have been aware of the Akeleys' and Johnsons' objection to the Hayden Snow film and the documentary of the Vanderbilt expedition, both which used questionable methods to capture footage of African animals. Or perhaps, he read Johnson's reports on *Ubangi* and *Africa Speaks*. Bell did not address those who critiqued jungle movies that promoted imperialism or besmirched the black character. His focus on natural history speaks to the public prominence of naturalists who decried African movies featuring fake heroes and dangerous animals. However, his silence on more politicized evaluations of jungle pictures does not undermine the importance and centrality of such critical appraisals, as his comfort with both Hollywood's and the British film industry's portrayals of Africans indicates. Bell's article bespoke his privileged position as a white male in a society where those who controlled mass communications shaped public attitudes on matters both mundane and profound.

That Pan-Africanists urged African American screen actors and filmmakers to use their talents to promote the "race" underscores the seriousness with which they approached media as propaganda tools. While they did not eschew the entertainment value of art, like Locke and Du Bois, many Pan-Africanists believed that the "Negro artist"—which beginning in the 1910s included those in the motion picture industry—had a duty to advance the struggle for equality. Criticisms of Robeson's appearance in *Sanders of the River* and later in *King Solomon's Mines* (1937) stemmed from this understanding of the political as well as cultural function of art. Pan-Africanists reasoned that white Americans could afford to turn a blind eye to "anti-Negro" cinema, as they enjoyed full citizenship rights and the freedom to express their manhood and womanhood. Unwarranted natural history lessons notwithstanding, American audiences' willingness to believe that *Ingagi* furnished indisputable proof that gorillas desired African women and indeed procreated with them weakens Bell's argument that jungle pictures were just entertainment.

Naturalists and Pan-Africanist understood the transformative power of film to shape and create new images of Africa. Naturalists, in their quest to convince the American public of Africa's brightness, not only criticized the film industry but seized on the technology to create their own cinematic counternarrative to the Dark Continent thesis. Pan-Africanists also used print media, notably black newspapers and periodicals, to censure anti-Africa films. However, unlike naturalists, they lacked the resources to produce their own "reel Africa." Those black filmmakers with resources like Oscar Micheaux produced films such as *Daughter of the Congo* (1930) aligned more with *Sanders* and *Ubangi*; however, instead of white heroes and heroines, lighter-skinned blacks played the hero and lost goddess, while the darker-skinned blacks played the savages. Micheaux's film was critiqued by African American newspapers. In the *Amsterdam News*, Theophilus Lewis lambasted Micheaux for casting all of the lighter-skinned African Americans in the "noble roles" replete with Western garb—including the mixed-raced Congolese girl raised by the "primitive" African tribe—and the darker-skinned blacks as half-naked savages."[56] Micheaux seems to have taken up the Congo question and found imperialist images of the region authentic and compelling. While he considered himself a "race man," he never claimed to be a Pan-Africanist. Also, the fervor surrounding his film never seemed to galvanize as much black criticism as Robeson's role in *Sanders of the River*, perhaps because Robeson espoused Pan-African ideas. It would take decades before a body of less problematic African films—both naturalistic and Pan-Africanist—emerged.

The public outcry against and criticism of films such as *Ingagi*, *Sanders of the River*, *Ubangi*, *Congorilla*, and *Hunting Big Game in Africa* highlighted America's appetites for authentic images of Africa, of its wildlife and people. This quest for authenticity in film, which producers promoted as either documentaries or commercial entertainments, occurred during a historical moment when Americans began reimagining Africa in the aftermath of its partition. Some viewers and critics proved uninterested in debunking the myth of Darkest Africa, seeking rather cinematic confirmation that in Africa lay the heart of darkness. Yet, these Americans wanted something new: not the old fare found in nineteenth-century novels and travel narratives, but rather footage of recently discovered African mysteries. Pan-Africanists and naturalists alike acknowledged the public's craving for portraits of Africa that reinforced long-standing stereotypes. For naturalists like Carl Akeley and the Johnsons, the goal was to capture African wildlife, landscapes, and peoples on film to present Africa "as God made it"—a primitive wonderland. In contrast, Pan-Africanists aimed to challenge cultural stereotypes of Africans as cannibals and savages, as well as to critique cinematic vindications of imperialism. The two objectives intersected so far as they criticized a film industry more interested in earning profit than educating the American public about Africa and Africans. The reel Africa was not real Africa.

CONCLUSION
The Wonders of Africa Brought to America

In December 1934 the *Pittsburgh Courier* announced: "Abyssinia, world's most extensive and populous Negro-governed country, is seriously menaced by the territorial and commercial ambitions of Italy and the diplomatic maneuverings of France." Recounting "secret designs against Abyssinia," the reporter concluded: "Doubtless Abyssinia will be left to fight its battles alone against Italian imperialism. It acquitted itself magnificently under Menelik at Adowa, as Italians painfully recall. It may do so again, despite Italy's air force." Indeed, in 1896 Italy attempted to add Ethiopia to its empire only to have its forces routed by soldiers armed with "feudal" weapons. Motivated by a desire to restore the Italian empire to its height during the Roman period and avenge the defeat at Adowa, Mussolini attempted to invade Ethiopia in 1935. The African nation found itself defending its borders against Italian invasion at Walwal. Ethiopia appealed to the League of Nations on January 3, 1935, to little avail. Britain and France did not want to agitate the Italians, fearing an alliance between Mussolini and Hitler. Additionally, Britain and France were imperial powers themselves with vast territories in Africa, and their delegates scoffed at Haile Selassie's demand that, as a member of the league, Ethiopia should be treated as an equal at the diplomatic bargaining table. In the end, Italy agreed to arbitrate the matter outside of the Permanent Court of International Justice (the World Court).[1]

The words of J. A. Rogers in his November 1934 "Ruminations" for the *New York Amsterdam News* appear predictive. Discussing the controversy over Emperor Selassie's objection to the use of the term *Negro* to describe Ethiopians, Rogers—a noted self-taught historian and race theorist—stated that most "Aframericans" agreed that the term was "disgraceful." However, Rogers argued that in the final analysis, nomenclature was of little consequence to the white imperialist. He remarked:

> As for the Ethiopians, or Abyssinians, or whatever name they choose to adopt, they will remain a black people, generally darker in skin-color and woollier in hair, than the average Aframerican. Because they are black, the hand of white imperialism is against them. The whites now insist that these Abyssinians are not Negroes, but Semites, Hamites, and heaven knows what. If, however, these whites ever get them in their power they are going to treat them as they have treated all the other natives of Africa, regardless of what category of "ite" they place them in now.

Rogers, a noted black internationalist, wrote several essays and articles emphasizing the imperative for "Negroes" to unify on the basis of their ties of consanguinity, especially in defense of Africa. His diatribe against Selassie reflected his main thesis in this work on race and "race-mixing"—that the one-drop rule imposed by whites exempted all members of the "dark races" from consideration as "Aryans."[2] Rogers's racial theories aside, because many Africans in the diaspora viewed Ethiopians as kindred, they rushed to aid and defend Ethiopia against imperialist aggression. Others did so because of their anticolonialist and/or Pan-Africanist politics.

July 1935 was a busy month for Pan-Africanists and other sympathizers with Ethiopians across America. The *Amsterdam News* called on "Negroes" in America, the West Indies, South America, and Africa to use the "power of protest"—partial boycotts of Italian goods, petitions to colonial governments, and demands that the U.S. State Department call in the Italian Great War debt—to pressure for international intervention in Il Duce's march on Ethiopia. Appealing to blood ties, Pan-Africanism, and Black Nationalism, the newspaper stated: "Negroes in the Western Hemisphere, who are related racially to the Ethiopians, have a profound and natural interest in the impending conflict. Most of them want to see the last real sovereign black nation in Africa remain free. They want Ethiopia to win." On July 15, the Committee for Ethiopia distributed 500,000 peace petitions, hoping to secure some 10,000,000 signatories to urge President Roosevelt to intervene in the Italian-Ethiopian conflict under the provisions of the Kellogg-Briand Pact (1928). The pact called for the isolation of nations that engaged in war not justified under the self-defense clause. The United States refused. When the U.S. government demanded that Americans evacuate Ethiopia's capital it became clear that neutrality would prevent direct black participation in the conflict. According to the *Washington Post*, as the committee began its petition campaign, Harlem was "rumbling to schemes for 'mobilization' of its man-power in defense of 'Africa for Africans.'" These plans included a rally led by the Pan-African Reconstruction Association. In an article for the *Amsterdam News*, Maurice Jennings asked "What is Africa to you?" in a clear reference to Countee Cullen's "Heritage." He begged his readers to reflect on the meaning of Africa to their lives as the "Legions of Rome" advanced on Ethiopia. Playing on Kipling's poem "The White Man's Burden," he called on black men to take up their burden, predicting that in a matter of time Liberia and Ethiopia would fall to European control. Jennings urged young people to read "Heritage," a poem that for him signaled "the coming day for a renascent Africa—a day when the black men of the world will reclaim it."[3]

The *New York Times*, in a July article titled "Harlem Ponders Ethiopia's Fate," reported on various activities taking place in Harlem to protest Italian encroachment on Ethiopian territory. Referring to mass meetings, planned and canceled parades, soap-box speeches, communist gatherings, and "racialist" orations, the reporter criticized the motives of a "small, highly articulate and aggressive minority" for advancing their causes under the pretense of defending Ethiopia. The article mocked the average Harlemite for joining the movements only because "black men are being threatened by white," asserting that African Americans had nothing to gain whether or not Ethiopia triumphed over the Italians. The author disparaged blacks who, like good patriots "in time of war," flocked to the streets to hear of "the white man's perfidy and chicanery" and pledged to boycott Italian businesses or to volunteer for Ethiopia's army. The reporter expressed skepticism about the success of an upcoming parade, where class consciousness would unite Italian Americans and African Americans to march in solidarity from Little Italy to Harlem to protest Italian aggression.[4] The newspaper's coverage of Harlem and African American internationalism underscored American fears of so-called radicalized Negroes.

African Americans' pledge to join Selassie's army and fight against the Italian invaders was no idle threat. The Neutrality Act of 1935 issued after Italy invaded Ethiopia proclaimed that "during any war in which the United States is neutral" the president could proclaim that "no citizen of the United States shall travel on any vessel of any belligerent nation except at his own risk." Although that statement was targeted at Americans traveling on Italian ships primarily, travel on Ethiopian vessels was also prohibited. Most important, American citizens could not fight in a foreign army without facing potential loss of citizenship, fines, and prison time. Selassie continued to accept African American volunteers for its army until the U.S. government pressured Ethiopia to stop all such activities.[5]

On August 4, the Provisional Committee for the Defense of Ethiopia and the American League against Fascism and War succeeded in organizing the rally in Harlem attended by members of the NAACP, the National Urban League, the Brotherhood of Sleeping Car Porters, Pioneers for Ethiopia, the International League for Peace, Father Divine's Angels, African American leaders, white elites, and members of the black and white working classes. Approximately twenty thousand demonstrators cried "Down with Mussolini!" and "Death to fascism!" as crowds cheered from the sidewalks and apartment windows. Ethiopian flags blew in the wind as speakers representing Jewish synagogues, Italian American newspapers, the Communist Party USA, various Protestant churches, and civil rights organizations took the podium at Bradhurst and Edgecombe avenues to pledge nonviolent fealty to Ethiopia in her struggle against Mussolini and urge the crowd to donate generously to the cause. The rally came to an end around seven that evening with demonstrators mobilized to fight against fascism and war in the days ahead. Two months later, Italy began its formal invasion of Ethiopia.[6]

In October, Ethiopia lost battles to Italy at Adowa and Axum. The country again appealed to the league, which declared Italy to be the aggressor nation and initiated sanctions that ultimately had little effect. Beginning in January 1936, a series of decisive battles took place that both devastated Ethiopian forces and dismayed their supporters in America, particularly Pan-Africanists whose dreams of a renascent Africa seemed to hinge on the outcome of the war. On May 2, Emperor Selassie and most of his army retreated into exile, where according to the Black Condor, John C. Robinson, they began the guerrilla warfare phase of the conflict. Selassie, now exiled in London, refused to meet with the London-based International African Friends of Ethiopia or with the resident Garvey. When the Italians captured Addis Ababa on May 5 and annexed Ethiopia to its empire two days later, Garvey spoke at Hyde Park denouncing Selassie for leaving his people at the mercy of the Italians and refusing to accept aid from "Negroes." The defeat of Ethiopia reverberated throughout Pan-Africanist and black anticolonialist circles and revived Black Nationalist ideology.[7]

On May 19, 1936, Harlemites continued to protest the Italian invasion (and now occupation) of Ethiopia, their last vestige of hope that Africa would emerge as a bright star among nations. In contrast to the peace rally held a year earlier, the nonviolent political gathering in front of Patsy's Fish Market that morning turned riotous after a white patrolman, Michael Ronan, shot a black man, Lee Cornish, while reportedly running to the aid of fellow patrolmen George Brennan and James Schowers. While more patrolmen and mounted policemen rushed to the scene, somewhere between three hundred to four hundred persons joined the crowd by either fighting with police in the streets, throwing stones and bricks from the tenement rooftops, or "raiding" Italian Americans' stores, including Joseph De Lucca's fruit and vegetable stand. According to the police, some of the protesters went in search of patrolman Charles Brown, an African American officer who arrested several demonstrators during meetings held at the corner in previous weeks. Meanwhile, mounted policemen pushed the crowd into the tenements or side streets. The disruption ended after thirty minutes, and the policemen took Cornish to a nearby hospital for treatment.[8]

It is not clear what motivated those who protested to defend Ethiopia to hold meetings for several weeks in front of Patsy's, an establishment owned by an Italian American. Perhaps they suspected the proprietor of being a former member of the defunct Fascist League of North America. Or, more likely, they noted the revelry and pride that many profascist New York City Italian Americans—especially businessmen—exhibited in the wake of the invasion and chose to demonstrate outside of Italian American establishments that economically "invaded" their neighborhoods. Whether in keeping with the politics of Pan-Africanism or Black Nationalism or expressing disdain for police crackdowns aimed at arresting African Americans for assembling at street corners, these protestors did not choose the site for their meetings arbitrarily. On this street corner in Harlem, they symbolically restaged Ethiopia's conflict with Italy.[9]

The Harlem events represented ongoing protest in the broader African American community against the Italian invasion. Ethiopia was a nation iconic for indigenous rule in Africa, and its invasion signified a devastating loss of black autonomy around the globe. Many African Americans, especially Pan-Africanists and communists, viewed Ethiopia's struggle as a collective black struggle against white supremacy and Western capitalism. Many blacks accused the United States of turning a blind eye to fascism. Linking imperialism and fascism to Jim Crow and other forms of racial inequality, these Harlem demonstrators took to the streets to defend themselves as much as Ethiopia.[10]

In the speech "What I Saw in Ethiopia," delivered before the Bethel A. M. E. Church in Detroit on June 11, Rogers declared: "What happened in Ethiopia was the worst example of international trickery, roguery, and unscrupulousness ever seen in history. England had one hand on Ethiopia, and France the other." However, he explained to the crowd, Ethiopia collapsed not because of white people, but rather because of "black people—that treacherous group who sell out their fellowmen for personal gain. The Italians did not really win the war. Rebellion among the Ethiopians was the cause." In his estimation, the lack of race consciousness and Pan-Africanist sentiment among some Ethiopians, led by the emperor, doomed the nation to conquest. When the white man did not come to the rescue of Ethiopia, the emperor changed his tactics. Rogers interviewed Selassie, who accused Italians of mounting propaganda campaigns in the United States to convince blacks that Ethiopians considered themselves whites and "superior to Americans Negroes." Rogers, who claimed to be the only "race" war correspondent for a black newspaper, vouched that the Ethiopians did not seek to be disunited from the rest of the "darker races."[11] Perhaps more important, he reiterated Pan-Africanist views that "Afric's sons" must face the realities of Du Bois's color line together. The dream of a revived Africa remained but became immersed in a broader set of black anticolonialist values in the wake of the annexation.

Disappointed that they could not come to the aid of Ethiopia, some African American men and women associated with the Communist Party joined the Abraham Lincoln Brigade in the fall of 1936 to fight in the Spanish Civil War. Interpreting the fascist takeover of Spain as an extension of fascist aggression that brought Mussolini to Addis Ababa, African Americans were willing to defy U.S. neutrality and fight in a foreign conflict. Robin D. G. Kelley argues: "for them Spain had become the battlefield to revenge the attack on Ethiopia and part of a larger fight for justice and equality that would inevitably take place on U.S. soil." The invasion of Ethiopia, rather than dampen efforts to redeem and regenerate Africa, transformed African American interest in Africa beyond Pan-Africanist circles.[12]

Imagining brightest Africa for Pan-Africanists in America and the diaspora, whether expressed in religious or messianic rhetoric or political discourse, composed part of the complex matrix of black liberation ideology. This Africa was not simply a tourist destination or exotic retreat but rather a site for political autonomy, regeneration, and expression, as well as cultural renewal or return. Although at times expressing a rather static view of African history, Pan-Africanist thinking was overall forward looking—at once acknowledging the glories of the continent's precolonial past and envisioning an Africa that could stand the test of modernity. As the world once again approached near-global war, mainstream Pan-Africanists abandoned Garvey's vision of a united sub-Saharan African polity as a "bright star"—an African empire or confederation like the United States—for arguably a more achievable goal of independent, cooperating African nations functioning on the international political stage.

While African Americans and worldwide sympathizers with Ethiopia pondered the ultimate fate of the fallen African empire in the Italo-Ethiopian War, other Americans looked to Africa for answers to nature's mysteries. Relatively unconcerned with the political status of the African continent, American scientific institutions and museums continued sponsoring expeditions into Africa. Unlike their European counterparts enmeshed in the buildup to World War II, American naturalist-environmentalists persisted in their quest to bring the "wonders of Africa to America." After over thirty years of safaris in Africa, the AMNH decided not to delay the 1936 opening of the still unfinished Akeley African Hall. The museum officials argued that if they postponed the dedication until the completion of the remaining dioramas (leopard and river hog, cheetah, colobus monkey, vulture, chimpanzee, and mandrill) it would be a long time before the hall opened. Despite the missing groups and incomplete structural work, some trustees suggested opening the African Hall for the overflow of the museum's dedication of the Roosevelt Memorial statue scheduled for January. However, Daniel Pomeroy and James Clark "emphatically" objected to the proposition, as they feared "it would kill the opening of African Hall." Echoing the sentiments of many of the naturalists who had worked with Akeley on his dream of capturing Brightest Africa for generations of Americans to come, they wanted the hall's opening to be spectacular, not overshadowed by the memory of the deceased president.[13]

The museum initially scheduled the opening for March. However, some museum officials suggested dedicating the hall on Akeley's birthday

(May 19), as it nearly coincided with the museum's Eighth Annual Members' Visiting Day. They reasoned that changing the date would "be desirable from the publicity standpoint," ensuring a sizable crowd for the opening. The museum's hope to generate as much public exposure for the launching ceremony as possible prompted them to invite *New Yorker* critic Morris Markey for an early viewing of the hall. Although the administrators sought to impress the museum-going public, they also arranged a private preview for the trustees, African Hall donors, and their families and friends the night before the opening. After the dedication ceremony, the hall would officially open to the public on May 20.[14]

Markey's review of African Hall characterized the exhibit as an "animal show," insinuating that it evoked feelings in its viewers akin to visiting a zoo, menagerie, or county fair. However, Markey clearly distinguished the hall from a live faunal exhibit, confessing "a certain pleasure in looking at those animals—a pleasure which is enhanced if they are dead, mounted, rather than alive, looking horribly unhappy, and smelling bad." The habitat diorama allowed naturalists to present an illusive portrait of nature, wherein animals appeared content rather than depressed by captivity. In this sense, Markey argued that the hall had "a three-way grip upon the mind and heart." It pleased visitors aesthetically, provided a "vivid lesson" in zoology, botany, and geography, and presented a historical "melodrama of enduring enthusiasms, of hardship, and of death."[15]

Explaining the aesthetic inspiration for the exhibition hall, Markey quoted the museum director, Roy Chapman Andrews: "'The idea was to give glimpses of Africa as they might be seen from a train window—the window of a sort of invisible train, which does not disturb the animals.'" The periodical *World Youth* also used the window as a metaphor, describing walking through the hall "as if one were looking through an open window across a living part of Africa—animals roaming, resting, browsing; colorful flowers, verdant woods, humid jungles, rolling plains, desert wastes and precipitous mountains." Markey commented that the "virtually invisible" glass protecting the exhibits, the backgrounds painted on "a sort of cyclorama," and the mounted specimens, along with a skillful use of lighting to simulate both the "twilight of the jungle" and tropical sunshine, created a "miraculous semblance of life of the African scene." The museum had succeeded in "mounting an imitation of Nature." Daniel Pomeroy concurred: "The American Museum has done more than merely keep a record of the animals of Africa. Each group is not alone an exhibit of the type of animal it features, but it is a complete cross-section of the region, which reveals the geology, botany, bird, and reptile life of the region. It goes so far as to cover even the meteorological features such as characteristic types of clouds."[16] African Hall left no aspect of Africa's "scene" uncovered. Every aesthetic detail of the hall had been orchestrated to perfection. Viewers would walk away from the exhibit feeling as if they had walked through Akeley's Brightest Africa and not Stanley's Dark Continent.

That Akeley's African Hall translated Brightest Africa as the white man's experience with nature appears clearly in Markey's melodramatic reading of the hall. For Markey, the exhibit acted as a travel narrative of sorts, conveying to spectators the enthusiasm, hardship, and death experienced by white hunter-naturalists on their quests to discover the authenticity of African nature. The hall expresses the travelers' amazement at seeing exotic animals up close and their exhaustion from long days and nights traveling through difficult terrains. Because the hall was dedicated to the deceased Akeley, an additional narrative was undergirded by its displays—man's conquest over and defeat by the environment. As Donna Haraway has argued, the view from the "invisible train" provides a visual account of Akeley's travels and demise on the continent—a privileged gaze of a white man traveling through Brightest Africa, witnessing its natural beauties with foreknowledge of their probable extinction.[17]

What the hall does not reveal is Akeley's original intention to document native life in his exhibit. In his travel narrative *In Brightest Africa* and plans sent to the AMNH board, Akeley made explicit this goal. Yet his narrative of Brightest Africa allocates no space to a systematic ethnography of Africans he encountered on his travels. However, he devotes an entire chapter to Uimba Gikungu, or "Bill," his "loyal" tent boy and later headman—a Kikuyu supposedly maligned by "conniving" Swahilis and Somalis who resented his position in the safari party. Akeley hired Gikungu as a gun boy (accounts vary as to whether Bill was nine or twelve) to serve him and aid the tent boy, Ali. Akeley described Gikungu as "my little Kikuyu friend" who "began his life as a little Kikuyu 'picaninny'"—a boy keen and agile—a "child of destiny." Referencing the derogatory caricature and term for a young black child, Akeley depicted Bill as a harmless, unkempt child engaged in playful antics while on safari. However, when Bill became a man, Akeley noticed disturbing trends in his behavior and began to write more critically of him. He portrayed Bill as sometimes shiftless, "cheeky," petulant, resentful, and untamed. Akeley recalled one of the few times he struck Bill, during an elephant hunt: "I wheeled and slapped Bill, because he had broken one of the rules of the game, which is that a black boy must

Advertisement for Akeley African Hall, 1937. Neg./Transparency no. 315382, courtesy the Library, American Museum of Natural History.

never shoot without orders unless his master is down and at the mercy of a beast. Of course it did not take long for me to come to the realization that Bill's shooting was done in perfectly good faith.... Bill's heart was broken and my apologies were forthcoming and were as humble as the dignity of a white man would permit." Despite his fondness for Bill, Akeley did not view him, or any African, as an equal. Akeley's overall portrait of Bill was of a faithful servant, a full-grown "boy" with an "exaggerated sense of loyalty" who would rather serve his master than one of his "own kind."[18]

Although Akeley devoted little discussion of Africans and their cultures in his written image of Brightest Africa (he mentioned only the Nandi by name; otherwise all Africans were "natives"), he attempted to incorporate Africans into his public display of the continent by sculpting Nandi bronzes to grace the hall and by promoting the Johnsons' film ventures. The unrealized *Songa, the Tale Bearer* was to be the museum's narrative of African life, a complement to the physical African Hall. However, the Johnsons could not capture native life on film in any methodical scientific fashion, instead choosing to depict Africans as comic relief in *Simba*. The museum decided to forgo displaying Akeley's sculptures and featured two life-sized bronzes of smiling male drummers sculpted by Malvina Hoffman, a former student of Rodin and employee of the Field Museum. This small representation of African life reflected images of Africans that most museum patrons and Americans in general found nonthreatening. As seen in the cover illustration for Leo E. Berliner's "Africana: A Ragtime Classic" (1904), images of "tribesmen" singing and dancing struck a chord with American consumers fascinated with primitive motifs. Visitors saw two happy "children of nature" making music instead of cannibals, poisoned-dart-throwing dwarfs, and slave traders, which populated fictional and nonfictional narratives of Darkest Africa.[19]

The museum depicts Africa as a continent filled with mysterious beasts and exotic flora. Mountain nyala emerges through shoulder-high heather on the mountains; a herd of elephants travels the plains following its leader; black-maned lions lie in tall grasses in the Serengeti; a family of zebra drink at a waterhole; and a male gorilla beats its chest to warn off encroachers. The invisible train would take its passengers across Africa without encountering a single human. Only the sound of distant drums would indicate that someone lived beyond the bright recesses of the jungle or the vast expanses of the plains. In African Hall, that person remained unseen and unknown.

Brightest Africa as imagined by naturalist-environmentalists in the mountains of Kivu, the rainforests of the Congo, and the veldts of the Serengeti and as invented on the silver screen and in the hallowed halls of Gotham's museum of natural history beckoned to a generation of Americans weary of city life, nostalgic for pastoral landscapes, and in search of a cause célèbre. From the Gilded Age to the Interwar Years, white American naturalists traveled to a continent that they were raised to believe was dark, inhabited by savages and dangerous animals, and filled with impenetrable jungles. Instead, they discovered "Congo Eden," "Lake Paradise," "Africa as God made it," and "gorilla trails in Paradise" as they savored "adventures" in the jungles, plains, and volcanic mountains. In their narratives of Brightest Africa, Africa came to represent earth's pristine past—Akeley's Africa of the Age of Mammals and Teddy Roosevelt's earth near the Pleistocene Epoch, when giant mammals roamed freely and primitive humanity just appeared. This Africa possessed no human civilizations, just humanity in its supposedly lowest/earliest form—wild men and women living in a natural state content with eking out subsistence off the land. As these naturalists made clear, Brightest Africa did not belong to these men and women inhabiting it, but rather to the white men and women equipped with the tools—diorama, film, and preserve—to "save" it.

As 1936 came to a close, those Americans who began reimaging Africa in the last decades of the nineteenth century as either a zoological wonderland or the site of a future black empire saw their dreams confront the stark reality of imperialism in Africa. Naturalists who sought to save Africa for themselves and future generations watched their vision of Brightest Africa progress from possibility to actuality. The successful opening of African Hall to critical acclaim and the development of similar African exhibits in other American museums of natural history, coupled with the founding of national parks in Africa, reinforced their assertion that the continent's brightness lay in its wide open spaces, jungle paradises, and faunal habitats. In contrast, Pan-Africanists who imagined Africa united under a confederation of powerful states witnessed the gradual conquest of a continent by European aggression. Although Liberia stood as the sole independent African nation on the eve of 1937, the loss of Ethiopia dealt a psychological blow to those seeking to preserve Africa for Africans.

In 1937, American trained scholar and future president of Nigeria, Nnamdi Azikiwe, published *Renascent Africa*, in which he contrasted "Old Africa" to the "New Africa" to come. Hailed by its publishers as a book "destined to revolutionize the ideas of Africans about Africans and the ideas of others about Africa," Azikiwe's monograph presented a new model of Pan-Africanism premised not on the ideas about Africa coming from the United States and West Indies but rather on African "self-analysis." Reviewed by Carter G. Woodson for the *Journal of Negro History* as critical reading for "students of Africa," the book represented an epistemological turn in Pan-Africanism as it urged Africans to look inward and embrace an indigenous self-help, racial-uplift ideology in realizing their own liberation.[20]

Whether flushed with success or defiant in the face of ostensible defeat, American naturalists and Pan-Africanists alike faced the coming years and decades resolved to carry on their preservation of and search for Brightest Africa, realizing that 1936 represented a watershed in their endeavors. Naturalist Mary Jobe Akeley recalled that "a great war, whose rumblings were even then shaking the continent from Abyssinia to the Cape, had occurred—cutting off both lines of *thought* and transport between America and Africa" (emphasis added). Although her husband's dream had come true according to the AMNH, more work needed to be done in Africa. Not until the end of World War II could she and other naturalists return to Africa to continue their environmentalist activities. In 1946, she returned to the "wilderness," to the "Congo Eden" that occupied her subconscious thoughts. Similarly, Pan-Africanists entered a new phase in their activism. Although many did not wait until the war ended to take up the banner of African liberation, they realized that the ante had been raised by Italy's aggression. On April 6, 1945, the Schomburg Library in Harlem hosted a "pan-African workshop" attended by members of the black intelligentsia, civil rights activists, and sympathetic whites. Among their many declarations, the attendees called for Italy to return occupied Ethiopian territory to indigenous rule.[21] The naturalist and Pan-Africanist ventures to save Africa would continue under different political and social contexts, as the aftermath of World War II brought into stark reality the global dimensions of colonialism and environmental destruction.

Renascent Africa

Discourses on Brightest and Darkest Africa have evolved since the end of World War II. The decolonizing of the continent, beginning with Ghanaian independence in 1957, proved to be a crucible not only for American Pan-Africanists who imagined a renascent Africa but also for the environmentalist movement in Africa led and controlled by white settlers and outsiders. The Organisation of African Unity founded in 1963 (later renamed the African Union) with its slogan "Africa Must Unite" on the surface appears to have realized Pan-African dreams of an African confederation and Garvey's call for African unity. While the organization operates somewhat similarly to the European Union, it has not gained the stature of the EU in international relations. The African Union brings together African nations—including those, such as Libya, criticized by various Western powers—without regard to racial categories. In this sense, the African Union exceeds the racialized prescription for African unity articulated by early twentieth-century Pan-Africanists. Today, almost all African nations are republics, with the exception of the kingdoms of Morocco, Lesotho, and Swaziland, and the socialist state of Libya. While all are not modelled exactly according to T. Thomas Fortune's vision of English civil government, republicanism has become the dominant form of government on the continent. These changes in the African political landscape, while bearing some markers of what American Pan-Africanists had imagined, resulted from African efforts to define their own models of the modern nation-state. Today, Pan-Africanist discourses engage issues of political corruption and unrest on the continent, but again Pan-African voices from within the continent dictate the parameters of that conversation.

Early Pan-Africanists argued that the political regeneration of Africa had to be accompanied by technological and commercial agricultural development. In African American forums, such as Tavis Smiley's "State of the Black Union," the development of Africa has continued to be a topic of discussion, particularly the technological gap. However, much of the foreign discussion on commercial agriculture in Africa is led by white-controlled agro-business and the World Bank. In 2008, the Organisation for Economic Co-Operation and Development (OECD) published a study on promoting commercial agriculture in Africa, focusing on Ghana, Senegal, Mali, Tanzania, and Zambia. The study concludes that efforts to transform agriculture in Africa using the business model have been ineffective. The World Bank has also noted the slow growth of commercial agriculture in the continent. African nations themselves are weighing the advantages and disadvantages of agro-business to their economic growth.[22]

With regard to environmentalism in Africa, Carl Akeley's and Mary Bradley's (among others) advocacy for gorilla preservation laid the groundwork for Jane Goodall's research on chimpanzees beginning in the 1960s, as well as famed zoologist Dian Fossey's work to save the gorillas beginning in 1978. Fossey's unsolved murder, which has been attributed to African poachers, underscores the historical tensions between Western ideas about environmental conservation, endangered species, and wildlife protection and some Africans' attempts to provide for their families via criminalized hunting. During and after the colonial period, poachers killed gorillas because the animals' parts commanded high prices in the trophy market. The resurgence of gorilla poaching in the twenty-first century in Rwanda has once again revealed how the illegal animal trade brings money to marginalized peoples. Although many of the postcolonial African states adopted conservationist programs, oftentimes in response to Western pleas, some policies have led the displacement of people from their traditional lands. African calls for community-controlled conservation seek to address the impact of resettlement.

The above cataloging of the ways in which Africa today resembles many of the imaginings of the continent by Pan-Africanists and naturalist-environmentalists from 1884 to 1936 is not meant to be evidence of the success of these two movements. Rather, it demonstrates how Africans themselves have shaped their own image of their individual countries, often in defiance of the Western trope of the Dark Continent. My objective in this study was to reveal the complexity of Euro-American and African American debates about Africa by situating them in visions of modernity in an era marked by technological innovation, global warfare, capitalist accumulation and imperialism. The transatlantic nature and scope of these debates impacted African political and environmental agendas for sure, but as Azikiwe expressed, the "New Africa" would be imagined by Africans.

CHRONOLOGY OF EVENTS

1884 Berlin Conference begins inaugurating the "scramble for Africa"
1885 General Act of Berlin Conference on West Africa is signed
 The Congo Free State is established
1890 The Great Migration of African Americans begins
 The U.S. Census Bureau declares the frontier closed
 George Washington Williams pens *An Open Letter to His Serene Majesty Leopold II* detailing the atrocities he witnessed in the Congo Free State
 Henry Morton Stanley publishes *In Darkest Africa*, his account of his mission to rescue Emin, the governor of Equatoria
 National Afro-American League is founded
1895 The Gammon Theological Seminary in Atlanta, Georgia, hosts the Congress on Africa in connection with the Cotton States and International Exposition
 The Cotton States and International Exposition features a Dahomey Village at Piedmont Park
1896 D. G. Elliot Expedition to British Somaliland for the Field Museum of Natural History in Chicago begins
 The Spanish-American War begins and ends
1897 Henry Sylvester Williams, a Trinidadian, founds the African Association, later called the Pan-African Association
1899 S. S. McClure Company publishes Theodore Roosevelt's *The Strenuous Life*
 The American Anti-Imperialist League is founded
1900 The First Pan-African Conference is held in London at Westminster Town Hall
1901 Xavier Pene's "Darkest Africa" exhibit opens at the Pan-American Exposition in Buffalo, New York
1902 The American Museum of Natural History (AMNH) receives the Western African Raff Collection of woodcarvings
1904 Ota Benga, a "Pygmy" from the Congo Free State, is exhibited at the St. Louis World's Fair
 The Congo Reform Association is founded in Great Britain and a sister branch in the United States

1905   Carl Akeley's British East Africa Expedition (Field Museum of Natural History in Chicago) begins
1906   (Richard) Tjäder Expedition to Africa (AMNH) begins
        The Fayum Expedition (AMNH) in search of fossils in Africa begins
1907   King Leopold II presents the AMNH with material culture from the Congo Free State
        The AMNH receives the Douglas African Collection and other ethnographic specimens
        Meta Warrick's *Landing of First Twenty Slaves at Jamestown* showcased at the Negro building at the 1907 Jamestown Tercentennial Exposition
1908   Henry Fairfield, prominent eugenicist, becomes president of the AMNH
        The Belgian government annexes the Congo Free State renaming it the Belgian Congo
1909   Akeley's British East Africa Expedition (AMNH) begins
        American Museum Congo Expedition, also called the Lang-Chapin Expedition (AMNH), begins
        Theodore Roosevelt's expedition to Africa for the Smithsonian begins
1910   The African Hall of Ethnology at the AMNH opens
        The National Association for the Advancement of Colored People is founded
        Roosevelt publishes *African Game Trails*
        William Sheppard returns to the United States after serving as a Presbyterian missionary
1911   Akeley proposes plan for African Hall
1914   Marcus Garvey founded the Universal Negro Improvement and Conservation Association and African Communities League (later UNIA) in Jamaica
        The first book edition of *Tarzan of the Apes* is published by Edgar Rice Burroughs
1915   Herbert Lang's Pygmy group is completed and displayed in the AMNH African Hall of Ethnology
1916   Marcus Garvey immigrates to Harlem
1917   The United States enters World War I
        New York Division of the UNIA opens
1919   World War I ends

"Red Summer," a summer of race riots and lynching of blacks, takes place
The 369th Infantry Regiment, the "Harlem Hellfighters," parade down Fifth Avenue in New York City after returning from fighting in France
W. E. B. Du Bois organizes the Pan-African Congresses and the first is held in Paris
Cyril V. Briggs forms the African Blood Brotherhood in New York City
1920 The Harlem Renaissance and the "Jazz Age" begin
1921 Akeley African Expedition the Belgian Congo (AMNH) begins
The Second Pan-African Congress in held in Paris
Meta Warrick Fuller creates *Ethiopia* for the America's Making Exposition
1922 Carlisle-Clark African Expedition (AMNH) begins
Carl Akeley films *Meandering in Africa*
1923 Martin Johnson African Expedition (AMNH) begins
Carl Akeley publishes *In Brightest Africa*
Martin and Osa Johnson release *Trailing Wild African Animals*
The Third Pan-African Congress is held in Lisbon and London
1924 Martin Johnson, Osa Johnson, Carl Akeley, and the AMNH release *Simba, King of Beasts*
1925 Prince Albert of Belgium signs a decree creating Parc National Albert to protect the mountain gorillas
Paul Louis Hoefler begins the Denver African Expedition to Namibia
1926 Eastman-Pomeroy-Akeley Expedition (AMNH) begins
Ruwenzori-Kivu Expedition (AMNH) begins
Carl and Mary in Africa is filmed, and left incomplete
Carl Akeley dies in Africa
James Chapin films *Mountains of the Moon* on the Ruwenzori-Kivu Expedition
1927 The Fourth Pan-African Congress is held in New York City
1928 Hoefler begins the Colorado African Expedition
1929 Sandford-Legendre Abyssinia Expedition (AMNH) begins
1930 Vernay-Lang Kalahari Expedition (AMNH) begins
The Négritude Movement begins under the leadership of Aimé Césaire, Léopold Senghor, and Léon Damas

Hoefler releases the film *Africa Speaks!*
1931   O'Donnell-Clark African Expedition (AMNH) begins
James Clark films *Adventures on the Upper Nile* while on expedition
1932   Martin and Osa Johnson release the film *Congorilla*
MGM's *Tarzan the Ape Man* premiers in New York City
1933   *King Kong* is released in movie theatres
1935   The Harlem Race Riot erupts
Martin and Osa Johnson release the film *Baboona*
1936   Akeley Memorial African Hall of the AMNH opens
Italy annexes Ethiopia
A riot breaks out in Harlem after a peaceful demonstration against the Italian invasion of Ethiopia
J. C. Robinson, the "Black Condor," returns to America from Ethiopia to train the Tuskegee Airmen

NOTES

Introduction

1. "Selassie's Air Aide Back from Africa," *New York Times*, May 19, 1936, 6; Garvey, *Philosophy and Opinions*, 4.

2. "Akeley Memorial Dedicated by Two Thousand," *New York Times*, May 20, 1936, 3; "Africa Comes to New York," *New York Times*, May 17, 1936, 16; "Mob of Four Hundred Battles the Police in Harlem; Italian Stores Raided, Man Shot in Crowd," *New York Times*, May 19, 1936, 6. The May 17 article was written before the opening at the AMNH and provided select media with an advance "behind-the-scenes" tour of the hall.

3. "New Negroes" were African Americans who claimed to be asserting a new forceful and unapologetic identity in early twentieth-century urban spaces (Baldwin, *Chicago's New Negroes*, 5).

4. Von Eschen, *Race against Empire*, 11–12.

5. Rydell, *All the World's a Fair*, 84–85; Brundage, "Meta Warrick's 1907 'Negro Tableaux,'" 1370.

6. For more on meme theories, see Blackmore, *The Meme Machine*.

7. Curtin, *The Image of Africa*; Hammond and Jablow, *The Africa That Never Was*; McCarthy, *Dark Continent*; Earle and Lowe, *Black Africans in Renaissance Europe*; Jordan, *White over Black*; Westhauser, "Revisiting the Jordan Thesis."

8. Adams and McShane, *The Myth of Wild Africa*; Beinart and Coates, *Environment and History*; Haraway, "Teddy Bear Patriarchy"; Teslow, "Representing Race to the Public"; Rony, *The Third Eye*.

9. Blyden referred to the "African Fatherland" and called for recognition of the manhood of the Negro in "The African Problem." The Universal Negro Improvement Association (UNIA) and Garvey referred to Africa as the "Motherland" in the "Declaration of the Rights of the Negro Peoples of the World," which contains several references to manhood.

10. Summers, *Manliness and Its Discontents*, 4.

11. See Wolcott, *Remaking Respectability*, and Baldwin, *Chicago's New Negroes*, for discussions of manhood, womanhood, and the politics of respectability.

12. Summers, *Manliness and Its Discontents*, 4.

13. Bederman, *Manliness and Civilization*, 207.

14. Said, *Orientalism*, 76–77, 87.

15. Blyden, "The African Problem"; Mudimbe, *The Invention of Africa*, 114–17.

16. Ranger, "Whose Heritage?" 221–22.

17. Akeley quoted in Albert, King of the Belgians, "To All Present and to Come," March 2, 1925, copy of translation, Box 3, Folder 13, CEA: Correspondence,

Gorilla Sanctuary, Mary Jobe Akeley Correspondence, Mary Jobe Akeley Collection, Archives, AMNH, New York.

18. Corbould, *Becoming African Americans*, 58.

19. Chirenje, *Ethiopianism and Afro-Americans*; Anthony, "Max Yergan and South Africa," 185–90.

20. See Stoler's discussion of "critical colonial studies" or the "new imperial history" in *Carnal Knowledge and Imperial Power*, 10.

21. Heilmann, ed., *Feminist Forerunners*, 1–2; Matthews, *The Rise of the New Woman*, 13–14.

One. A Cry from Africa

1. "A Noble African," *Virginia Star*, December 9, 1882; Iliffe, *Africans*, 155.
2. Ibid.
3. "A Cry from Africa," *Virginia Star*, December 23, 1882; Mitchell, *Righteous Propagation*, 53–54.
4. Mitchell, *Righteous Propagation*, 53–54.
5. Painter, *Standing at Armageddon*, 143–48.
6. Lewis, *The Race to Fashoda*, 16–18; Iliffe, *Africans*, 187–93; Shillington, *History of Africa*, 294–95.
7. W. D. Boyce quoted in McCarthy, *Dark Continent*, 137. Boyce was the founder of the Boy Scouts of America and the editor of *Blade*.
8. Brooks, "Prince Hall, Freemasonry, and Genealogy," 197–98.
9. McCartney, *Black Power Ideologies*, 28–32.
10. Logan, *The Negro in American Life and Thought*; Hooker, "The Pan-African Conference 1900"; Shepperson, "Pan-Africanism and 'Pan-Africanism,'" 349–55. See Neal's discussion of the Black Public Sphere in *What the Music Said*, 3–9, and see Harris-Lacewell's discussion of the counterpublic in *Barbershops, Bibles, and bet*, 5–6.
11. Meyer, *The Farther Frontier*, 7–9.
12. Turner, "The Significance of the Frontier in American History," 2, 5, 11, 45.
13. Roosevelt, *The Strenuous Life*, 11, 14, 24, 29. *The Strenuous Life* was originally a speech delivered before the Hamilton Club in Chicago, Illinois, on April 10, 1899. The speech was subsequently published in 1900. Roosevelt, *African Games Trails*, xi.
14. Akeley, *In Brightest Africa*, 19.
15. Scholars have long debated the dates for the emergence or the rise of Modern America, with Schlesinger and Nevins both setting the beginning in 1865. See Singal, "Towards of Definition of American Modernism"; Nevins, *The Emergence of Modern America, 1865–1878*; and Schlesinger, *The Rise of Modern America, 1865–1951*. Pedagogically, many historians begin in 1890 with the official closing of the frontier and end in 1930, the first full year of the Great Depression.
16. See Schlesinger, *The Rise of Modern America*.

17. Baldwin, *Chicago's New Negroes*, 8; Levine, *Highbrow/Lowbrow*.

18. Ogren, "What Is Africa to Me?" 19–20, 23–25, 30.

19. Dumenil, *The Modern Temper*, 6, 12.

20. Pauline Hopkins quoted in Jill Bergman, "'A New Race of Colored Women': Pauline Hopkins at the *Colored American Magazine*," in Heilmann, ed., *Feminist Forerunners*, 87–100.

21. Brantlinger, "Victorians and Africans," 198; Wesseling, *Divide and Rule*, 81–83; Driver, "Henry Morton Stanley and His Critics," 136–38.

22. Hickey and Wylie, *An Enchanting Darkness*, 8–10.

23. Du Chaillu, *Explorations and Adventures in Equatorial Africa*; Speke, *Journey of the Discovery of the Source of the Nile*; Livingstone and Livingstone, *Narrative of an Expedition to the Zambesi and Its Tributaries*.

24. Hickey and Wylie, *An Enchanting Darkness*, 188; Jarosz, "Constructing the Dark Continent," 105–7.

25. Stanley, *In Darkest Africa*, in Murray, *Wild Africa*, 140–41.

26. Oerlemans, *Romanticism and the Materiality of Nature*, 148–52.

27. Stanley, *In Darkest Africa*, in Murray, *Wild Africa*, 147.

28. See Fritzell, *Nature Writing and Africa*.

29. Leigh, *Frontiers of Enchantment*, ix–xi.

30. See Devlin, "The Eye and the Gaze in *Heart of Darkness*."

31. "A Thrilling Experience: Forty-eight Hours in the African Jungles," *New York Freeman*, June 19, 1886; "A Noted African Trader," *New York Freeman*, September 11, 1886.

32. Williams, "Black Journalism's Opinions about Africa," 227; "He Saw Stanley in Africa," *New York Age*, August 17, 1889; Phillips Exeter Academy, *General Catalogue of the Officers and Students*, 155; "A Thrilling Experience," *New York Freeman*, June 19, 1886; "A Noted African Trader: The Richest Man in Central Africa and Greatest Slave and Ivory Dealer in the World—His Visit to the Sultan of Zanzibar," *New York Freeman*, September 1, 1886; "Tidings from the Congo: A Letter from a Female Missionary," *New York Freeman*, September 3, 1887.

33. "His Bloody Life: The Man Who Has Ended Many Careers," *National Reflector*, March 27, 1887.

34. Adams, "Recent Discoveries in the Congo Basin," 37–38.

35. "Dr. Bowen on Ethnology," *New York Age*, December 13, 1890.

36. Blyden, "The African Problem," 24, 17.

37. "Our African Contingent," *New York Freeman*, July 31, 1886. See Fortune, *Black and White*.

38. "Our African Contingent," "Growing Too Soon," and "Colored Men of Mark," *N.C. Republican and Civil Rights Advocate*, May 22, 1884; "The Afro-American League: Editor Bonaparte's Open Letter to the Race," *New York Age*, July 9, 1887; Summers, *Manliness and Its Discontents*, 1–4.

39. "Future for Africa," *Northwestern Recorder*, March 1893, 2–3.

40. "The Liberia Fever Again," *New York Times*, February 8, 1888; "Major M'Gill's Version," *New York Times*, February 6, 1888; "Fifty Days in Africa," *National Baptist World*, October 26, 1894, November 2, 1894; Upchurch, *Legislating Racism*, 23–44.

41. "The African Baptist Foreign Mission Convention at Xenia, Ohio," *National Baptist World*, November 9, 1894; Chirenje, *Ethiopianism and Afro-Americans*, 1–5, 63–65; "'Ethiopianism's' Menace in Africa," *New York Age*, March 15, 1906, reprinted from the *London Spectator*; "Relation of England to the Natives of South Africa," *New York Age*, August 16, 1906.

42. "The African Baptist Foreign Mission Convention," *National Baptist World*, November 9, 1894; Turner, "A 'Black-White' Missionary on the Imperial Stage," 1–2.

43. National Association of Colored Women's Clubs (hereafter NACW), *National Federation of Afro-American Women, Convention Minutes and Reports, 1896*, sess. 2, 43–45; Ogren, "'What Is Africa to Me?'" 20.

44. NACW, *Minutes and Reports, 1896*, 34–35.

45. Schlesinger, *The Rise of Modern America*, 114; Carby, "'On the Threshold of Woman's Era,'" 246–65; Heilmann, ed., *Feminist Forerunners*, 1.

46. "The Negro's Future in the South," *New York Times*, September 1, 1889, 3.

47. Shufeldt, "The Practicability of Transporting the Negro back to Africa," 48; "Carrying forward Darwinism," *New York Times*, June 19, 1887, 14. See the chapter "Human Physiognomy" in Cope, *Origin of the Fittest*, 281–93.

48. Cope, *Origin of the Fittest*, 287–88.

49. Shufeldt, "The Practicability of Transporting the Negro back to Africa," 48.

50. "The Negro's Proper Home," *New York Times*, August 25, 1892, 9.

51. See "Future for the Negro: Philippine Islands Suggested as a Solution," *Washington Post*, February 16, 1900, 11.

52. See Dumenil, *The Modern Temper*, 168; Douglas, *Terrible Honesty*, 282–83, 288; Torgovnick, *Gone Primitive*, 29; Rosetti, *Imagining the Primitive in Naturalist and Modernist Literature*, 4–5, 174–75; Lemke, *Primitivist Modernism*, 27–28, 148; and Lewis, *When Harlem Was in Vogue*.

53. Review of *Negro Myths from the Georgia Coast*, 169–70; Oertel, "Notes on Six Negro Myths from the Georgia Coast," 309.

54. Chatelain, "African Races," 289.

55. Ibid., 298–99, 302.

56. These topics are covered in the *Journal of American Folklore* based on my survey of the journal's publications from 1891 to 1900. Other mentions of Africa can be found in articles on African American, Caribbean, and South American cultures during the same period.

57. See the official Web site of the American Ethnological Society at http://www.aesonline.org/ and "Anthropological Society of Washington Records 1879–1980," Manuscript 4821, Smithsonian Institution National Anthropological

Archives at http://siris-archives.si.edu; Risjord, "The Politics of Explanation and the Origins of Ethnography," 29.

58. Baker, *From Savage to Negro*, 38, 104; "Human Sacrifices in Dahomey" and "Worship of Prehistoric Stone Implements in Yoruba, West Coast of Africa," 96.

59. See Campbell, *Middle Passages*, 99–135.

60. See Newman's discussion of Sheldon in *White Women's Rights*; Boisseau, *White Queen*.

61. "Obituary: May French Sheldon," 288; "What She Was in Africa," *New York Times*, March 22, 1892, 8.

62. Sheldon, *Sultan to Sultan*; Sheldon, "Customs among the Natives of East Africa," 358–62, 389–90.

63. The term "anti-colonial Pan-Africanists" comes from Sundiata, *Brothers and Strangers*, 11.

Two. To Bunco a Yankee

1. Iliffe, *Africans*, 189; Shillington, *History of Africa*, 196.

2. Mr. Francis to M. Frelinghuysen, May 15, 1883, in House Committee on Foreign Relations, *Papers Relating to the Foreign Relations of the United States, Transmitted to Congress, with the Annual Message of the President, December 4, 1883*, 48th Cong., 1st sess., House Executive Document 1, 1884, 739–41.

3. House Committee, *Papers Relating to the Foreign Relations of the United States*.

4. Brooks, *Yankee Traders, Old Coasters, and African Middlemen*, vii, 180–86, 194–95, 204, 257.

5. Ibid., 291–93.

6. Driver, "Henry Morton Stanley and His Critics," 159–64.

7. Ibid.

8. Ibid.

9. Jeal, *Stanley*, 10–11.

10. Louis, "Roger Casement and the Congo," 99–100; Hawkins, "Mark Twain's Involvement with the Congo Reform Movement," 148–49; Brantlinger, "Victorians and Africans," 193, 196, 198; Schurz, "Platform of the Anti-Imperialist League."

11. Senate Committee on Foreign Relations, *Occupation of the Congo Country in Africa*, 48th Cong., 1st sess., 1884, S. Rep. 393, 1–7; Fry, *John Tyler Morgan*, 76–80.

12. Senate Committee, *Occupation of the Congo*, 1–2.

13. Ibid., 6–7.

14. Ibid.

15. Ibid., 1–7.

16. Ibid., 7.

17. Ibid., 7–9.

18. Ibid., 8–9.

19. *Senate Miscellaneous Document no. 59*, 48th Cong., 1st sess., 1884.

20. "The Dark Continent: Shrewd Americans Likely to Capture All the Plums," *Chicago Daily Tribune*, November 30, 1884, 9.

21. "The Congo Conference," *Washington Post*, November 27, 1884, 1; "The Powers and the Congo," *New York Times*, November 27, 1884, 1.

22. "The Dark Continent," *Chicago Daily Tribune*, November 29, 1884, 5.

23. Ibid.; "The Dark Continent," *Chicago Daily Tribune*, December 10, 1884, 5; "The Dark Continent," *Chicago Daily Tribune*, January 10, 1885, 5.

24. "The Congo Conference Closed," *New York Times*, February 27, 1885, 5.

25. "The Negro's Peculiar Work," *New York Freeman*, January 15, 1887; "To Consider African Questions; America to Be Represented at the Congo Conference," *New York Times*, October 21, 1884, 1.

26. Chester A. Arthur, *Message from the President of the United States Transmitting a Report from the Secretary of State in Relation to the Congo Conference at Berlin*, 48th Cong., 2nd sess., House Executive Document 156, 1885, 1–2, 10; House Committee on Foreign Relations, *Participation of the United States in the Congo Conference*, 48th Cong., 2nd sess., 1885, H. Rep. 2655, 1–2, 21.

27. De Leon, "The Conference at Berlin on the West-African Question," 103, 119–21, 138–39.

28. The European plenipotentiaries represented Great Britain, Austria-Hungary, Belgium, Denmark, France, Germany, Italy, the Netherlands, Portugal, Russia, Spain, and Sweden and Norway.

29. De Leon, "The Conference at Berlin," 109–13, 135–36.

30. Ibid., 136–39; Wesseling, *Divide and Rule*, 99–103, 113–19.

31. Williams quoted in Franklin, *George Washington Williams*, 202.

32. Hochschild, *King Leopold's Ghost*, 101–6; Franklin, *George Washington Williams*, xvi, 201–2.

33. Williams, "An Open Letter to Leopold II," in Franklin, *George Washington Williams*, 243–53.

34. Adams, "Recent Discoveries in the Congo Basin," 37.

35. Ibid., 37–38.

36. Ibid., 38–40.

37. Franklin, *George Washington Williams*, 231–34, 238, 241; Blyden, "The African Problem," 128; Shepperson, "Pan-Africanism and 'Pan-Africanism,'" 353.

38. Parliament, *Correspondence and Report from His Majesty's Consul at Boma*, 21, 33.

39. Hochschild, *King Leopold's Ghost*, 203–7; Hawkins, "Mark Twain's Involvement in the Congo Reform Movement," 153–56.

40. "Worse Than the Sixteenth Century," *Harper's Weekly*, March 26, 1904; Congo Committee, "The Real Issue in Re Congo Intervention," 1.

41. Whiteley, "The Congo Free State," 129.

42. Wack, *The Story of the Congo Free State*, 473–74.

43. Twain, *King Leopold's Soliloquy*, 6–10.

44. Ibid., 10–14.

45. Hochschild, *King Leopold's Ghost*, 154, 158; "Redeeming Africa," *New York Age*, January 19, 1905; Booker T. Washington, "Industrial Education in Africa," *New York Age*, March 22, 1906.

46. Cureau, "William H. Sheppard," 340; "Congo Libel Suits Deferred," *New York Times*, June 4, 1909, 5; Turner, "A 'Black-White' Missionary on the Imperial Stage," 1–2.

47. Schildkrout, "Art as Evidence," 155–56.

48. Osborn, "The Congo Expedition," xvi–xix.

49. Ibid., xx–xxii, xxvi–xxvii.

50. Lowie, "Industry and the Art of the Negro Race," 13–14.

51. Stocking, *The Ethnographer's Magic*, 132, 135, 139; Lowie, "Industry and Art of the Negro Race," 12–15.

52. Lowie, "Industry and Art of the Negro Race," 13.

53. Ibid., 16; Wissler, "The Douglas African Collection," 67–68.

54. "Benin Bronzes" is the term the museum curators gave Benin art in the late nineteenth century. It is a misnomer; twentieth-century technology showed that the works were made of brass, an alloy of copper and zinc; bronze is an alloy of copper and tin. See Mowat, *Symbols of Kings*.

55. Coombes, *Reinventing Africa*, 17.

56. Pitt-Rivers, *Antique Works of Art from Benin*, iv.

57. "Collections from Africa" in Sherwood, *General Guide to the Exhibition Halls*, 41; Lowie, "Industry and the Art of the Negro Race," 16, 18–19; Stocking, *The Ethnographer's Magic*, 120; Baker, *From Savage to Negro*, 148.

58. Osborn, "The Congo Expedition," xx–xxii, xxvi–xxvii.

59. Lang, "An Explorer's View of the Congo," 379–80.

60. Ibid., 380, 382–83.

61. Lang, "Nomad Dwarfs and Civilization," 697–98; Lang, "An Explorer's View of the Congo," 379–80.

62. Lang, "Nomad Dwarfs and Civilization," 699.

63. Ibid., 697; "Pygmy Group in Exhibit Halls—African People's Hall," neg. 333305, Photographic Print Collection, AMNH, New York.

64. Schildkrout, "The Spectacle of Africa through the Lens of Herbert Lang," 71. The editor of the *American Museum Journal* quoted in the introduction of Lang, "An Explorer's View of the Congo," 379.

65. Lang, "Famous Ivory Treasures of a Negro King," 527–29; Lang, "Nomad Dwarfs and Civilization," 697–98; Lang, "An Explorer's View of the Congo," 379; Rony, "Those Who Squat and Those Who Sit," 279.

66. "'American Congo' to Be Subject at This Gathering," *Cleveland Advocate*, December 12, 1919, 1.

Three. Written on the Wall

1. "An African Empire," *New York Freeman*, January 15, 1887.
2. Ibid.
3. Ibid.
4. Ibid.
5. "Many Facts in Brief about the Negro," *AME Quarterly Almanac, 1893.*
6. Fortune, "The Negro's Peculiar Work," *New York Freeman*, January 15, 1887.
7. Mudimbe, *The Invention of Africa*, 88–91, 114–17, 130–33; Lewis, *W. E. B. Du Bois: Biography of a Race*, 161–62.
8. Edwards, *The Practice of Diaspora*, 1–3, 10; Plummer, *Rising Wind*, 13–14; Lewis, *W. E. B. Du Bois: Biography of a Race*, 248; Baldwin, *Beyond the Color Line and the Iron Curtain*, 2–4. For information on Marcus Garvey amassing a Pan-Africanist following see Hill and Bair, *Marcus Garvey, Life and Lessons*; Martin, *Race First*; Stein, *The World of Marcus Garvey*; Rolinson, *Grassroots Garveyism*; Sundiata, *Brothers and Strangers*.
9. Plummer, *Rising Wind*, 12; Edwards, *The Practice of Diaspora*, 243–44.
10. Plummer, *Rising Wind*, 12.
11. Baldwin, *Beyond the Color Line and the Iron Curtain*, 46, 55, 96.
12. Martin, *Race First*, 13, 236–43, 249.
13. Edwards, *The Practice of Diaspora*, 2–5; Stein, *The World of Marcus Garvey*, 273, 277.
14. Peete, "The Problem of Liberia," *New York Age*, March 17, 1888.
15. Bowser, "More about Liberia," *New York Age*, March 17, 1888; Sundiata, *Black Scandal*, 4–7.
16. Clegg, *The Price of Liberty*, 301; Price, "Price's Rejection of Position," 234.
17. Blyden, "The African Problem," 126–31; Lewis, *W. E. B. Du Bois: Biography of a Race*, 248.
18. Blyden, "The African Problem," 126–31.
19. Blyden, "The Call of Providence to the Descendants of Africa in America," 125; Blyden, "The African Problem," 126, 131, 133–34, 136; Upchurch, *Legislating Racism*, 23–44.
20. Thirkield, "Opening Remarks" in "Africa, the Continent: Its Peoples, Their Civilization and Evangelization," 13.
21. Ibid., 14.
22. Moses, *The Golden Age of Black Nationalism*, 200.
23. Fortune, "The Nationalization of Africa," 199–201.
24. Ibid., 201.
25. Ibid.
26. Mason, "The Methodist Episcopal Church and the Evangelization of Africa," 143–48.
27. Holderness, "Sketch of My Life in Africa," 113–15.
28. Washington, Wood, and Williams, *A New Negro for a New Century.*

29. Hamedoe, "The First Pan-African Conference of the World," 223–31; Edwards, *The Practice of Diaspora*, 1; Lewis, *W. E. B. Du Bois: Biography of a Race*, 250; Plummer, *Rising Wind*, 14.

30. Hamedoe, "The First Pan-African Conference of the World," 223–31.

31. Ibid.; Lewis, *W. E. B. Du Bois: Biography of a Race*, 248–51; Edwards, *The Practice of Diaspora*, 1; Plummer, *Rising Wind*, 14–15.

32. Plummer, *Rising Wind*, 15.

33. Edwards, *The Practice of Diaspora*, 9; Martin, *Race First*, 5–10, 122.

34. "Hostility to Europeans," *New York Age*, December 13, 1906.

35. "Leopold's European Rivals in African Atrocities," *New York Age*, January 10, 1907.

36. "Relation of England to the Natives of South Africa," *New York Age*, August 16, 1906.

37. Ibid.

38. Ibid.; Erhagbe, "African-Americans and the Defense of African States against European Imperial Conquest," 56.

39. "Liberia Still on Trial," *New York Age*, January 31, 1907; "News of Europe and Africa," *New York Age*, June 20, 1907.

40. "Liberia: Frontier Agreement between France and Liberia," in Department of State, *Papers Relating to the Foreign Relations of the United States with the Annual Message of the President Transmitted to Congress, December 3, 1907*, 830–32; "Commissioners from Republic of Liberia," *New York Age*, June 4, 1908; "Conditions in Liberia," in Theodore Roosevelt, *Message from the President of the United States*, 60th Cong., 2nd sess., 1909, House Executive Document 666; Erhagbe, "African-Americans and the Defense of African States against European Imperial Conquest," 57.

41. Erhagbe, "African-Americans and the Defense of African States against European Imperial Conquest," 56–58.

42. "Conditions in Liberia," in Roosevelt, *Message from the President*.

43. Department of State, *Papers Relating to the Foreign Relations of the United States*; "Affairs in Liberia," in William H. Taft, *Message from the President of the United States Transmitting a Letter of the Secretary of State Submitting a Report of the Commission Which Visited Liberia in Pursuance of the Provisions of the Deficiency Act of March 4, 1909, "To Investigate the Interests of the United States and Its Citizens in the Republic of Liberia, with the Consent of the Authorities of Said Republic,"* 61st Cong., 2nd sess., House Executive Document 457.

44. Lewis, *W. E. B. Du Bois: The Fight for Equality*, 37–84.

45. "International Conference at Tuskegee Institute," *Chicago Defender*, February 3, 1912, 1.

46. Evans, "International Conference on the Negro," 417.

47. "An Announcement of a Conference at Tuskegee Institute," March 1911; Isaiah Goda Sishuba, Queenstown, South Africa, to Booker T. Washington, July 25,

1911; "The Opening Address of the International Conference on the Negro," April 17, 1912, all in the Booker T. Washington Papers Online, 72, 273, 520–22; Evans, "International Conference on the Negro," 420–23.

48. Evans, "International Conference on the Negro," 423–24.

49. "Declarations of the First International Conference on the Negro," in Evans, "International Conference on the Negro," 425–27.

50. Mary Rolinson, "Declaration of the Rights of the Negro Peoples of the Word," in Wintz, ed., *African American Political Thought*, 208–14; Rolinson, *Grassroots Garveyism*, 151.

51. Summers, *Manliness and Its Discontents*, 77–78; Du Bois, "Marcus Garvey," in Wintz, ed., *African American Political Thought*, 123; Mboukou, "The Pan-African Movement," 275–77; Stein, *The World of Marcus Garvey*, 273–77; Rolinson, *Grassroots Garveyism*, 150–51.

52. Du Bois, "Marcus Garvey" and "Marcus Garvey: Information Exclusively from the Files of the Military Intelligence Division and State Department," in Wintz, ed., *African American Political Thought*, 123, 194; Martin, *Race First*, 280.

53. "Marcus Garvey: Information Exclusively from the Files of the Military Intelligence Division and State Department" and "Address to UNIA Supporters in Philadelphia, October 21, 1919," in Wintz, ed., *African American Political Thought*, 194, 199, 200–204.

54. "Address to UNIA Supporters in Philadelphia," in Wintz, ed., *African American Political Thought*, 206; Rolinson, *Grassroots Garveyism*, 154–60.

55. "Declaration of the Rights of the Negro Peoples of the World" and "Address to the Second UNIA Convention, New York, April 31, 1921," in Wintz, ed., *African American Political Thought*, 208–14, 218–23; Stein, *The World of Marcus Garvey*, 86–87.

56. "The Negro's Greatest Enemy" and "Address to the Second UNIA Convention," in Wintz, ed., *African American Political Thought*, 171, 222; Martin, *Race First*, 41–62, 192–94.

57. Campbell, *Middle Passages*, 230–31; Du Bois, "The African Roots of War," 1–6.

58. Campbell, *Middle Passages*, 231; Du Bois, "The African Roots of War," 6–10; Lewis, *W. E. B. Du Bois: The Fight for Equality*, 59–60.

59. Worley and Contee, "The Worley Report on the Pan-African Congress of 1919," 140–42; Martin, *Race First*, 122, 146; Stein, *The World of Marcus Garvey*, 49, 117.

60. Campbell, *Middle Passages*, 231; Contee, "Du Bois, the NAACP, and the Pan-African Congress of 1919," 15–16; Contee, "The 'Statuts' of the Pan-African Association of 1921," 410, 412–14.

61. Du Bois, "The African Roots of War," 10; Edwards, *The Practice of Diaspora*, 136–38; Rolinson, *Grassroots Garveyism*, 150–54; Stein, *The World of Marcus Garvey*, 277.

62. Kelley, "Afric's Sons with Banner Red," 106; Lewis, *W. E. B. Du Bois: The Fight for Equality*, 335, 336; Ogren, "'What Is Africa to Me?'" 19–20.

63. African Blood Brotherhood, "Programme of the African Blood Brotherhood," 1; Kelley, "Afric's Sons with Banner Red," 106, 108.

64. Martin, *Race First*, 13, 236–43, 249; Kelley, "Afric's Sons with Banner Red," 108.

65. African Blood Brotherhood, "Programme of the African Blood Brotherhood," 1–2.

66. Ibid., 2–3, 5; Martin, *Race First*, 241; Lewis, *W. E. B. Du Bois: The Fight for Equality*, 72; Chirenje, *Ethiopianism and Afro-Americans*.

67. African Blood Brotherhood, "Programme of the African Blood Brotherhood," 5.

68. Ibid.; Garvey, "Speech on Disarmament Conference," 4; Stein, *The World of Marcus Garvey*, 142–45; Martin, *Race First*, 138, 294.

69. Garvey, "Speech Delivered at Madison Square Garden," 1–3; Grey, "The Fourth Pan-African Congress and Harlem," *New York Amsterdam News*, July 20, 1927, 14; Stein, *The World of Marcus Garvey*, 211–18.

70. "Negro Workers Protest Race Discrimination," *New York Amsterdam News*, January 20, 1926, 16; Baldwin, *Chicago's New Negroes*, 50; Chalk, "The Anatomy of an Investment," 12–13, 17–20; Akpan, "Liberia and the Universal Negro Improvement Association," 122; Renda, *Taking Haiti*, 10, 189–90; Edwards, *The Practice of Diaspora*, 9; Martin, *Race First*, 136–37; Stein, *The World of Marcus Garvey*, 213–14.

71. "Exposure of Communists Is Promised," *New York Amsterdam News*, July 28, 1934, 1; Martin, *Race First*, 262–63; Sundiata, *Black Scandal*, 122–23.

72. "Form League to Suppress Oppression in Colonies," *Pittsburg Courier*, October 30, 1926, 4; "To Send Delegates to Oppression Conference," *New York Amsterdam News*, June 5, 1929, 2; Edwards, *The Practice of Diaspora*, 251, 254.

73. Du Bois, "Pan-Africa and the New Racial Philosophy," in Wintz, ed., *African American Political Thought*, 152–53; Lewis, *W. E. B. Du Bois: The Fight for Equality*, 335–36; Du Bois, *The Souls of Black Folk*, 17.

74. Du Bois, "Pan-Africa and the New Racial Philosophy," in Wintz, ed., *African American Political Thought*, 154–55; Lewis, *W. E. B. Du Bois: The Fight for Equality*, 335–36.

75. Edwards, *The Practice of Diaspora*, 275–76; Kelley, "This Ain't Ethiopia, But It'll Do," 123–31; Plummer, *Rising Wind*, 37; Scott, *Sons of Sheba's Race*, 100.

76. Du Bois, "Forum Fact and Opinion," *Pittsburgh Courier*, February 29, 1936.

77. Edwards, *The Practice of Diaspora*, 136–37; Penny, *Objects of Culture*, 7.

78. Rydell, *All the World's a Fair*, 61, 66, 84–85, 95, 145–46.

79. Ibid.; Brundage, "Meta Warrick's 1907 'Negro Tableux,'" 1370.

80. Ater, "Making History," 13; Brundage, "Meta Warrick's 1907 'Negro Tableux,'" 1369–1370; Painter, *Creating Black Americans*, 8.

Four. To Capture a Vanishing World

1. "Protection of Wild Animals in Africa," 275–76.

2. Elliot, "African Expedition Report," 23, and "Specimens Obtained on African Expedition as Shown in Customs List Made at Aden, for Export Duty," D. G. Elliot Africa Expedition, 5 January 1897, in Registrar Accession Records, Zoology, Acc. 151, Field Museum of Natural History, Chicago; Akeley and Akeley, *Adventures in the African Jungle*, 75–91.

3. Akeley, *The Wilderness Lives Again*, 368; Akeley, *In Brightest Africa*, 254.

4. Neumann, *Imposing Wilderness*.

5. C. W. Hobley, Acting Secretary of the Society for the Preservation of the Fauna of the Empire, September 20, 1929, in Public Record Office, CO 691/101/10, Big Game Hunting, Hunting by Motor Car, Tanganyika, 1929.

6. Akeley, *In Brightest Africa*, 7–8; Bodry-Sanders, *Carl Akeley*, 21, 172.

7. Akeley, *In Brightest Africa*, 7; "Just Like Jumbo: What Professor Ward Has Patiently Accomplished," *Union and Advertiser*, February 25, 1886.

8. Akeley, *In Brightest Africa*, 8; Kohlstedt, "Henry A. Ward," 655; Lurie, *A Special Style*, 13; "Just Like Jumbo"; Record of Proceedings of the Board of Trustees of the Public Museum of the City of Milwaukee, 25 June 1886, 15 February 1887, 23 March 1887, 20 December 1887, 20 December 1888, 25 January 1890, 26 August 1890, 29 December 1890, 20 January 1891, 21 April 1891; the Carl E. Akeley Co. to the Board of Trustees of the Public Museum of the City of Milwaukee, n.d., Carl Akeley Correspondence, 1887–1912, Milwaukee Public Museum Library and Archives.

9. Record of Proceedings, 21 July 1891; Resignation Letter: Carl E. Akeley to Henry Wehrling, 21 May 1892, Carl Akeley Correspondence; Akeley, *In Brightest Africa*, 10; Bodry-Sanders, *Carl Akeley*, 41; "Akeley of Africa," 121.

10. Conn, *Museums and American Intellectual Life*, 77–78.

11. Bodry-Sanders, *Carl Akeley*, 48.

12. Robinson, Gallagher, and Denny, *Africa and the Victorians*, 151–52; D. G. Elliot, New York, to F. J. V. Skiff, Chicago, 1 March 1896, Director's Correspondence, General Alpha, 1893–1907, D. G. Elliot, Curator, Zoology, Folder 1, Library and Archives, Field Museum of Natural History (hereafter LAFMNH), Chicago; Bodry-Sanders, *Carl Akeley*, 48; McCarthy, *Dark Continent*, xvi–xvii.

13. Elliot to Skiff, 1 March 1896; Smith authored *Through Unknown African Countries*, an account of his 1896 safari. Iliffe, *Africans*, 195; D. G. Elliot, South Kensington, to F. J. V. Skiff, Chicago, 15 March 1896, Director's Correspondence, General Alpha, 1893–1907, D. G. Elliot, Curator, Zoology, Folder 1, LAFMNH; VanOnselen, "Reactions to Rinderpest in Southern Africa"; Pitts, "Rinderpest and Rebellion in Southern Rhodesia, 1896"; Ofcansky, "The 1889–97 Rinderpest Epidemic"; Phoofolo, "Epidemics and Revolutions."

14. Elliot to Skiff, 15 March 1896.

15. Bodry-Sanders, *Carl Akeley*, 48; Elliot to Skiff, 15 March 1896; Elliot, "African Expedition Report," n.d., 3, Field Museum of Natural History, Historical Files, Chicago.

16. Elliot, "African Expedition Report," 5, 8, 19, 20; Akeley and Akeley, *Adventures in the African Jungle*, 75–91; Bodry-Sanders, *Carl Akeley*, 68.

17. Elliot, "African Expedition Report," 23; "Specimens Obtained on African Expedition," January 5, 1897, Registrar Accession Records; Akeley and Akeley, *Adventures in the African Jungle*, 75–91.

18. Bodry-Sanders, *Carl Akeley*, 68–69, 71, 73–75.

19. W. A. Dorsey, Curator of Anthropology, Chicago, to F. J. V. Skiff, Director, Chicago, 1 August 1905, British East Africa Expedition, Director's Office, Expedition Files, Box z-1036, Folder 4, LAFMNH; Elliot, "African Expedition Report," 22.

20. Dorsey to Skiff, 1 August 1905; Stauder, "The 'Relevance' of Anthropology to Colonialism and Imperialism," 408–10, 416–17; Asad, "Afterword," 314–15.

21. H. N. Higinbotham, Chicago, to Honorable John Hay, Washington, D.C., 20 February 1905; Francis A. Loomis, Assistant Secretary to H. K. [sic] Higinbotham, 27 February 1905; Alvey A. Adee, Acting Secretary, Washington, D.C., to H. K. [sic] Higinbotham, 6 April 1905 [with enclosures]; Alvey A. Adee, Acting Secretary, Washington, D.C., to H. K. [sic] Higinbotham, 25 April 1906, British East Africa Expedition, Director's Office, Expedition Files, Box z-1036, Folder 4, LAFMNH. The enclosures included copies of the East Africa Game Relations, 1900; Proclamation 16th January 1901; Game Ordinance, 1904; East Africa Fire Arms Ordinance, 1904; East Africa Fire Arms Regulations, 1896; and *Deutsches Kolonialblatt* no. 14 (July 15, 1903).

22. C. E. Akeley, Nairobi, BEA, to F. J. V. Skiff, Director, 7 November 1905, British East African Expedition, Director's Office, Expedition Files, Box z-1036, Folder 1, LAFMNH.

23. "List of contents of eighty-four packages numbered from 1 to 84 inclusive, packed by C. E. Akeley for export from the East Africa Protectorate"; C. E. Akeley, Gilgil, BEA, to F. J. V. Skiff, Director, Chicago, 8 March 1906; C. E. Akeley, Molo, BEA, to F. J. V. Skiff, Director, Chicago, 4 April 1906; "List of contents," British East African Expedition, Director's Office, Expedition Files, Box z-1036, Folder 1, LAFMNH; Bodry-Sanders, *Carl Akeley*, 99–106; Akeley, *In Brightest Africa*, 164; Conn, *Museums and American Intellectual Life*, 32–74.

24. Stauder, "The 'Relevance' of Anthropology to Colonialism and Imperialism," 409, 416; Miller, *Hunting Big Game in the Wilds of Africa*, iii; Rexer and Klein, *American Museum of Natural History*, 112–13; Pringle, *Theodore Roosevelt*, 492; Hartzell, "Mr. Roosevelt's Safety," 822.

25. Ybarra, "Africa's Latest Case of Sleeping Sickness," 696; "Mr. Roosevelt in Africa," 248; Roosevelt, *The Strenuous Life*, 11, 14, 24, 29; Jenkins, "Theodore Roosevelt," 2; Hartzell, "Mr. Roosevelt's Safety," 821. Roosevelt delivered "The

Strenuous Life" as a speech before the Hamilton Club in Chicago, Illinois, on April 10, 1899, and it was subsequently published in 1900. Platt quoted in Pringle, *Theodore Roosevelt*, 508, 509.

26. Bodry-Sanders, *Carl Akeley*, 122–24; Rexer and Klein, *American Museum of Natural History*, 114; Akeley, *In Brightest Africa*, 161–62; Roosevelt, *African Game Trails*, 399; "Roosevelt Disappointed," *New York Times*, October 27, 1909, 4; Akeley, "Theodore Roosevelt and Africa," 12–13; Roosevelt, *African Game Trails*, 400–402.

27. Akeley, *In Brightest Africa*, 162; Roosevelt, *African Game Trails*, 403–4.

28. Bodry-Sanders, *Carl Akeley*, 129–30; Akeley, *In Brightest Africa*, 47–48; Rexer and Klein, *American Museum of Natural History*, 116.

29. Roosevelt, *African Game Trails*, 404.

30. Ibid.; Haraway, "Teddy Bear Patriarchy," 50–51; "Mrs. Akeley's Big Elephant (Kenya)," Akeley Expedition, British East Africa, neg. 211518, Photographic Print Collection, AMNH, New York.

31. Akeley, *In Brightest Africa*, 55.

32. Roosevelt, *African Game Trails*, xi, ix; Rotundo, *American Manhood*, 226, 231, 247, 259; Lears, *No Place of Grace*, 27, 30, 96.

33. Roosevelt quoted in "Mr. Roosevelt in Africa," 248; Roosevelt, *African Game Trails*, x. Akeley, "Theodore Roosevelt and Africa," 19; Rotundo, *American Manhood*, 228; Haraway, "Teddy Bear Patriarchy," 54; Torgovnick, *Gone Primitive*, 29.

34. Roosevelt, *African Game Trails*, x.

35. Ibid., 56.

36. Bender, *New York Intellect*, 170; Rexer and Klein, *American Museum of Natural History*, 24–32.

37. Osborn, *The American Museum of Natural History*, 85, 103–4.

38. Akeley, *In Brightest Africa*, 251; Osborn, "Report of the President," 21.

39. Lowie, "Industry and the Art of the Negro Race," 12, 15; Schildkrout, "Art as Evidence," 157.

40. Appel, "Science, Popular Culture, and Profit," 237–67; Bronner, *Consuming Visions*, 15–16; Conn, *Museums and American Intellectual Life*, 4–21; Welch, *The Book of Nature*, 2–9.

41. Conn, *Museums and American Intellectual Life*, 4–30.

42. Rexer and Klein, *American Museum of Natural History*, 24; Osborn, *The American Museum of Natural History*, 9–10.

43. Osborn, *The American Museum of Natural History*, 10; Alexander, *Museums in Motion*, 19–20; Welch, *The Book of Nature*, 195, 221; Rosenzweig and Blackmar, *The Park and the People*, 351; Tipple, "Big Business and a New Economy," 13–30; Bronner, *Consuming Visions*, 26–29; Harris, *Cultural Excursions*, 267.

44. *New York Times*, February 10, 1898, 7.

45. Osborn, *The American Museum of Natural History*, 85, 103; Schildkrout, "Art as Evidence," 154.

46. Osborn, *The American Museum of Natural History*, 103–4; Schildkrout, "Art as Evidence," 154–55; Iliffe, *Africans*, 190.

47. Iliffe, *Africans*, 193–94; Schildkrout, "Art as Evidence," 155; Wissler, "The Douglas African Collection," 67, 76–80, 83.

48. Osborn, "Report of the President," 21.

49. Tjäder, *The Big Game of Africa*, 26; "The Tjäder East Africa Expedition," 214; "The Results of the Tjäder Expedition," 61; Allen, "Mammals from British East Africa," 147–48.

50. "The Results of the Tjäder Expedition," 62.

51. Osborn, "The Fayum Expedition of the American Museum," 513–14; Osborn, "New Fossil Mammals," 265.

52. Osborn, "The Fayum Expedition of the American Museum," 513, 515–16; Osborn, "New Fossil Mammals," 265; Osborn, "New Carnivorous Mammals," 415.

53. Rexer and Klein, *American Museum of Natural History*, 210–18.

54. Akeley, *In Brightest Africa*, 251.

55. Ibid., 19.

56. Ibid., 251–53, 256; Akeley, "Plans for the African Hall [corrected version]," n.d., A.A31 Box 1, Folder 3, AMNH, Carl Ethan Akeley Papers, Department of Rare Books and Special Collections, University of Rochester Library, New York, 2; AMNH, *Presidents' Annual Reports*, 1911, 21; Osborn, *The American Museum of Natural History*, 103–4; "New African Hall Planned by Carl E. Akeley," 181.

57. Carl Ethan Akeley, New York, to Henry Fairfield Osborn, New York, 3 March 1913, A.A31, Box 6, Folder 21, Carl Ethan Akeley Papers.

58. Akeley, *In Brightest Africa*, 252.

59. "New African Hall," 177–81; Akeley, "Plans for the African Hall," 1.

60. Akeley, "Plans for the African Hall," 1; "New African Hall," 180–82; Akeley, *In Brightest Africa*, 257–58.

61. "New African Hall," 177–81; Stauder, "The 'Relevance' of Anthropology to Colonialism and Imperialism," 417.

62. "The Work of Carl E. Akeley," 173; "New African Hall," 186; Akeley, *In Brightest Africa*, 261; Akeley, "Plans for the African Hall," 2.

63. Akeley, "Plans for the African Hall," 2–3; Akeley, *In Brightest Africa*, 262–63.

64. Rexer and Klein, *American Museum of Natural History*, 126–27; Clark, "The Image of Africa," 70.

65. Pringle, *Theodore Roosevelt*, 602; Carl Akeley, "Theodore Roosevelt and Africa," 12–14; Akeley, *In Brightest Africa*, 254.

66. Akeley, *In Brightest Africa*, 253–54.

67. Ibid., 251.

68. Henry Fairfield Osborn, New York, to Carl Akeley, New York, 2 July 1921, A.A31, Box 7, Folder 14, Carl Ethan Akeley Papers; Akeley, *In Brightest Africa*, 198–200; Bradley, *On the Gorilla Trail*, 97.

69. Akeley, *In Brightest Africa*, 200–201.
70. Bradley, *On the Gorilla Trail*, 98, 107; Akeley, *In Brightest Africa*, 201–3.
71. Akeley, *In Brightest Africa*, 205–6.
72. Ibid., 206.
73. Ibid., 196–97.
74. Ibid., 215–24.
75. Bradley, *On the Gorilla Trail*, 114, 116; Akeley, *In Brightest Africa* 225, 229.
76. Akeley, *In Brightest Africa*, 229–30.
77. Bradley, *On the Gorilla Trail*, 116–17; "Large Male Gorilla," 45-Akeley African Hall–Gorilla Group, Exhibition Halls–Mammals, neg. 315078, Photographic Print Collection, AMNH.
78. Akeley, *In Brightest Africa*, 231; Bradley, *On the Gorilla Trail*, 118, 121.
79. Akeley, *In Brightest Africa*, 235; Bradley, *On the Gorilla Trail*, 132.
80. Ranger, "Whose Heritage?" 221–22.
81. Carl Akeley to Robert Yerkes, 31 April 1922, A.A31, B7/F29, Carl Ethan Akeley Papers; Berkhofer, *The White Man's Indian*, 166–74. For more on advocates for creating preserves for endangered tribes see Powell-Cotton, "Notes on a Journey through the Great Ituri Forest," 1–12; Thomas, "Sir Harry Johnston on 'George Greenfell and the Congo,'" 21–30; and Bradford and Blume, *Ota Benga: The Pygmy in the Zoo.*
82. Akeley to Yerkes, 31 April 1922.
83. Belgian Congo, *Parc National Albert*, 10, 12, 14.
84. Wils Glydenstople to Captain A. Gyde, 14 September 1923, Box 3, Folder 11, Mary Jobe Akeley Collection, Archives, AMNH, New York.
85. Akeley, *In Brightest Africa*, 216.
86. Glydenstople to Gyde, 14 September 1923.
87. Herbert E. Bradley, Chicago, to Carl E. Akeley, New York, 5 November 1923, Box 3, Folder 11, CEA: Correspondence, Gorilla Sanctuary, Mary Jobe Akeley Collection.
88. Carl Akeley to James Whiteley, 1 July 1924; James Whiteley to Carl Akeley, New York, 29 July 1924; draft of James Whiteley, "A Gorilla Sanctuary," *Times* (London), 5 September 1924; all in Box 3, Folder 12, Mary Jobe Akeley Collection.
89. Alexander T. Barnes quoted in Carl Akeley, New York, to His Excellency, Baron de Cartier de Marchienne, Washington, D.C., 5 June 1925, Box 3, Folder 13, CEA: Correspondence, Gorilla Sanctuary, Mary Jobe Akeley Collection.
90. Akeley to Marchienne, 5 June 1925.
91. Belgian Congo, Parc National Albert, 18; Derscheid, *La Protection Scientifique de la Nature*, 15, 23–24; AMNH, *Presidents' Annual Report*, 14; Akeley, "Darkest Africa Becomes a Wonderland," *New York Times Magazine*, 1932, in *Bulletin of the Belgian Chamber of Commerce in the United States*, Box 6, Mary Jobe Akeley Collection, 1, 3, 5; Leigh, *Frontiers of Enchantment*, 31, 48, 65–93.
92. Akeley, *The Wilderness Lives Again*, 368.

Five. Reel Africa

1. UNIA, Declaration of Rights of the Negro Peoples of the World, New York, August 13, 1920.

2. AMNH, *The Martin Johnson African Expedition*; Carl E. Akeley, New York, to Gifford Pinchot, Harrisburg, Pennsylvania, 4 April 1923, A.A31, Box 7, Folder 41, Carl Ethan Akeley Papers, Department of Rare Books and Special Collections, University of Rochester Library, New York.

3. Everett, *Returning the Gaze*, 1–3, 11, 284, 287; Cameron, *Africa on Film*, 98, 217, 222; Reddick, "Educational Programs," 367–72. Note that Everett cites Reddick's essay as "Of Motion Pictures" from an edited anthology.

4. Reddick, "Educational Programs," 369, 375; Gordon, *Picturing Bushmen*, 89–100.

5. Reddick, "Educational Programs," 382–86.

6. Ibid.; "Collecting for Museum Exhibition," James Lippitt Clark Radio Talks, Transcripts, Special Collections, AMNH, New York, 8.

7. "Radio Waves and Ripples," *Washington Post*, June 10, 1934, B6; Dixon-Stowell, "The Hatch-Billops Collection," 49.

8. Anne O'Hare McCormick, "New Dreams of African Empire," *New York Times*, June 16, 1935, SM1.

9. Nelson B. Bell, "The Jungles: A Vogue and a Tear for Some Old Friends," *Washington Post*, March 22, 1931, A4; Mitman, *Reel Nature*, 29–31; Roberts, "The Changing Images of Africa," 6, 77, 87, 91, 242, 260, 265; Rony, *The Third Eye*, 85–90; Roberts, "Africa on Film to 1940," 208; McCarthy, *Dark Continent*, xvii–xviii, 24, 45, 125; Dunn, "Lights . . . Camera . . . Africa," 149–75; *"Paul J. Rainey's African Hunt," "Common Beast of Africa," "Sport and Travel in Central Africa,"* and *"Lady MacKenzie's Big Game Pictures,"* in Hanson and Gevinson, eds., *The American Film Institute Catalog*; *"With Eustace in Africa,"* in Munden, ed., *The American Film Institute Catalog*. Although Dunn's article focuses on the 1930s, he includes a brief discussion of 1920s jungle films.

10. *"The Jungle Princess"* and *"Jungle Trail of the Son of Tarzan,"* in Munden, ed., *The American Film Institute Catalog*; *"The Jungle Lover," "The Jungle Master," "The Jungle Trail,"* and *"Judgment of the Jungle"* in Hanson and Gevinson, eds., *The American Film Institute Catalog*; Cameron, *Africa on Film*, 218–19; Hickey and Wylie, "'Heart of Darkness," 249–63; 250; Edward Schallert, "The Jungle Trail," *Los Angeles Times*, August 25, 1919, sec. 2, 10; "Lionesque Temperament," *Los Angeles Times*, October 2, 1921, sec. 3, 16; "Post Carrier to See Play," *Washington Post*, April 4, 1923, 3.

11. Kasson, *Houdini, Tarzan, and the Perfect Man*, 7, 215–18.

12. "Tarzan and the Black Boy" in Burroughs, *Jungle Tales of Tarzan*, 292.

13. "Tarzan of the Apes," *New York Times*, January 28, 1918, 13; "Strand—'Tarzan of the Apes,'" *Washington Post*, May 19, 1918, SM6; Mae Tinée, "'Tarzan' a 'Pill'?" *Chicago Daily Tribune*, May 14, 1918; Tinée, "Being Final Chronicles of a Monkey Man," *Chicago Daily Tribune*, October 3, 1918; Dunn, "Lights . . . Camera . . .

Africa," 155–59; Cameron, *Africa on Film*, 225–26; "*Tarzan of the Apes*," in Hanson and Gevinson, eds., *The American Film Institute Catalog*.

14. Walt Morton, "Tracking the Sign of Tarzan," in Kirkham and Thumin, eds., *You Tarzan*, 106–11; Kasson, *Houdini, Tarzan, and the Perfect Man*, 215–18.

15. "Tarzan of the Apes," *New York Times*, January 28, 1918, 13; "Cost of Atmosphere in Big Motion Pictures," *Los Angeles Times*, May 12, 1918, sec. 3, 4; "Strand—'Tarzan of the Apes,'" *Washington Post*, May 19, 1918, SM6.

16. Carl Ethan Akeley, New York, to Martin Johnson, Nairobi, BEA, 23 June 1922, A.A31, Box 7, Folder 28, Carl Ethan Akeley Papers; Mitman, *Reel Nature*, 29–31; Carl E. Akeley, New York, to Gifford Pinchot, Harrisburg, Pennsylvania, 4 April 1923, A.A31, Box 7, Folder 41, Carl Ethan Akeley Papers.

17. Tinée, "Wild Animal Pictures by Snow Great," *Chicago Daily Tribune*, April 28, 1923, 15; "'Hunting Big Game' Film at Rialto, Real Thriller," *Washington Post*, April 24, 1923, 4; Schallert, "Playdom: In the African Wild," *Los Angeles Times*, sec. 2, 7; "Close-Ups of Great Untamed," *Los Angeles Times*, April 22, 1923, sec. 1, 13; "Animals Pose Just Like Folks before Camera," *Los Angeles Times*, April 29, 1923, sec. 3, 35.

18. Snow, "Getting Animal 'Close-ups,'" 24; *Hunting Big Game in Africa with Gun and Camera*, in Munden, ed., *The American Film Institute Catalog*, 369; Carl Akeley, New York, to Herbert E. Bradley, Chicago, 22 May 1923, Box 3, Folder 16, CEA: Correspondence, Martin Johnson Expedition, 1923–1925, Mary Jobe Akeley Collection, Archives, AMNH, New York; Carl Akeley to Samuel L. Rothapfel, 10 March 1923, Box 2, Folder 16, CEA: Correspondence, Martin Johnson Expedition, 1923–1925, Mary Jobe Akeley Collection.

19. Herbert E. Bradley, Chicago, to Carl E. Akeley, New York, 29 May 1923, Box 3, Folder 16, CEA: Correspondence, Martin Johnson Expedition, 1923–1925, Mary Jobe Akeley Collection.

20. Carl E. Akeley, New York, to George Eastman, Rochester, New York, 26 July 1923, Box 3, Folder 17, CEA: Martin Johnson Expedition, Correspondence with George Eastman, 1923–1925, Mary Jobe Akeley Collection.

21. Carl E. Akeley, New York, to Herbert E. Bradley, Chicago, 13 November 1923 and Carl Akeley, New York, to Mr. ——, 22 January 1924, Box 3, Folder 16, CEA: Correspondence, Martin Johnson Expedition, 1923–1925, Mary Jobe Akeley Collection; Martin Johnson quoted from *World's Work* in Carl E. Akeley, "Martin Johnson and His Expedition to Lake Paradise," 288.

22. Akeley, "Plans for the African Hall [corrected version]," n.d., A.A31 Box 1, Folder 3, AMNH, Carl Ethan Akeley Papers, 3–4, 6.

23. Ibid., 3–6.

24. Félix-Louis Regnault quoted in Rony, "Those Who Squat and Those Who Sit," 274–75; Carl Akeley quoted in Preston, "Shooting in Paradise," 16; Sklar, *Movie-Made America*, 1–9.

25. Martin Johnson quoted from *World's Work* in Akeley, "Martin Johnson and His Expedition to Lake Paradise," 288; Rexer and Klein, *American Museum of Natural History*, 119; Johnson, *Camera Trails in Africa*, 304–5.

26. Johnson, *I Married Adventure*, 203, 206–7.

27. Ibid., 262.

28. Ibid., 273; Akeley, "Martin Johnson and His Expedition to Lake Paradise," 288; Johnson, *Camera Trails in Africa*, 335.

29. Martin Johnson quoted in Carl E. Akeley, "Martin Johnson and His Expedition to Lake Paradise," 288.

30. *Simba*.

31. Ibid.; Johnson, *I Married Adventure*, 228, 283; "Mr. and Mrs. Johnson, Motion Picture Camera and Native Porters, Entrance to Lake Paradise," 122–Johnson–BEA–Lae Pardise–1921, neg. 128755, Photographic Print Collection, AMNH, New York.

32. Poster for *Simba*, Martin and Osa Johnson Papers, Martin and Osa Johnson Safari Museum, Chanute, Kansas; Webb, *Martin and Osa Johnson*.

33. *Simba*.

34. Ibid.; Johnson, *I Married Adventure*, 289–93.

35. See Bogle, "Black Beginnings," 13, and Cripps, *Slow Fade to Black*, 10.

36. *Simba*.

37. Schallert, "Museum Opus, 'Simba,' Seen in New York," *Los Angeles Times*, January 22, 1928, C13; Ralph Flint, "Martin Johnson's African Film," *Christian Science Monitor*, February 7, 1928, 8; Tinée, "'Simba' Shows Jungle Life in Africa as It Is," *Chicago Daily Tribune*, 17.

38. "Extracts from the Diary of Martin Johnson," 571–78.

39. Akeley, *Congo Eden*.

40. "Martin Johnson's Pictures of African Game," 301; Martin Johnson quoted in *Adventure Lovers*; Ernest Hemingway quoted in *Adventure Lovers*.

41. "Display Ad 9—No Title," *Chicago Daily Tribune*, May 24, 1930, 12; "Wild Game Hunt Film Exhibited," *Los Angeles Times*, April 13, 1930, B15; "Behind the Screens with Nelson B. Bell," *Washington Post*, April 24, 1930, 8; "Ban on Jungle Picture Ignored by Exhibitors," *Los Angeles Times*, June 11, 1930, A12.

42. "Jungle Thrills Shown," *Los Angeles Times*, April 15, 1930, A13; "Behind the Screens with Nelson B. Bell," *Washington Post*, April 24, 1930, 8; "African Film Continues to Pack Keith's," *Washington Post*, May 4, 1930, A4; "Barnum Would Have Gobbled Such a Freak," *Washington Post*, April 27, 1930, A2.

43. "Ban on Jungle Picture Ignored by Exhibitors," *Los Angeles Times*, June 11, 1930, A12; "Make Monkey of Gorilla? No!" *Los Angeles Times*, June 12, 1930, A1; "Who Put the Gag in 'Ingagi'?" *Los Angeles Times*, June 15, 1930, B9; "Behind the Screens with Nelson B. Bell," *Washington Post*, April 24, 1930, 8.

44. Cripps, *Slow Fade to Black*, 133. See Schechter's discussion of Ida B. Wells and the film committee of the Urban League in *Ida B. Wells-Barnett and American Reform, 1880–1930*.

45. Mordaunt Hall, "Review Summary: Trader Horn," *New York Times Review*, February 4, 1931; Carveth Wells, "The Voice of the Fan," *Chicago Daily Tribune*, March 15, 1931.

46. "Film 'Africa Speaks' (Objectionable Incidents)," in Public Record Office, CO 822/34/4, "African Game," *East Africa Correspondence, 1931*; "Erreurs dans le film sur la jungle dénoncées par les autorités," in le Ministre, Le Directeur, Brussels, to Monsieur le Ministre des Colonies, 23 March 1932, in "Film Americaine 'Ubangi,'" *Informations relatives aux puissance d'Amérique*—E.U.A., 1275–1393, Etats-Unis d'Amérique, Ministère des Colonies, AE/II no. 1388 (3240) 8516, AA, Brussels; Roberta Nangle, "Here's Splendid Picture of Life in the Jungle," *Chicago Daily Tribune*, September 21, 1930, F1; "'African Film' Warning Issued," *Los Angeles Times*, February 15, 1932, 5.

47. *Congorilla*; *Adventure Lovers*.

48. *Adventure Lovers*.

49. *Baboona*; F. Trubee Davison, New York, to Martin Johnson, New York, 14 January 1935, Box 22, Folder 3, the Clark H. Getts Papers (4941), American Heritage Center, Laramie, Wyoming.

50. *Sanders of the River*; Sennwald, "'Sanders of the River,' a British Film Based on Edgar Wallace Stories," *New York Times Review*, June 27, 1935.

51. Roi Ottley, "Propaganda Pictures," *New York Amsterdam News*, July 27, 1935, 11.

52. Ottley, "King Jaja Exiled," *New York Amsterdam News*, July 27, 1935, 11; Ofonagoro, "Commercial Revolution in the Niger Delta," 137–39.

53. Bourne, *Black in the British Frame*, 11, 14, 16–18; Lewis, *W. E. B. Du Bois: The Fight for Equality*, 168–66; T. R. Poston, "Robeson to Play King Christophe," *New York Amsterdam News*, October 5, 1935, 1.

54. Nelson B. Bell, "A Hollywood Secret—Jungle License—A Pointed Analogy," *Washington Post*, May 24, 1931, A4.

55. Ibid.

56. Gaines, *Fire and Desire*, 147–48.

Conclusion

1. "The Menace to Abyssinia," *Pittsburg Courier*, December 22, 1934, 10; Haile, "The Unity and Territorial Integrity of Ethiopia," 470; Plummer, *Rising Wind*, 13, 37; Scott, *Sons of Sheba's Race*, 54, 57.

2. J. A. Rogers, "Ruminations," *New York Amsterdam News*, November 10, 1934, 8; Edwards, *The Practice of Diaspora*, 132; Scott, *Sons of Sheba's Race*, 25, 199–200. See Rogers's later work, *Sex and Race*.

3. "Aid for Ethiopia," *New York Amsterdam News*, July 13, 1935, 12; "Giant Petition for U.S. to Help Ethiopia Starts," *Washington Post*, July 16, 1935, 9; Maurice Jennings, "Vignettes of Color: What Is Africa to You?" *New York Amsterdam News*, July 20, 1935, A7; Von Eschen, *Race against Empire*, 11; Plummer, *Rising Wind*, 44; Kelley, "'This Ain't Ethiopia, But It'll Do,'" 130–31.

4. "Harlem Ponders Ethiopia's Fate," *New York Times*, July 14, 1935, E10; Scott, *Sons of Sheba's Race*, 144–45.

5. Senate, *Report Accompanying Senate Joint Resolution 198, Extending Joint Resolution Approved August 31, 1935 (Public Res. 67, 74th Cong.), Together with Other Amendments, January 16 (calendar day, Feb. 12), 1936*, 74th Cong., 2nd sess., S. Rep. 1557; Kelley, "'This Ain't Ethiopia, But It'll Do,'" 130.

6. "White and Negro Join Peace Rally," *New York Times*, August 4, 1935, 28; Kelley, "'This Ain't Ethiopia, But It'll Do,'" 130–31; Scott, *Sons of Sheba's Race*, 144–45.

7. Scott, *Sons of Sheba's Race*, 75, 79, 217; "Selassie's Air Aide Back from Africa," *New York Times*, May 19, 1936, 6; Von Eschen, *Race against Empire*, 11; Stein, *The World of Marcus Garvey*, 269–70; Plummer, *Rising Wind*, 37; Edwards, *The Practice of Diaspora*, 246, 276, 295–305.

8. "Mob of Four Hundred Battles the Police in Harlem," *New York Times*, May 19, 1936, 6.

9. On Italian Americans and fascism see Cannistraro, "Fascism and Italian-Americans in Detroit, 1933–1935," and *Blackshirts in Little Italy*; Nazarro, *Fascist and Anti-Fascist Propaganda in America*; and Saverino, "Italian in Public Memory," 96–97. See also Pugliese's review of *Blackshirts in Little Italy*.

10. Kelley, "'This Ain't Ethiopia, But It'll Do,'" 130–31; Plummer, *Rising Wind*, 40–60.

11. S. T. Holland, "J. A. Rodgers Thrills Capacity Crowd in Detroit," *Pittsburgh Courier*, June 13, 1936, 10.

12. Kelley, "'This Ain't Ethiopia, But It'll Do,'" 124; Plummer, *Rising Wind*, 60–64.

13. As of December 1936, these groups remained "uncollected and unfinanced." I. W. Schlesinger and his brother, M. A. Schlesinger, expressed interest in helping with the completion of the hall. See F. Trubee Davison, New York, to Mrs. Carl Akeley, New York, 15 December 1936; "African Hall: Work Required to Complete Second and Third Floors in Preparation for Opening May 15, 1936"; R. C. Andrews, New York, to Professor Louis E. Akeley, Vermillion, South Dakota, 2 March 1936; and James L. Clark, New York, to R. C. Andrews, New York, 13 January 1936, all in Letters: African Hall, Central Archives, AMNH, New York.

14. Vice-Director, New York, to Daniel Pomeroy, 4 April 1936; "Extract from letter from Mr. Faunce to Dr. Andrews, Dated April 18, 1936"; and C. J. O'Connor, New York, to William Hanemann, New Jersey, 14 May 1936, all in Letters: African Hall, Central Archives.

15. Markey, "A Reporter at Large, Africa Brought to Town," 45.

16. Ibid., 48–50; Pomeroy quoted in Markey, "The Wonders of Africa Brought to America."

17. Haraway, "Teddy Bear Patriarchy," 26–46.

18. Ibid., 53–54; Akeley, *In Brightest Africa*, 131–34, 141–44; Bogle, "Black Beginnings," 16; Akeley and Akeley, *Adventures in the African Jungle*, 25–45.

19. Markey, "The Wonders of Africa Brought to America"; Teslow, "Representing Race"; Smith, New York, to R. C. Andrews, 24 December 1936, Letters: African Hall, Central Archives; Berliner, "Africana. A Ragtime Classic"; "Gorilla Group, African Hall, with lettering (October 1937)," 45–Akeley African Hall–Gorilla Group, Exhibition Halls–Mammals, neg. 315382, Photographic Print Collection, AMNH, New York.

20. Mudimbe, *The Invention of Africa*, 90; Woodson, review of *Renascent Africa*, 244–45.

21. Von Eschen, *Race against Empire*, 11; Lewis, *W. E. B. Du Bois: The Fight for Equality*, 499–500; Akeley, *Congo Eden*, xviii–xix.

22. See Organisation for Economic Co-Operation and Development, *Business for Development 2008: Promoting Commercial Agriculture in Africa*.

BIBLIOGRAPHY

Manuscript Collections

African Hall. Letters. Central Archives, American Museum of Natural History, New York.

Akeley, Carl. Correspondence. Milwaukee Public Museum Library and Archives.

Akeley, Carl Ethan. Papers (A.A31). Department of Rare Books and Special Collections. University of Rochester Library. New York.

Akeley, Mary Jobe. Collection (MSS.A342). Archives. American Museum of Natural History, New York.

American Museum of Natural History (New York) Collection. Correspondence with H. C. Bumpus and H. F. Osborn. Natural History Museum Archives. Natural History Museum, London.

Biography Files. Archives. American Museum of Natural History, New York.

Booker T. Washington Papers Online. Open Book Edition. University of Illinois Press. http://www.historycooperative.org/btw/index.html.

Chapin, James P. Papers. Archives. The Natural History Museum, London.

Clark, James Lippitt. Diaries, 1907–1948. Rare Book Room. American Museum of Natural History, New York.

———. Diary; British East Africa, 1909–1910. Rare Book Room. American Museum of Natural History, New York.

———. Radio Talks, Transcripts. Special Collections. American Museum of Natural History, New York.

Director's Correspondence, General Alpha, 1893–1907. Library and Archives. Field Museum of Natural History, Chicago.

Director's Office. Expedition Files. Library and Archives. Field Museum of Natural History, Chicago.

Eastman, George. Papers. George Eastman House, Rochester, New York.

Field Museum of Natural History. Historical Files. Library and Archives, Chicago.

Foreign Office. Records. Public Record Office, Kew, United Kingdom.

Getts, Clark H. Papers (4941). American Heritage Center, Laramie, Wyoming.

Johnson, Martin and Osa. Films. The Martin and Osa Johnson Safari Museum, Chanute, Kansas.

———. Papers. The Martin and Osa Johnson Safari Museum, Chanute, Kansas.

Lang, Herbert. (MSS. C661) Congo Expedition of the American Museum of Natural History (1909). Correspondence, 1918–1920. Archives. American Museum of Natural History, New York.

———. (MSS. C662) Congo Expedition of the American Museum of Natural History (1909). Papers. American Museum of Natural History Archives, New York.

———. Various Papers of the American Museum Congo Expedition. Special Collections. American Museum of Natural History, New York.

Ministère des Affaires Étrangères du Commerce Extérieur et de la Coopération au Développement. Archives Africaines. Brussels, Belgium.

The National Association of Colored Women's Clubs. Records. LexisNexis.

The Natural History Museum. Archives. London.

Photographic Print Collection. Archives. American Museum of Natural History, New York.

Record of Proceedings of the Board of Trustees of the Public Museum of the City of Milwaukee, 1883 to ———. Library and Archives. Milwaukee Public Museum.

Registrar Accession Records, Zoology, Acc. 151, Library and Archives. Field Museum of Natural History, Chicago.

Smithsonian Institution National Anthropological Archives. http://siris-archives.si.edu.

Town of Clarendon Historic Records. Town Hall, Clarendon, New York.

United Kingdom. Parliament. *Correspondence and Report from His Majesty's Consul at Boma Respecting the Administration of the Independent State of the Congo.* Cd. 1933. 1904.

———. Public Record Office. Colonial Office. Records. Kew.

Vernay, A. S. Correspondence on the Vernay-Lang Expedition to the Kalahari Desert, 1930–1932. Archives. The Natural History Museum, London.

———. Miscellaneous Papers. Archives. The Natural History Museum, London.

———. Papers. Archives. The Tring Library via the Natural History Museum, London.

Ward, Henry Augustus. Papers, 1840–1933, A.W23. Department of Rare Books and Special Collections. University of Rochester Library, New York.

Ward's Natural Science Establishment Papers, Addition, D.258. Department of Rare Books and Special Collections. University of Rochester Library. New York.

Newspapers

Chicago Daily Tribune, November 29, 1884–March 15, 1931
Chicago Defender, February 3, 1912
Christian Science Monitor, February 7, 1928
Cleveland Advocate, December 12, 1919
Los Angeles Times, May 12, 1918–February 15, 1932
National Baptist World, October 26, 1894–November 9, 1894
National Reflector, March 27, 1887
N.C. Republican and Civil Rights Advocate, May 22, 1884

New York Age, August 17, 1889–June 4, 1908
New York Amsterdam News, January 20, 1926–October 5, 1935
New York Freeman, June 19, 1886–September 3, 1887
New York Times, November 27, 1884–May 20, 1936
Northwestern Recorder, March 1893
Pittsburgh Courier, February 29, 1936–June 13, 1936
Union and Advertiser, February 25, 1886
Virginia Star, December 9, 1882–December 23, 1882
Ward's Natural Science Bulletin, January 1, 1883
Washington Post, November 27, 1884–July 16, 1935

Printed Primary Sources

Aborigines Protection Society. *The Treatment of Natives in the Congo; a Statement Submitted to His Majesty's Government on Behalf of the Aborigines Protection Society*. London: n.p., 1902.

Adams, C. C. "Recent Discoveries in the Congo Basin." *Harper's Weekly*, January 18, 1890, 37.

African Blood Brotherhood. "Programme of the African Blood Brotherhood." *Communist Review* 2, no. 6 (April 1922). www.marx.org.

Akeley, Carl. *In Brightest Africa*. Garden City, N.Y.: Doubleday, Page, 1924.

———. "Martin Johnson and His Expedition to Lake Paradise: A Culminating Chapter in the History of Wild-Life Photography, with a Survey of Some of the Earlier Stages in the Development of its Technique." *Natural History* 21, no. 4, (May–June 1924): 284–88.

———. "Theodore Roosevelt and Africa: The Man Who Felt the Attraction of Life in the Silent Places and the Wide Waste Spaces of the Earth." *Natural History* 19 (January 1919): 12–14.

Akeley, Carl, and Mary L. Jobe Akeley. *Adventures in the African Jungle*. New York: Dodd, Mead, 1930.

———. *Lions, Gorillas and Their Neighbors*. New York: Dodd, 1932.

Akeley, Delia J. *"J.T., Jr.": The Biography of an African Monkey*. 1928. Reprint, New York: Macmillan, 1939.

———. *Jungle Portraits*. 1930. Reprint, New York: Robert M. McBride, 1933.

Akeley, Mary L. Jobe. *Carl Akeley's Africa: The Account of the Akeley-Eastman-Pomeroy African Hall Expedition of the American Museum of Natural History*. New York: Blue Ribbon Books, 1929.

———. *Congo Eden: A Comprehensive Portrayal of the Historical Background and Scientific Aspects of the Great Game Sanctuaries of the Belgian Congo with the Story of Six Months Pilgrimage throughout That Most Primitive Region in the Heart of the African Continent*. 1950. Reprint, New York: Dodd, Mead, 1961.

———. *The Wilderness Lives Again: Carl Akeley and the Great Adventure*. New York: Dodd, Mead, 1940.

"Akeley of Africa." *True: The Man's Magazine*, June 1952, 120–21.

Allen, J. A. "Mammals from British East Africa, Collected by the Tjäder Expedition of 1906." *Bulletin of the American Museum of Natural History* 24 (1908): 147–75.

American Museum of Natural History. *Catalog of the American Museum of Natural History Film Archives*. New York: Garland Publishers, 1987.

———. *The Complete Book of the African Hall*. New York: American Museum of Natural History, 1936.

———. *The Martin Johnson African Expedition under the Supervision of the American Museum of Natural History*. New York: American Museum of Natural History, 1923.

———. *Presidents' Annual Reports, 1907–1932*. New York: American Museum of Natural History, 1933–1935.

Arthur, Chester A. *Message from the President of the United States Transmitting a Report from the Secretary of State in Relation to the Congo Conference at Berlin*. 48th Cong., 2nd sess., 1885. House Executive Document 156.

Battel, Andre. Ernest George Ravenstein, Samuel Purchas, and Anthony Knivet. *The Strange Adventures of Andrew Battel of Leigh, in Angola and the Adjoining Regions*. London: Hakluyt Society, 1901.

Belgian Congo. *Parc National Albert*. Brussels, Belgium: n.p., 1934.

Berliner, Leo E. "Africana. A Ragtime Classic." In *African-American Sheet Music, 1850–1920*. http://memory.loc.gov.

Blyden, Edward W. "The African Problem, and the Method of Its Solution." In *Negro Social and Political Thought, 1850–1920: Representative Texts*, edited by Howard Brotz, 126–39. New York: Basic Books, 1966.

Bowen, John Wesley Edward, ed. *Africa and the American Negro: Addresses and Proceedings of the Congress on Africa: Held under the Auspices of the Stewart Missionary Foundation for Africa of Gammon Theological Seminary in Connection with the Cotton States and International Exposition December 13–15, 1895*. Electronic Edition. Documenting the American South. http://docsouth.unc.edu/church/bowen/menu.html.

Bradley, Mary Hastings. *On the Gorilla Trail*. New York: D. Appleton-Century, 1936.

The Brockport Directory for the Year Beginning January 1, 1901. Brockport, N.Y.: Curvin and Parker, 1901.

Brooklyn City Directory, 1879/1880. Brooklyn, N.Y.: Lain, 1880.

Burroughs, Edgar Rice. *Jungle Tales of Tarzan*. Chicago: A. C. McClurg, 1919.

———. *Tarzan of the Apes*. New York: Ballantine Books, 1990.

Burrows, Guy, and Edgar Canisius. *The Curse of Central Africa*. London: R. A. Everett, 1903.

Chapman, Abel. *On Safari: Big-Game Hunting in British East Africa with Studies of Bird-Life*. London: Edward Arnold, 1908.

Chatelain, Heli. "African Races." *Journal of American Folklore* 7, no. 27 (October–December 1894): 289–302.

Clark, James L. *The Giant Eland of Southern Sudan*. New York: American Museum of Natural History, 1931.

———. *Good Hunting: Fifty Years of Collecting and Preparing Habitat Groups for The American Museum*. Norman: University of Oklahoma Press, 1966.

———. "The Image of Africa." In *The Complete Book of the African Hall*, 70. New York: American Museum of Natural History, 1936.

Coles, John J. *Africa in Brief*. New York: New York Freeman Steam Printing Establishment, 1886.

Congo Committee, Massachusetts Commission for International Justice. "The Real Issue in Re Congo Intervention." *Congo News-Letter* (1904). www.memory.loc.gov

Congo Reform Association. *Will Civilisation Hearken? The Appeal of Fifty-two Pioneers of Christianity on the Congo, Comprising Englishmen, Canadians, Americans, Germans, Swedes, Danes, and Norwegians*. Liverpool, U.K.: John Richardson and Sons, 1906.

Conrad, Joseph. *Heart of Darkness*. Edited by Ross C. Murfin. Boston, Mass.: Bedford Books of St. Martin's Press, 1996.

Contee, Clarence G. "The 'Statuts' of the Pan-African Association of 1921: A Document." *African Historical Studies* 3, no. 2 (1970): 409–17.

Cope, E. D. *The Origin of the Fittest: Essays on Evolution*. New York: D. Appleton, 1886.

Crummell, Alexander. "The Relations and Duties of Free Colored Men in America to Africa." In *Negro Social and Political Thought, 1850–1920: Representative Texts*, edited by Howard Brotz, 171–80. New York: Basic Books, 1966.

De Leon, Daniel. "The Conference at Berlin on the West-African Question." *Political Science Quarterly* 1, no. 1 (March 1886): 103–39.

Derscheid, J. M. *La Protection Scientifique de la Nature*. Brussels, Belgium: n.p., 1927.

Du Bois, W. E. B. "The African Roots of War." *Atlantic Monthly* 115, no. 5 (May 1915): 707–14. www.webdubois.org.

———. *The Souls of Black Folk*. Edited by Henry Louis Gates Jr. and Terri Hume Oliver. New York: W. W. Norton, 1999.

Du Chaillu, Paul Belloni. *Explorations and Adventures in Equatorial Africa*. New York: Harper, 1861.

Evans, Maurice S. "International Conference on the Negro." *Journal of the Royal African Society* 11, no. 44 (July 1912): 416–29.

"Extracts from the Diary of Martin Johnson." *Natural History* 25, no. 6 (November–December 1925): 571–94.

Field Museum of Natural History. *Annual Report of the Director to the Board of Trustees*. Chicago: Field Museum of Natural History, 1908–1935.

———. *Zoological Series.* Vol. 10. Chicago: Field Museum of Natural History, 1909–1923.

Fortune, Timothy Thomas. *Black and White: Land, Labor, and Politics in the South.* New York: Fords, Howard and Hulbert, 1884.

———. "The Nationalization of Africa." In Bowen, ed., *Africa and the American Negro,* 199–204.

Garvey, Marcus. "Declaration of the Rights of the Negro Peoples of the World." In *Philosophy and Opinions of Marcus Garvey,* edited by Amy Jacques Garvey. New York: Arno Press, 1923.

———. *Philosophy and Opinions of Marcus Garvey.* Edited by Amy Jacques-Garvey. 1923. Reprint, New York: Arno Press, 1963.

———. "Speech Delivered at Madison Square Garden." In *Philosophy and Opinions of Marcus Garvey,* edited by Amy Jacques Garvey. New York: Arno Press, 1923.

———. "Speech on Disarmament Conference." In *Philosophy and Opinions of Marcus Garvey,* edited by Amy Jacques Garvey. New York: Arno Press, 1923.

Gregory, J. W. *The Foundation of British East Africa.* London: H. Marshall and Son, 1901.

Haggard, H. Rider. *King Solomon's Mines.* London: Cassell, 1885.

———. *She.* London: Hodder and Stoughton, 1886.

Hamedoe, S. E. F. C. C. "The First Pan-African Conference of the World." *Colored American Magazine* 4 (September 1900): 223–31.

Harris, Captain William Cornwallis. *The Wild Sports of Southern Africa: Being the Narrative of an Expedition from the Cape of Good Hope through the Territories of the Chief Moselekatse, to the Tropic of Capricorn.* 1841. Reprint, Cape Town, South Africa: C. Struik, 1963.

Hartzell, J. H. "Mr. Roosevelt's Safety." *Outlook* 91 (April 10, 1909): 821–22.

Henty, G. A. *By Sheer Pluck: A Tale of the Ashanti War.* London: Blackie and Son, 1884.

———. *With Buller in Natal, or, A Born Leader.* London: Blackie and Son, 1901.

———. *With Kitchener in the Soudan: A Story of Atbara and Omburman.* London: Blackie and Son, 1902.

Holderness, Etna. "Sketch of My Life in Africa." In Bowen, ed., *Africa and the American Negro,* 113–16.

"Human Sacrifices in Dahomey." *American Anthropologist* 4, no. 1 (January 1891): 96.

Johnson, Martin. *Camera Trails in Africa.* New York: Century, 1924.

———. *Congorilla: Adventures with Pygmies and Gorillas in Africa.* New York: Brewer, Warren, and Putnam, 1931.

Johnson, Osa. *Four Years in Paradise.* Philadelphia: J. B. Lippincott, 1941.

———. *I Married Adventure: The Lives and Adventures of Martin and Osa Johnson.* Philadelphia: J. B. Lippincott, 1940.

Kearton, Cherry, and James Barnes. *Through Central Africa from East to West.* London: Cassell, 1915.

Knox, Thomas W. *The Boy Travellers on the Congo: Adventure of Two Youths in a Journey with Henry M. Stanley "Through the Dark Continent."* London: Sampson, Low, Marston, Searle, and Rivington, 1888.

Lang, Herbert. "An Explorer's View of the Congo." *American Museum Journal* (1915): 379–88.

———. "Famous Ivory Treasures of a Negro King." *American Museum Journal* (1919): 696–713.

———. "Nomad Dwarfs and Civilization." *Natural History* 19, no. 6 (1919): 527–52.

Legendre, Gertrude Sanford. *The Time of My Life.* Charleston, S.C.: Wyrick, 1987.

Leigh, W. R. *Frontiers of Enchantment: An Artist's Adventures in Africa.* New York: Simon and Schuster, 1938.

Livingstone, David, and Charles Livingstone. *Narrative of an Expedition to the Zambesi and Its Tributaries and of the Discoveries of Lakes Shirwa and Nyassa, 1858–1864.* New York: Harper and Bros., 1866.

Lowie, Robert H. "Industry and the Art of the Negro Race." *American Museum Journal* 11 (1911): 12–19.

"Many Facts in Brief about the Negro." *AME Quarterly Almanac 1893*, 18–20. http://memory.loc.gov/cgi-bin/query/r?ammem/murray:@field(DOCID+@lit(lcrbmrpt2316div4))

Markey, Morris. "A Reporter at Large, Africa Brought to Town." *New Yorker*, May 2, 1936, 45.

———. "The Wonders of Africa Brought to America." *World Youth: International News Review*, May 30, 1936.

"Martin Johnson's Pictures of African Game." *Natural History* (1923): 301.

Mason, M. C. B. "The Methodist Episcopal Church and the Evangelization of Africa." In Bowen, ed., *Africa and the American Negro*, 143–48.

Miller, J. Martin. *Hunting Big Game in the Wilds of Africa, Containing Thrilling Adventures of the Famous Roosevelt Expedition . . . the Whole Comprising a Vast Treasury of All That Is Marvelous and Wonderful in Darkest Africa.* Philadelphia: National, 1909.

Mitchell, Augustus. *A System of Modern Geography, Comprising a Description of the Present State of the World, and Its Five Great Divisions, America, Europe, Asia, Africa, and Oceanica, with Their Several Empires, Kingdoms, States, Territories, etc.* Rev. ed. Philadelphia: Cowperthwait, Desilver, and Butler, 1873.

"Mr. Roosevelt in Africa." *Outlook* 93 (October 2, 1909): 247–49.

"New African Hall Planned by Carl E. Akeley." *American Museum Journal* 14 (May 1914): 175–87.

New York City Directory, for the Year Ending May 1, 1879. New York: Trow City Directory, 1879.

"Obituary: May French Sheldon." *Geographical Journal* 87, no. 3 (March 1936): 288.

Oertel, Hanns. "Notes on Six Negro Myths from the Georgia Coast." *Journal of American Folklore* 2, no. 7 (October–December 1889): 309.

Osborn, Henry Fairfield. *The American Museum of Natural History: Its Origins, Its History, the Growth of Its Departments to December 31, 1909.* New York: Irving Press, 1911.

———. "The Congo Expedition of the American Museum of Natural History." *Bulletin of the American Museum of Natural History* 39 (1919): xv–xxviii.

———. The Fayum Expedition of the American Museum." *Science* 25, no. 639 (March 29, 1907): 513–16.

———. "New Carnivorous Mammals from the Fayum Oligocene, Egypt." *Bulletin of the American Museum of Natural History* 26 (1909): 415–24.

———. "New Fossil Mammals from the Fayum Oligocene, Egypt." *Bulletin of the American Museum of Natural History* 24 (1908): 265–72.

———. "Report of the President, 1911." In *Presidents' Annual Reports, 1907–1932.* New York: American Museum of Natural History, 1933–1935.

"Le Parc National Albert." *Bulletin de la Société d'Études Géographiques*, May 1934, 18–26.

Patterson, J. H. *The Man-Eaters of Tsavo and Other East African Adventures.* London: MacMillan, 1907.

Phillips Exeter Academy. *General Catalogue of Officers and Students, 1783–1903.* Exeter, N.H.: The News-Letter Press, 1903.

Pitt-Rivers, Augustus. *Antique Works of Art from Benin.* 1900. Reprint, New York: Dover, 1976.

Powell-Cotton, P. H. G. "Notes on a Journey through the Great Ituri Forest." *Journal of the Royal African Society* 7, no. 25 (October 1907): 1–12.

Price, J. C. "Price's Rejection of Position." *Journal of Negro History* 63, no. 3 (July 1978): 234.

Pringle, Henry F. *Theodore Roosevelt: A Biography.* New York: Harcourt, Brace, 1931.

"Protection of Wild Animals in Africa." *Science*, n.s., 12, no. 294 (August 17, 1900): 275–76.

Rainsford, William Stephen. *The Land of the Lion.* New York: Doubleday, Page, 1909.

Reddick, L. D. "Educational Programs for the Improvement of Race Relations: Motion Pictures, Radio, the Press, and Libraries." *Journal of Negro Education* 13, no. 3 (Summer 1944): 367–89.

"The Results of the Tjäder Expedition." *American Museum Journal* 7, no. 4 (March 1907): 58–62.

Review of *Negro Myths from the Georgia Coast*, by Charles C. Jones Jr. *Journal of American Folklore* 1, no. 2 (July–September 1888): 169–70.

Rogers, J. A. *Sex and Race: Negro-Caucasian Mixing in All Ages and All Lands.* New York: J. A. Rogers, 1940–1944.

Roosevelt, Theodore. *African Game Trails: An Account of the African Wanderings of an American Hunter-Naturalist.* New York: C. Scribner's Sons, 1910.

———. *Message from the President of the United States.* 60th Cong., 2nd sess., 1909. House Executive Document 666.

———. *The Strenuous Life.* Bedford, Maine: Applewood Books, 1991.

Schurz, C. "Platform of the Anti-Imperialist League." *Speeches, Correspondence and Political Papers.* Edited by Frederic Bancroft. World Civilizations. http://www.wwnorton.com/college/history/ralph/workbook/ralprs30a.htm.

Sheldon, May French. "Customs among the Natives of East Africa, from Teita to Kilimegalia, with Special Reference to Their Women and Children." *Journal of the Anthropological Institute of Great Britain and Ireland* 21 (1892): 358–90.

———. *Sultan to Sultan: Adventures among the Masai and Other Tribes of East Africa.* 1892. Reprint, Manchester, England: Manchester University Press, 1999.

Sherwood, George H. *General Guide to the Exhibition Halls of the American Museum of Natural History.* New York: American Museum of Natural History, 1911.

Sherwood, Robert E. *The Best Moving Pictures of 1921–22, also Who's Who in the Movies and the Yearbook of the American Screen.* 1922. Reprint, New York: Revisionist Press, 1974.

Shufeldt, R. W. "The Practicability of Transporting the Negro back to Africa." *Science* 17, no. 146 (January 23, 1891): 48.

Smith, Arthur Donaldson. *Through Unknown African Countries: The First Expedition from Somaliland to Lake Tamu.* London: Edward Arnold, 1897.

Snow, H. A. "Getting Animal 'Close-ups'." *Film Yearbook* (1924): 24.

Speke, John Hanning. *Journey of the Discovery of the Source of the Nile.* New York: Harper, 1864.

Stanley, Henry M. *The Congo and the Founding of Its Free State: A Story of Work and Exploration.* New York: Harper and Brothers, 1885.

———. *How I Found Livingstone: Travels, Adventures, and Discoveries in Central Africa.* New York: Scribner, Armstrong, 1872.

———. *In Darkest Africa: Or, the Quest, Rescue, and Retreat of Emin, Governor of Equatoria.* New York: Charles Scribner's Sons, 1890.

———. *Through the Dark Continent; or, The Sources of the Nile around the Great Lakes of Equatorial Africa and Down the Livingstone River to the Atlantic Ocean.* London: Sampson Low, Marston, Searle, Rivington, 1878.

Swinton, William. *Elementary Course in Geography Designed for Primary and Intermediate Grades, and as a Complete Shorter Course.* New York: Ivison, Blakeman, 1875.

Taft, William H. *Message from the President of the United States Transmitting a Letter of the Secretary of State Submitting a Report of the Commission Which Visited*

Liberia in Pursuance of the Provisions of the Deficiency Act of March 4, 1909, "To Investigate the Interests of the United States and Its Citizens in the Republic of Liberia, with the Consent of the Authorities of Said Republic." 61st Cong., 2nd sess., 1910. House Executive Document 457.

"Taxidermists Wanted." *Ward's Natural Science Bulletin* 2, no. 1 (January 1, 1883): 1.

Thirkield, Wilbur P. "Opening Remarks" in "Africa, the Continent: Its Peoples, Their Civilization and Evangelization." In Bowen, ed., *Africa and the American Negro*, 13–14.

Thomas, N. W. "Sir Harry Johnston on 'George Greenfell and the Congo.'" *Journal of the Royal African Society* 8, no. 21 (October 1908): 21–30.

Tjäder, Richard. *The Big Game of Africa*. New York: D. Appleton, 1910.

"The Tjäder East Africa Expedition." *American Museum Journal* 6, no. 4 (October 1906): 214–16.

Turner, Frederick Jackson. "The Significance of the Frontier in American History." Chap. 1 in *The Frontier in American History*. New York: Holt, Rinehart, and Winston, 1962.

Twain, Mark. *King Leopold's Soliloquy: A Defense of His Congo Rule*. Boston, Mass.: P.R. Warren, 1905.

Universal Negro Improvement Association. "Declaration of Rights of the Negro Peoples of the World." *History Matters*. http://historymatters.gmu.edu/d/5122/.

U.S. Congress. House. Committee on Foreign Relations. *Papers Relating to the Foreign Relations of the United States, Transmitted to Congress, with the Annual Message of the President, December 4, 1883.* 48th Cong., 1st sess., 1884. House Executive Document 1, pt. 1.

———. Committee on Foreign Relations. *Participation of the United States in the Congo Conference*. 48th Cong., 2nd sess., 1885. H. Rep. 2655.

U.S. Congress. Senate. 48th Cong., 1st sess., 1884. S. Misc. Doc. 59.

———. *Occupation of the Congo Country in Africa*. 48th Cong., 1st sess., 1884. S. Rep. 393.

———. *Report Accompanying Senate Joint Resolution 198, Extending Joint Resolution Approved August 31, 1935 (Public Res. 67, 74th Cong.), Together with Other Amendments, January 16 (calendar day, Feb. 12), 1936*. 74th Cong., 2nd sess., S. Rep. 1557.

U.S. Department of State. *Papers Relating to the Foreign Relations of the United States with the Annual Message of the President Transmitted to Congress, December 3, 1907*. Washington, D.C.: GPO, 1910.

Wack, Henry Wellington. *The Story of the Congo Free State: Social, Political, and Economic Aspects of the Belgian System of Government in Central Africa*. New York: G. P. Putnam's Sons, 1905.

Washington, Booker T., Norman Barton Wood, and Fannie Barrier Williams. *A New Negro for a New Century*. New York: Arno Press, 1990.

Whiteley, James Gustavus. "The Congo Free State." *New York Times Book Review*, March 4, 1905, 129.

Wissler, Clark. "The Douglas African Collection." *American Museum Journal* 7, no. 5 (May 1907): 67–83.

Woodson, Carter G. Review of *Renascent Africa*, by Nmamdi Azikiwe. *Journal of Negro History* 23, no. 2 (April 1938): 243–45.

"The Work of Carl E. Akeley." *American Museum Journal* 13, no. 4 (April 1913): 173–78.

Worley, H. F., and C. G. Contee. "The Worley Report on the Pan-African Congress of 1919." *Journal of Negro History* 55, no. 2 (April 1970): 140–43.

"Worse Than the Sixteenth Century." *Harper's Weekly*, March 26, 1904, 457–58.

"Worship of Prehistoric Stone Implements in Yoruba, West Coast of Africa." *American Anthropologist* 4, no. 1 (January 1891): 96.

Ybarra, Thomas R. "Africa's Latest Case of Sleeping Sickness." *Current Literature* 46 (June 1909): 696–700.

Secondary Sources

Adams, Jonathan S., and Thomas O. McShane. *The Myth of Wild Africa: Conservation without Illusion*. New York: W. W. Norton, 1992.

Akpan, M. B. "Liberia and the Universal Negro Improvement Association: The Background to the Abortion of Garvey's Scheme for African Colonization." *Journal of African History* 14, no. 1 (1973): 105–27.

Alexander, Edward P. *Museums in Motion: An Introduction to the History and Function of Museums*. Nashville, Tenn.: American Association for State and Local History, 1979.

Alvey, Mark. "The Cinema as Taxidermy: Carl Akeley and the Preservation Obsession." *Journal of Cinema and Media* 48, no. 1 (Spring 2007): 23–45.

Anderson, David, and Richard Grove, eds. *Conservation in Africa: People, Policies, and Practice*. Cambridge: Cambridge University Press, 1987.

Anthony, David H. "Max Yergan and South Africa: A Transatlantic Interaction." In *Imagining Home: Class, Culture, and Nationalism in the African Diaspora*, edited by Sidney J. Lemelle and Robin D. G. Kelley, 185–206. London: Verso, 1994.

Appel, Toby A. "Science, Popular Culture, and Profit: Peale's Philadelphia Museum." *Journal of the Society for the Bibliography of Natural History* 9, no. 4 (1980): 629–34.

Asad, Talal. "Afterword: From the History of Colonial Anthropology to the Anthropology of Western Hegemony." In *Colonial Situations: Essays on the Contextualization of Ethnographic Knowledge* by George W. Stocking Jr. Madison: University of Wisconsin Press, 1991.

Asma, Stephen T. *Stuffed Animals and Pickled Heads: The Culture and Evolution of Natural History Museums*. New York: Oxford University Press, 2001.

Ater, Renée. "Making History: Meta Warrick Fuller's *Ethiopia*." *American Art* 17, no. 3 (Autumn 2003): 13–31.

Bair, Barbara. "Pan-Africanism as Process: Adelaide Casely Hayford, Garveyism, and the Cultural Roots of Nationalism." In *Imagining Home: Class, Culture and Nationalism in the African Diaspora*, edited by Sidney J. Lemelle and Robin D. G. Kelley, 121–44. London: Verso, 1994.

Baker, Lee D. *From Savage to Negro: Anthropology and the Construction of Race, 1896–1954*. Berkeley: University of California Press, 1998.

Baldwin, Davarian L. *Chicago's New Negroes: Modernity, the Great Migration, and Black Urban Life*. Chapel Hill: University of North Carolina Press, 2007.

Baldwin, Kate A. *Beyond the Color Line and the Iron Curtain: Reading Encounters between Black and Red, 1922–1963*. Durham, N.C.: Duke University Press, 2002.

Bederman, Gail. *Manliness and Civilization: A Cultural History of Gender and Race in the United States, 1880–1917*. Chicago: University of Chicago Press, 1995.

Beinart, William, and Peter A. Coates. *Environment and History: The Taming of Nature in the USA and South Africa*. London: Routledge, 1995.

Bender, Thomas. *New York Intellect: A History of Intellectual Life in New York City, from 1750 to the Beginnings of Our Own Times*. New York: Knopf, 1987.

Berkhofer, Robert F. *The White Man's Indian: Images of the American Indian from Columbus to the Present*. New York: Knopf, 1978.

Blackmore, Susan J. *The Meme Machine*. New York: Oxford University Press, 1999.

Blyden, Edward W. "The Call of Providence to the Descendants of Africa in America." In *African American Social and Political Thought, 1850–1920*, edited by Howard Brotz. 112–26. New Brunswick, N.J.: Transaction Publishers, 1992.

Bodry-Sanders, Penelope. *Carl Akeley: Africa's Collector, Africa's Savior*. New York: Paragon House, 1991.

Bogle, Donald. "Black Beginnings: From *Uncle Tom's Cabin* to *The Birth of a Nation*." In *Representing Blackness: Issues in Film and Video*, edited by Valerie Smith. 13–24. New Brunswick, N.J.: Rutgers University Press, 1997.

Boisseau, Tracey Jean. *White Queen: May French Sheldon and the Imperial Origins of American Feminist Identity*. Bloomington: Indiana University Press, 2004.

Bourne, Stephen. *Black in the British Frame: Black People in British Film and Television, 1896–1996*. London: Cassell, 1998.

Bradford, Phillipe Verner, and Harvey Blume. *Ota Benga: The Pygmy in the Zoo*. New York: Dell, 1992.

Brantlinger, Patrick. "Victorians and Africans: The Genealogy of the Myth of the Dark Continent." In *"Race," Writing, and Difference*, edited by Henry Louis Gates Jr., 185–217. Chicago: University of Chicago Press, 1986.

Bravo, Michael T. "Ethnological Encounters." In *Cultures of Natural History*, edited by N. Jardine, J. A. Secord, and E. C. Spary, 338–39. Cambridge: Cambridge University Press, 1996.

Bronner, Simon J. *Consuming Visions: Accumulation and Display of Goods in America, 1880–1920.* New York: Norton, 1989.

Brooks, George E. *Yankee Traders, Old Coasters, and African Middlemen: A History of American Legitimate Trade with West Africa in the Nineteenth Century.* Brookline, Mass.: Boston University Press, 1970.

Brooks, Joanna. "Prince Hall, Freemasonry, and Genealogy." *African American Review* 34, no. 2 (Summer 2000): 197–216.

Brotz, Howard. *Negro Social and Political Thought, 1850–1920.* New York: Basic Books, 1966.

Brundage, W. Fitzhugh. "Meta Warrick's 1907 'Negro Tableaux' and (Re)Presenting African American Historical Memory." *Journal of American History* 89, no. 4 (March 2003): 1368–1400.

Cameron, Kenneth M. *Africa on Film: Beyond Black and White.* New York: Continuum, 1994.

Campbell, James T. *Middle Passages: African American Journeys to Africa, 1787–2005.* New York: Penguin Books, 2006.

Cannistraro, Philip V. *Blackshirts in Little Italy: Italian Americans and Fascism, 1921–1929.* West Lafayette, Ind.: Bordighera, 1999.

———. "Fascism and Italian-Americans in Detroit, 1933–1935." *International Migration Review* 9, no. 1 (Spring 1975): 29–40.

Carby, Hazel V. "'On the Threshold of Woman's Era': Lynching, Empire, and Sexuality in Black Feminist Theory." *Critical Inquiry* 12, no. 1 " (Autumn 1985): 262–77.

Carruthers, Jane. "Dissecting the Myth: Paul Kruger and Kruger National Park." *Journal of Southern African Studies* 20, no. 2 (June 1994): 263–83.

Chalk, Frank. "The Anatomy of an Investment: Firestone's 1927 Loan to Liberia." *Canadian Journal of African Studies/Revue Candienne des Ètudes Africaines* 1, no. 1 (March 1967): 12–32.

Chirenje, J. Mutero. *Ethiopianism and Afro-Americans in Southern Africa, 1883–1916.* Baton Rouge: Louisiana State University Press, 1987.

Clegg, Claude A., III. *The Price of Liberty: African Americans and the Making of Liberia.* Chapel Hill: University of North Carolina Press, 2004.

Comaroff, Jean, and John Comaroff. *Of Revelation and Revolution: Christianity, Colonialism, and Consciousness in South Africa.* Chicago: University of Chicago Press, 1991.

Conn, Steven. *Museums and American Intellectual Life, 1876–1926.* Chicago: University of Chicago Press, 1998.

Contee, Clarence G. "Du Bois, the NAACP, and the Pan-African Congress of 1919." *Journal of Negro History* 57, no. 1 (January 1972): 13–28.

Coombes, Annie E. *Reinventing Africa: Museums, Material Culture, and Popular Imagination in Late Victorian and Edwardian England.* New Haven, Conn.: Yale University Press, 1994.

Cooter, Roger, and Stephen Pumfrey. "Separate Spheres and Public Places: Reflections on the History of Science Popularization and Science in Popular Culture." *History of Science* 32 (1994): 237–67.

Corbould, Clare. *Becoming African American: Black Public Life in Harlem, 1919–1939*. Cambridge, Mass.: Harvard University Press, 2009.

Cripps, Thomas. *Slow Fade to Black: The Negro in American Film, 1900–1942*. 1977. Reprint, New York: Oxford University Press, 1993.

Cureau, Harold G. "William H. Sheppard: Missionary to the Congo, and Collector of African Art." *Journal of Negro History* 67, no. 4 (Winter 1982): 340–52.

Curtin, Philip D. *The Image of Africa: British Ideas and Actions, 1780–1850*. Madison: University of Wisconsin Press, 1964.

Danto, Arthur Coleman, ed. *Art/artifact: African Art in Anthropology Collections*. New York: Center for African Art, 1988.

Devlin, Kimberly J. "The Eye and the Gaze in *Heart of Darkness*: A Symptomological Reading." *Modern Fiction Studies* 40, no. 4 (Winter 1994): 711–35.

Dixon-Stowell, Brenda. "The Hatch-Billops Collection." *Dance Research Journal* 15, no. 2 (Spring 1983): 49–50.

Douglas, Ann. *Terrible Honesty: Mongrel Manhattan in the 1920s*. New York: Farrar, Straus, and Giroux, 1995.

Driver, Felix. "Henry Morton Stanley and His Critics: Geography, Exploration, and Empire." *Past and Present* 133 (November 1991): 134–66.

Dumenil, Lynn. *The Modern Temper: American Culture and Society in the 1920s*. New York: Hill and Wang, 1995.

Dunn, Kevin. "Lights . . . Camera . . . Africa: Images of Africa and Africans in Western Popular Films of the 1930s." *African Studies Review* 39 (1996): 149–75.

Earle, T. F., and K. J. P. Lowe, eds. *Black Africans in Renaissance Europe*. Cambridge: Cambridge University Press, 2005.

Edwards, Brent Hayes. *The Practice of Diaspora: Literature, Translation, and the Rise of Black Internationalism*. Cambridge, Mass.: Harvard University Press, 2003.

Ellingson, Terry Jay. *The Myth of the Noble Savage*. Berkeley: University of California Press, 2001.

Erhagbe, Edward O. "African-Americans and the Defense of African States against European Imperial Conquest: Booker T. Washington's Diplomatic Efforts to Guarantee Liberia's Independence." *African Studies Review* 39, no. 1 (April 1996): 55–65.

Everett, Anna. *Returning the Gaze: A Genealogy of Black Film Criticism, 1909–1949*. Durham, N.C.: Duke University Press, 2001.

Franklin, John Hope. *George Washington Williams: A Biography*. Chicago: University of Chicago Press, 1985.

Frederickson, George M. *The Black Image in the White Mind: The Debate on Afro-American Character and Destiny, 1817–1914.* New York: Harper and Row, 1971.

Fritzell, Peter A. *Nature Writing and America: Essay upon a Cultural Type.* Ames: Iowa University Press, 1990.

Fry, Joseph A. *John Tyler Morgan and the Search for Southern Autonomy.* Knoxville: University of Tennessee Press, 1992.

Gaines, Jane. *Fire and Desire: Mixed-Race Movies in the Silent Era.* Chicago: University of Chicago Press, 2001.

Gates, Henry Louis, Jr., ed. *"Race," Writing, and Difference.* Chicago: University of Chicago Press, 1986.

Gordon, Robert J. *Picturing Bushmen: The Denver African Expedition of 1925.* Athens: Ohio University Press, 1997.

Gould, Stephen Jay. *The Mismeasure of Man.* New York: Norton, 1981.

Haile, Getatchew. "The Unity and Territorial Integrity of Ethiopia." *Journal of Modern African Studies* 24, no. 3 (September 1986): 465–87.

Hamilton, Angus. *Somaliland.* 1911. Reprint, Westport, Conn.: Negro Universities Press, 1970.

Hammond, Dorothy, and Atla Jablow. *The Africa That Never Was.* 1970. Reprint, Prospect Heights, Ill.: Waveland Press, 1992.

Hanson, Patricia King, and Alan Gevinson, eds. *The American Film Institute Catalog of Motion Pictures Produced in the United States: Feature Films, 1911–1920, Film Entries.* Berkeley: University of California Press, 1988.

Haraway, Donna. "Teddy Bear Patriarchy: Taxidermy in the Garden of Eden, New York City, 1908–1936." Chap. 3 in *Primate Visions: Gender, Race, and Nature in the World of Modern Science.* New York: Routledge, 1989.

Harris, Neil. *Cultural Excursions: Marketing Appetites and Cultural Tastes in Modern America.* Chicago: University of Chicago Press, 1990.

Harris-Lacewell, Melissa Victoria. *Barbershops, Bibles, and bet: Everyday Talk and Black Political Thought.* Princeton, N.J.: Princeton University Press, 2004.

Hawkins, Hunt. "Mark Twain's Involvement with the Congo Reform Movement: 'A Fury of Generous Indignation.'" *New England Quarterly* 51, no. 2 (June 1978): 147–75.

Heilmann, Ann, ed. *Feminist Forerunners: New Womanism and Feminism in the Early Twentieth Century.* London: Pandora, 2003.

Hickey, Dennis, and Kenneth Wylie. *An Enchanting Darkness: The American Vision of Africa in the Twentieth Century.* East Lansing: Michigan State University Press, 1993.

———. "'Heart of Darkness' or 'Mother of Light'? American Perceptions of the African Rainforest." *Centennial Review* 35 (1991): 249–63.

Hill, Robert A. "Before Garvey: Chief Alfred Sam and the African Movement, 1912–1916." In *Pan-African Biography*, edited by Robert A. Hill, 58–77. Los

Angeles: African Studies Center and Crossroads Press, African Studies Association, 1987.

Hill, Robert A., and Barbara Bair. *Marcus Garvey, Life and Lessons: A Centennial Companion to the Marcus Garvey and Universal Negro Improvement Association Papers*. Berkeley: University of California Press, 1987.

Hochschild, Adam. *King Leopold's Ghost: A Story of Greed, Terror, and Heroism in Colonial Africa*. Boston, Mass.: Houghton Mifflin, 1998.

Hooker, J. R. "The Pan-African Conference 1900." *Transition* 46 (1974): 20–24.

Iliffe, John. *Africans: The History of a Continent*. Cambridge: Cambridge University Press, 1995.

JanMohamed, Abdul R. "The Economy of Manichean Allegory: The Function of Racial Difference in Colonialist Literature." In *"Race," Writing, and Difference*, edited by Henry Louis Gates Jr. 78–106. Chicago: University of Chicago Press, 1986.

Jarosz, Lucy. "Constructing the Dark Continent: Metaphor as Geographic Representation of Africa." *Geografiska Annaler*, series B, *Human Geographa* 74, no. 2 (1992): 105–15.

Jeal, Tim. *Stanley: The Impossible Life of Africa's Greatest Explorer*. New Haven, Conn.: Yale University Press, 2007.

Jenkins, Deborah Gail. "Theodore Roosevelt: American Hunter-Naturalist in Africa." PhD diss., Georgia Southern College, 1985.

Jones, Jeannette Eileen. "'Gorilla Trails in Paradise': Carl Akeley, Mary Bradley, and the American Search for the Missing Link." *Journal of American Culture* 29, no. 3 (September 2006): 321–36.

———. "'In Brightest Africa': Naturalistic Constructions of Africa in the American Museum of Natural History, 1910–1936." In *Images of Africa: Stereotypes and Realities*, edited by Daniel M. Mengara, 195–208. Trenton, N.J.: Africa World Press, 2001.

Jordan, Winthrop. *White over Black: American Attitudes toward the Negro, 1550–1812*. Chapel Hill: University of North Carolina Press, 1968.

Kasambira, Tafadzwa Sila. "An Analysis of the Treatment of Africa and Africans in American Secondary School Geography Textbooks." PhD diss., Kent State University, 1980.

Kasson, John F. *Houdini, Tarzan, and the Perfect Man: The White Male Body and the Challenge of Modernity in America*. New York: Hill and Wang, 2001.

Katz, Wendy R. *Rider Haggard and the Fiction of Empire: A Critical Study of British Imperial Fiction*. Cambridge: Cambridge University Press, 1987.

Kelley, Robin D. G. "Afric's Sons with Banner Red." In *Race Rebels: Culture, Politics, and the Black Working Class*. New York: The Free Press, 1994.

———. "'This Ain't Ethiopia, But It'll Do': African Americans and the Spanish Civil War." Chap. 6 in *Race Rebels: Culture, Politics, and the Black Working Class*. New York: Free Press, 1994.

Kirkham, Pat, and Janet Thumim, eds. *You Tarzan: Masculinity, Movies, and Men.* London: Lawrence and Wishart, 1993.

Knowles, Joan N., and D. P. Collett. "Nature as Myth, Symbol, and Action: Notes toward a Historical Understanding of Developmental Conservation in Kenyan Maasailand." *Journal of the International African Institute* 59, no. 4 (1989): 433–60.

Kohlstedt, Sally Gregory. "Henry A. Ward: The Merchant Naturalist and American Museum Development." *Journal of the Society for the Bibliography of Natural History* 9, no. 4 (1980): 647–61.

Lears, T. J. Jackson. *No Place of Grace: Antimodernism and the Transformation of American Culture, 1880–1920.* New York: Pantheon Books, 1981.

Lemke, Sieglinde. *Primitivist Modernism: Black Culture and the Origins of Transatlantic Modernism.* New York: Oxford University Press, 1998.

Levine, Lawrence W. *Highbrow/Lowbrow: The Emergence of Cultural Hierarchy in America.* Cambridge, Mass: Harvard University Press, 1990.

Lewis, David Levering. *The Race to Fashoda: European Colonialism and African Resistance in the Scramble for Africa.* New York: Weidenfeld and Nicolson, 1987.

———. *W. E. B. Du Bois: The Biography of a Race, 1868–1919.* New York: Holt, 1993.

———. *W. E. B. Du Bois: The Fight for Equality and the American Century, 1919–1963.* New York: Holt, 2000.

———. *When Harlem Was in Vogue.* New York: Alfred A. Knopf, 1981.

Logan, Rayford Whittingham. *The Negro in American Life and Thought: The Nadir, 1877–1901.* New York: Dial Press, 1954.

Louis, William Roger. "Roger Casement and the Congo." *Journal of African History* 1 (1964): 99–120.

Lurie, Nancy Oestreich. *A Special Style: The Milwaukee Public Museum, 1882–1982.* Milwaukee, Wis.: Milwaukee Public Museum, 1983.

Lutz, Catherine A., and Jane L. Collins. *Reading National Geographic.* Chicago: University of Chicago Press, 1993.

Martin, Tony. *Race First: The Ideological and Organizational Struggles of Marcus Garvey and the Universal Negro Improvement Association.* Westport, Conn.: Greenwood Press, 1976.

Matthews, Jean V. *The Rise of the New Woman: The Women's Movement in America, 1875–1930.* Chicago: Ivan R. Dee, 2003.

Mboukou, Alexandre. "The Pan-African Movement, 1900–1945: A Study in Leadership Conflicts among the Disciples of Pan Africanism." *Journal of Black Studies* 13, no. 3 (March 1983): 275–88.

McCarthy, Michael. *Dark Continent: Africa as Seen by Americans.* Westport, Conn.: Greenwood Press, 1983.

McCartney, John T. *Black Power Ideologies: An Essay in African-American Political Thought.* Philadelphia, Pa.: Temple University Press, 1992.

Meyer, Lysle E. *The Farther Frontier: Six Case Studies of Americans and Africa, 1848–1936*. Selinsgrove, Pa.: Susquehanna University Press, 1992.

Mitchell, Michele. *Righteous Propagation: African Americans and the Politics of Racial Destiny after Reconstruction*. Chapel Hill: University of North Carolina Press, 2004.

Mitman, Gregg. *Reel Nature: America's Romance with Wildlife on Film*. Cambridge, Mass.: Harvard University Press, 1999.

Morton, H. Wayne. "Toward National Unity." In *The Gilded Age*, edited by H. Wayne Morton. 1–12. Syracuse, N.Y.: Syracuse University Press, 1970.

Moses, Wilson Jeremiah. *The Golden Age of Black Nationalism, 1850–1925*. Hamden, Conn.: Archon Books, 1978.

Mowat, Linda. *Symbols of Kings: Benin Art at the Pitt-Rivers Museum*. Oxford: Pitt-Rivers Museum, University of Oxford, 1991.

Msiska, Mpalive-Hangson, and Paul Hyland, eds. *Writing and Africa*. LondonNew York: Longman, 1997.

Mudimbe, V. Y. *The Invention of Africa: Gnosis, Philosophy, and the Order of Knowledge*. Bloomington: Indiana University Press, 1988.

Munden, Kenneth W., ed., *The American Film Institute Catalog of Motion Pictures Produced in the United States: Featured Films, 1921–1930*. New York: R. R. Bowker, 1971.

Murray, John A. *Wild Africa: Three Centuries of Nature Writing from Africa*. New York: Oxford University Press, 1993.

Nazarro, Pellegrino. *Fascist and Anti-Fascist Propaganda in America: The Dispatches of Italian Ambassador Gelasio Caetani*. Youngstown, N.Y.: Cambria Press, 2008.

Neal, Mark Anthony. *What the Music Said: Black Popular Music and Black Public Culture*. New York: Routledge, 1999.

Neumann, Roderick P. *Imposing Wilderness: Struggles over Livelihood and Nature Preservation in Africa*. Berkeley: University of California Press, 1998.

Nevins, Allan. *The Emergence of Modern America, 1865–1878*. New York: Macmillan, 1927.

Newman, Louise Michele. *White Women's Rights: The Racial Origins of Feminism in the United States*. New York: Oxford University Press, 1999.

Oerlemans, Onno. *Romanticism and the Materiality of Nature*. Toronto: University of Toronto Press, 2002.

Ofcansky, Thomas P. "The 1889–97 Rinderpest Epidemic and the Rise of British and German Colonialism in Eastern and Southern Africa." *Journal of African Studies* 8, no. 1 (1981): 31–38.

Ofonagoro, Walter Ibekwe. "Commercial Revolution in the Niger Delta: A Review Article." *asa Review of Books* 3 (1977): 135–54.

Ogren, Kathy J. "'What is Africa to Me?' African Strategies in the Harlem Renaissance." In *Imagining Home: Class, Culture, and Nationalism in the African*

Diaspora, edited by Sidney J. Lemelle and Robin D. G. Kelley, 19–34. London: Verso, 1994.

Organisation for Economic Co-Operation and Development, *Business for Development 2008: Promoting Commercial Agriculture in Africa*. OECD Publishing, 2008.

Painter, Nell Irvin. *Creating Black Americans: African-American History and Its Meanings, 1619–Present*. New York: Oxford University Press, 2006.

———. *Standing at Armageddon: The United States, 1877–1919*. New York: W. W. Norton, 1987.

Penny, H. Glen. *Objects of Culture: Ethnology and Ethnographic Museums in Imperial Germany*. Chapel Hill: University of North Carolina Press, 2002.

Phoofolo, Pule. "Epidemics and Revolutions: The Rinderpest Epidemic in Late Nineteenth-Century Southern Africa." *Past and Present* 138 (1993): 112–43.

Pieterse, Jan Nederveen. *White on Black: Images of Africa and Blacks in Western Popular Culture*. New Haven, Conn.: Yale University Press, 1992.

Pitts, Delia. "Rinderpest and Rebellion in Southern Rhodesia, 1896." *Potomac Review* 8, no. 1 (1978): 22–34.

Plummer, Brenda Gayle. *Rising Wind: Black Americans and U.S. Foreign Affairs, 1935–1960*. Chapel Hill: University of North Carolina Press, 1996.

Posnock, Ross. *Color and Culture: Black Writers and the Making of the Modern Intellectual*. Cambridge, Mass.: Harvard University Press, 1998.

Pratt, Mary Louise. *Imperial Eyes: Travel Writing and Transculturation*. London: Routledge, 1992.

Preston, Douglas J. "Shooting in Paradise." *Natural History* 93 (December 1984): 14–19.

Pugliese, Stanislao G. Review of *Blackshirts in Little Italy: Italian Americans and Fascism, 1921–1929*, by Philip V. Cannistraro. H-Net Review, November 2002. http://www.h-net.org/reviews/showrev.cgi?path=17661066521831.

Ranger, Terence. "Whose Heritage? The Case of Matobo National Park." *Journal of Southern African Studies* 15, no. 2 (January 1989): 217–49.

Raphael, Lois A. C. *The Cape-to-Cairo Dream: A Study in British Imperialism*. New York: Octagon Books, 1973.

Renda, Mary A. *Taking Haiti: Military Occupation and the Culture of U.S. Imperialism, 1915–1940*. Chapel Hill: University of North Carolina Press, 2001.

Rexer, Lyle, and Rachel Klein. *American Museum of Natural History: 125 Years of Expedition and Discovery*. New York: H. N. Abrams in association with the American Museum of Natural History, 1995.

Risjord, Mark W. "The Politics of Explanation and the Origins of Ethnography." *Perspectives on Science* 8, no. 1 (Spring 2000): 29–52.

Roberts, Andrew. "Africa on Film to 1940." *History in Africa* 14 (1987): 189–227.

———. "Americans and Africans." *Journal of African History* 28 (1987): 295–99.

Roberts, Norman Phillip. "The Changing Images of Africa in Some Selected American Media from 1930 to 1969." PhD diss., American University, 1970.

Roberts, Robert P. "Popular Culture and Public Taste." In *The Gilded Age*, edited by H. Wayne Morton, 272–82. Syracuse, N.Y.: Syracuse University Press, 1970.

Robinson, Ronald, John Gallagher, and Alice Denny. *Africa and the Victorians*. New York: St. Martin's Press, 1967.

Rogers, Ben F. "William E. B. Du Bois, Marcus Garvey, and Pan-Africa." *The Journal of Negro History* 40, no.2 (April 1955): 154–65.

Rolinson, Mary G. *Grassroots Garveyism: The Universal Negro Improvement Association in the Rurural South, 1920–1927*. Chapel Hill: University of North Carolina Press, 2007.

Rony, Fatimah Tobing. *The Third Eye: Race, Cinema, and Ethnographic Spectacle*. Durham: North Carolina University Press, 1996.

———. "Those Who Squat and Those Who Sit: The Iconography of Race in the 1895 Films of Félix-Louis Regnault" *Camera Obscura* 28 (1993): 263–89.

Rosenzweig, Roy, and Elizabeth Blackmar. *The Park and the People: A History of Central Park*. Ithaca, N.Y.: Cornell University Press, 1992.

Rosetti, Gina M. *Imagining the Primitive in Naturalist and Modernist Literature*. Columbia: University of Missouri Press, 2006.

Rotundo, E. Anthony. *American Manhood: Transformations in Masculinity from the Revolution to the Modern Era*. New York: HarperCollins, 1993.

Rydell, Robert W. *All the World's a Fair: Visions of Empire at American International Expositions, 1876–1916*. Chicago: University of Chicago Press, 1984.

Said, Edward W. *Orientalism*. New York: Vintage Books, 2004.

Saverino, Joan. "Italians in Public Memory: Pageantry, Power, and Imagining the Italian American." *Italian American Review* 8 (Autumn/Winter 2001): 83–111.

Schechter, Patricia. *Ida B. Wells-Barnett and American Reform, 1880–1930*. Chapel Hill: University of North Carolina Press, 2001.

Schiebinger, Londa. *Nature's Body: Gender in the Making of Modern Science*. Boston, Mass.: Beacon Press, 1993.

Schildkrout, Enid. "Art as Evidence: A Brief History of the American Museum of Natural History African Collection." In *Art/artifact: African Art in Anthropology Collections*, edited by Arthur Danto et al. 153–92. New York: Center for African Art, 1988.

———. "The Spectacle of Africa through the Lens of Herbert Lang." *African Arts* 24, no. 4 (October 1991): 70–85.

Schlesinger, Arthur M. *The Rise of Modern America, 1865–1951*. 4th ed. New York: Macmillan, 1951.

Scott, William R. *The Sons of Sheba's Race: African-Americans and the Italo-Ethiopian War, 1935–1941*. Bloomington: Indiana University Press, 1993.

Shepperson, George. "Pan-Africanism and 'Pan-Africanism': Some Historical Notes." *Phylon* 23, no. 4 (4th Qtr., 1962): 346–58.

Shillington, Kevin. *History of Africa.* New York: St. Martin's Press, 1995.
Singal, Daniel Joseph. "Towards a Definition of American Modernism." *American Quarterly* 39, no. 1 (Spring 1987): 7–26.
Sklar, Robert. *Movie-Made America: A Cultural History of American Movies.* 1975. Reprint, New York: Vintage Books, 1994.
Slotkin, Richard. *Regeneration through Violence: The Mythology of the American Frontier, 1600–1860.* Middletown, Conn.: Wesleyan University Press, 1973.
Stansell, Christine. *American Moderns: Bohemian New York and the Creation of a New Century.* New York: Metropolitan Books, 2000.
Stauder, Jack. "The 'Relevance' of Anthropology to Colonialism and Imperialism." In *The "Racial" Economy of Science: Toward a Democratic Future,* edited by Sandra Harding. 408–32. Bloomington: Indiana University Press, 1993.
Stein, Judith. *The World of Marcus Garvey: Race and Class in Modern Society.* Baton Rouge: Louisiana State University Press, 1986.
Stepan, Nancy Leys. "Race and Gender: The Role of Analogy in Science." *Isis* 77 (1986): 261–77.
Stocking, George W., Jr. *The Ethnographer's Magic and Other Essays in the History of Anthropology.* Madison: University of Wisconsin Press, 1992.
———. *Race, Culture, and Evolution: Essays in the History of Anthropology.* New York: Free Press, 1968.
Stoler, Ann Laura. *Carnal Knowledge and Imperial Power: Race and the Intimate in Colonial Rule.* Berkeley: University of California Press, 2002.
Strachey, Lytton. *Eminent Victorians.* New York: Modern Library, 1999.
Summers, Martin. *Manliness and Its Discontents: The Black Middle Class and the Transformation of Masculinity, 1900–1930.* Chapel Hill: University of North Carolina Press, 2004.
Sundiata, Ibrahim. *Brothers and Strangers: Black Zion, Black Slavery, 1914–1940.* Durham, N.C.: Duke University Press, 2003.
Sundiata, I. K. *Black Scandal: America and the Liberian Labor Crisis, 1929–1936.* Philadelphia, Pa.: ISHI, 1980.
Teslow, Tracy Lang. "Representing Race to the Public: Physical Anthropology in Interwar American Natural History Museums." PhD diss., University of Chicago, 2002.
Tipple, John. "Big Business and a New Economy." In *The Gilded Age,* edited by Wayne Morton, 13–30. Syracuse, N.Y.: Syracuse University Press, 1970.
Torgovnick, Marianna. *Gone Primitive: Savage Intellects, Modern Lives.* Chicago: University of Chicago Press, 1990.
Turner, John G. "A 'Black-White' Missionary on the Imperial Stage: William H. Sheppard and Middle-Class Black Manhood." *Journal of Southern Religion* 9 (2006): 1–19. http://jsr.fsu.edu.
Upchurch, Thomas Adams. *Legislating Racism: The Billion Dollar Congress and the Birth of Jim Crow.* Lexington: University Press of Kentucky, 2004.

VanOnselen, C. "Reactions to Rinderpest in Southern Africa." *Journal of African History* 13, no. 3 (1972): 473–88.

Von Eschen, Penny M. *Race against Empire: Black Americans and Anticolonialism, 1937–1957.* Ithaca, N.Y.: Cornell University Press, 1997.

Webb, Dave. *Martin and Osa Johnson.* S.I.: Kansas Heritage Center, 1985.

Welch, Margaret. *The Book of Nature: Natural History in the United States, 1825–1875.* Boston, Mass.: Northeastern University Press, 1998.

Wesseling, H. L. *Divide and Rule: The Partition of Africa, 1880–1914.* Translated by Arnold J. Pomerans. London: Praeger, 1996.

Westhauser, Karl E. "Revisiting the Jordan Thesis: 'White over Black' in Seventeenth-Century England and America." *Journal of Negro History* 85, no. 3 (Summer 2000): 112–22.

Williams, Walter L. "Black Journalism's Opinions about Africa during the Late Nineteenth Century." *Phylon* 34, no. 3 (3rd Qtr., 1973): 224–35.

Wintz, Cary D., ed. *African American Political Thought, 1890–1930: Washington, Du Bois, Garvey, and Randolph.* Armonk, N.Y.: M. E. Sharpe, 1995.

Wolcott, Victoria W. *Remaking Respectability: African American Women in Interwar Detroit.* Chapel Hill: University of North Carolina Press, 2001.

Zwick, Jim, ed. "Stereoviews of the Congo Free State and Belgian Congo." In *Stereoscopic Visions of War and Empire.* http://www.bbondocksnet.com/stero/congo.html.

Films

Adventure Lovers. Videocassette. Produced and directed by Sébastien Degenne and Michel Viotte. France: La Septe ARTE and Nestor Productions, 2000. The Martin and Osa Johnson Safari Museum, Chanute, Kans.

Adventure on the Upper Nile. Special Collections. American Museum of Natural History, New York, 1931.

Akeley in Camp: Carl and Mary Akeley in Africa. Special Collections. American Museum of Natural History, New York, 1926.

Baboona: An Aerial Epic over Africa. Videocassette. Produced and directed by Martin and Osa Johnson. Fox Films, 1935. The Martin and Osa Johnson Safari Museum, Chanute, Kans.

Congorilla: Adventures among the Big Apes and Little People of Central Africa. Videocassette. Produced and directed by Martin and Osa Johnson. Morro Films, 1932. The Martin and Osa Johnson Safari Museum, Chanute, Kans.

Meandering in Africa. Videocassette. Produced and directed by Carl Ethan Akeley. AMNH, 1921–1922. AMNH Film Archives, New York.

Sanders of the River. Videocassette. Directed by Zoltan Korda. 1935.

Simba, the King of Beasts: A Saga of the African Veldt. Videocassette. Produced and directed by Martin Johnson, Osa Johnson, Carl Ethan Akeley, and Alfred J. Klein. AMNH, 1928. AMNH Film Archives, New York.

Tarzan and His Mate. Directed by Cedric Gibbons. Metro-Goldwyn-Mayer, 1934.
Tarzan Escapes. Directed by Richard Thorpe. Metro-Goldwyn-Mayer, 1936.
Tarzan of the Apes. Directed by Scott Sidney. National Film Corporation of America. 1918.
Tarzan the Ape Man. Directed by W. S. Van Dyke. Metro-Goldwyn-Mayer, 1932.
Tarzan the Fearless. Directed by Robert Hill. Principal Distributing Corporation. 1933.
The William D. Campbell African Expedition. 1938. Special Collections. American Museum of Natural History, New York.

INDEX

Page numbers in italics refer to illustrations.

ABB (African Blood Brotherhood), 89, 118–24, 206, 229
Abolition of Slave Trade Act, 49, 61
Abraham Lincoln Brigade, 216
Abyssinia. *See* Ethiopia
Adams, C. C., 64
Adams, Jonathan S., 5–6
"Adventures on Mt. Mikeno" (Akeley), 166
AES (American Ethnological Society), 42
Africa: community-controlled conservation, 224; culture, 139–40; as Fatherland, 36, 45, 56, 84, 127, 231n9; internationalization, 87–88, 98–99, 103–4, 106–7, 115–17, 125, 128, 215–17; as Motherland, 109, 119–20, 122, 123, 126, 127, 231n9; political context, 2–9, 223–25; racial connection for African Americans, 35–36, 56, 103. *See also* Darkest Africa myth; internationalization of Africa; *specific countries and colonies*
Africa in Brief (Coles), 26
African Americans: and African nationalism, 9, 106, 115, 117, 118, 121; Africa's significance for, 45, 46, 86, 87, 92–93, 107–9, 131; and anti-imperialism, 17–18, 80, 215–16; art and identity, 130; and Berlin Conference, 82; in British colonies, 29, 33, 103; characterization of, 126, 128, 179–80, 182–83; citizenship and rights for, 30–31; on Congo atrocities, 69, 71; and Congress on Africa, 92–93; and Darkest Africa myth, 17, 178–80, 201, 206, 209; and deportation movement, 33, 36–38; and Ethiopia, 213–15; films and images, 179–80, 182–83, 209; and Harlem, 2, 109–10, 123, 127–28, 214, 215, 228; Harlem Renaissance, 5, 10, 21, 39, 89, 229; and internationalist framework for racial justice, 87–88, 98–99, 103–4, 215–17; and Islam, 21, 97; journeys to Africa, 43–44; and Liberian independence, 14, 32, 92, 101; manhood, link to Africa, 29–30; media ownership, 21, 100–104; missionaries in Africa, 13–14, 21, 26–28, 32–33; and museum exhibits' racial hierarchy myths, 73–76; and naturalist-environmentalist discourses, 3, 4, 131; race riots, 17, 177, 229, 230; racial connection to Africa, 35–36, 56, 103; racial tensions, 3, 213; radio propaganda, 7, 179, 180–81; self-determination, 15–18, 28, 45, 81, 97–98, 99; in South Africa, 33, 103; and Spanish Civil War, 216; terminology for, 34–35, 45, 98; white American's debt to, 29–30; and whiteness, 39–45. *See also* Harlem; Pan-Africanism
African American womanhood: and art, 130; citizenship and rights, 30–31; cultural traditions, 35, 45; historical context, 12; idealized, 8; inspiration for, 21; and missionaries, 33–34; New Women identity, 22, 35; and Pan-Africanism, 7–8, 11–12, 33–34, 110, 130; and regeneration of race, 29, 97, 106, 231n9; and terminology for African

277

Americans, 98; and Victorianism, 8, 21, 33–34
"Africana: A Ragtime Classic" (Berliner), 221
African Blood Brotherhood (ABB), 89, 118–24, 206, 229
"African Empire, An" (editorial), 83–85
African Game Trails (Roosevelt), 19, 228
African Hall: advertisement, 220; Akeley's BEA Expedition, 144–45, 228; author's childhood visits, xii; dedication ceremonies, 2, 217–18, 228, 230, 231n2; design, 73, 158–59; Eastman-Pomeroy-Akeley Expedition, 162, 175, 229; Elephant Group Exhibition "The Herd," xii, 2, 146, 157–59, 160; ethnography depicted in, 150, 151, 159–60, 175, 219, 220, 221; Expedition to the Belgian Congo, 52, 163–69, *168*, 175, 229; finances, 157, 217, 251n13; goals, 151, 219; gorilla group exhibit, 163–69; history of, 73, 135, 136, 156, 157, 228; Johnsons' films commission, 189–91; Lang-Chapin Expedition, 71–73, 76–80, *79*, 157, 161, 228; museum personnel, 158, 160–61, 162; O'Donnell-Clark African Expedition, 163, 230; okapi habitat exhibit, 71, 72, 76, 159; planning, 2, 73, 157–60, 161; reviews of, 2, 175, 218–19; as Roosevelt memorial, 2, 161–62, 217; Sanford-Legendre Abyssinia Expedition, 162–63, 229; Vernay-Lang Kalahari Expedition, 163, 229; Western knowledge production, 144, 218–19, 221–22. *See also Simba, The King of Beasts* (film)
African nationalism: African American leadership, 9, 106, 115, 117, 118, 121; African leadership, 17, 18, 215–16, 224; Belgian Congo and, 117; political organization for, 84–89, 94–97, 99, 117, 120, 223
"African Races" (Chatelain), 40–41
"African Roots of War" (Du Bois), 115, 118
Africans: characteristics, 163, 164, 166, 219–20; characterizations, 126, 128; cultural traditions, 1–2, 7–8, 39–45, 129–30; as "endangered species," 170, 203; ethnography as extension of fauna in museum exhibits, 150, 159–60, 175, 198; films dispelling negative characteristics, 1, 76, 134, 177–78, 179, 204, 207, 208–10; and gorillas, myths, 200, 201; hunting rights, 135; and Islam, 91, 108; militant activities in British colonies, 16, 27, 94, 120, 138; naturalist-environmentalist discourses on cultural traditions of, 139–40, 142; racial hierarchy myths, 73–76; racialized discourses in films on, 183–85; reserves for protection of, 170; ridicule of, 192, 194–97, 203–4, 220–21; women's bodies in films, 195–96
African Union (Organisation of African Unity), 223
Africa Speaks! (*When Africa Speaks*; film), 180, 182, 202, 208, 230
Afro-American League, 30, 227
AFS (American Folklore Society), 39–40
Akeley, Carl E.: "Adventures on Mt. Mikeno," 166; African Expedition to the Belgian Congo, 52, 163–69, *168*, 175, 229; on African natural history at AMNH, 150, 157; on Africans' characteristics, 163, 164, 166, 219–20; on Africans' cultural traditions, 139–40; BEA expeditions for AMNH, 140–43, 144–45, 228;

biography, 136, 229; on Darkest Africa myth, 151, 188–89, 197, 210, 219; on "disappearing continent" and fauna collections, 139–40, 142–43, 146–47, 149, 156–57, 162, 169; on documenting African life, 150, 151, 159–60, 175, 219, 220, 221; Eastman-Pomeroy-Akeley Expedition, 162, 175, 229; elephant attack on, 145–46; elephant diorama at FMNH, 143; on elephants as icon, 145–47, 156–57; and Elliot, 135–36; Elliot Expedition to British Somaliland, 137–40, 227; ethnological specimen collections, 141, 143, 150; on fauna collections, 140–41; gorilla group specimen expedition, 163–69, *168*, 175, 229; and gorilla preserves, 10, 163, 170–75, 224; humanization of gorillas, 165–67, 170–71, 172; *In Brightest Africa*, 171, 219, 229; on jungle films, 186–88; professional training, 135–36; on realism in Johnsons' films, 185–88; on regeneration in African primitivism, 162; on Roosevelt's contributions, 161–62; Ruwenzori-Kivu Expedition, 163, 229; on shooting film and photographs, 139–40; and taxidermy, 135, 136–37, 158; on zoology specimens, 143, 149, 156. *See also* African Hall

Akeley, Delia Julia Reiss (née Denning), 7, 141, 145, 146, *147*

Akeley, Mary Jobe, 175, 222–23

Akeley Memorial Hall of African Mammals. *See* African Hall

Akka ("Pygmies"), 65, 78–80, *79*, 85, 170, 203–4, 228

Albert (King of Belgium), 171, 229

Albert National Park (Parc National Albert), 10, 135, 163, 171, 174, 229

alcohol, as imperialist tool, 59, 84, 120

American Anthropological Association, 42, 81

American Anthropologist, 42–43

American Colonization Society, 29, 53, 54, 90–91

American Ethnological Society (AES), 42

American Folklore Society (AFS), 39–40

American Museum Congo Expedition, 71–73, 76–80, *79*, 157, 161, 228

American Museum of Natural History: African Hall of Ethnology, 155, 156, 228; and African natural history, 150, 157; Akeley African Expedition to Belgian Congo, 52, 163–69, *168*, 175, 229; Akeley's BEA Expedition, 144–45, 228; authenticity of film images, 178, 198, 204; author's childhood visits, xii; board of trustees, 152–53; collections history, 150, 152–53, 156; "disappearing continent" exhibits, 134–35, 149, 175; Douglas African Collection, 74, 153–54, 228; ethnological specimens collected, 52, 72, 81, 150, 153, 154, 156; fauna collection expeditions, 156; Fayum Expedition, 153–56, 157, 228; and films dispelling Darkest Africa myth, 1, 76, 134, 178, 197, 198, 204; fossil collecting expeditions, 153–56, 157, 228; history, 149–52, 153; Johnsons' AMNH African Expedition, 188–91, *193*, 229; Lang-Chapin Expedition to Congo, 71–73, 76–80, *79*, 157, 161, 228; and naturalist-environmentalist discourses, 134, 135; North American collections and exhibits, 150; "Pygmies" diorama, 78–79, *79*; Ruwenzori-Kivu Expedition, 163, 229; Tjäder Expedition, 153–55, 157, 228; Western African Raff

Index 279

Collection, 153, 227. *See also* African Hall; *Simba, The King of Beasts* (film)
American South, 14, 15, 38, 45, 81
America's Making Exposition, 130, 229
AMNH (American Museum of Natural History). *See* American Museum of Natural History
Amsterdam News, 119, 205, 209, 212–13, 223
Anderson, Walter, 123, 124
animal kingdom. *See* fauna
Anthropological Society of Washington (ASW), 42
anthropological studies. *See* ethnographic studies
anti-imperialism: in Africa, 4, 18; African Americans' role, 17–18, 80, 215–16; Berlin Conference, 46; Congo and, 46, 51–52, 59, 63, 64–65; 80, 81; and emigration movement, 57, 81; in Germany, 124; Pan-Africanism and, 81, 87, 93, 94, 97, 125, 127
Anti-Imperialist League, 52, 125, 227
Antique Works of Art from Benin (Pitt-Rivers), 75
Arabs, 26, 77–78, 91, 121
Arthur, Chester A., 48–50, 69, 80
Ashanti people, 16, 27, 94
Association Internationale Africaine (International African Association; IAA), 48–49, 50, 53–58, 62–63, 68
ASW (Anthropological Society of Washington), 42
Ater, Renée, 130
Azikiwe, Nnamdi, 222, 225

Baboona (film), 178, 180, 190, 198, 199, 204, 230
Bair, Barbara, 87
Baker, Lee D., 18
Baldwin, Davarian, 7

Baltimore American, 30
Bancroft, George, 54–55
Barclay, Arthur, 103–4
Barnes, T. Alexander, 172, 174
Batwa (Twa; "Pygmies"), 65, 78–80, 79, 85, 170, 203–4, 228
BEA (British East Africa): expedition for FMNH, 140–43, 228; sphere of influence, 133, 139, 140, 142
Bederman, Gail, 9
Beinart, William, 6
Belgian Congo: Africans' hunting rights, 135; Albert (King) on game preserve in, 171, 229; and American South, 81; Denis-Roosevelt expedition, 179; films about, 179, 180, 182, 202, 203–4, 208, 230; game preserves, 10, 134–35, 163, 171, 174; game reserves, use of term, 170; gorilla specimen collecting expeditions, 52, 163–69, *168*, 175, 229; history, 71, 228; Hoeffler's African Expedition, 180, 182, 202, 208, 230; and imperialism, 51, 52; Lang-Chapin Expedition for AMNH, 71–73, 76–80, *79*, 157, 161, 228; Lowie on ethnographic specimens from, 72–76; Parc National Albert game preserve, 10, 134–35, 163, 171, 174. *See also* Congo Free State
Bell, Nelson B., 182, 207–8
Benga, Ota, 79, 227
Benin Bronzes, 75, 153, 237n54
Berlin Conference (Kongokonferenz): African Americans and, 82; anti-imperialism and, 46; Congo question, 16, 46, 58, 59, 60–62, 65–66; dates, 57, 227; European nations at, 236n28; and General Act, 16, 59, 65, 227; Leopold II on, 59; U.S. position at, 57–58, 59, 60, 61–62

Berliner, Leo E., "Africana: A Ragtime Classic," 221
Bickmore, Albert, 152
bin Hamid, Muhammad (Tippu Tib), 26, 65
Birth of a Nation (film), 179
Bismarck, Otto von, 59, 60–61. *See also* Germany
Black and White (Fortune), 29
Black Condor (J. C. Robinson; Brown Condor), 1–2, 214, 230
black manhood. *See* New Negro identities
Blyden, Edward Wilmot: on African American freedom in Liberia, 14, 32, 91, 92; on imperialism, 65, 90–91; and Islam, 97; on manhood, 29, 91–92, 126–27, 231n9; and paternalistic rhetoric of Pan-Africanism, 9, 13–14, 86, 88
Bonaparte, W. H., 30–31
Boston Advocate, 30
Bourne, Stephen, 206
Bowen, John Wesley Edward, 28–29
Bradley, Herbert, 164, 165, 167, 170, 172–73, 187
Bradley, Mary, 164, 167, 169, 170, 224
Briggs, Cyril, 118, 119, 120, 124, 229
Brightest Africa narrative: and Darkest Africa myth, 4–5, 46, 197–98; described, 2–3, 45, 46, 175, 223; elephants as icon of, 145–47, 156–57; films and, 1, 76; imperialism and, 12; museum exhibits and, 128, 219; naturalist-environmentalist discourses and, 133–35, 221–22; Pan-Africanism and, 97, 128, 217
British East Africa (BEA), 133, 139, 140, 142
British Empire. *See* Great Britain
British Museum, 137, 164
British Society for the Preservation of Fauna of the Empire, 135, 173
British Somaliland, 133, 138, 139, 153, 160, 219
British South Africa. *See* South Africa
Brooks, George, 50
Brown Condor (J. C. Robinson; Black Condor), 1–2, 214, 230
Brundage, W. Fitzhugh, 129–30
Bumpus, H. C., 72, 150–51
Burroughs, Edgar Rice, 183, 184, 228
Butler Bill, 32, 91

Cain, R. H., 14–15
Cameron, Verney L., *Across Africa*, 26
Camp, Eugene M., 29–30
Campbell, James T., 43
Camphor, Alexander, "A Hymn of Sympathy and Prayer for Africa," 95–96
cannibalism: Dahomey village exhibit and, 129; eradication, 61, 65, 76, 77–78; ethnographic studies, 77; eugenics and, 77; films and images, 177, 182–83, 189, 210; gorilla meat-eating and quasi, 169; media images of, 182–83, 189, 210; missionaries' role in eradicating, 61; myth of, 23, 39, 42, 64–65, 67, 71, 81, 169; "Pygmies" and, 78, 80
Carson, W. R., 14
Casement, Roger, 51, 66
Casement Report, 51, 66–67
Chapin, James, 71–73, 76, 161, 228, 229
Chatelain, Heli, 40–41
Chicago Daily Tribune, 57–58, 184, 202
Chicago Defender, 100, 107
Christianity, and Pan-African paternalistic rhetoric, 9, 13–14, 21, 26–28, 32–33, 86, 88, 106. *See also* missionaries

chronology of events, 227–30
Clark, James L., 180–81, 217
Cleveland administration, 62, 90, 106
Coates, Peter A., 6
Coles, John J., *Africa in Brief*, 26
Colored American Magazine, 98, 100
color line, 125–26, 216
communism, 88, 117, 119–20
community-controlled conservation, 224
Congo Free State: African Americans on atrocities in, 69, 71; alcoholic beverages and, 59; anti-imperialism and, 46, 51–52, 59, 63, 64–65, 80, 81; atrocities in, 51, 62, 66–69, 71, 77; cannibalism in, 64–65; and Darkest Africa myth, 25–27, 72, 73–76; in defense of, 67–68, 76–78; emigration movement and, 46, 55–56, 57; ethnographic studies, 25–27, 72–81, 79; expeditions' role in enlightenment, 69, 71; founding, 46, 50; and France, 47–48; and Germany, 59–62; and Great Britain, 51, 66, 67, 69; IAA sovereignty in, 53–57, 58, 62; imperialism myth in, 50–51; Ituri forest, 79, 79, 203–4; missionaries and, 63, 67, 68, 69, 71; naturalist-environmentalist discourses and, 52, 57; racial discrimination, 65, 72, 74–75, 80–81; rubber trade, 51, 59, 62, 66–69, 71, 169, 170; slave trade, 56, 58–59, 62, 65; U.S. foreign policy and trade interests, 48–49, 57–58, 59–60, 61–62, 72; and white manhood regeneration, 50, 56–57, 68, 76–78, 80. *See also* Belgian Congo; Berlin Conference; Leopold II
Congo question. *See* Congo Free State
Congo Reform Association, 51, 52, 66, 72, 81, 108, 170, 227

Congo region, and Portugal, 47–49, 56, 58, 61, 78
Congorilla (film), 178, 190, 198, 199, 203, 204, 230
Congress on Africa, 45, 92–97, 101, 106, 109, 127, 229. *See also* Pan-African Congresses
conservation movement, white, 3–4, 18–20, 24–25, 28, 57, 131. *See also* game preserves
Cope, E. D., 36–37
Corbould, Clare, 10–11
Cotton States and International Exposition, 129, 227
Crummell, Alexander, 7, 86
Cullen, Countee, "Heritage," xii, xiii, 213
cult of primitivism: and white manhood regeneration, 8–9, 19, 50, 56–57, 68, 76–78, 80, 144, 147–49; and whiteness, 22, 35–39, 41, 44
culture, African. *See* ethnographic studies
"Customs among the Natives of East Africa" (Sheldon), 44

Dahomey village exhibit, 129, 227
Darkest Africa myth: African Americans' criticism of, 17, 178–80, 201, 206, 209; and Brightest Africa narrative, 4–5, 46, 197–98; counternarratives of, 25, 52–53; ethnographic studies dispelling, 25–27, 72, 73–76, 81; films dispelling, 1, 76, 177–79, 197–99, 204, 207–10; films replicating, 178, 183, 197, 199, 204, 210; as geographic location, 2–3; and human sacrifices, 27, 65, 81, 200; and imperialism, 46, 204–6; and naturalist-environmentalist discourses, 1, 24–25, 76, 181, 185, 207,

209–10; Pan-Africanism's challenges to, 1, 76, 181, 204, 207, 208–10; scholarship on, 5–7; Western images, 4–7, 16–17, 20, 23–28, 90, 126, 178, 183, 199, 210. *See also* cannibalism

Dark Rapture (film), 179

Dark Sands (film), 179

Darwinism, 38–39, 128

Daughter of the Congo (film), 209

De Brazza, Pierre Savorgnan, 47, 48, 57, 83

"Declaration of Rights of the Negro People of the World" (Garvey), 106, 112, 177, 231n9

De Leon, Daniel, 60–62

democratic-republicanism, 88, 90, 97, 106, 109, 110–11, 120, 124

Denis-Roosevelt expedition, 179

Denver African Expedition of 1925, 180

deportation movement, of African Americans, 33, 36–38

Derscheid, J. M., 174–75

Diagne, Blaise, 116, 122

"disappearing continent" myth: and ethnographic studies, 141–42; and fauna collections, 134, 139–40, 142–43, 146–47, 149, 156–57, 162, 169; in films, 134; and imperialism, 162; and museum exhibits, 131, 134–35, 144, 149, 175, 218–19, 221–22; and naturalist-environmentalist discourses, 9–10, 45, 133–35, 169, 175; sport hunters on, 132, 133, 171, 172, 174

Dixon-Stowell, Brenda, 181

Dorsey, W. A., 141, 142

Douglas, Richard, 153–54

Douglas African Collection, 74, 153–54, 228

Du Bois, W. E. B.: "African Roots of War," 115, 118; on characterization of Africans and African Americans, 126, 128; on color line, 125–26, 216; on conferences on Africa, 92; on Garvey, 110; on leadership for African nationalism, 115, 117, 118; and NAACP, 119; "Pan-Africa and the New Racial Philosophy," 125; Pan-Africa defined, 126; Pan-Africanism's influence, 87; philosophy, 106–7, 115–17, 125, 128; on racial discrimination in U.S., 81; *The Souls of Black Folk*, 87, 125. *See also* Pan-African Congresses

Du Chaillu, Paul Belloni, 19, 23, 164

"dwarfs" ("Pygmies"), 65, 78–80, 79, 85, 170, 203–4, 228

Eastman, George, 175, 187, 195

Eastman-Pomeroy-Akeley Expedition, 162, 175, 229

"Educational Programs . . ." (Reddick), 179

Edwards, Brent Hayes, 87

Elephant Group Exhibition "The Herd," xii, 2, 146, 157–59, 160

elephants: Akeley's mauling, 145–46; *The Fighting Bulls* diorama, 143; "The Herd" Elephant Group Exhibition, xii, 2, 146, 157–59, 160; humanization of, 193, 198; icon of Brightest Africa narrative, 145–47, 156–57; trophies for white manhood, 146; white New Women, and killing, 146, *147*, 157

Elliot, D. G., 133, 135–36, 138, 139, 140, 141

Elliot Expedition to British Somaliland for FMNH, 133, 137–40, 227

emigration movement: and anti-imperialism, 57, 81; and Butler Bill, 32, 91; and Congo, 46, 55–56, 57; history, 15, 20, 32, 227; and Liberia,

14, 32, 54, 89–90; and the Negro question, 46, 55–56; and Pan-Africanism, 17, 21; and Pan-Negro Nationalists, 17, 85; and voluntary repatriation, 38
Emin Pasha of Equatoria, 50–51, 227
Enchanting Darkness, An (Hickey and Wylie), 6
England. *See* Great Britain
Erhagbe, Edward O., 104–5
Ethiopia: African Americans and invasion of, 2, 127–28, 212–15; and France, 211, 216; and Great Britain, 211; and Haile Selassie, 1, 10, 211–16; as icon for indigenous rule, 17, 18, 215–16; as independent state, 16; and Italian imperialism, 1–3, 89, 119, 127–28, 211–16, 230; and Kellogg-Briand Pact, 213; and Menelik II, 10, 206, 211; Sanford-Legendre Abyssinia Expedition, 162–63, 229; U.S. neutrality during invasion, 213–14; and white supremacy, 212, 216
Ethiopia Awakening (sculpture), 129–30, 229
Ethiopian Church of South Africa, 33, 108–9
Ethiopianism, 33
ethnographic studies: of cannibalism, 77; in Congo, 25–27, 72–81, 79; and Darkest Africa myth, 25–27, 72, 73–76, 81; and "disappearing continent" myth, 141–42; ethnography as extension of fauna, 150, 159–60, 175, 198; and imperialism, 40–41, 141–42; missionaries' role in, 40–42; and naturalist-environmentalist discourses, 10–11, 135, 139–40, 142; Pan-Africanism's influence, 10–11, 89, 98–99; and whiteness, 39–45
ethnological specimen collections: for AMNH, 52, 72–76, 81, 141, 143, 150, 153,

154, 156; for FMNH, 141, 143; Lowie's analysis of Congo, 72–76; "Pygmies" and, 78–80, 79
eugenics, 38, 72, 74, 77, 78, 228
European nations: alcohol as imperialist tool, 59, 84, 120; at Berlin Conference, 236n28; imperialism, 3, 15–16, 28, 45, 59, 83–84, 90, 120; reserves for protection of endangered tribes, 170. *See also specific nations*
Evans, Maurice S., 108–9
Everett, Anna, 178–79
exhibits. *See* African Hall; museum exhibits; *specific museums*
expeditionary films, 179, 180, 182, 185, 202, 208, 230
expeditions, 16, 40–41, 131, 141; from France, 47, 57; and naturalist-environmentalist discourses, 71–72. *See also specific expeditions*
"Explorer's View of the Congo, An" (Lang), 76

Fatherland concept, of Africa, 36, 45, 56, 84, 127, 231n9
fauna: Akeley on collections, 140–41; ethnography as extension of, 150, 159–60, 175, 198; film misrepresentations of, 1, 76, 178–80, 181, 185, 201, 207, 209–10; illegal animal trade, 224; killing fauna, use of term, 167; and naturalist-environmentalist discourses, 156. *See also* fauna collections; game preserves; *specific expeditions*; *specific fauna*; *specific mammals*
fauna collections: Akeley on, 140–41; and "disappearing continent" myth, 131, 134–35, 139–40, 142–44, 146–47, 149, 156–57, 162, 169, 175, 218–19, 221–22. *See also* fauna; game

284 Index

preserves; *specific expeditions*; *specific mammals*
Fayum Expedition, 153–56, 157, 228
Field Museum of Natural History (FMNH), 133, 137–43, 227, 228
Fighting Bulls (elephant diorama), 143
films: African Americans' criticism of, 178–80, 201, 206, 209; African Americans' images in, 179–80, 182–83, 209; artificiality of jungle realism in, 184, 185, 192–94, 199, 210; audiences for, 182, 185, 187, 189, 190, 198, 207; authenticity of images in, 178, 181, 199, 201, 202–3, 207–8, 209; award nominations for, 201; banning of, 199, 200, 201; and Brightest Africa narrative, 1, 76; cannibalism images in, 177, 182–83, 189, 210; and Darkest Africa myth stereotypes, 179, 183, 199, 210; and "disappearing continent" myth, 134; dispelling Darkest Africa myth and negative characterizations of Africans, 1, 76, 134, 177–79, 181, 185, 197–98, 204, 207–10; editing, 190; ethnography as extension of fauna in, 175, 198; expeditionary, 179, 180, 182, 185, 202, 208, 230; fauna, misrepresentation in, 1, 76, 178–80, 181, 185, 201, 207, 209–10; and gorillas myth, 200, 201; hoax, 200–201; imperialism legitimized in, 178, 204, 205; jazz symbolism in, 196, 203; jungle films, 181–88, 207; and National Better Business Bureau, 201, 202; naturalist-environmentalist discourses in, 1, 76, 181, 185, 207, 209–10; Pan-Africanism and, 1, 76, 204, 207; racial hierarchy in, 191–92, 195, 197–98, 203–4; racialized discourses on manhood in, 183–85; reviews of, 199–200; ridicule of Africans in, 194–97, 203–4, 220–21; silent, 182–85; support for, 182, 207–8; and Western knowledge production, 189, 208; white New Women in, 182–83, 191–92, 194, 195, 197; women's bodies as African specimens in, 195–96. *See also* Johnson, Martin and Osa, films by; *specific films*
FMNH (Field Museum of Natural History), 133, 137–43, 141, 143, 227, 228
foreign policy and trade interests in Africa: of France, 49, 50; rubber trade and, 51, 59, 62, 66–69, 71, 169, 170; of U.S., 48–50, 57–58, 59–60, 61–62, 72, 213–14
Fortune, T. Thomas, 29–30, 69, 86, 94–96, 100, 101, 223
Fossey, Dian, 224
France: atrocities under, 71; colonies in Africa, 47–48, 49, 103, 107, 112; and Ethiopia, 211, 216; expeditions from, 47, 57; foreign policy and trade interests in Africa, 49, 50; and imperialism, 111; and Liberian sovereignty, 104; and Pan-African Congresses, 116, 117, 122
Francis, John M., 47–49
Frelinghuysen, Frederick, 47, 48, 60
Fuller, Meta Warrick, 129–30, 228

game preserves: and community-controlled conservation, 224; for gorillas, 10, 134–35, 163, 170–75, 171, 174, 224; Great Britain and, 135, 170, 173; and naturalist-environmentalist discourses, 1, 76, 170, 173, 222; Parc National Albert, 10, 134–35, 163, 171, 174; and white conservation movement, 3–4, 18–20, 24–25, 28, 57, 131. *See also* fauna
Garvey, Marcus: on African American leadership for African nationalism, 9, 106, 118; on aid to Ethiopia,

Index 285

214–15; Black Star Line, 110, 111, 112; charisma, 110; Constitution for Negro Rights, *113*; criticism of film propaganda, 206; "Declaration of Rights of the Negro People of the World," 106, 112, 177, 231n9; on films, 206; in Harlem, 109–10, 123, 228; on indigenous knowledge, 11; on Motherland concept, 109, 122, 123; "The Negro's Greatest Enemy," 114; and Pan-Africanism, 87; philosophy, 109, 111–12, 114, 122–23, 231n9; photograph, *113*; as "Provisional President of Africa," 11, 114, 122; in West Indies, 109–10. *See also* Universal Negro Improvement Association (UNIA)

General Act, and Berlin Conference, 16, 59, 65, 227

Germany: anti-imperialism, 124; and atrocities in Africa, 100–101; and Congo, 59–62; and German East Africa Protectorate, 142; and imperialism, 16, 84, 111; and Liberian sovereignty, 104; redistribution of colonies of, 87, 112, 116, 117, 124, 127; and U.S. immigrants from, 62. *See also* Berlin Conference

Gladden, W. E., 32

Glydenstople, Wils, 172

gorillas: Akeley African Expedition for specimens, 52, 163–69, *168*, 175, 229; and film myths, 200, 201; game preserves for, 10, 134–35, 163, 171, 174, 224, 229; Heller-Collins expedition for specimens, 173, 174; humanization of, 165–67, 170–71, 172; quasi-cannibalism on expedition, 169; sport hunters and, 171, 172, 174

Great Britain: and African militancy, 16, 27, 94, 120, 138; BEA influence, 133, 139, 140, 142; Benin Bronzes seized by, 75, 153, 237n54; and British Museum, 137, 164; Casement Report, 51, 66; colonies, 29, 33, 40, 49, 84, 102–4, 109, 112, 154; Congo atrocities reports, 51, 66, 67, 69; Congo Reform Association of, 66, 227; and Ethiopia, 211; films and imperialist propaganda, 178, 204–6; game preserves and, 135, 170, 173; and Native Americans, 53; racial discrimination, 98, 99, 100, 101–3, 108–9; slave trade, 49, 61, 115. *See also specific colonies*

Great War, the (World War I), 115, 116, 127, 228

Griffith, D. W., 179

Haile Selassie, 1, 10, 211–16

Haiti, 97, 99, 114, 123, 126

Hamedoe, S. E. F. C. C., 98, 99

Haraway, Donna, 6, 219

Harlem, 2, 109–10, 123, 127–28, 214, 215, 228. *See also* African Americans

Harlem Renaissance, 5, 10, 21, 39, 89, 229

Harper's Weekly, 57–58, 64, 66–67

Heller-Collins gorilla expedition, 173, 174

Hemphill, J. C., 37

"Herd, The" Elephant Group Exhibition, xii, 2, 146, 157–59, 160

Hickey, Dennis, 6, 23

Higinbotham, H. N., 142, 243n21

Hill, Robert, 87

History of the United States (Bancroft), 54–55

Hoeffler, Paul, 180, 202, 229, 230; African Expedition film, 180, 182, 202, 208, 230

Hoffman, Malvina, 221

Holderness, Etna, 96

"Hollywood Secret, A" (Bell), 207

Horn, Aloysius "Trader," 201–2
"Hostility to Europeans" (newspaper article), 100
human sacrifices myth, 27, 65, 81, 200
hunters, sport: on "disappearing continent" myth, 132, 133, 171, 172, 174; elephants as trophies, 146; and gorillas, 171, 172, 174; and imperialism, 20; and naturalist-environmentalist discourses, 1, 76, 132, 133, 171, 172, 174
Hunting Big Game in Africa . . . (film), 186–87
"Hymn of Sympathy and Prayer for Africa, A" (Camphor), 95–96

IAA (International African Association; Association Internationale Africaine), 48–49, 50, 53–58, 62–63, 68
illegal animal trade, 224
imperialism: benevolent, 50, 57, 63, 170, 171; Blyden on, 29, 65, 90–91; and Brightest Africa narrative, 12; Congo, and myth of, 50–51; and Darkest Africa myth, 46, 204–6; and "disappearing continent" myth, 162; and ethnographic studies, 40–41, 141–42; in films, 178, 204, 205; France and, 111; IAA and, 53, 54; and naturalist-environmentalist discourses, 40–41, 141–42
In Brightest Africa (Akeley), 171, 219, 229
In Darkest Africa (Stanley), 23, 227
indigenous knowledge, 10–11, 17, 18, 215–16, 224
industrial education, and Pan-Africanism, 107–8, 109, 224
"Industry and Art of the Negro Race" (Lowie), 73
Ingagi (film), 180, 182, 199–201, 207, 208–9
International African Association (IAA; Association Internationale Africaine), 48–49, 50, 53–58, 62–63, 68
International Conference on the Negro, 98, 107–9
internationalization of Africa, 87–88, 98–99, 103–4, 106–7, 115–17, 125, 128, 215–17
Islam, 21, 91, 97, 108
Italian Americans, 213, 215
Italian imperialism, 1–3, 89, 119, 127–28, 211–16
Ituri people ("Pygmies"), 65, 78–80, 79, 85, 170, 203–4, 228

Jamaica, 86, 100, 107, 109, 228
Jamestown Tercentennial Exposition, 4, 129–30, 228
Jazz Age, 39, 196, 203, 229
Jeal, Tim, 51
Jennings, Maurice, 213
Jesup, Morris K., 72, 152
Johnson, Martin: elephants, humanization of, 193, 198; on films by others, 202–3. *See also* Johnson, Martin and Osa, films by
Johnson, Martin and Osa, films by: African women's bodies as specimens , 195–96; AMNH African Expedition, 188–91, *193*, 229; artificiality of African jungle realism, 192–94, 195, 198; authenticity of images, 190, 199, 202–3, 204, 210; *Baboona*, 178, 180, 190, 198, 199, 204, 230; competition for audiences, 187, 190; *Congorilla*, 178, 190, 198, 199, 203, 204, 230; criticism of, 186–87, 190, 204; and Darkest Africa myth, 178, 197–99, 204; environment, manipulation of, 203–4; misrepresentation in, 186–88, 203–4; Osa as white heroine and hunter, 191–92, 194, 195, 197; racial hierarchy,

Index 287

191–92, 195, 197–98; realism, 185–88; reviews, 197; ridicule of Africans, 194–97, 203–4, 220–21; *Songa, the Tale Bearer* (film project), 198, 220–21. See also *Simba, The King of Beasts* (film)
Jones, Charles C., Jr., *Negro Myths from the Georgia Coast*, 39
Jordan, Winthrop, *White over Black*, 5
journalism, and reimagining Africa, 5, 17–18, 26–28, 98, 100–104, 116. See also specific articles
jungle films, 181–88, 207
Jungle Goddess, The (film), 183
Jungle Princess, The (film), 183
"Jungles, The" (Bell), 182
Jungle Trail, The (film), 182, 183

Kasson, John A., 58–60, 183, 184
Kelley, Robin D. G., 87, 216
King Jaja of Opobo, 205–6
King Kong (film), 179–80
King Leopold's Soliloquy (Twain), 68, 70, 72, 80
King Solomon's Mines (film), 186, 208
knowledge production. See white Western knowledge production
Kongokonferenz. See Berlin Conference
Kykunkor (*Witch Woman*; opera), 181

labor exploitation: Pan-Africanist critique of, 119, 123–25, 128; rubber trade and, 51, 59, 62, 66–69, 71, 169, 170
Lang, Herbert, 71–73, 76–81, 128, 153, 156, 161, 228
Lang-Chapin Expedition for AMNH, 71–73, 76–80, 79, 157, 161, 228
League against Cruelties and Oppression in the Colonies, 124
League against Imperialism, 124
League of Nations, 211

Leigh, William Robinson, 25
Leopold II: on Berlin Conference, 59; and Congo, 50; criticism of, 50–51, 62–63, 66, 68–69, 80; and gorilla sanctuary, 171; Morgan on, 56–57; and Stanley, 50–51; and U.S., 72. See also Congo Free State
"Leopold's European Rivals in African Atrocities" (newspaper article), 101
Lewis, David Levering, 86–87, 106
Lewis, Theophilus, 209
Liberia: African Americans, and freedom in, 14, 32, 92; democratic-republicanism, 124; emigration movement, 14, 32, 54, 89–90; as independent state, 13, 16, 126, 222; and Pan-African Congresses, 116–17; and Pan-Africanism, 90, 116–17, 124–25, 127; as political model for Africa nationalization, 85; rubber industry in, 123–24; sovereignty threatened, 101, 103–4; transatlantic alliance, 31–32; UNIA, and colonization plan for, 122–24; and U.S., 16, 28, 49, 53–54, 54–55, 104–6, 116, 117; and U.S. Commission on Liberia, 104–6
literature, and reimagining Africa, 5, 17–18, 26–28, 98, 116. See also specific literature
Livingstone, David, 16, 22–23, 25
Los Angeles Times, 183
Lowie, Robert H., 72–76, 81, 128, 150, 156

manhood, black. See New Negro identities
manhood, white. See white manhood
Markey, Morris, 218–19
Martin, Tony, 87, 110, 120
Mason, M. C. B., 95
Matobo National Park, 9–10

McCormick, Anne O'Hare, 181
McKinney, Nina Mae, 204–5, 206
McShane, Thomas O., 5–6
media, 7, 11, 20–21, 100–104, 179, 180–81. *See also* films
men. *See* New Negro identities; white manhood
Menelik II, 10, 206, 211
Micheaux, Oscar, 179, 209
Middle Passages (Campbell), 43
Milwaukee Public Museum (MPM), 136, 137
missionaries: African Americans in Africa, 13–14, 21, 26–28, 32–33; and African American womanhood, 33–34; and cannibalism, eradication of, 61; and Congo, 63, 67, 68, 69, 71; and ethnographic studies, 40–42; indigenous knowledge dismissed by black missionaries, 11; and manhood, 33–34; and Pan-Africanism, 92–94, 95–96, 100, 106, 109, 121, 127; and paternalistic rhetoric, 9, 13–14, 21, 26–28, 32–33, 86, 88, 106; on slave trade, 11; on white redemption of Africa, 4, 21
Mitchell, Michele, 14
Mitman, Gregg, 182
modernity dates, in U.S., 20, 232n15
Montgomery Advertiser, 36
Morel, E. D., 66, 108
Morgan, John Tyler, 53–57, 58, 62
Morton, Kasson and Walt, 184
Moses, Wilson Jeremiah, 93
Motherland concept, of Africa, 109, 119–20, 122, 123, 126, 127, 231n9
MPM (Milwaukee Public Museum), 136, 137
Mudimbe, V. Y., 86
Mungo Park, expeditions, 16, 83
Munsey, Frank, 183
Musée de Congo Belge, 72, 128

museum exhibits: and Brightest Africa narrative and, 128, 219; and "disappearing continent" myth, 131, 134, 144, 175, 218–19, 221–22; ethnography as extension of fauna in, 150, 159–60, 175, 198; and naturalist-environmentalist discourses, 10, 217, 221; and racial hierarchy myths, 73–76; in urban museums, 20, 151, 152; and Western knowledge production, 128–29, 131, 144, 151–52, 175, 218–19, 221–22. *See also* African Hall; naturalist-environmentalist discourses; *specific museums*
museums, urban, 20. *See also specific museums*
Mussolini, Benito, 211. *See also* Italian imperialism
Myth of Wild Africa, The (Adams and McShane), 5–6

NAACP (National Association for the Advancement of Colored People), 119, 124–25, 179, 214, 228
National Association of Colored Women (NACW), 34, 35
National Baptist World, 31, 33
National Better Business Bureau, 201, 202
"Nationalization of Africa, The" (Fortune), 94
National Reflector, 27
Native Americans, 43, 53, 54–55, 136, 150, 170
natural history museums, 20, 151–52. *See also specific museums*
naturalist-environmentalist discourses: African Americans, 3, 4, 7, 131; Brightest Africa narrative, 133–35, 221–22; community-controlled conservation, 224; Congo, 52, 57;

Index 289

Darkest Africa myth, 1, 24–25, 76, 134–35, 175, 181, 185, 207, 209–10; defined, 3; "disappearing continent" myth, 9–10, 45, 133–35, 169, 175; ethnographic studies, 10–11, 135, 139–40, 142; ethnography as extension of fauna in, 150, 159–60, 175, 198; expeditions, and effects on, 71–72; fauna, and importance in, 156; game preserves, 1, 76, 134–35, 170, 173, 222; hunters for sport, 1, 76, 132–33, 171, 172, 174; imperialism, 40–41, 141–42; media, role in, 21; museums and, 10, 20, 151, 152, 217, 221; radio broadcasts and, 180–81; Rinderpest epidemic, 132, 139; South Africa, 6, 10; the West, comparisons with Africa, 19, 57, 133, 146–47, 170, 227; white conservation movement and, 3–4, 18–20, 24–25, 28, 57, 131; white manhood, 7, 135, 146; white New Women, 7, 44–45, 135, 146. *See also* museum exhibits; *specific expeditions*; *specific fauna*; *specific museums*; *specific naturalists-environmentalists*

N. C. Republican and Civil Rights Advocate, 30

Negro, use of term, 102

Negro Myths from the Georgia Coast (Jones), 39

Negro question, 30, 46, 55–56, 59, 91, 98

"Negro's Greatest Enemy, The" (Garvey), 114

"Negro's 'Peculiar Work,' The" (editorial), 85–86

"Negro's Proper Home, The" (newspaper article), 36

Neumann, Roderick P., 135

Nevins, Alan, 232n15

New Negro for a New Century, A (Washington, Wood, and Williams), 97

New Negro identities: described, 12, 34, 114, 231n3; historical context, 12; inspiration, 21; manhood, 29–30, 33–34, 35, 45, 91–92, 98, 126–27, 231n9; and Pan-Africanism, 7–8, 11–12, 31–32, 33–34, 110; pride in, 28–29; race regeneration for, 106, 231n9; and racialized discourses in films, 184–85; and self-determination, 15–18, 28, 45, 81, 97–98, 99; and Victorianism, 8, 33–34. *See also* African American womanhood

newspapers, and reimagining Africa, 5, 17–18, 26–28, 98, 100–104, 116. *See also specific articles*

New Women. *See* African American womanhood; white New Women

New York Age, 26, 30, 69, 89, 100, 103, 104

New York Amsterdam News, 119, 205, 209, 212–13, 223

New York Freeman, 29, 83, 86

New York Sun, 26, 69, 85–86

New York Times, 2, 36, 43–44, 57–58, 59, 213

Nobbs, E. A., 9–10

"Nomad Dwarfs and Civilization" (Lang), 77, 78

"Notes on Six Negro Myths from the Georgia Coast" (Oertel), 39

O'Donnell-Clark African Expedition, 163, 230

OECD (Organisation for Economic Co-Operation and Development), 224

Oerlemans, Onno, 24

Oertel, Hanns, 39–40

Ogren, Kathy, 21

Open Letter to His Serene Majesty Leopold II . . . , An (Williams), 62, 227

operas, 181

Organisation for Economic Co-Operation and Development (OECD), 224
Organisation of African Unity (African Union), 223
Origin of the Fittest, The (Cope), 37
Osborn, Henry Fairfield, 72–73, 155–58, 187, 228
Ota Benga, and exhibit at St. Louis World's Fair, 79, 227
Other, the, 9, 23, 129–30
Ottley, Roi, 205–6
"Our African Contingent" (Camp), 29

Pacific imperialism, 15–16, 38
Padmore, George, 124
Painter, Nell Irvin, 130
paleontology specimens, 153–56, 157, 228
Pan-Africa, defined, 126
"Pan-Africa and the New Racial Philosophy" (Du Bois), 125
Pan-African Association, 17, 99, 117, 227
Pan-African Congresses: 1919, 100, 106, 110, 116, 117, 122, 229; 1921, 117, *118*, 122, 229; 1923, 229; 1927, 229; ABB, and criticism of, 121–22; delegates to, 116–17, 122; goals of, 125; in London, 1900, 17, 87, 98–99; obstacles for, 99–100; transnational, 87; U.S. reports on, 116–17. *See also* Congress on Africa
Pan-Africanism: African Americans' role in, 95; and African American womanhood, 7–8, 11–12, 110, 130; Africa reimagined, 21–22, 86–89, 99, 119, 130–31; and anti-imperialism, 81, 87, 93, 94, 97, 125, 127; and Brightest Africa narrative, 97, 128, 217; and color line, 125–26, 216; and communism, 88, 117, 119–20; and Congress on Africa, 45, 92–97, 101, 106, 109, 127, 229; Darkest Africa myth dispelled by, 1, 76, 181, 204, 207, 208–10; and democratic-republicanism, 88, 90, 97, 106, 109, 110–11, 120, 124; and emigration movement, 17, 21; equality struggles in, 208; and Ethiopian invasion, 127–28; and ethnographic studies, 10–11, 89, 98–99; and Fatherland concept, 36, 45, 56, 84, 127, 231n9; and films, 1, 76, 204, 207, 208–10; and gender identities, 7–8, 33–34; goals and origins, 1, 17, 21, 76; and industrial education, 107–8, 109, 224; and International Conference on the Negro, 98, 107–9; internationalist framework for racial justice, 7–8, 87–88, 98–99, 103–4; and Islam, 97; and labor exploitation, 119, 123–25, 128; and leadership for African nationalism, 9, 106, 115, 117, 118, 121, 224; and Liberia, 90, 116–17, 124–25, 127; and media owned by African Americans, 21, 100–104; missionary, 92–94, 95–96, 100, 106, 109, 127; and Motherland concept, 119–20, 122, 123, 126, 127, 231n9; New Negro identities, intersection with, 7, 11–12, 31–32, 110; and paternalistic rhetoric about saving Africa, 13–14, 21, 26–28, 32–33, 106; and political philosophies, 84–89, 94–97, 99–100, 120, 223; and political regeneration, 222–25; radicalization of, 107–9, 123, 127; and Versailles Conference, 116, 127; and Victorianism, 33–34, 84–89, 94–97, 99–100, 120, 223. *See also* Universal Negro Improvement Association (UNIA); *specific Pan-Africanists*
Pan-African Reconstruction Association, 213
Pan-American Exposition, 129
Pan-Negro Nationalism, 17, 85

Index 291

Parc National Albert (Albert National Park), 10, 135, 163, 171, 174, 229
paternalistic rhetoric about saving Africa, 9, 13–14, 21, 26–28, 32–33, 86, 88, 106
Patterson, J. H., 25
Payne, Daniel, 33
Pene, Xavier, "Darkest Africa" exhibit, 129, 227
Percival, Blaney, 190–91
Pitt-Rivers, Augustus, *Antique Works of Art from Benin*, 75
Pittsburgh Courier, 119, 180, 211
Plummer, Brenda Gayle, 87, 88, 99, 127–28
political context for Africa, 2–9; communism, 88, 117, 119–20; democratic-republicanism, 88, 90, 97, 106, 109, 110–11, 120, 124; internationalization, 87–88, 98–99, 103–4, 106–7, 115–17, 125, 128, 215–17; Pan-Africanism, political philosophies of, 84–89, 94–97, 99–100, 120, 223; political regeneration by Africans, 223–25. See also African nationalism
Pomeroy, Daniel E., 175, 217, 218
Price, J. C., 85–86, 88, 90
primitivism: narratives, 130–31, 162; and white manhood regeneration, 8–9, 19, 50, 56–57, 68, 76–78, 80, 144, 147–49
Prince of Sweden, 164, 172
"Pygmies," 65, 78–80, 79, 85, 170, 203–4, 228

race riots, 17, 177, 229, 230
racial discrimination: color line, 125–26, 216; in Congo, 65, 72, 74–75, 80–81; and Great Britain, 98, 99, 100, 101–3, 108–9; in South Africa, 98, 100, 101–3, 108–9; in U.S., 3, 15, 38, 45, 81, 213
racial hierarchy myths, 73–76, 191–92, 195, 197–98
radio broadcasts, 7, 179, 180–81
Ranger, Terence, 9
Reddick, L. D., 179–80, 183
Regnault, Félix-Louis, 189
Renascent Africa (Azikiwe), 222
research methodologies, 11
Returning the Gaze (Everett), 178–79
Rhodesia, 102, 138
Rinderpest epidemic, 132, 139
Robeson, Paul, 178, 179, 204–7, 208, 209
Robinson, J. C. (Black Condor; Brown Condor), 1–2, 214, 230
Rogers, J. A., 212, 216
Rolinson, Mary, 87, 109
Romanticism, 23–24
Rony, Fatimah Tobing, 6
Roosevelt, Teddy: *African Game Trails*, 19, 228; African Hall as memorial to, 2, 161–62, 217; death of, 161; on "disappearing continent" myth, 149; and Liberian sovereignty, 104–5; Smithsonian African Expedition, 143–46, *147*; statue of, 2, 217; "The Strenuous Life" speech and doctrine, 9, 19, 144, 162, 227, 232n13, 243–44n25; on white manhood and primitivism, 8–9, 19, 144, 147–49
Root, Elihu, 28, 105
Rotundo, E. Anthony, 8
rubber trade, 51, 59, 62, 66–69, 71, 169, 170
"Ruminations" (Rogers), 212
Ruwenzori-Kivu Expedition, 163, 229

Safari (*Trailing African Wild Animals*; film), 185–86, 189, 229

Sanders of the River (film), 178, 179, 199, 204–6, 208, 209
Sanford-Legendre Abyssinia Expedition, 162–63, 229
Schlesinger, Arthur M., 232n15
Science (magazine), 132
Scott, William R., 128
Seaman, Louis L., 101
self-determination, 15–18, 28, 45, 81, 97–98, 99
Sheldon, May French, 43–45, 96
Sheppard, William H., 33–34, 71, 228
Shufeldt, R. W., 36–37
Sierra Leone colony, 49, 84, 103–4
silent films, 182–85
Simba, The King of Beasts (film): Africans ridiculed, 194–97, 220–21; African women's bodies as specimens, 195–96; AMNH contract with Johnsons, 190; artificiality of African jungle realism, 192–94, 195, 198; Darkest Africa myth replicated, 178, 197, 199, 204; racial hierarchy in, 191–92, 195, 197–98; release date, 229; reviews, 197; white heroine and hunter, 191–92, 194, 195, 197
slave trade: Abolition of Slave Trade Act, 49, 61; in Congo, 22, 26, 56, 58–59, 62, 65; missionaries on, 11; transatlantic, 5, 45, 49, 54, 56, 57, 61, 115
Smith, Arthur Donaldson, 138
Smith, Charles, 102–3, 104
Smith, Frederick Nicholas, 26–27, 29
Smithsonian African Expedition, 143–46, 228
Snow, H. A., 186–88, 208
social Darwinism, 38–39, 128
Somaliland, British, 133, 138, 139, 153, 160, 219
Songa, the Tale Bearer (film project), 198, 220–21

Souls of Black Folk, The (Du Bois), 87, 125
South, American, 14, 15, 38, 45, 81
South Africa: African Americans in, 33, 103; Ethiopian Church of, 33, 108–9; Great Britain, governance of, 102; naturalist-environmentalist discourses in, 6, 10; racial discrimination and tension, 98, 100, 101–3, 108–9
Spanish Civil War, 216, 227
Speke, 16, 19, 23
Stanley, Henry Morton: biography, 22; in Congo, 25–27; criticism of, 50–51; and Darkest Africa myth, 23–28; Emin Pasha rescue mission, 50–51, 227; expeditions of, 16, 22–28; and imperialism, 50; *In Darkest Africa*, 23, 227; and Leopold II, 50–51; publications, 22–23; on slave trade, 58–59
Stein, Judith, 87
stereotypes. *See* Darkest Africa myth
St. Louis World's Fair, Ota Benga exhibit, 79, 227
Story of the Congo Free State, The (Wack), 67–69
"Strenuous Life, The" Roosevelt speech and doctrine, 9, 19, 144, 162, 227, 232n13, 243–44n25
Summers, Martin, 7, 8
Sundiata, Ibrahim, 87
Sweden, Prince of, 164, 172

Taft, William Howard, 104–6, 123
Tarzan (films), 183–85, 230
Tarzan (radio serial), 181
Tarzan of the Apes (Burroughs), 183, 228
Tarzan of the Apes (film), 183–84
Tarzan the Ape Man (Burroughs), 184
Teslow, Tracy Lang, 6
Thirkield, Wilbur P., 92–93

Times (London, newspaper), 51, 132, 133, 173
Tinée, Mae, 184, 186, 197, 202
Tippu Tib (Muhammad bin Hamid), 26, 65
Tjäder Expedition for AMNH, 153–55, 157, 228
Tobias, D., 98, 99, 106
Trader Horn (film), 180, 182, 201–2
Trailing African Wild Animals (*Safari*; film), 185–86, 189, 229
Turner, Frederick Jackson, "The Significance of the Frontier in American History," 19
Turner, Henry McNeal, 30, 86
Turner, John G., 33
Tuskegee Institute, 1, 102, 107, 230
Twa (Batwa; "Pygmies"), 65, 78–80, 79, 85, 170, 203–4, 228
Twain, Mark: on atrocities in Congo, 68–69, 80, 81; and Congo Reform movement, 52, 81; *King Leopold's Soliloquy*, 68, 70, 72, 80; on U.S. role in Congo, 69, 80

Ubangi (film), 202–3
UNIA (Universal Negro Improvement Association). *See* Universal Negro Improvement Association (UNIA)
United Kingdom. *See* Great Britain
United States: on atrocities in Congo, 67–68, 69, 80; and Berlin Conference, 57–58, 59, 60, 61–62; Commission on Liberia, 104–6; cultural relativism, 18; Darkest Africa myth images, 16–17, 20, 23–28, 178; Ethiopian invasion by Italy, neutrality of, 213–14; foreign policy and trade interests, African, 48–50, 57–58, 59–60, 61–62, 72, 213–14; German immigrants in, 62; and IAA, 48–49, 50, 57, 68; and imperialism, 15–16, 38, 45, 105–6, 124; and Leopold II, 72; and Liberia, 16, 28, 49, 53–55, 104–6, 116, 117, 124; modernity, dates of, 20, 232n15; Pan-African Congress reports for, 116–17; and racial connection between Africa and African Americans, 35–36, 56; racial discrimination and tensions, 3, 15, 38, 45, 81, 213; and slave trade, 5, 45, 54, 56, 57, 115; and Stanley expeditions, 22–28; western frontier compared with Africa, 19, 57, 133, 146–47, 170, 227; white Americans' debt to African Americans, 29–30. *See also* African Americans; African American womanhood; white manhood; white New Women
Universal Negro Improvement Association (UNIA): ABB criticism of, 121–22; Africa's significance to African Americans, 87; black capitalism, 114; black elite guidance, 117; complex class dimensions, 110; conventions, 112, *113*; films challenging stereotypes of Africa and Africans, 177–78, 179; history, 100, 109, 228; and labor exploitation, 124; Liberia colonization plan, 122–24; and Pan-African Congresses, 116; and paternalistic rhetoric about saving Africa, 106; philosophy, 109, 111; race regeneration, 106, 231n9; race solidarity, 112; redemption from European imperialism, 112. *See also* Garvey, Marcus; Pan-Africanism
urban museums, 20. *See also specific museums*
U.S. Census Bureau, 18, 227

Vernay-Lang Kalahari Expedition, 163, 229

Versailles Conference, 116, 127
Victorianism: Africa as inspiration for changes in, 21–22; and African American womanhood, 8, 21, 33–34; and New Negro identities, 8; and Pan-Africanism, 33–34, 84–89, 94–97, 99–100, 120, 223; and white New Women, 21–22
Virginia Star, 13, 14
Von Eschen, Penny, 3

Wack, Henry Wellington, 67–69, 80, 81
Washington, Booker T., 69, 97–98, 105; on African Americans' ideas about Africa, 107–9; on criticism of Congo, 69, 71; International Conference on the Negro, 1912, 107–9; *A New Negro for a New Century*, 97
Washington Post, 57–58, 182, 184, 213
Wells, Carveth, 202
West, American, compared with Africa, 19, 57, 133, 146–47, 170, 227
Western African Raff Collection, 153, 227
West Indians, 86, 109–10, 114, 212, 222
"What I Saw in Ethiopia" (Rogers), 216
When Africa Speaks (*Africa Speaks!*; film), 180, 182, 202, 208, 230
white conservation movement, 3–4, 18–20, 24–25, 28, 57, 131
Whiteley, James Gustavus, 67, 68, 72, 171, 173–74
white manhood: Africa, as inspiration for regeneration of, 22; elephants as trophies for, 146; and films, 1, 76, 181, 183–85, 207, 209–10; freedom to express, 208; and naturalist-environmentalist discourses, 7, 135, 146; regeneration in primitivism, 50, 56–57, 68, 76–78, 80. *See also* whiteness

whiteness: and cult of primitivism, 35–39, 41, 44; as mediated through ethnographic studies of Africa, 39–45; as racial identity, 35–36, 56. *See also* white manhood; white New Women
white New Women: Africa, as inspiration for, 22; African travels, 43–45, 96; and elephant trophies, 146, *147*, 157; as heroine and hunter in films, 182–83, 191–92, 194, 195, 197; historical context, 22, 35; identity of, 12, 21, 22, 35, 43–45, 96, 208; and naturalist-environmentalist discourses, 7, 135, 146; and Victorianism, 21–22. *See also* whiteness
White over Black (Jordan), 5
white supremacy: Africans' acceptance of, 100; Ethiopia's struggle against, 216; and Fuller's sculptures, 130; in museum exhibits and narratives, 128–29, 135; reimagining Africa and, 35–36, 45; scientific evidence for, 18, 38–39, 46, 128; and social Darwinism, 38–39, 128
white Western knowledge production: films and, 189, 208; museum exhibits and, 128–29, 131, 144, 151–52, 175, 218–19, 221–22. *See* Western knowledge production
white womanhood. *See* white New Women
wildlife. *See* fauna
Williams, Fannie Barrier, 97
Williams, George Washington, 62–64, 66, 227
Williams, Henry Sylvester, 17, 92, 98, 227
Wilson administration, 123
Wissler, Clark, 74, 154
Witch Woman (*Kykunkor*, opera), 181

Within Our Gates (film), 179
womanhood, African American. *See* African American womanhood
womanhood, white. *See* white New Women
Wood, Norman Barton, 97
Woodson, Carter G., 222
World War I, 115, 116, 127, 228
Worley, Harry F., 116–17

"Worse Than the Sixteenth Century" (magazine article), 66
Wylie, Kenneth, 6, 23

Ybarra, Thomas R., 144
Yergan, Max, 11

zoology. *See* fauna

RACE IN THE ATLANTIC WORLD, 1700–1900

The Hanging of Angélique: The Untold Story of Canadian Slavery and the Burning of Old Montréal
by Afua Cooper

Christian Ritual and the Creation of British Slave Societies, 1650–1780
by Nicholas M. Beasley

African American Life in the Georgia Lowcountry: The Atlantic World and the Gullah Geechee
Edited by Philip Morgan

The Horrible Gift of Freedom: Atlantic Slavery and the Representation of Emancipation
by Marcus Wood

The Life and Letters of Philip Quaque, the First African Anglican Missionary
edited by Vincent Carretta and Ty M. Reese

In Search of Brightest Africa: Reimagining the Dark Continent in American Culture, 1884–1936
by Jeannette Eileen Jones

Contentious Liberties: American Abolitionists in Post-Emancipation Jamaica, 1834–1866
by Gale L. Kenny

We Are the Revolutionists: German-Speaking Immigrants and American Abolitionists after 1848
by Mischa Honeck

The American Dreams of John B. Prentis, Slave Trader
by Kari J. Winter

Missing Links: The African and American Worlds of R. L. Garner, Primate Collector
by Jeremy Rich